Civil-Military Conflict
in Imperial Russia
1881-1914

Civil-Military Conflict in Imperial Russia

1881-1914

William C. Fuller, Jr.

PRINCETON UNIVERSITY PRESS
PRINCETON, NEW JERSEY

Published by Princeton University Press,
41 William Street, Princeton, New Jersey 08540
In the United Kingdom: Princeton University Press,
Guildford, Surrey

Library of Congress Cataloging in Publication Data
will be found on the last printed page of this book

ISBN 0-691-05452-5

Publication of this book has been aided by a grant from the
Whitney Darrow Fund of Princeton University Press

This book has been composed in Linotron Aldus

Clothbound editions of Princeton University Press books
are printed on acid-free paper, and binding materials
are chosen for strength and durability

Printed in the United States of America
by Princeton University Press, Princeton, New Jersey

To Lt. Col. and Mrs. William C. Fuller

CONTENTS

LIST OF ILLUSTRATIONS

(following p. 164)

1. The personal pennant of the War Minister, adopted in 1892. From *Chertezhi i risunki k polnomu sobraniiu zakonov Rossiiskoi Imperii*, St. Petersburg, 1892. Courtesy of International Legal Studies, Law Library, Harvard University.

2. A soldier of the engineers in full combat dress, 1898. From *Chertezhi i risunki k polnomu sobraniiu zakonov Rossiiskoi Imperii*. St. Petersburg, 1898. Courtesy of International Legal Studies, Law Library, Harvard University.

3. Repression. Cossack soldiers burning down a peasant hut in Georgia, 1906. From Kellogg Durland, *The Red Reign: The True Story of an Adventurous Year in Russia* (New York: The Century Company, 1908).

4. An infantry patrol, Warsaw 1906. From Kellogg Durland, *The Red Reign: The True Story of an Adventurous Year in Russia* (New York: The Century Company, 1908).

5. Three soldiers to guard each policeman, Warsaw 1906. From Kellogg Durland, *The Red Reign: The True Story of an Adventurous Year in Russia* (New York: The Century Company, 1908).

6. Revolutionary terrorism. A horse killed by a small bomb in the course of a politically motivated robbery. From Kellogg Durland, *The Red Reign: The True Story of an Adventurous Year in Russia* (New York: The Century Company, 1908).

7. The Russo-Japanese War. Entrenched Russian infantry during the battle of Liao-Yang, August, 1904. From *The Russo-Japanese War* (New York: P. C. Collier and Sons, 1905).

8. Gen. A. N. Kuropatkin, former War Minister and commander-in-chief of Russia's forces in the east, awards a soldier a decoration during the battle of Liao-Yang. From *The Russo-Japanese War* (New York: P. F. Collier and Sons, 1905).

9. The Ministry of War with St. Isaac's Cathedral in the background. From *Stoletie voennogo ministerstva. Istoricheskii ocherk deiatel'nosti kantseliarii voennogo ministerstva i voennogo soveta* (St. Petersburg, 1903).

LIST OF TABLES

A NOTE ON STYLE

All dates in this book are given in Old Style unless otherwise indicated. The Julian Calendar used in Imperial Russia lagged twelve days behind the Gregorian Calendar used in the West in the nineteenth century and thirteen days in the twentieth. The transliteration system employed is that used by the Library of Congress with one exception: in the text English versions of the names of well-known Russian figures have been employed, while other names have been directly transliterated. Hence Tsar Nicholas II, Witte, but also Nikolai Nikolaevich.

ABBREVIATIONS

The following abbreviations have been used in the text and the notes:

BE *Entsiklopedicheskii slovar'*. Published by F. A. Brokhauz and I. A. Efron. 43 volumes. St. Petersburg, 1890-1907. (Brokhauz/Efron encyclopedia)

GVSU Glavnoe voenno-sudnoe upravlenie (Main Administration of Military Justice)

MVD Ministerstvo vnutrennykh del (Ministry of the Interior)

OPPS Osoboe prisutsvie pravitel' stvuiushchego senata

PSZ *Polnoe sobranie zakonov Rossiiskoi Imperii* (Complete Collected Laws of the Russian Empire)

SEER *Slavonic and East European Review*

SGO Sovet gosudavstvennoi oboroni

SI *Slavianskie izvestiia* (Slavic News)

SR *Slavic Review*

SZ *Svod zakonov* (Code of Laws)

TsGVIA Tsentral'nyi gosudarstvennyi voenno-istoricheskii arkhiv (Central State Archive of Military History)

TsGAOR Tsentral'nyi gosudarstvennyi arkhiv Oktiabr'skoi Revoliutsii (Central State Archive of the October Revolution)

VAK Vyshaia attestatsionnaia komissiia (Higher Commission on Performance Reviews)

VE *Voennaia entsiklopediia* (The Military Encylopedia)

VG *Voennyi golos* (The Military Voice)

VM Voennoe ministerstvo (Ministry of War)

VS *Voennyi sbornik* (Military Journal)

For archival citations:

f. fond (collection)

op. opis' (catalogue)

d. delo (file)

l. or ll. list, listy (sheet, sheets)

INTRODUCTION

> Ever since the Grand Duchy of Muscovy became a
> considerable power in the sixteenth century, Russia
> has been, and still remains, a great military Empire.
>
> G.H.N. Seton-Watson[1]

ONE of the most persistent themes in the historiography of the Russian Empire is the interlocking of military necessity and state decision making. That the needs of the army preceded all other concerns in the thinking of successive Russian governments has been repeated so often by historians that one might well assume that solicitude for the military was an unchanging principle of Russian administration. Scholars have invoked this principle to elucidate a great number of historiographical problems. In part, Richard Hellie has maintained that the final establishment of serfdom in 1649 was the direct consequence of the government's need for revenue to fund the rearmament of the military.[2] The great Russian historian, V. O. Kliuchevskii, defined the majority of Petrine reforms as improvisations arising out of the exigencies of war with Sweden and Turkey.[3] S. M. Troitskii stressed the enormity of military expenditures during the eighteenth century, and demonstrated the symbiotic relationship between the rise in state revenues due to military requirements and the imposition of increasingly draconian measures of tax collection, in which the military often played a part.[4] In discussing the same century, S. M. Solov'ev often pointed to the rapid changes in the governmental system occasioned by war, while Marc Raeff has emphasized the manner in which the "military ethos" molded the character of Russian administration, while simultaneously imprinting itself on the consciousness of the Russian gentry.[5] The best recent

[1] G.H.N. Seton-Watson, "Russia: Army and Aristocracy," in *Soldiers and Governments. Nine Studies in Civil-Military Relations*, ed. Michael Howard (London, 1957), p. 101.

[2] Richard Hellie, *Enserfment and Military Change in Muscovy* (Chicago, 1971).

[3] Vasili Klyuchevsky, *Peter the Great*, trans. Liliana Archibald (New York, 1958), p. 77.

[4] S. M. Troitskii, *Finansovaia politika russkogo absoliutizma v XVIII veke* (Moscow, 1966), pp. 25, 28, 228-230.

[5] See, for example, S. M. Solov'ev, *Istoriia Rossii s drevneishikh vremen*, vol. 12 (Moscow, 1964), pp. 321-323; Marc Raeff, "L'état, le gouvernement et la tradition politique

study of the reign of Nicholas I devotes considerable attention to Russia as a militarized state, and to the Emperor's preference for military men in civilian posts.[6] In explaining one of the most significant events in modern Russian history—the emancipation of the serfs—Alfred Rieber once again invoked the military imperative: Alexander II, in his view, appreciated the fact that a modern army composed of citizen soldiers was fundamental to Russia's survival as a great power.[7] Writing in 1877, Herbert Spencer could find no better example of the "militant type of society" in Europe than Russia: "Modern Dahomey and Russia, as well as ancient Peru, Egypt and Sparta, exemplify that owning of the individual by the state in life, liberty and goods which is proper for a social system adapted for war."[8]

That the satisfaction of military requirements by the state is one of the motors of Russian history is unquestionable. However, is it necessarily the case that Russia was always some sort of "garrison state?"[9] Is it reasonable to suppose that the government's commitment to the army was static and unshakable? Is it true that the same slavish devotion to the military interest and the same harmony, if not identity, of military and civilian elites characterized the Russian Empire from beginning to end? These questions could be asked with profit about the entire course of modern Russian history, or about any of its subdivisions. But it seems particularly appropriate to pose them about the last decades of the monarchy. It is of course methodologically unsound to deduce the intentions behind a policy in terms of the outcome of that policy. Yet surely the connection (or lack of it) between intentions and outcomes deserves attention in historical writing. And if the government of the Russian Empire was thoroughly promilitary, it is remarkable that the vast majority of officers in the last years of the regime were ill-paid and ill-educated.[10] The fact that this presumably militarist empire suffered such

---

en Russie imperiale avant 1861," *Revue d'Histoire moderne et contemporaine* 9 (Oct.-Dec. 1962): 302; Marc Raeff, *The Origins of the Russian Intelligentsia: The Eighteenth-Century Nobility* (New York, 1966), pp. 48-50.

[6] W. Bruce Lincoln, *Nicholas I: Emperor and Autocrat of All the Russias* (Bloomington, Ind., 1978), pp. 88, 183-185, 164, 230.

[7] Alfred J. Rieber, ed., *The Politics of Autocracy: Letters of Alexander II to Prince A. I. Bariatinskii, 1857-1864* (The Hague, 1966), pp. 23, 59, 96. For a critique of this explanation see Daniel Field, *The End of Serfdom: Nobility and Bureaucracy in Russia, 1855-1861* (Cambridge, Mass., 1976), pp. 53-54, 386.

[8] Herbert Spencer, *Principles of Sociology*, vol. 2 (New York, 1895), p. 602.

[9] Richard Hellie, in "The Structure of Modern Russian History: Toward A Dynamic Model," *Russian History* 4, pt. 1 (1977): 1-22, argues that Muscovy, Imperial Russia, and the Soviet Union all represent varieties of the "garrison state."

[10] See for example P. A. Zaionchkovskii, *Samoderzhavie i russkaia armiia na rubezhe XIX-XX stoletii* (Moscow, 1973), pp. 168-248.

resounding defeats in twentieth-century wars with Japan and the Central Powers is also somewhat disturbing. Yet perhaps tsarist Russia was both militarist and incompetent. This was the view adopted by V. I. Lenin. To Lenin, although militarism and tsarism were inseparable, the Imperial government was frankly incapable of building up a strong army and navy. As Lenin wrote in early 1905 with reference to the Russo-Japanese War: "the military might of autocratic Russia has proved to be a sham. Tsarism has proved to be a hindrance to the organization of up-to-date efficient warfare, that very business to which tsarism dedicated itself wholeheartedly, of which it was so proud, and for which it offered such colossal sacrifices in defiance of all opposition on the part of the people."[11] There is some truth in these remarks, for as we shall see, structural peculiarities of the autocracy did impede military reform and military improvement in Russia. But as an assessment of tsarist military policy Lenin's statement is unsatisfactory. Clearly the Imperial regime was relatively efficient in a variety of areas of endeavor, such as industrialization and famine relief.[12] This being so, why should the state fail so stunningly in "that very business to which it devoted itself wholeheartedly"?

Considerations other than the implausibility of Lenin's argument drew me to reconsider state military policy in the later Imperial period and to probe more deeply into the relationships between Russian soldiers and civilian bureaucrats in the same years. The first of these considerations was some work I did on the Russian army before 1881 and the army during the First World War. At least until the late seventies, the Russian War Ministry was ebullient, vigorous, and influential enough to intervene in matters of state only remotely connected to the military. An examination of the Ministry from 1914 to 1917, however, revealed a contrary picture. The Ministry was weak, politically isolated, and unable to wrest even the authority it needed to wage war from a suspicious monarchy and equally suspicious Duma. What accounted for this precipitous reversal?

The second consideration was my reading in the sociology of civil-military relations. This field has been accurately described as a growth industry. Kurt Lang's 1972 bibliography of military sociology listed 351

[11] V. I. Lenin, *Collected Works*, 4th ed., vol. 8, trans. Bernard Isaacs and Isidor Lasker (Moscow, 1962), p. 51.

[12] See for example Richard G. Robbins, *Famine in Russia, 1891-1892* (New York, 1975), pp. 168-175; T. H. von Laue, *Sergei Witte and the Industrialization of Russia* (New York, 1963), passim; Patricia Herlihy, "Death in Odessa: A Study of Population Movements in a Nineteenth-Century City," *Journal of Urban History* 4, no. 4 (Aug. 1978): 426-427, 430-431.

significant contributions to the subject.[13] Although little of this socio-logical literature exactly fits with the Russian historical experience, much of this work is highly provocative for historians of Russia.[14] This is so because many of the models devised by the sociologists of necessity imply the existence of a great degree of civil-military tension in late Imperial Russia. M. D. Feld, for instance, while admitting that nothing is known about civil-military conflict in Russia in this period, observes that "an apolitical officer corps is a direct consequence of a stable political order."[15] Tsarist military memoirists almost in unison insisted that the Russian officer corps was apolitical; it is indubitable, however, that the political order which obtained in the last decades of the Empire was not stable. Perlmutter's recipe for military intervention in politics states that officers are most likely to take political action when the "integrity of military professionalism" is weakened. This integrity weakens as a result of a decline in the status of officers, military defeat, and the rise of radical movements.[16] All of these latter phenomena were features of late Imperial Russian history. Finer's description of some optimum condi-tions for military intervention in politics is also striking. These condi-tions include an upsurge in military professionalism, an overreliance by the state on the army in dealing with internal enemies, and humiliating defeat in war perceived by soldiers to be the outcome of civilian bun-gling.[17] In other words, Finer has painted a rather accurate picture of the Russian army circa 1906 or 1907. No military coup occurred in

[13] Kurt Lang, *Military Institutions and the Sociology of War: A Review of the Literature with Annotated Bibliography* (Beverly Hills, 1972).

[14] I will discuss my problems with some of the leading sociological works in the first chapter. Among the most important studies are Samuel P. Huntington, *The Soldier and the State: The Theory and Politics of Civil Military Relations* (Cambridge, 1954); Morris M. Janowitz, *The Professional Soldier: A Social and Political Portrait*, 2nd ed. (New York, 1971); S. E. Finer, *The Man on Horseback: The Role of the Military in Politics*, 2d ed. (London, 1976); Amos Perlmutter, *The Military and Politics in Modern Times: On Profes-sionals, Praetorians and Revolutionary Soldiers* (New Haven, 1977); John J. Johnson, ed., *The Role of the Military in Underdeveloped Countries* (Princeton, 1962); Jacques van Doorn, ed., *Armed Forces and Society: Sociological Essays* (The Hague, 1968); *Armed Forces and Society in Western Europe, Archives européenes de sociologie*, vol. 6, no. 2 (The Hague, 1965); S. N. Eisenstadt, *The Political System of Empires* (London, 1963); Bengt Abrahamsson, *Military Professionalisation and Political Power* (Stockholm, 1971); Stanislaw Andreski, *Military Organization and Society*, 2d ed. (Berkeley, 1968); Jacques van Doorn, ed., *Military Profession and Military Regimes: Commitments and Conflicts* (The Hague, 1969); A. R. Luckham, "A Comparative Typology of Civil-Military Rela-tions," *Government and Opposition* 6, no. 1 (Winter 1971): 5-35.

[15] M. D. Feld, "Professionalism, Nationalism and the Alienation of the Military" in van Doorn, *Sociological Essays*, pp. 65, 68.

[16] Perlmutter, *Military and Politics*, pp. 34-35.

[17] Finer, *Man on Horseback*, pp. 41-49, 55.

Russia in these years, yet was the Russian officer corps, so aptly described by Finer, completely immune to politics? Even if it had been apolitical in the past, could it have remained so, in the face of such serious challenges to its interests and prestige?

The issue of the apparent decline in the power of the War Ministry, along with questions suggested by sociological theory, then, provided the starting point for this book. My main contention is that Russia, while a great military empire in the period from 1881 to 1914, was not a militarist or militant state. By this I mean that, in the eyes of the army leadership, the Russian state did not serve military interests before all else and did not in fact satisfy the most pressing of the army's needs. On the face of it, this would seem to be a paradoxical assertion, for from 1881 to 1914, as in the previous two hundred years, the Russian military appeared to enjoy privileged status, while the distinction between "military" and "civilian" elites appeared, at least superficially, to be just as indistinct as in the past.

Just as their predecessors, the last autocrats and members of the Imperial house occupied ceremonial posts as colonels of elite regiments, frequently wore military uniforms dripping with medals and insignia, and issued proclamations which underscored their devotion to the Russian army. Nicholas II told A. N. Kuropatkin (War Minister, 1898-1904) in January 1898 to include even the smallest details of military life in his reports since "everything about the army interests me."[18] A few months later, Nicholas's eyes would fill with tears as he relived the emotions which had swept over him upon viewing the enthusiasm of his troops during the Belostok maneuvers.[19] Although less demonstrative than his son, Alexander III publicly hailed military affairs as "one of the areas of state administration most important and closest to me."[20]

But the autocrats' testimony is not the only evidence for the military character of the Imperial Russian state. As was true in earlier periods of Russian history, military officers under the late Empire often occupied high civilian posts while retaining army rank. Officers were to be found working for the Ministry of Finance, the State Control, or the Ministry of Foreign Affairs. They served in the Chancellery of the Ministry of the Interior (MVD) and administered Russian provinces as governors in provincial capitals. The Gendarmes, subordinate to the Interior Ministry, were technically part of the Russian army. Further, the Gendarmes, like the police and the Frontier Guard, largely consisted of former regular

[18] TsGVIA, f. 165, op. 1, d. 1868, ll. 6-7.
[19] Ibid., l. 19.
[20] TsGVIA, f. 409, op. 1, d. ps. 79-176, l. 5.

army soldiers and officers. The governor-generalships of Warsaw, Kiev-Podol'ia-Volynia, Moscow, and St. Petersburg were often held by the commanders of the corresponding military districts. In the Caucasus, Central Asia, and the Far East vast territories were under direct military rule. From the Pacific to the Baltic, from ministerial offices to the Senate and the Council of State, present and former military officers were numerous and powerful.

Appearances can of course be deceiving. The apparent interchangeability of officers and civilian bureaucrats, the many officers in civilian jobs, the promilitary utterances of the autocrats—all of these things actually masked acute civil-military conflicts. Where there is identity of interest of course there can be no conflict. But the fact is that the military as opposed to the civilian interest became more and more sharply defined in the last half of the nineteenth century. This was itself because the Ministry of War had lost that favored status it had enjoyed in the past. Especially under Nicholas I, the tsarist state had effectively been a militarized regime: the military model was prized above all others as an organizational principle, and civilian and military elites had also been intertwined. After Nicholas I's "system" had been discredited in the Crimean war and most strikingly after the accession of Alexander III in 1881, however, there was increasing functional differentiation between the various branches of the government. The administrative history of tsarist Russia came to be the history of competing institutional points of view. Each ministry was a quasi-independent organization: each minister was responsible to the sovereign rather than to his ministerial colleagues, and each ministry charted its own policies, regardless of whether these complemented or contradicted the policies of the other branches of government.[21] The War Ministry, which had once stood above such interministerial squabbling, was now reduced to the position of yet another special interest group. For a variety of reasons to be outlined in this book, chiefly the necessity for economic modernization and the growing threat of internal unrest, the autocracy came to promote the goals of such institutions as the Ministries of Finance, Justice, and the Interior over the goals of the Ministry of War. The Ministry of War accordingly had to fight for what it wanted in ways it had rarely had to fight before. Yet there is a further point of even greater importance: the Ministry of War had also changed its military goals in the last decades

---

[21] For discussions of this problem see George L. Yaney, "Some Aspects of the Imperial Russian Government on the Eve of the First World War," *SEER* 43 (Dec. 1964): 69-87; Jacob W. Kipp and W. Bruce Lincoln, "Autocracy and Reform: Bureaucratic Absolutism and Political Modernization in Nineteenth Century Russia," *Russian History* 6, pt. 1 (1979): 16.

of Imperial power. And this was due to the increasing professionalization of the highest echelons of the tsarist military elite. Russia's military professionals demanded not only an army which was well-funded and well-equipped, but also an army which would be exclusively devoted to preparing for war and which would fulfill no internal police functions. It is for this reason that military professionalism became the greatest source of conflict both between the army and the autocracy and between the army and the bureaucracy. The incapacity of the Imperial government to reconcile the civilian and military interests, in short to *digest* military professionalism, represented one of the gravest weaknesses of tsarism, for it undermined the repressive efforts of the regime, politicized key members of the military elite, and seriously undermined Russia's ability to wage war.

I have chosen to concentrate primarily on civil-military conflict engendered by military professionalism at the center of power—St. Petersburg—and have further chosen to examine only two facets of that conflict: finance and repression. In the provinces, of course, there existed many arenas of civil-military dispute: conscription boards, zemstvo and town committees on troop accommodation, uezd military chiefs' offices, and the like.[22] To study all of these local conflicts would clearly mandate an unwieldy and lengthy book. My decision to examine the development of conflict in St. Petersburg (while not excluding consideration of conflicts which began in the provinces but which ended in the Imperial capital) is therefore a logical one. My decision to investigate just two areas of conflict at the center perhaps requires a more substantial defense. For example, I have little to say about civil-military friction over foreign affairs. This subject calls for a detailed treatment in its own right. Nonetheless, the rationale for avoiding a discussion of foreign affairs is not only the unavailability of archival material on this subject, but also my supposition that the army in fact played a minor role in the formulation of foreign policy towards Europe from 1881 to 1914. This was chiefly the consequence of the compartmentalization of the affairs of state. Now it is true that certain prominent soldiers did help to smooth the way for the signing of the Franco-Russian Alliance of 1892. However, as late as June of 1892, P. S. Vannovskii (War Minister, 1881-1898) was still unaware of the content of the Franco-Russian diplomatic talks then taking place.[23] Because of the division of the General Staff from the War

[22] For just one example of civil-military conflict, in this case over accommodations for troops, see N. M. Maskevich, comp., *Raz"iasneniia glavnogo shtaba i drugikh uchrezhdenii po kvartirnomu dovol'stviiu voisk* (St. Petersburg, 1896).

[23] V. N. Lamzdorff, *Dnevnik, 1891-1892*, ed. F. A. Rotshtein (Moscow and Leningrad, 1934), p. 343.

Ministry in 1906, A. F. Rediger (War Minister, 1905-1911) was thoroughly ignorant of the extent of Russia's foreign obligations as late as November 1908.[24] And on the very eve of the First World War, Russia's diplomats were largely unaware of the Empire's true state of readiness, while Russia's generals were largely in the dark about the objectives of foreign policy.[25]

The reason for studying financial conflict needs no explanation. Every institution in the Russian state needed money, but money was especially important to the Ministry of War, confronted as it was by the technological revolution in armaments and the necessity for competing with the wealthier powers of Western Europe. With regard to internal repression, my emphasis on this problem is predicated on the fact that in its acceptance or rejection of heavy internal repressive service, an army is confronted with a true identity crisis: should it be an armed force designated to protect the state against external foes, or a corps of internal police?[26]

The subject of civil-military conflict in Russia has never before been treated in depth. This gap in the historiography is partially explained by the fact that scholars have only comparatively recently undertaken serious studies of the Imperial administration. Work on the civilian bureaucracy has now borne fruit in a whole range of important articles and monographs.[27] Even more recently, works have appeared that point the way towards a reinterpretation of the Imperial army. Stein, Kenez, and Wildman, for instance, have effectively exploded the myth that the late nineteenth-century officer corps was the bastion of aristocracy and privilege. Zaionchkovskii has provided an excellent description of the army on the eve of the war with Japan. Beskrovnyi has discussed the armament and supply of the Imperial forces in great detail. Stone's

[24] TsGVIA, f. 230, op. 1, d. 7, p. 768.

[25] See my essay, "The Russian Empire, 1909 to 1914," in *Knowing One's Enemies: Intelligence Assessment Before the Two World Wars*, ed. Ernest May (Princeton, 1985).

[26] One curious exception is the American army in the late nineteenth century. After 1877 professional American officers stressed their eagerness to uphold "public order"— by crushing strikes, etc.—in order to justify the army's existence to a skeptical Congress. See Jerry M. Cooper, *The Army and Civil Disorder, Federal Military Intervention in Labor Disputes, 1877-1900* (Westport, Conn., 1980), pp. xiv, 251-253, 257-258.

[27] See for example Walter M. Pintner and Don Karl Rowney, eds., *Russian Officialdom from the Seventeenth through the Twentieth Centuries: The Bureaucratization of Russian Society* (Chapel Hill, 1980); Daniel T. Orlovsky, *The Limits of Reform: The Ministry of Internal Affairs in Imperial Russia, 1802-1881* (Cambridge, Mass., 1981); Neil B. Weissman, *Reform in Tsarist Russia: The State Bureaucracy and Local Government, 1900-1914* (New Brunswick, 1981); Roberta Thompson Manning, *The Crisis of the Old Order in Russia: Gentry and Government* (Princeton, 1982); George Yaney, *The Urge to Mobilize: Agrarian Reform in Russia, 1861-1930* (Urbana, 1982).

revisionist history of World War I on the Eastern front includes some provocative observations about the relationship between the military and society. And Bushnell is currently engaged in path-breaking work on the social history of the army, on the attitudes and perceptions of common soldiers and officers.[28] I have been able to draw on all of these studies with profit. Yet few of these works overlap with mine. Stein and Kenez are chiefly interested in the social profile of the officer corps. Wildman's true focus is the revolution of 1917, while Stone's is operational history. Bushnell focuses chiefly on the revolution of 1905-1907. Further, his perspective is very different from mine. His vantage point is that of the provincial garrison, while mine is that of the chancellery, more often than not.

In writing this book I have made use of the standard memoirs, journals, newspapers, and other published sources. But in the main I have founded the monograph on material from two Soviet archives: the Central State Archive of the October Revolution (TsGAOR) and, most importantly, the Central State Archive of Military History (TsGVIA). TsGAOR provided me with personal papers of the last two emperors and with significant police reports concerning both repression and the political mood within the army. However, TsGVIA furnished me with the bulk of the archival files used: a complete listing of the collections examined is provided in the bibliography. I am much indebted to the staff at TsGVIA for helpfulness and generosity; however, I am constrained to observe that I was never given archival catalogues (*opisi*). Further, Soviet authorities consistently denied my requests to use the Central State Historical Archive of the Soviet Union in Leningrad (TsGIA SSSR), where the working papers of almost all the civilian tsarist ministries are housed. I cannot therefore pretend to have mastered all of the documents which bear on my subject. Yet I am confident that I have seen enough of them to offer here an analysis of the contours of civil-military conflict in the

---

[28] Hans-Peter Stein, "Der Offizier des Russischen Heeres im Zeitabschnitt zwischen Reform und Revolution (1861-1905)," *Forschungen zur Osteuropäischen Geschichte* (Berlin) 13 (1967): 346-504; Peter Kenez, "A Profile of the Pre-Revolutionary Officer Corps," *California Slavic Studies* 7 (1973): 121-158; Allan K. Wildman, *The End of the Russian Imperial Army: The Old Army and the Soldiers' Revolt (March-April, 1917)* (Princeton, 1980); Zaionchkovskii, *Samoderzhavie*; Norman Stone, *The Eastern Front, 1914-1917* (New York, 1975); John Bushnell, "Mutineers and Revolutionaries: Military Revolution in Russia, 1905-1907," Ph.D. diss., Indiana University, 1977; John Bushnell, "Peasants in Uniform: The Tsarist Army as a Peasant Society," *Journal of Social History* 13, no. 4 (Summer 1980): 565-576; John Bushnell, "The Tsarist Officer Corps, 1881-1914: Customs, Duties, Inefficiency," *American Historical Review* 86, no. 4 (Oct. 1981); L. G. Beskrovnyi, "Proizvodstvo vooruzheniia i boepripasov dlia armii v Rossii v period imperializma (1898-1917 gg.)" *Istoricheskie zapiski* (Moscow) 99 (1977): 88-139.

late Russian Empire. Rich opportunities for further scholarship exist. The Russian army, its internal arrangements, and its place in society and state have not been exhausted as topics for historical research.

I have accumulated many debts while writing this book. First, I would like to thank those institutions which provided funding, typing and/or office space: the International Research Exchanges Board and the Fulbright/Hays Commission, which between them defrayed the costs of research in Moscow during the 1978-1979 academic year; the History Department of Colgate University; and Harvard University's Russian Research Center, which honored me with several summer fellowships. I should also like to express my gratitude to those colleagues and senior scholars who took the time to read the manuscript or offer valuable suggestions: Harley Balzer, Thomas Fallows, Daniel Field, Gregory Freeze, John Erickson, Samuel Kassow, John Keep, Edward L. Keenan, Jr., Daniel Orlovsky, Norman Stone, and Jonathan Zorn. A special thanks goes to John Bushnell, who generously shared with me a manuscript copy of his book on military mutinies in Russia from 1905 to 1907 before its publication.

I am most particularly indebted to my teacher and friend, Richard Pipes. It was his example of scholarship, professionalism, and general culture which inspired me to embark on the serious study of Russian history in the first place. He was, further, an unfailing source of support and advice during my long years as a graduate student at Harvard.

What I owe my wife, Sarah, is of course beyond expression.

Hamilton, N.Y.
April 1984

Civil-Military Conflict
in Imperial Russia
1881-1914

ONE

Military Professionalism,
the Imperial War Ministry,
and the Officers

IN IMPERIAL RUSSIA, as elsewhere, professional soldiers represented a distinct subgroup of professional men. The chief differences between the military profession and the associative professions such as medicine, law, and engineering are too obvious to review in detail. One distinction, of course, is that the struggle to monopolize the market for a particular service is foreign to the officer. As absolutist European states came to trammel the power of their nobilities and suppress private armies, so they raised their own standing forces, officered by men whose monopoly over the management of violence was secured to them by central authority. European army officers therefore never had to strive for official recognition: the value of the services they performed was never questioned by the modern state.[1]

If military professionalism is therefore a separate type of professionalism, how ought it to be characterized? Theoretical debates about the nature of military professionalism have been common among military sociologists. In my view, however, military sociologists often have been less interested in refining the theory of military professionalism as a study in its own right than in considering it in terms of its presumed outcomes. Thus, for instance, some of the most prominent scholars in the field have elected to analyze military professionalism largely as a factor either precipitating or forestalling military intervention in politics. Huntington, with the example of the American army uppermost in mind, argues that professionalism is a strong bulwark against the military coup, while Finer, who derives much of his evidence from the history of officer corps in the Third World, argues the reverse.[2] Janowitz, Perlmutter, van

---

[1] On this subject see Geoffrey Parker, "The 'Military Revolution,' 1560-1660—A Myth," *The Journal of Modern History* 48 (June 1976): 195-214, and Andre Corvisier, *Armies and Societies in Europe, 1494-1789*, trans. Abigail T. Siddal (Bloomington, Ind., 1949).

[2] Huntington, *Soldier and the State*, pp. 463-464; Finer, *Man on Horseback*, pp. 21-23; 188-189.

Doorn, Abrahamsson, and others have contributed to this dispute.[3] More recently the Dutch scholar G. Teitler has broken with the tradition of discussing military professionalism in relation to modern politics. Insisting on a broader temporal dimension, Teitler harks back to the fifteenth century in his search for the genesis of military professionalism. Although he advances the somewhat dubious hypothesis that the rise of military professionalism is solely dependent on the embourgeoisement of the officer corps, he does remind us that professionalism must be studied more as a dynamic than a static condition—a point of view which persuasively recommends itself to historians.[4]

Teitler aside, however, most sociologists have been concerned more with military professionalism in its twentieth-century maturity than in its nineteenth-century infancy. This has led many of them to assume that a sort of transnational uniformity in professionalization resulted in the triumph of military professionalism everywhere in Europe by 1900 or so. Even Finer and Huntington, who disagree on so many other matters, are in full accord here.[5] Further, many definitions of military professionalism proposed by sociologists place an inordinate stress on objective standards. A professional officer is said to possess an objectively measurable quantity of specialized knowledge or an objectively certifiable quantity of competence. Some historians have appropriated this method: Dietrich Beyrau, for instance, has recently supplied an objective definition of military professionalism in Russia.[6]

---

[3] Janowitz, *Professional Soldier*; Perlmutter, *Military and Politics*; van Doorn, *Armed Forces and Society*; van Doorn, *Military Profession*; Abrahamsson, *Military Professionalisation*.

[4] G. Teitler, *The Genesis of the Professional Officers' Corps* (London, 1977), pp. 6-8, 40-41, 226-227.

[5] "By 1875 the Prussian officer corps was fully professionalized. The qualification for entrance was educational, an examination system was in full swing, and the provision of centres of military education was complete. Advancement proceeded by merit. A General Staff had been formed. All these features formed part of one interlocking system and the officer corps which was the product enjoyed to the highest degree a sense of corporate identity.

France followed Germany, but at one remove. Britain was still slower. Nevertheless it would be true to say that at the beginning of the nineteenth century none of the three countries possessed a professional officer corps. By 1914 all did." Finer, *Man on Horseback*, p. 199.

"Prior to 1800 there was no such thing as a professional officer corps. In 1900 such bodies existed in virtually all major countries." Huntington, *Soldier and the State*, p. 19.

[6] Dietrich Beyrau, "Zur Ausbildung des russischen Offiziersstandes in 19. Jahrhundert: Von der 'Militarisierung' zur 'Professionalisierung,' " unpublished manuscript, 1980, p. 1; Huntington, *Soldier and the State*, p. 19; Feld, "Professionalism," pp. 62-63; Teitler, *Professional Officers' Corps*, p. 41; Janowitz, *Professional Soldier*, p. 6. I regret that I was unable to obtain a copy of Dr. Beyrau's recently published book in time to use it in my study.

Professionalism is, of course, superior to amateurism and the professional officer is more competent than the feudal amateur he supplanted, much as a professional physician today is superior to the itinerant barber-surgeon of the past. But competence is in this sense a relative concept only. At any given time military professionalism is not necessarily the guarantee of superb achievement, victory in the field, or even competence, for we must not gloss over the possibility that the standards of performance promoted by professional officers might be deluded or irrational. For professions like medicine, we might measure competence in terms of the doctors' ability to adapt to technological or scientific innovations. Yet if we attempt to apply this measure to the military establishments of nineteenth-century Europe we are left with a large problem. The late nineteenth and early twentieth centuries witnessed an enormous military technical revolution—the introduction of smokeless powder, quick-firing artillery, machine guns, etc.—whose implications were largely misunderstood by the General Staffs of Europe. Despite the warnings of such civilian prophets as Ivan Bliokh that the new weaponry would lead to trench warfare, deadlock, and unheard of levels of casualties, and despite episodes in the Russo-Japanese War such as the battle of Mukden which foreshadowed the bloodbaths of 1914-1918, the European military establishments were firmly in the grip of what has been called the "short war illusion."[7] European military leaders conducted their training, stockpiling, and planning in tune with the belief that the coming war would be a brief campaign resolved by an annihilating battle such as Sedan or Sadowa, and they thus disregarded broader questions of military potential. As no European army accurately foresaw World War I or adequately prepared for it, one could plausibly criticize them all for lack of imagination if not signal incompetence.[8]

Because of the difficulties which confuse objective evaluations of military competence in this period, I prefer a definition of military professionalism in which competence is deemphasized while *consciousness* is stressed. I see military professionalism as being defined by five criteria. First, the military professional acquires special knowledge and skill in schools of military learning or by experience in the field. Second, the military professional insists on the upgrading of standards of perform-

[7] On Bliokh, see Merze Tate, *The Disarmament Illusion. The Movement for a Limitation of Arms to 1907* (New York, 1942), pp. 171-173; also, I.S. Block (*sic*), *The Future of War*, trans. R. C. Long (Boston, 1902).

[8] On this, see John Gooch, *Armies in Europe* (London, 1980), pp. 143-144; also, May, *Knowing One's Enemies*. In *Forward into Battle: Fighting Tactics from Waterloo to Vietnam* (Chichester, 1981), Paddy Griffith offers some stimulating comments about why the impact of military technology on warfare in the late nineteenth century was misperceived. See pp. 43-72.

ance within the officer corps. In the third place, a professional officer corps has a strong sense of group identity which is expressed in a high degree of self-esteem and confidence in its ability to fulfill military tasks. The fourth criterion is the officers' recognition and articulation of the special interests of the military. Finally, there is the criterion of autonomy. If the army cannot itself control admissions to the officer corps or promotion within it, it nonetheless demands that considerations of "military expertise" weight heavily in these decisions.

In adopting this definition, then, we dismiss the idea that professionalism is always the equivalent of excellence or even competence. We may therefore also recognize that the "rightness" or "wrongness" of the tsarist army's military doctrine is likewise an invalid measure of its professionalism. The received views on tactics until 1905 were still those which Gen. M. I. Dragomirov propounded in his *Lectures on Tactics* (1864). One of the most popular and respected figures in the Russian army, Dragomirov had been the Russian military attaché during the Franco-Austrian War of 1859, a war climaxed at Solferino by one of the last successful bayonet charges against entrenched positions in European military history. At the Nicholas Academy of the General Staff, which he headed from 1878 to 1889, and thereafter in countless articles and pamphlets, Dragomirov tirelessly argued that the decisive factor in warfare was morale, not technology. This deduction led him to undervalue the significance of such weapons as quick-firing artillery and the machine gun in modern war.[9] In strategy, the dominant personality was Gen. G. A. Leer, whose textbook *Strategy* (1867) was in its sixth edition by 1898. Although he did perceive the military applications of such modern innovations as the railroad, Leer obdurately maintained that strategy was a finite art, that there was no point in studying the history of the most recent wars when all known strategic principles could be learned from an analysis of the campaigns of Republican Rome. He took this position even though he was the author of two very successful volumes on the Franco-Prussian War.[10] But the fact that both Dragomirov's and Leer's teachings (in hindsight) contained damaging elements provides no information about the professionalism of the army they served.

Yet even in the terms of this definition, just how professional was the

[9] G. P. Meshcheriakov, *Russkaia voennaia mysl' v XIX v.* (Moscow, 1973), pp. 200-204. Dragomirov is one of the most fascinating figures in Russian military history. Perhaps the best reminiscences of Dragomirov are those written by his son-in-law, Gen. A. S. Lukomskii, Hoover Institution Archives, Lukomskii collection, box 2, "Ocherki iz moei zhizni," pp. 13, 329-333, 400-401, 402-440, 465-446.

[10] Ibid., pp. 186-187, 192, 246. Peter von Wahlde, "Military Thought in Imperial Russia," Ph.D. diss., Indiana University, 1966, pp. 133-136.

tsarist officer corps in the late nineteenth century? To tackle this question we must begin with a consideration of the military reforms of the 1860s and 1870s, since these reforms represented in part a first attempt to professionalize Russia's military establishment. But further, because the reforms created the key military-administrative institutions which were to persist until the collapse of the Imperial regime, an examination of them is an indispensable foundation for the present study.

THE MILIUTIN REFORMS

In 1863 Emperor Alexander II confirmed Gen. D. A. Miliutin as sole War Minister. During the next seventeen years Miliutin implemented a series of liberal, imaginative, and integrally related reforms which had as their goal the infusion of efficiency and competence into every aspect of Russian military life.[11] Under his leadership the army was rearmed twice, abandoning the unreliable musket for the muzzle-loading rifle, and the latter for the breechloader. In the area of military administration, Miliutin thoroughly overhauled his ministry. By 1880 the central organs of the ministry comprised the Military Council (*Voennyi sovet*), the Main Staff, the Main Administrations (Cossacks, Intendancy, Engineers, Artillery, Military Medical, Military Justice, Military Educational), plus two separate Inspectorates—one for the Cavalry and the other for Marksmanship.[12] The Military Council, chaired by the War Minister, consisted of generals personally appointed by the Emperor. The Council drafted military legislation which it could submit directly to the autocrat, and made final decisions with regard to military expenditure. The War Ministry Chancellery was attached directly to the Council, acted as its secretariat, and further conducted correspondence with the civilian ministries and administrations.[13]

The Main Staff, an elephantine organization, had multifarious duties: it oversaw personnel, deployment, recruitment, military expenditure,

---

[11] On the Miliutin reforms generally, see P. A. Zaionchkovskii, *Voennye reformy 1860-70 godov v Rossii* (Moscow, 1952); Forrest A. Miller, *Dmitrii Miliutin and the Reform Era in Russia* (Nashville, Tenn., 1968), and N. A. Danilov, comp., *Istoricheskii obzor razvitiia voennogo upravleniia v Rossii*, vol. 1 of D. A. Skalon et al., eds., *Stoletie voennogo ministerstva, 1802-1902* (St. Petersburg, 1902), pp. 427-570. See also W. Bruce Lincoln, ''D. A. Miliutin's Views on Russia and Reform,'' in D. A. Miliutin, *Vospominaniia*, ed. W. Bruce Lincoln (Newtonville, Mass., 1980), pp. 1-14.

[12] *Obzor deiatel'nosti voennogo ministerstva v tsarstvovanie Imperatora Aleksandra III (1881-1894)* (St. Petersburg, 1903), p. 59.

[13] A. Rediger and A. Gulevich, *Komplektovanie i ustroistvo vooruzhennoi sily*, 3rd ed. (St. Petersburg, 1900), p. 466.

education, military statistics, and strategic planning.[14] The Chief Military Court had a prominent consultative role in the preparation of military legislation; since 1867, it had been the final court of cassation for all military judicial cases.[15] The Main Administrations represented powerful fiefdoms within the Ministry, each the nexus of its own particular technical specialty.

Yet Miliutin's most lasting reform (the Soviet Union retains it to this day) was the creation of military districts incorporating all of the provinces of the Empire. In 1881 there were thirteen of these districts—St. Petersburg, Finland, Vil'na, Warsaw, Kiev, Odessa, Khar'kov, Moscow, Kazan', Turkestan, Western Siberia, Eastern Siberia, the Caucasus, plus the territory (*oblast'*) of the Don Cossack Army, which enjoyed military district status. In 1888, the Khar'kov District was abolished, its provinces reassigned to Moscow and Kiev. In 1884 the Eastern Siberian region was split into two—Amur District and Irkutsk District. In 1890 yet another territory with district status (Transcaspian) joined the list. Each of these districts and territories was headed by a district commander, de jure responsible to none but the Emperor himself, de facto dependent on the War Minister. Each district, as well, possessed its own council, staff, and administrations of intendency, artillery, engineers, and medicine, in exact parallel to the organization of the central War Ministry in Petersburg.[16] Before Miliutin, the Russian army, in terms of its organizational redundancies and structural defects, had been one of the most backward institutions in the Imperial state. Under Miliutin's brilliant tutelage, the army and the War Ministry at one bound matched the most sophisticated of the Empire's governmental agencies.

Of utmost significance to Miliutin personally were those of his innovations that directly affected the quality of both officers and men in the army. To Miliutin, professionalism began with education. In the period 1825-1855, less than 30 percent of officers commissioned into the service had any strictly military education.[17] Miliutin made military education a requirement for a commission, and further altered the existing military educational system. The old cadet corps, that combination primary and secondary school for future officers which had emphasized brutal discipline and automatic obedience, gave way to the military *Gymnasium* staffed with civilian instructors and distinguished by its

[14] A. Kavtaradze, "Iz istorii russkogo general'nogo shtaba," *Voenno -istoricheskii zhurnal* 13, no. 12 (Dec. 1971), p. 77.

[15] See chap. 4 for a more complete account of the military judicial system.

[16] *Obzor deiatel'nosti*, pp. 59-60, 68-69, 70.

[17] Oliver Allen Ray, "The Imperial Russian Army Officer," *Political Science Quarterly* 76, no. 4 (Dec. 1961): 577.

breadth of required courses in the sciences and liberal arts. A *Gymnasium* graduate matriculated at a so-called military school (*voennoe uchilishche*) where he studied special military subjects such as strategy, tactics, and fortification, but simultaneously continued with work in foreign languages, Russian literature, and natural science.[18] At the same time, Miliutin also regularized the old, less elite, junker schools, and opened them and some of the military schools to the previously "bound" classes—including the peasantry. Quite obviously, Miliutin's goal had been to create a broadly educated, socially responsible officer corps, and to some extent he was successful. One Soviet scholar has in fact ascribed the notable liberalism and even radicalism of certain officers of the sixties and seventies to Miliutin's educational system.[19]

Concern for improving standards among the rank-and-file officers was paralleled by a concern for transforming the officers of the General Staff into a true military elite. The vehicle of that transformation, once again, was education—in this case substantive changes in the curriculum and status of the Nicholas Academy of the General Staff. Miliutin's plan was to make the Staff Academy the school for the most intellectually able officers in the army, officers who were to be selected, if possible, without regard to social class or wealth.[20]

After Miliutin's reform of the Academy, two tiers of competitive examinations controlled admissions. Any officer with four (later three) years' field service was eligible. An officer who announced his intention of applying received a discharge from duty for three months in which to prepare. He then sat for an examination in the headquarters of the military district in which he served. If successful, he received an invitation to participate in written and oral examinations conducted by the Academy professoriate in St. Petersburg. These examinations, lasting for several days, included military subjects, foreign languages, and mathematics. Beating out his competitors, the officer was then enrolled in the first of his two years of general courses. If he completed these in the first academic group (*vyshii razriad*), he was both rewarded with one year's salary and made eligible to continue into the final third year

---

[18] Zaionchovskii, *Voennye reformy*, pp. 227-253, passim.

[19] V. R. Leikina-Svirskaia, *Intelligentsiia v Rossii vo vtoroi polovine XIX veka* (Moscow, 1971), p. 98. On junker schools, see Kenez, "Pre-Revolutionary Officer Corps," p. 126.

[20] On the role of the Staff generally, see Matitiahu Mayzel, "The Formation of the Russian General Staff, 1880-1917: A Social Study," *Cahiers du Monde russe et sovietique* 16, nos. 3-4 (July-Dec. 1975): 294-321; also Mayzel, "Generals and Revolutionaries, the Russian General Staff during the Revolution: A Study in the Transformation of a Military Elite," in *Studien zur Militärgeschichte, Militärwissenschaft und Konfliktforschung* (Osnabruck) 19 (1979): 16-18.

of his training. His class rank at the end of this year would determine whether he would be allowed to join the Staff or not. If he was permitted to do so, he was granted an immediate promotion of one full rank, plus the right to wear a special uniform which would distinguish him forever as a member of the eminent fraternity of Staff officers.[21] Staff officers not only held down staff jobs in Petersburg or the military districts; their visibility and credentials placed them squarely in the recruitment pool for high command in the Imperial army. Then, too, the same factors enabled them to abandon military service if they so chose in favor of lucrative and responsible employment in the civilian ministries of state. In view of the brilliant career prospects open to Staff officers it was not surprising that admission to the Academy was dearly prized.[22] Although there was a structural bias in favor of wealthy applicants, since they could afford superior secondary education and coaching to prepare themselves for the Academy's entrance examinations, the fact is that the Staff did accept candidates from every social background. This then made the Academy one of the most democratic institutions in the Russian army. In 1871, for instance, the year future War Minister V. A. Sukhomlinov enrolled in the junior class, over 37 percent of the Academy's entering students were officers of the regular army infantry, which, as we will see somewhat later in this chapter, was the most socially inferior branch of the service.[23]

What Miliutin had done for the General Staff he replicated on a smaller scale for three other intellectually prestigious groups of officers: the lawyers, the engineers, and the artillerists. The Alexander Academy of Military Justice, the Nicholas Engineering Academy, and the Michael Artillery Academy all came to feature strict two- to three-year courses and rigorous competitive examinations for admission. Just as it was true for the General Staff, entry into these technical specialties was to be preserved for a small group of intellectual mandarins culled from the entire officer corps.[24]

---

[21] Mayzel, "Russian General Staff," pp. 303-306; Major General Chistiakov, comp., *Nikolaevskaia akademiia general'nogo shtaba. Naznachenie akademii* (St. Petersburg, 1904), pp. 3, 5, 8, 10, 15, 32, 34, 35, 37; M. Grulev, *Zapiski generala evreia* (Paris, 1930), p. 136.

[22] E. I. Martynov, *Iz pechal'nogo opyta russko-iaponskoi voiny* (St. Petersburg, 1906), p. 36; F. F. Novitskii, *Na puti k usovershenstvovaniiu gosudarstvennoi oborony* (St. Petersburg, 1909), pp. 30-33; A. Rediger, *Zametki po voennoi administratsii* (St. Petersburg, 1885), p. 135; TsGVIA, f. 544, op. 1, d. 1208, ll. 15, 26; A. Samoilo, *Dve zhizni*, 2d ed. (Moscow, 1963), p. 65.

[23] TsGVIA, f. 544, op. 1, d. 711, l. 35.

[24] On the Alexander Academy, see chap. 4; "Mikhailovskaia artilleriiskaia akademiia," *VE*, vol. 16 (St. Petersburg, 1914), pp. 355-356; "Nikolaevskaia inzhenernaia akademiia," *VE*, vol. 16 (St. Petersburg, 1914), p. 611.

Miliutin's interests in military reform, however, ran deeper than the mere betterment of Russian officers. In fact, his greatest achievement of all was doubtless the enactment of the universal conscription law of January 4, 1874. Miliutin's success here was due to widespread astonishment among Russia's governing elite about the achievements of Prussia, which had crushed the Austrians decisively in 1866 and had emerged after 1871 as the dominant force in the newly established German Empire. It was held by many in St. Petersburg that failure to imitate Prussia's universal draft system might be to court the risk of military disaster in some future conflict. Miliutin capitalized on these worries to outmatch his political opponents and force his bill into law: by its provisions all estates (*sosloviia*), including the previously exempt gentry, became liable for service in the ranks. There was a further refinement, however. The law also deducted time from the prescribed tour of active duty in correspondence with the recruit's education; the higher the level of education, the shorter the term of service with the colors.[25] The conscription law, then, was both an act of military reform and an act of social reform, since Miliutin hoped with its aid to drive the peasantry of Russia into the schools. The act of 1874 was the quintessential illustration of Miliutin's reformism: while using the resources of the Empire to modernize the army, Miliutin also wished to use the resources of the army to modernize the Empire.

The Miliutin period was a time of promise for the Russian army. Insofar as military education had been standardized and made a requirement for admission to the officer corps, the Russian army had taken its first step towards professionalization. However, the Miliutin system did not survive Miliutin's fall from power intact. When Alexander III came to the throne after the assassination of his father in 1881, he swiftly forced Miliutin from office, replacing him with Gen. P. S. Vannovskii. Within a few months of this event, the new autocrat convened a commission under the presidency of Adjutant General Kotsebu to review the Miliutin reforms *in toto*. Although the majority of the members of the commission favored dismantling Miliutin's War Ministry organization, fiduciary prudence argued against such sweeping changes.[26] Thus Miliutin's administrative institutions—in the central Ministry itself, and in the military districts—remained largely unaltered. Such was not the case, however, with military secondary education. Military *Gymnasien* were replaced with resuscitated cadet corps, and civilian instructors were purged from their faculties. Vannovskii narrowed curricula both in the

[25] Zaionchkovskii, *Voennye reformy*, pp. 257-303, passim.
[26] Zaionchkovskii, *Samoderzhavie*, pp. 93-102; Danilov, *Istoricheskii obzor*, pp. 578-587, 615.

cadet corps and the military schools and tightened discipline, reintroducing corporal punishment.[27]

But most importantly, access to the cadet corps and hence to the military schools was severely limited for boys who were not of the gentry. Miliutin had envisioned his conscription law and his opening of schools and officers' messes to non-nobles as blows against the very idea of the estate, as a movement away from the antiquated concept of estates towards a more general concept of citizenship. Indeed, the idea of citizenship had underpinned many of the "Great Reforms" which followed in the wake of the abolition of serfdom in 1861. Such novel institutions as the jury, the zemstvo, and the town council were designed to include members of all estates and thus to blur the distinctions between them. But the more conservative autocracy of Alexander III rejected this schema and enacted law after law to sharpen the differentiation between the estates and to prop up the tottering edifice of gentry privilege. Thus, after 1881 the only practicable means of entering the officer corps for the non-noble became matriculation at one of the sixteen junker schools. These were not under the control of the Main Military Educational Administration, but were rather run by each military district separately. Upon graduation, junkers emerged not as commissioned officers but as *podpraporshchiki* (subensigns), and had to serve several years as essentially glorified NCOs before being granted true officer status. Representatives of the more lowly estates soon became more numerous in the educationally inferior junker schools while the cadet corps and military schools came to be populated chiefly by scions of the gentry.[28] Since graduates of the military schools were better educated and connected than pupils at the junker schools, they had greater opportunities for service in the Guards and in the elite technical services, and they had obvious advantages in the examinations for admission to any of the military institutions of higher learning. In short, the Imperial government was quite brazenly skewing the military educational system to favor the gentry. Although one criterion of professionalism was satisfied after 1881 as it had been in the Miliutin years, since military education

---

[27] Zaionchkovskii, *Samoderzhavie*, pp. 294-337, passim. Aleksandr Kuprin gives a lurid account of these "counterreformed" schools in his novella, "The Kadets." See Aleksandr Kuprin, "Kadety," *Na perelome* (Nizhnyi Novgorod, 1929), pp. 11-101 (esp. 98-101).

[28] Whereas in 1877 74 percent of the junkers were children of nobles, either hereditary or personal, by 1894 only 53 percent of the junkers were of noble origin. By contrast, in 1895 87 percent of all the boys in the cadet corps and 85 percent of all students in the military schools had fathers who were either hereditary or personal nobles. See Kenez, "Pre-Revolutionary Officer Corps," p. 127; *Vsepoddanneishii otchet o deistviiakh voennogo ministerstva za 1895 g. Otchet o sostoianii voenno-uchebnykh zavedenii* (St. Petersburg, 1897), pp. 8-9.

was still mandatory for admission to the officer corps, it is certain that the institutionalization of inequality of opportunity represented by this bifurcated military educational system was both socially and professionally retrograde.

Self-Improvement

If the first condition of military professionalism—special education—was technically met after 1881, what of the second—a concern for raising standards and self-improvement? We may justly conclude that the majority of army officers in the eighties and nineties were indifferent to these pursuits. Contemporaries charged that the bulk of the officers were disinclined to read and study; this statement gains credibility from a glance at Russian book statistics.[29] In 1894 only 2 percent of all titles and .9 percent of all copies of books printed in the Russian Empire treated military themes. There were then about thirty-four thousand officers on active duty, roughly twice the Empire's complement of doctors. Yet in 1894, 9 percent of all titles and 3.7 percent of all books published in the Empire dealt with medicine. As late as 1903 and 1904 there were only 165 and 124 military titles published respectively.[30]

The resistance to self-improvement suggested by these figures was in part a function of the army's poor performance after 1881 in the competition with other occupations for bright young men. The Russian War Ministry, quite simply, was unable to attract the sort of candidates it needed. In 1898, for instance, the military district commander of Kiev complained of the numerous "failures" (*neudachniki*) who were entering the junker schools and hence the officer corps since their poor talents had disqualified them from civilian careers.[31] In its annual report for 1904, the Ministry of War itself emphasized that the majority of Russia's military district commanders were perturbed by the "low mental level" of the bulk of the officers.[32]

Low quality went hand in hand with inadequate quantity. The complement of serving officers varied from 3 to 8 percent lower than the norm established by law in the last fifteen years of the nineteenth

---

[29] For a couple of representative remarks, see Iu. Lazarevich, "Zametki o boevoi pogotovke nashei pekhoty," *VS*, no. 8 (Aug. 1905): 78; Col. Ladyzhenskii, "O mirnoi podgotovke kavalerii k voine i o nastavlenii dlia vedeniia zaniatii v kavalerii," *VS*, no. 2 (Feb. 1906): 96. See also Bushnell, "Tsarist Officer Corps," pp. 763-764.

[30] *Knizhnyi vestnik*, no. 9 (Sept. 1894): 329; "Ukazatel'novykh knig," *Knizhnyi vestnik*, no. 12 (Dec. 1894): "Ukazatel'novykh knig," *Knizhnyi vestnik*, no. 12 (Dec. 1904): 107-110; Leikina-Svirskaia, *Intelligentsiia v Rossii*, pp. 140-141.

[31] TsGVIA, f. 1, op. 2, d. 511, l. 1.

[32] TsGVIA, f. 1, op. 2, d. 163, l. 32.

century.[33] Recruitment difficulties were not unique to Russia, for in other European armies, notably the Italian and French, there were substantial increases in the number of officer vacancies around the turn of the century.[34] In the Russian case, however, there were three distinctive reasons why the officer's career lost its attractiveness. The first of these was ideological. After Vannovskii took over the War Ministry in 1881, the antiprogressive spirit of the military counterreforms he introduced severely cropped the prestige of military service among liberal and idealistic Russian youths. For young educated Russians who desired to serve society, the calling of army officer was falling into disrepute.

Another reason for the unpopularity of officer service was the extremely low pay of Russian officers. Officers in the Italian and French armies also voiced complaints about inadequate pay.[35] But Russian officers chose to compare themselves with their better-compensated German counterparts abroad, and civilian bureaucrats at home. Officers' emolument, figured as a complex combination of salary, plus "housing," "table," and sometimes "forage" money, had been set by law in 1859 lower than levels for civilian bureaucrats of comparable position in the table of ranks. Alexander III was to add a piddling amount to officers' pay packets in 1883, but significant improvement in compensation had to wait for 1888.[36] Since the cost of living was not stable in late nineteenth-century Russia, officers below the rank of lieutenant colonel were under increasing economic pressure as the years went by. War Minister Vannovskii was not exaggerating very much when in 1893 he described the great mass of Russian officers as "impoverishing themselves in the service." Low wages were clearly demoralizing, as Grand Duke Vladimir Aleksandrovich, commander of St. Petersburg Military District, noted in 1897.[37] More than this, however, given the stunning growth and opportunities in Russia's trade and industrial sectors, many young men elected against underpaid military service; many others, who did enter,

[33] TsGVIA, f. 1/L, op. 2, d. 1140, l. 8.

[34] See John Whittam, *The Politics of the Italian Army, 1861-1918* (London, 1977), p. 152.

[35] Ibid., p. 150.; Raoul Girardet, *La Societé militaire dans la France contemporaine, 1815-1939* (Paris, 1953), p. 269; Douglas Porch, *March to the Marne: The French Army, 1871-1914* (Cambridge, 1981), pp. 89-90.

[36] Zaionchkovskii, *Samoderzhavie*, pp. 223-224; Stein, *Der Offizier*, pp. 417-418; "Dovol'stvie voisk," *VE*, vol. 9 (St. Petersburg, 1912), pp. 146-147.

[37] *Izvlechenie iz vsepoddanneishego otcheta Ego Imperatorskogo Vysochestva, Glavnokomanduiushchego voiskami gvardii i peterburgskogo voennogo okruga za 1897* (St. Petersburg, n.d.), pp. 1-2; *Vsepoddanneishii doklad po voennomu ministerstvu 1893 goda. Sekretno* (St. Petersburg, 1894), p. 224.

soon fled to better paying posts in the Frontier Guard, the Gendarmes, or the Ministry of the Interior.[38]

The last factor which discredited the officer corps was the thorough redeployment of the army in the eighties and nineties. To counterbalance Germany's alarming superiority in mobilization speed, P. S. Vannovskii and Main Staff Chief N. N. Obruchev devised a plan which was to remain at the heart of Russian strategic thinking until almost 1914. Germany's advantage, resulting from her ability to mobilize her forces rapidly in the east, they reasoned, would be offset were Russia to permanently station a large proportion of her active army on her Western frontier. Accordingly, from 1881 to 1894 the Russian War Ministry fulfilled the task of concentrating over 45 percent of the army in the western military districts of Kiev, Odessa, and Warsaw.[39] As a consequence of this westward shift of the Russian army, thousands of officers accustomed to the diversions of Petersburg, Kiev, Warsaw, or Moscow suddenly found themselves assigned to miserable little hamlets in western Poland and the Ukraine. The shock of this redeployment caused the exodus of many officers from the army.[40]

Of course for the scions of that highest Imperial elite for whom wealth was allied with social prestige, the suitability of a young man's start in life as a Guards officer was unquestioned. The Preobrazhenskii Guards, Izmailovskii Guards, Life Guard Hussars, Horse Guards, etc., were never to complain of difficulty in attracting officers. And at the bottom of the social scale, the grandson of an emancipated peasant, like Denikin, might eagerly grasp at officer's rank as tangible proof of social mobility. For many, however, a life in the army was a career decision enforced by lack of alternatives. And such people had little desire to improve either their special military knowledge or their level of general culture.[41] In this respect the Russian officer corps was unprofessional.

GROUP IDENTITY

With regard to a sense of group identity, the third point in our definition of military professionalism, the notorious disunity of the Russian officer

[38] *Izvlechenie*, pp. 1-2. Also, A. P. Martynov, *Moia sluzhba v otdel'nom korpuse zhandarmov. Vospominaniia*, ed. Richard Wraga (Stanford, 1972), pp. 10-16.

[39] *Vsepoddanneishii doklad po voennomu ministerstvu 1892 goda. Sekretno* (St. Petersburg, 1893), pp. 13-41. See also: *Obzor deiatel'nosti*, appendix, "Mobilizatsionnaia gotovnost' voik. ves'ma sekretno," p. 10.

[40] V. A. Sukhomlinov, *Vospominaniia Sukhomlinova* (Moscow and Leningrad, 1926), p. 63.

[41] A. Kersnovskii, *Istoriia russkoi armii*, pt. 3 *(1881-1917 g.g.)* (Belgrade, 1935), pp. 614-615; A. I. Denikin, *Staraia armiia*, vol. 2 (Paris, 1931), pp. 7-8.

corps militated against a highly articulated corporate spirit. Unlike English and Prussian officers, Russian officers were not all cut from the same mold.[42] They were, rather, distinguished from each other by striking differences in outlook, social standing, educational attainments, and wealth. The antithesis of the smart young lieutenant of the Horse Guards in St. Petersburg, attending fashionable entertainments, dining at the best restaurants, and playing polo, was the half-educated staff captain in Turkestan on a drunken spree. The Russian army contained a hierarchy of subservices, each with a different status, each competing for limited resources. And an officer's life, privileges, and conditions of service varied in strict dependence on the sort of unit in which he served.[43]

We have already seen how Miliutin invested the General Staff, the military lawyers, engineers, and ordnance specialists with favors and privileges. Each of these services had a separate Main Administration within the War Ministry; and each of them represented an independent hierarchy in which educational standards were higher, promotions faster, working conditions better, and the work itself more intellectually demanding than that in the infantry. The natural outcome of this was the perpetuation of caste spirit. And caste spirit of each of these services was duplicated down the line in other technical specialties—the Intendancy, the Corps of Military Veterinarians, the Military Medical Corps, the Corps of Military Topographers.[44]

The officers in the technical services or staff could at least argue that they had earned preferential treatment. But members of other elite groups in the army could not offer the same rationalization. Consider, for instance, the most exclusive organization within the army: the Imperial suite. To be one of the roughly one hundred and fifty officers who comprised the suite, or more precisely the Imperial Chief Apartment (later the Imperial Field Chancellery), was to be attached directly to the person of the Emperor and consequently to be an official courtier. There were three levels of membership: aide-de-camp (ADC) for officers not

[42] See for instance Gwyn Harries-Jenkins, *The Army in Victorian Society* (London, 1977), pp. 247-248; Gordon A. Craig, *The Politics of the Prussian Army, 1640-1945* (London, 1964), pp. 218, 237, 238.

[43] Almost all Russian military memoirists have emphasized this distinctly. The divisions among the Russian officers are especially well treated in Stein, "Der Offizier," pp. 378-389. For a contemporary foreign perspective, see also [Anon.], *L'Armee russe et ses chefs en 1888* (Paris, 1888), p. 57.

[44] A. V. von Shwartz, "Vospominaniia," in *Russian Emigre Archives*, ed. Alexander Pronin, vol. 3 (Fresno, Calif., 1973), pp. 57-64; Rediger, *Komplektovanie*, p. 240; *Istoriia 'dvorian' i 'Konstantinovtsev' 1807-1907* (Petersburg, n.d.), app. 1, pp. 4-5; Denikin, *Staraia armiia*, vol. 2, pp. 10, 116-118.

of general's rank, major general of the suite, and adjutant general of His Imperial Highness, for lieutenant generals, full generals, and field marshals. Such officers were subordinate to the Commander of the Imperial Chief Apartment, an official of no mean power, who also had jurisdiction over the Commandant of the Imperial palace and the Imperial convoy. Under Alexander III, Adjutant General Rikhter occupied this post; under Nicholas II, it was filled by Baron Frederiks, who after 1902 was simultaneously Minister of the Imperial Court.[45]

Frederiks once wrote Nicholas II that the purpose of the suite was to serve "as an organ for the personal contact of Your Highness with your army," a rather comical assertion in view of the fact that the officers who dwelt in the giddying atmosphere of the court were as far removed as possible from the realities of Russian military life.[46] Membership in the suite was entirely at the Emperor's pleasure. Although he could theoretically appoint anyone to the suite, he usually chose people with high social standing. All members of the Imperial family who acquired military rank were promptly inducted into the suite. But if an officer did not happen to be a Romanov, his chances of entering the suite were better than average if his last name was Sheremet'ev, Orlov, or Osten-Saken. The Emperor might tap a less exalted officer for the suite in recognition of some signal act of loyalty or heroism.

Membership in the suite conferred more than the distinction of sporting the Emperor's monogram on one's uniform. An officer of the suite held a court appointment and drew a handsome salary whether he had any other employment or not. On August 30, 1892, there were nine adjutant generals, four major generals, and nine ADCs who served in no other state institution than the suite. At the end of the century, the salary of a major general of the suite was 3,300 rubles per annum, while that of an adjutant general was almost 6,000 rubles.[47] Associated with the court, a young officer might catch the eye of one of the ministers of the Imperial government, or even attract the attention of the Emperor himself. If so, such an officer might be offered a lucrative and visible post—in the diplomatic corps, the Ministry of Finance, or the Ministry of the Interior. Thus Durnovo appointed ADC Colonel Kosach vice-governor of Petersburg Province in August 1892. And Nicholas II made ADC Dzhunkovskii the acting governor of Moscow. In fact, almost all

[45] Count Eric Lewenhaupt, trans., *The Memoirs of Marshall Mannerheim* (New York, 1954), p. 77; A. A. Mossolov, *At the Court of the Last Tsar*, trans. E. W. Dickes (London, 1935), pp. 120-127, 182-183; TsGVIA, f. 970, op. 3, d. 300, ll. 89-92; A. A. Ignatyev, *A Subaltern in Old Russia*, trans. Ivor Montagu (London, 1944), p. 17.

[46] TsGVIA, f. 970, op. 3, d. 678, l. 61.

[47] TsGVIA, f. 970, op. 3, d. 300, ll. 42, 91-92; TsGVIA, f. 970, op. 3, d. 999, l. 279.

of Nicholas II's choices of military men for civilian posts alighted on members of the suite. Sviatopolk-Mirskii came from the suite to the Ministry of the Interior, as did Trepov, Veretennikov, and many others.[48]

The Imperial Guards were but one rung beneath the suite in status. The Guards consisted of three infantry and two cavalry divisions, four rifle regiments, a sappers regiment, and four artillery brigades, all of which comprised 4 percent of the officers and men in the Russian army.[49] In 1692, Peter I had founded the first two Guards regiments, the Preobrazhenskii and Semenovskii, in direct imitation of the military traditions of Western Europe.[50] In the West, the Guards both performed the function which had historically given them their name—e.g., the protection of the monarch's person—and fulfilled other duties on the battlefield consonant with their status as crack troops. Although in Russia, as in the West, any military justification for the Guards had vanished by the mid-nineteenth century (since they performed no better in combat than any other units), they persisted in enjoying high prestige. Technically, Guards service was supposed to be the reward for superb performance in military secondary schools. In fact, however, due to both the high cost of Guards service and an overt patronage network, Guards officers were selected almost exclusively from among the richest and most ancient families in the Empire. No officer without a private source of income could dream of serving in the Guards. The officers' lists for such regiments as the Horse Guards or the Chevalier Guards resemble pages from a book of heraldry.[51] As one might expect, the Guards officer possessed valuable privileges. First, he could depend on speedy promotions, due in part to the fact that there was no statutory limit on the number of officers who could hold the rank of colonel and above in the corps of Guards officers.[52] Further, until 1884, a Guards captain was technically equal in rank to a lieutenant colonel in the regular army, a Guards colonel the equivalent of any army major general, and so forth.[53]

Like the beneficiaries of the old Muscovite system of *mestnichestvo*,

[48] TsGVIA, f. 970, op. 3, d. 300, l. 120; TsGVIA, f. 970, op. 3, d. 999, ll. 1, 17, 51, 55; TsGVIA, f. 970, op. 3, d. 1505, passim.

[49] M. Lyons, *The Russian Imperial Army* (Stanford, 1968), pp. 7-58; Denikin, *Staraia armiia*, vol. 2, p. 144.

[50] M. D. Rabinovich, *Polki petrovskoi armii. Kratkii spravochnik, 1698-1725* (Moscow, 1977), p. 25.

[51] Samoilo, *Dve zhizni*, pp. 46, 55; Prince Felix Youssoupoff, *Lost Splendour*, trans. Ann Green and Nicholas Katkoff (London, 1953), p. 112; Ignatyev, *Subaltern in Old Russia*, pp. 9, 14, 15, 66.

[52] B. V. Gerua, *Vospominaniia o moei zhizni*, vol. 1 (Paris, 1969), p. 62; Rediger, *Komplektovanie*, p. 238.

[53] Mayzel, "Russian General Staff," p. 302.

which assigned state posts according to an elaborate code of family precedence, the Guardist's social standing tended to give him a natural claim on high military command. All too often, a general of the Guards cavalry became commander of a regular army infantry division, even though he was egregiously ignorant of the most elementary principles of infantry tactics. As late as 1910, 51 of the 145 army infantry divisions were commanded by generals of the Guards.[54] The gorgeous chevrons of the Guards also provided as many opportunities for transfer into other areas of state service as the black velvet and aiguillette of the General Staff. When Baron Frederiks, former commander of the Horse Guards, took over the Ministry of the Imperial Court in 1902, he initiated the policy of hiring exclusively officers from his old regiment.[55] This latter example highlights another noteworthy point about the Guards. Even though the corps of the Guards had a separate corporate existence within the Russian army, and even though all Guards units in the Empire were subordinate to the same person, the commander of St. Petersburg Military District, the Guards did not themselves represent an entirely unified group. Rivalry poisoned the relations between the Guards. The Warsaw Guards frequently articulated their contempt for their confreres in St. Petersburg, and vice versa.[56]

Another greatly indulged group within the Russian army, and indeed one of that army's chief peculiarities, was the Cossacks. This hereditary warrior estate was bound to universal adult military service in exchange for corporate existence and certain other rights. Cossacks were organized in twelve armies (voiska)—the Don, Kuban, Orenburg, Terek, Transbaikal, Ural, Siberian, Semirech'e, Astrakhan', Ussur'ia, Irkutsk and Krasnoiarsk. A Cossack army was not only a military unit but also a corporate identity and a territorial division. The armies, each headed by an ataman, varied in territory, population, and the number of troops they could furnish for active duty. In 1894, for instance, the Army of the Don, the largest army, had almost 22,000 men on active service; Ussur'ia, the smallest, supplied only 198.[57] Each Cossack ranker spent four years on active duty with a first-line (ochered') regiment. Thereafter, he moved to a second-line regiment, and after a few years, to a

[54] Denikin, Staraia, vol. 2, p. 115; A. P. Skugarevskii, Ocherki i zametki, vol. 3 (St. Petersburg, 1913), p. 27.

[55] Mossolov, Court of the Last Tsar, p. 127.

[56] Samoilo, Dve zhizni, p. 55.

[57] A. I. Nikol'skii et al., "Glavnoe upravlenie kazach'ikh voisk. Istoricheskii ocherk," in Stoletie voennogo ministerstva, ed. D. A. Skalon, vol. 11, pt. 1 (St. Petersburg, 1902), pp. 1-17, 551-768, passim. A. M. Zolotarev, Zapiski voennoi statistiki Rossii, 2d ed., vol. 1 (St. Petersburg, 1894), p. 402.

third-line regiment, for a total of eight to ten years' additional reserve service. Regiments of the second and third line were supposed to be called up only in the event of a general mobilization.[58]

Although a Cossack private could only serve in a Cossack regiment, the Imperial government did make some feeble efforts to integrate Cossack officers into the rest of the officer corps. In the late 1870s, non-Cossack officers were permitted to serve in Cossack regiments, while Cossack officers were allowed to accept military posts outside their own armies. Yet this experiment did not result in much mingling between Cossacks and outsiders. Cossack officers, with their distinctive traditions, were still very much members of an ingrown elite.[59]

The regular army cavalry, roughly 10 percent of the peacetime army, lost favor during the reign of Alexander III. General Sukhotin, an enthusiastic student of the American Civil War, convinced his sovereign that the day of the massed cavalry charge was over, and that the only conceivable role for the cavalry in the future was for scouting parties (a la Jeb Stuart) or as a source of mounted infantrymen. Alexander was impressed enough by these arguments to transform all of the regular cavalry uhlan and hussar regiments into dragoon (or mounted infantry) regiments. The gorgeous uniforms, feathered shakos, and gilded braiding, such tempting targets for the infantryman's bullet, gave way to drab army green. But if this diminished the snob appeal of cavalry service, the Imperial Russian state was nevertheless kinder to the cavalry officer than to his infantry counterpart. In the first place, the cavalry enjoyed protection under both Alexander III and Nicholas II from the most influential military men within the Romanov family. Nikolai Nikolaevich the elder and his son Nikolai Nikolaevich the younger each served in turn as Inspector General of the Cavalry. The cavalry could therefore rely on these two Grand Dukes to defend its interests within the councils of state; perhaps as a result, promotions within the army cavalry were faster than within the army infantry, and perhaps for the same reason, the cavalry were often issued better equipment than the infantry. Indeed, some regular cavalry regiments, such as the Sumskii Hussars of General Zeslavin, were so prestigious and exclusive that they were virtually interchangeable within the Guards.[60]

Far beneath the ADC, the Guards cornet, the Staff officer, the military

[58] Nikol'skii, *Glavnoe*, pp. 460-477; V. M. Bribovskii, *Gosudarstvennoe ustroistvo i upravlenie Rossiiskoi Imperii* (Odessa, 1912), pp. 186-187.

[59] V. D. Novitskii, *Iz vospominanii zhandarma* (Priboi, 1929), pp. 13, 62.

[60] Zolotarev, *Zapiski*, p. 388; Kersnovskii, *Istoriia*, pp. 498-499, 504; Sukhomlinov, *Vospominaniia*, p. 61; Novitskii, *Na puti*, pp. 135-136; Vladimir S. Littauer, *Russian Hussar* (London, 1965), pp. 43-44, 56, 100.

prosecutor, and all the rest stood the officer of the regular Russian infantry. The officers in the line infantry regiments made up the majority of the Russian officer corps. Although graduates of the military schools were to be found among them, in the main they were products of the junker schools (as late as 1908 over three-quarters of regular army captains had been trained in junker schools) and as such were people who technically had not even completed secondary education. It was in the junker schools and the line infantry that the real social dilution of the tsarist army in the late nineteenth and early twentieth centuries occurred: the growing predominance of non-noble officers in the regular infantry explains why the proportion of non-nobles in the entire officer corps rose from 26 percent in 1895 to over 45 percent in 1910.[61]

Promotions for these men came more slowly than for any other group in the army. For example, whereas an officer of the General Staff might expect to be a lieutenant colonel after 15 to 18 years of active service, most infantry officers had to wait much longer. Of the 932 army infantry captains confirmed in lieutenant colonel's rank between 1900 and 1905, only 8.9 percent (83) had served 15 to 20 years; 51.2 percent (477) had served 20 to 25 years; and 39.9 percent (372) had served 25 to 30 years. By contrast, a Staff officer who served 30 years could expect to be a major general at least. Over half of the regular army captains never became active-duty lieutenant colonels at all, receiving this rank, as was customary in the Russian Empire, only as a retirement present.[62] The places in which these forgotten men had to reside added to their distress: as we have seen, the plurality of Russia's army was quartered in Poland and the Ukraine, and a large percentage of the rest of the army infantry was stationed in desolate outposts strewn along the border regions in the Caucasus, Turkestan, or Eastern Siberia. Unlike the Staff officer or military lawyer, who might mark time temporarily in such a place awaiting an eventual transfer, the officer of a line infantry regiment could anticipate spending his entire life in some such gloomy backwater. When poor, ignorant, and sometimes unstable people collide with depressing environments, in Russia, as everywhere, the results could be alcoholism,

---

[61] Wildman, *Russian Imperial Army*, pp. 22-23. Indeed, by 1910 a higher proportion of students in the military elementary schools were the sons of peasants (17.92 percent) rather than the sons of hereditary nobles (15.77 percent). See *Vsepoddanneishii otchet o deistviiakh voennogo ministerstva za 1910 g. Otchet o sostoianii voenno-uchebnykh zavedenii* (St. Petersburg, 1912), p. 3. For more extensive prosopographical data on the *sosloviia* represented in the officer corps, see Dmitry Ponomareff, "Political Loyalty and Social Composition of the Military Elite: The Russian Officer Corps, 1861-1903," RAND Paper, ser. P-6052 (Nov. 1977).

[62] Novitskii, *Na puti*, pp. 113, 105.

mental illness, suicide, or criminality. While endorsing Martynov's criticism of Kuprin's famous exposé of military life in *The Duel*—that the regiment Kuprin described was grotesquely atypical—one can hardly doubt that analogues for each drunkard, sadist, or fool in the novel could be met with in the regular army infantry regiments.[63] How else can one account for the fact that Second Lieutenant Ivanov drowned Ivan Savel'kov at the climax of an all-night debauch? Or that Capt. B. F. Soroko tortured his orderly by pouring boiling water over his extended hands? Or that Lieutenant Colonel Ignatev attempted to murder Lieutenant Vysin? Or that Lieutenant Saakadze gunned down Collegiate Assessor Kasatkin and his wife in a psychotic fit?[64] Cases like these were of course abnormal. But they were not all that abnormal: things were far from well in the infantry regiments of the line.

There were vast differences, then, in the status, career prospects, and privileges of the various subservices of the tsarist army. These differences were further embodied in behavior, since an officer's affiliation to his subservice was often considerably stronger than his affiliation to the officer corps as a whole. The Guards believed themselves to be the true patrician military elite, the officers of the General Staff deemed themselves the intellectual cream of the service, the cavalry despised the infantry, and the technical services such as engineers and artillery reviled cavalry and infantry alike. The Imperial government was alive to the disunity of tsarist officers and developed two strategies for overcoming it. The first of these was the foundation of officers' clubs. Introduced gradually in the 1880s and 1890s, these institutions were especially encouraged during the ministry of A. N. Kuropatkin (1898-1904). Ranging from the sumptuous (the Army-Navy Club in St. Petersburg) to the exceedingly modest (two rented rooms in a log cabin near Irkutsk), the clubs generally featured a buffet, a dining hall, a library with newspapers and magazines, and perhaps a billiard table. Membership and the payment of dues were obligatory. The model charter for these clubs declared in part that the goal of the clubs was to "afford the officers the means for drawing closer together, while supporting among the officers correct comradely relations, consonant with the spirit and demands of military service."[65] Unfortunately this goal was only fulfilled on paper. The failure of the officers' clubs can be ascribed to the fact that the clubs

---

[63] Martynov, *Iz pechal'nogo*, p. 165. See also Bushnell, "Tsarist Officer Corps," pp. 753-754. For more on *The Duel*'s impact on the military self-image, see chap. 5.

[64] TsGVIA,, f. 801, op. 56/79, d. 3 (1904), l. 6; TsGVIA, f. 400, op. 15, d. 1832 (1899-1900), ll. 17, 52; TsGVIA, f. 400, op. 15, d. 2040 (1901), l. 83; TsGVIA, f. 400, op. 15, d. 2157 (1902), l. 8; also TsGVIA, f. 400, op. 15, d. 2290, ll. 43-44 (1903).

[65] This model charter is reproduced in *Polozhenie ob ofitserskom sobranii ofitserskoi strelkovoi shkoly* (St. Petersburg, 1907). See esp. pp. 1, 15.

were organized by service and unit—and hence did nothing to bridge the gaps between artillery and infantry, infantry and Staff, Staff and Guards.[66]

The second strategy was more subtle. The government was aware that it could not reasonably expect to have an officer corps solely composed of nobles. But it attempted to compensate for this by promoting norms of officer behavior which were at least theoretically "aristocratic," norms which revolved around the officers' adherence to a special code of honor. In theory, honor (*chest'*) for Russian officers was supposed to be synonymous with knightliness (*rytsarstvo*), a way of life governed by lofty ideals of chivalry and self-sacrifice and incidentally a transparent borrowing of a foreign word and a foreign code which never indigenously developed in Russia. *Chest'* could also embrace such British public school virtues as manliness, forthrightness, and fair play. In practice, however, honor existed for officers chiefly as a commodity which could be lost. And the principal way in which an officer could lose his honor was by failing to defend it. The concept was circular: an honorable officer was one who protected his honor.[67] On the most primitive level, this meant protecting his epaulettes. These pads of pasteboard, metal, and cloth were presumed to be the physical emblem of an officer's honor and were accorded a totemic devotion. Woe to the civilian who tried to rip an epaulette from an officer's shoulder, for military custom, tolerated by the state, obliged the officer to repay him with death.[68]

In a Riga brothel on the afternoon of February 23, 1893, two officers of the 115th Viazemskii infantry got involved in a drunken confrontation with some students from the local polytechnic school. During the brawl one student, Berezovskii, tore away the epaulette of Lieutenant Khalkiopov and stubbornly refused to return it. Khalkiopov's response was to shoot Berezovskii. Military judicial personnel at once initiated proceedings against Khalkiopov, even though his regimental commander, Colonel Baranovskii, maintained that the lieutenant had merely defended his honor, for there could be no doubt that Berezovskii's deed had been both ill-timed and extremely provocative. Baranovskii further hailed Khalkiopov as an outstanding officer and was especially effusive about Khalkiopov's high standards of morality (*nravstvennost'*). Although one might wonder about the morals of a person who was a habitué of whorehouses and had additionally just confessed to the commission of a brutal murder, the colonel did not. On a report submitted to him about this case, War Minister Vannovskii penned a note in which he expressed

---

[66] Kersnovskii, *Istoriia*, pp. 520-521.
[67] See the discussion of honor in M. Dragomirov, *Dueli* (Kiev, 1900), p. 4.
[68] Littauer, *Russian Hussar*, pp. 49, 93-94.

sympathy for this fine officer and wondered what could be done to mitigate his guilt. On June 2, 1893, the Temporary Military Court in Riga stripped Khalkiopov of rank, orders, and rights and exiled him to remote Yenisei Province. Twenty-one days later, Alexander III commuted this sentence to six weeks' confinement in a fortress without loss of rights. Five years after, Nicholas II indulgently ordered that all references to this affair be expunged from the service record of Staff Captain Khalkiopov.[69] Khalkiopov and Baranovskii obviously believed that Berezovskii's insult to the honor of an officer's uniform at least partially exonerated his murderer. Alexander III, Nicholas II, and Vannovskii all shared this point of view.

But the autocracy did more than merely show clemency to officers like Khalkiopov who were swift to defend the military honor, for the regime tried to promote its concept of the officers' honor code by establishing regimental officers' courts. These courts had jurisdiction over the actions of officers up to the rank of lieutenant colonel, actions which, though not criminally punishable, were still unbecoming to an officer's honor. Consisting of seven judges elected by the officers and two appointed by the colonel, the courts dispensed an entire range of punishments, including expulsion from the regiment. The enactment of the notorious dueling law of May 13, 1894 enhanced the applicability of the latter penalty. Apparently the brainchild of P. S. Vannovskii, and warmly endorsed by Nicholas II, who informed Kuropatkin in 1899 that it was essential to "cling" to the law of 1894, this decree not only legalized the dueling for officers, it *required* them to duel over points of honor. If an officer refused to duel, the local regimental officers' court could discharge him from the service. The rationale behind this decree, of course, was to increase the cohesiveness and caste spirit of the officer corps. Regiments had in the past expelled officers who declined to duel (such an episode figures in Dostoevskii's *Krotkaia*), but now the state was officially sanctioning this practice.[70] This sanction was taken quite seriously.

In the mid-nineties, Second Lieutenants Dukhnovskii and Aliksanderov of the Novogeorgievsk fortress battalion publicly insulted each other in a quarrel. Although the two men subsequently made their peace, in the opinion of the officers' court a duel was necessary. The two

[69] TsGVIA, f. 400, op. 15, d. 1424, ll. 1-6, 8-10, 13.

[70] Zaionchkovski, *Samoderzhavie*, p. 240; *Ministerstvo voennoe. Glavnoe voenno-sudnoe upravlenie. otdelenie 1. 31 avgusta 1894 no. 4025* (St. Petersburg, n.d.), pp. 1-2, 13-14, 18; TsGVIA, f. 165, op. 1, d. 1868, l. 55. On dueling in Germany, see Karl Demeter, *The German Officer Corps in Society and State, 1640-1945*, trans. Angus Malcolm (New York, 1965), pp. 117-147; F. M. Dostoevskii, "Krotkaia" (1876) *Peterburgskie povesti i rasskazy* (Leningrad, 1973), pp. 738-739.

lieutenants were forced to comply and accordingly staged a sham duel from which both walked away unscathed. The temporary commander of Warsaw Military District was dissatisfied with this outcome and wrote War Minister Vannovskii requesting the discharge of these officers, since neither had displayed "an urge to uphold the dignity of an officer and . . . [since] the only stimulus for the duel was their fear of being cashiered, rather than a consciousness of the need to wash [with blood] the insults they had received."[71] In March 1899 the officers' court of the 43rd Tver' dragoons (Tiflis) expelled Lieutenant Prince Abkhazi since he did not challenge Cornet Prince Dzhandieri, even though the former was aware that the latter was slandering his wife.[72] The court of the 5th Zacaspian rifle battalion passed a similar sentence on Lt. N. P. Nebratov in 1900. Nebratov had goaded Lieutenant Buiko into striking him on the back with the flat of his sword, yet no duel had transpired.[73] Other examples could be added. Of the twenty-one regimental officers' court cases from 1898 to 1901 which the Judicial Section of the Main Staff found worthy of archival preservation, nine of them concerned officers who were fired from their regiments for their reluctance to duel.[74]

Under these circumstances it is not surprising that some officers preferred the risk of dueling to the certainty of disgrace. Yet despite its legalization, dueling did not really catch on among officers. The best statistics we have list 320 duels fought by 1910 in accord with the provisions of the 1894 act, which averages out to 20 per year. This figure becomes even less impressive when we compare it to the number of army officers—roughly thirty five thousand—on active duty in any given year. Further, although on 30 occasions from 1894 to 1910 duels resulted in serious injury or death, 104 of the duels during this period were totally bloodless, which suggests that a good number of officers managed to feign dueling and got away with it, unlike Dukhnovskii and Aliksanderov.[75]

The tsarist government's experiments in indoctrinating the officers with a sense of honor were thus not entirely successful. The dueling law, for instance, failed to unite the Russian officer corps in any positive way, if we except those officers who united to conspire against its intent. Further, we may well wonder just how professionally functional duels

[71] TsGVIA, f. 801, op. 39/45, d. 39, l. 69.

[72] TsGVIA, f. 400, op. 15, d. 1859, l. 2.

[73] TsGVIA, f. 801, op. 30/45, d. 39, l. 73.

[74] Ibid., ll. 9-11; also see TsGVIA, f. 400, op. 15, d. 2290, ll. 1, 24, 32, 35, 109-110, 125.

[75] "Poedinok," VE, vol. 18 (Petrograd, 1915), p. 512. Compare with Imperial Germany where, in 1885, a full 12 percent of all officers in the army were disciplined for dueling. Demeter. German Officer Corps, 1640-1945, p. 141.

were for the Russian officers at this time. A hundred years or so previously, when personal valor was perhaps the highest quality an officer
could bring to the battlefield, dueling may have been useful in promoting
a cult of bravery.[76] However, given the technological conditions of late
nineteenth-century warfare, valor was quite possibly of less relevance
to the military occupation than such attributes as intelligence, patience,
and organizational ability.[77]

Insofar as corporate identity or consciousness existed for the entire
Russian officer corps at all, it existed *only* in relation to perceived menaces
from the distrusted outside world. I would like to dub this phenomenon
negative corporatism. Negative corporatism meant hostility to outsiders,
which was justified by the presumption (shared by many officers) that
civil society nourished an unquenchable antagonism towards the army
and the officer corps. With regard to segments of the intelligentsia this
presumption may, in fact, have been correct. An anonymous officer
essayist writing in 1890 bitterly noted that recent Russian novels and
plays (perhaps those of Shcheglov-Leont'ev?) tended to characterize officers as careerists, playboys, and buffoons.[78]

But educated society was not the only target of army mistrust, for
officers suspected that civilian *officials* of the state were themselves guilty
of antimilitary bias: at times, the bureaucrats seemed too willing to
believe ill of the army; at times, insufficiently staunch in protecting the
dignity of the armed forces. Tension between the army and the civilian
police, which boiled over in the post-1905 period, had already begun to
brew in the early 1890s. In 1891 gendarme NCO Sukonnikov convinced
the Ministry of the Interior that soldiers of the 43rd Tver' dragoons had
run amuck in the settlement of Tsarskie Kolodtsy (Tiflis Province) and
had savaged the civilian residents. Although Durnovo of the Interior
Ministry testified to the probity of gendarme Sukonnikov, the investigators of Major General Sheremetko, Chief of Staff of Caucasus District,
denounced Sukonnikov's report as malicious slander. Sukonnikov, a former dragoon in the 43rd Tver' regiment, had been cashiered for repeated
drunkenness; it was quite probable that he had falsified his report in
order to bring his old regiment into disrepute.[79] Again, in the summer
of 1890 in a village near the Khodynka parade ground in Moscow, a

[76] See Demeter, *German Officer Corps, 1640-1945*, p. 114.

[77] This may have been understood abroad. Dueling, once epidemic in the German officer
corps, became less and less common between regular officers after the turn of the century.
Ibid., p. 147; also, Martin Kitchen, *The German Officer Corps, 1890-1914* (Oxford, 1968),
pp. 55-56.

[78] "V sem'e ne bez urodov," *Razvedchik*, no. 34 (Oct. 11, 1890): 339.

[79] TsGVIA, f. 400, op. 15, d. 1286, ll. 1-3, 4, 6-7, 8-18, 20, 22, 24, 27-28; for similar
examples, see TsGVIA, f. 400, op. 15, d. 1224, ll. 1, 9-11.

mob of peasants screaming insults directed "at the entire military cor-poration" assaulted two lieutenants of the 1st Life Grenadiers and beat them senseless. Alexander III himself wrote that this episode "is such an outrage that I hope the guilty parties will be given exemplary pun-ishment." Yet the Staff of Moscow Military District was furious with the outcome of this case in civilian court: only one peasant was convicted, and he was convicted under an article of the criminal code which assumed an assault without either premeditation or any intention of committing an injury. If this were not bad enough, the felonious peasant was con-demned to only six months in prison, as opposed to the statutory eight to fifteen months required by even this article.[80]

Although there may have been sound reasons for the War Ministry's anger over the Sukonnikov and Khodynka cases, the negative corporatist mentality often jumped to unwarranted conclusions. After all, negative corporativism was in its essence a siege mentality—irrational and steeped in paranoia. Minor slights were puffed up into threats and isolated events invested with all the significance of sinister trends. This cast of thought pervades a report the Commander of Warsaw Military District, Adjutant General Chertkov, filed for 1903. In it, he averred that the number of attacks by civilians on soldiers was increasing, and that this increase was unchecked by the lenient punishments prescribed for the offense. War Minister V. M. Sakharov took these complaints earnestly enough to query Minister of the Interior Prince P. D. Sviatopolk-Mirskii about them in November 1904. On the basis of police documents, the Prince responded that street clashes between soldiers and civilians in Warsaw Military District for 1903 had totalled exactly seven. This figure had "even less meaning if it was considered in relation to the enormous number of troops quartered in Warsaw Military District." Mirskii also confessed his bewilderment at Chertkov's implicit call for sterner pun-ishments; it would be difficult to concoct anything more severe than forced labor (katorga), the existing penalty.[81]

But negative corporatism was as much a way of acting as a style of thinking. In the first place, some officers reacted to real or imagined civilian provocation with behavior ranging from verbal rudeness to phys-ical violence. Two cases suggest the lower and upper limits of such conduct. In 1903, falsely believing that he was being snubbed by a railway ticket vendor, Lieutenant Colonel Galitsinkii roared back: "You have no right to address me like that. I am a staff officer, a military investigator, and if I were to report this you would be kicked out of your job within

[80] TsGVIA, f. 400, op. 15, d. 1223, ll. 1-6, 17-18, 23, 28, 37.
[81] TsGVIA, f. 400, op. 15, d. 2443, ll. 1-2, 4, 8-9.

twenty-four hours!"[82] One year later in the Kostroma city theater Lieutenant Vasich of the 245th Soligalichsk infantry regiment insulted the daughter of a local brewery owner. Boris Rostovskii, the *Gymnasium* student who was her escort, called Vasich "impudent." The officer seized the student by the ear, and the student punched his tormentor in the face. The berserk lieutenant now drew his saber and chased Rostovskii all the way down the stairs of the theater and into the street. When Rostovskii's father refused Vasich's challenge to a duel (Rostovskii himself was underage), Vasich stormed into the elder Rostovskii's home and thrashed the old man.[83]

Of course, although the typical tsarist officer might insult civilians with the mocking (and untranslatable) epithets of army slang, he was unlikely to violently assault them, as Vasich did.[84] However, the negative corporatist feelings of the typical officer would most commonly be expressed in a Pavlovian *defense* of officers like Vasich against civilian charges, whether justified or not. The Ministry of War itself often automatically extended its protection to an officer or officers accused of misconduct either by private persons or by civilian bureaus of government. For instance, in 1900 a command of the Semenovskii Guards on maneuver had billeted in the village of Begunitsy, Petersburg Province, without notifying the police. The officers treated the peasants like a conquered population, damaged property, and amused themselves with the village women while the soldiers' behavior at a village wedding led to a riot, accompanied by knife fights. As Count Tol' wrote for the Police Department on January 23: "the cause of the disorders was the total abdication by the officers of their primary obligations . . . as military commanders, as a result of which the police and the village authorities were not in a position, due to their small numbers, to forestall the disorders, which were committed by a significant number of drunken soldiers." Although the available evidence indicated that Tol's interpretation of these events was the correct one, the officials of St. Petersburg Military District did not hesitate to lie by brazenly denying any military wrongdoing at all.[85]

In the end, negative corporatism conferred no more than a fictive unity on Russian officers. Unlike true military professional corporatism, which binds officers together on a foundation of shared pride, self-esteem, and a sense of mission, negative corporatism links the officers

[82] TsGVIA, f. 801, op. 56/79, d. 26, ll. 6-7.

[83] TsGVIA, f. 400, op. 15, d. 2442, ll. 4, 14. For a painstakingly thorough catalogue of similar incidents of military violence, see V. G. Korolenko, *Tragediia generala Kovaleva i nravy voennoi sredy* (Moscow, 1906), pp. 6-18.

[84] Zaionchkovskii, *Samoderzhavie*, pp. 238-239.

[85] TsGVIA, f. 400, op. 15, d. 1941, ll. 6-7.

one to another exclusively on the basis of shared fear. While corporatist officers see themselves as being outside civil society and perhaps superior to it because they are experts, negative corporatist officers see themselves as separate from society in the sense that they are society's victims, or potential victims. There is yet another way in which negative corporatism was an antiprofessional, rather than a professional impulse. While professionalism might require the ruthless expulsion from the officer corps of perceived incompetents, negative corporatism worked to shelter the least worthy. As we have already seen, high military officials were capable of excusing tactlessness, battery, and even homicidal criminality in their subordinate officers if such behavior was presumed a response to civilian attack.[86]

Other European armies at this time were not immune to negative corporatism, even the German army, which many contemporaries adjudged to be the best. Consider the Zabern incident of 1913, in which an officer's slanderous speech about the people of Alsace touched off serious public disturbances. Instead of chastising the officer responsible, the garrison commander imposed martial law, replete with stern repressive measures, against the civilian population. These tactics were supported by both the army High Command and Kaiser Wilhelm II, despite the stormy domestic and international outcry they elicited. But there was more at issue in Zabern than the defense of the "army's honor" since, believing that war with France was inevitable, the German officer corps held that the people of Alsace were potential fifth columnists who could only be governed with an iron hand.[87] Even if the attitude of German officers during the Zabern affair was otherwise stupid and reactionary, it did at least also reflect a professional strategic consensus. It is this that highlights the difference between German and Russian officers, for unlike the German officer corps, the Russian officers lacked the cohesion to pursue a program of corporate interests or even to develop such a program.[88]

[86] It will be noted that my distinction between positive and negative corporatism owes something to Alfred Vagts' celebrated distinction between "militarism" and "the military way." "An army so built that it serves military men, not war, is militaristic; so is everything in an army which is not preparation for fighting, but which merely exists for diversion," A History of Militarism, rev. ed. (New York, 1959), p. 15.

[87] For an excellent brief account of the affair, see Gordon A. Craig, Germany, 1866-1945 (New York, 1978), pp. 297-301; also Kitchen, German Officer Corps, 1890-1914, pp. 197-221.

[88] Bushnell, "Tsarist Officer Corps," pp. 753-780, also discusses many features of the behavior I identify as negative corporatism. My view of the Russian officer corps is, however, somewhat different than Professor Bushnell's. I can get at the difference best by pointing out some problems which I have with this article.

a) Bushnell's method, which is perforce impressionistic, relies on the accretion of masses

Special Interests and Autonomy

The disunity of the Russian officers, then, contributed to their failure to satisfy the fourth condition of professionalism: the recognition and articulation of innate military interests. But another capital obstacle here was a full-blown cult of the Emperor which encouraged officers to confuse the dynastic and military interest and which discouraged them from criticism of state military policy or any political thinking at all.[89] That

---

of damning detail from memoirs, belles lettres, fiction, etc. However, although I agree that the officer's milieu was characterized by heavy drinking, thievery, etc., I find Professor Bushnell's portrait of the extent of these vices among the officers to be somewhat over-drawn. We should be very leery of accepting impressionistic observations as definitive statements about the group behavior of 35,000 individuals, all the more so since some of the evidence Bushnell adduces is frankly contradictory: officers are seen both as notoriously heavy drinkers (pp. 755-756) and as clerks assiduously preoccupied with regimental house-keeping (pp. 768-769); similarly, officers are depicted both as prone to violence (760-761) and as pacifistic (pp. 770, 773).

b) The extremely negative judgment of the competence of the Russian officer corps might have been tempered if Professor Bushnell had introduced a comparative perspective into his account. Many of the behavior patterns which Bushnell sees as peculiar to Russian officers were in fact *not* peculiar to them alone. For instance, there was a high rate of suicide in the Russian officer corps (although we have no statistics which allow us to judge exactly how high). But in the German Empire, suicides in the army were fourteen times more prevalent than in civilian society (Kitchen, *German Officer Corps, 1890-1914*, p. 181). Bushnell sees the Russian officers as "swaddled in red tape" (p. 768). But, although the regimental economy was more burdensome in Russia than elsewhere, French officers, among others, were just as distracted from training as Russian ones by the minute bu-reaucratic demands of administration (Porch, *March to the Marne*, p. 201).

c) With the model of military inefficiency presented in this article, Bushnell is able to explain the "ineptitude and panic" (p. 778) of the Russian army during the first few months of World War I. However, what Bushnell cannot account for is that same army's successes: victory over the Germans at Gumbinnen (August 1914), substantial victories over the Austrians (August-September 1914), not to mention the Brusilov offensive of 1916.

d) Bushnell cannot account very well for military professionalism with his model. Yet at least one half of the sources he cites are the writings of professional, reform-minded tsarist officers who were self-consciously criticizing (and perhaps exaggerating) the defects of the army in the hope of improving it.

In summation, while Bushnell sees the tsarist officer corps as perhaps the worst in Europe in 1914 (due to the persistence of the regimental economy), I see the tsarist officers as manifesting behavior patterns which were not all that dissimilar from behavior patterns in other officer corps. What did distinguish the tsarist officers from other officers was an extremely low sense of self-esteem and an absence of cohesion. On the other hand, the military professionals who did serve within the tsarist officer corps were the military equals of any professional officers in Europe, in my opinion.

[89] Stein, *Der Offizier*, pp. 467-468, for a good discussion of this cult. Illustrations of this cult, including extravagant professions of loyalty and gratitude, can be found in A. N. Petrov, ed., *Istoricheskii ocherk Pavlovskogo voennogo uchilishcha, Pavlovskogo kadetskogo korpusa i Imperatorskogo voenno-sirotskogo doma 1798-1898 gg.* (St. Peters-

this cult had a hold over the officers is not surprising, for it was not so much the state which the officer was sworn to uphold as the autocracy and the dynasty. An officer's oath of allegiance detailed his obligation to defend the dynasty to his last drop of blood, tucking in his duty to the nation almost as an afterthought.[90] In a sense the reigning monarch was the proprietor of the Russian army and serving officers were in vassalage to him. The Emperor was the supreme commander of the Russian land forces, the source of all rewards and all punishments; the granting or removal of any commission was technically an act of the Imperial will. This was of course true in other armies. United States army officers always have been commissioned by presidential order. But in Russia law required the army officer to describe any unusual occurrences in the unit under his command—drownings, suicide, even cases of dog bites—in a personal report addressed to the Emperor.[91] This format was followed even though these reports were intercepted and channelled, unread by the tsar, into neat, blue-bound files in the Main Staff.

That this Imperial supremacy over the army also restricted professional autonomy requires no elaborate proof. The Emperor's prerogative to disburse military appointments, for example, could and often did lead to their distribution on the basis of criteria which were both exogenous and irrelevant to the military art: high birth, wealth, social grace, and zealous fealty. Such Imperial meddling was especially noticeable under Nicholas II, who reasserted the martial traditions of the Romanov dynasty which had somewhat decayed under Alexander III. A vivid example occurred in 1902 when Nicholas II made his suite a repository for performance reviews of officers considered for corps command and above. This move enhanced the power of the court in the military promotion process, while simultaneously degrading the authority of the Ministry of War.[92]

MILITARY PROFESSIONALS

We are now able to return to the question posed at the beginning of this chapter. How professional was the tsarist officer corps in the late

---

burg, 1898), pp. 687-689; *Aleksandrovskoe voennoe uchilishche za XXV let 1863-1898* (Moscow, 1900), pp. 21-22, 25; TsGVIA, f. 400, op. 15, d. 1345, ll. 9, 13.

[90] See *Spravochnaia kniga dlia iunkerov 2-go voennogo Konstantinovskogo uchilishcha po 1889/93 uchebnyi god (sic)* (St. Petersburg, 1888), pp. iv-v, on the oath.

[91] See, for instance, TsGVIA, f. 400, op. 15, d. 1264 (events in the army for the second half of October 1891); TsGVIA, f. 400, op. 15, d. 1197 (events in the army for the first half of November 1890); TsGVIA, f. 400, op. 15, d. 1241, l. 1.

[92] TsGVIA, f. 970, op. 3, d. 648, ll. 3, 48, 60-61.

nineteenth century? In view of all the foregoing—lack of interest in upgrading standards, poor cohesion, indifference to special military interests, absence of autonomy—we must answer, not very. It might even be plausibly argued that a military profession as profession in late Imperial Russia simply did not exist. Of course many of the antiprofessional conditions we have identified in the Russian army also obtained in armies abroad. Social dilution, for instance, was a feature of even the German army. By 1913, if those holding reserve commissions are tallied in, the Prussian officer corps was 70 percent bourgeois.[93] But the German officer corps was able to digest its nonaristocratic officers in a way that the Russian corps did not. In Germany, unlike Russia, there was an endogenous acceptance of written standards for officer conduct within the corps. German officers further had a strongly positive image of themselves as builders and preservers of the Reich, whatever their social origin.[94] The French army, too, was characterized by social heterogeneity (in 1899, 89 percent of army lieutenants were nonpatrician) and negative corporativism (e.g., the Dreyfus case). Yet in the 1880s the government of France reformed military education and attempted to equalize the status of the various arms of service, actions which produced a growing professional consciousness among the French officers.[95] In Italy, as in Russia, there was vastly preferential treatment extended to the officers of the Staff at the expense of those of the line. But even in Italy, officers were united by a common sense of their purpose as the educators of the nation; Russian officers had no such source of cohesion.[96] If we rank the great European armies in terms of their professionalism, then, the German army would head the list, while the Russian would come near the bottom.[97]

Although there may have been no military profession in Russia, there were, however, military professionals, albeit a small layering of them. In the main, these people were officers who had graduated from one of the four elite military academies: The Alexander Academy of Military Justice, the Nicholas Engineering Academy, the Michael Artillery Academy, and, most especially, the Nicholas Academy of the General Staff. These institutions, which, as we have seen, had been substantively upgraded by D. A. Miliutin, continued to graduate class after class of elite experts in the years after Miliutin left power. The most important source of professional officers was the Staff Academy, since its graduates were

[93] Demeter, *German Officer Corps, 1640-1945*, p. 28.
[94] Kitchen, *The German Officer Corps, 1890-1914*, pp. 28, 38, 120, 145.
[95] Porch, *March to the Marne*, pp. 18, 42-43, 58.
[96] Whittam, *Italian Army*, pp. 148, 150-152, 154-155.
[97] On superior German professionalism, see Gooch, *Armies in Europe*, p. 69.

the most likely to seriously ponder the condition of the entire army rather than the condition of one particular subservice. Then, too, the military jurist and possibly the military engineer were people for whom there existed powerful magnets of professionalism outside the military world: the civilian legal profession, the civilian engineers. Such persons participated in occupational cultures in which civilians had influence over the norms of performance. In other words, it was possible for the military lawyer, and in some cases the military engineer, to be purely a military professional, purely a civilian professional, or a hybrid of both.[98] As for the artillerists, many of them were narcissistically absorbed with the issues confronting their own technical specialty. We are therefore left with a small group—a few thousand officers—in which the General Staff officers predominated. These were officers who had special education and a sense of group cohesion, which gave them an understanding of innate military interests and a desire for self-improvement and more autonomy for the army. The military professionals in Russia were alarmed precisely by the degree to which the bulk of the Russian officer corps did not partake of these values. The military professional program was therefore at first an educational program, for it consisted in efforts to persuade the great inert and slothful mass of Russian officers to study and upgrade standards. There are numerous examples of professionally conscious officers who, like Benthamite agitators, tried to awaken their compatriots to the love of learning and education through articles, pamphlets, even short stories. One of the earliest and best examples of this sort of educational professionalism was *Razvedchik* (The Scout), the first private military journal in the history of Russia.

Retired Staff Captain V. A. Berezovskii founded the journal in the mid-1880s. Its purpose was to provide "the familiarity with military literature" which the editorial board deemed "essential for every officer."[99] The pseudonymous officer contributors who wrote for *Razvedchik* sugared the didactic pill by sending in "amusing" short stories, poems, and feuilletons in addition to technical articles. In any event, the purpose of the literary articles of *Razvedchik* was the same as that of the technical contributions: the promotion of seriousness, self-education, and military scholarship. Typical of the sort of piece which *Razvedchik* published was a short story by future War Minister V. A. Sukhomlinov. In the course of "The Pen" (1894), Lieutenant Makhov, who serves in a cavalry reg-

---

[98] For information on "military-legal" professionalism, see chap. 4. It was not unheard of for military lawyers to make the transition to civilian legal practice. See S. S. Anisimov, *Kak eto bylo. Zapiski politicheskogo zashchitnika o sudakh Stolypina* (Moscow, 1931), p. 92; on the military engineers, see von Shwartz, "Vospominaniia."

[99] *Razvedchik*, no. 220 (Dec. 15, 1894): 1 and advertisement on back cover.

iment where the overwhelming majority of officers "did not even find it worthwhile to read the promotion list" in the army's daily newspaper comes to value military learning so much that he zealously applies himself to his books and earns admission to the Staff Academy.[100]

The authorities first looked askance at *Razvedchik*. After all, the voicing of private opinions by military men smacked of insubordination, however well-intentioned. But "difficulties" with the censorship abruptly disappeared in 1890 when the Emperor Alexander III himself subscribed. Nicholas II kept his copies close at hand, for as he said, "everybody reads it." By 1894, *Razvedchik* had 4,004 (chiefly military) subscriptions at the rather stiff price of six rubles a year. By 1896, there were over eight thousand. Yet these numbers do not convey a sense of *Razedchik's* total readership among the officers, since regimental libraries and officers' clubs regularly ordered it.[101] Nor was *Razvedchik* an isolated phenomenon. Throughout the 1890 high-minded officers founded a great number of new military journals devoted to educating the officer corps. In 1899 the *Warsaw Military District Journal*, the *Intendancy Journal*, and *Russian Invalid Supplement* first appeared; the first issues of the *Herald of the Cossack Armies*, the *Herald of the Officers' Rifle School* and *News of Foreign Military Literature* came off the presses in 1900.[102]

Another more exclusive nexus of military professionalism was the *Obshchestvo revnitelei voennykh znanii* (Society of Zealots of Military Knowledge). The society grew out of a private study group organized in St. Petersburg in 1896 by a tiny group of Staff and Guards officers. As more and more officers started to attend the meetings, it occurred to the founders that an officially chartered organization might be of some use. Once again, there was friction with higher military and civilian officials over this idea. But, owing to the intercession of Grand Duke Vladimir Aleksandrovich, the Commander of St. Petersburg Military District, Nicholas II was persuaded to issue his formal consent in 1898. The purpose of the society was not too dissimilar from that of *Razvedchik*—the dissemination of technical knowledge among as many serving officers as possible.[103] The society rapidly attracted members. By the end

[100] V. Sukhomlinov, *Piat' voennykh rasskazov* (St. Petersburg, 1894), pp. 1, 20-21.

[101] Denikin, *Staraia armiia*, vol. 1, pp. 118-120; "Novye knigi," *Knizhnyi vestnik*, no. 2 (Feb. 1893): 74-75; TsGVIA, f. 280, op. 1, d. 5, p. 547; TsGVIA, f. 165, op. 1, d. 1868, l. 17; Anton I. Denikin, *The Career of a Tsarist Officer: Memoirs, 1872-1916*, trans. Margaret Patoski (Minneapolis, 1975), pp. 185-192.

[102] Z. P. Levasheva et al., comps., *Russkaia voennaia pechat' 1702-1916 gg.* Nos. 87, 89, 92, 95, 99 (Moscow, 1959).

[103] V. N. Domanevskii, "Revniteli voennykh nauk. chastnyi pochin v voenno -nauchnoi dele," *Chasovoi* (Paris), nos. 5-6 (March): 15-17; E. F. Novitskii, "K 30-letiiu sozdaniia obshchestva revnitelei voennykh znanii," *Voennyi sbornik* (Belgrade), 10 (1929): 140-154.

of 1899, the membership was over 1,300; over 1,600 by 1900; 1,800 by 1903, and over 3,000 by 1905, by which point the society was larger than the Imperial Geographic Society.[104] The chief voice of the society was its *Vestnik* (Herald). Appearing irregularly but often (sometimes as frequently as twice in one week), *Vestnik* featured articles with a heavy emphasis on the most current military technologies. Discussions of the triple expansion engine, the dumdum bullet, the torpedo boat, and the machine gun regularly appeared on its pages.[105] Another activity was the sponsorship of free public lectures on military subjects. The society sold through the mails the printed texts of the approximately 150 lectures delivered before 1905. Among the lecturers were V. I. Gurko, N. A. Danilov, A. F. Rittikh, A. P. Skugarevskii, V. A. Sukhomlinov, E. F. Novitskii, E. I. Martynov, and N. N. Golovin.[106] In short, the roster of the society's lecturers is an honor roll of most of those who emerged as the capital military thinkers and administrators of Russia in the last seventeen years of the Imperial regime. The "military renaissance" in Russia, that heightened interest in military affairs which is usually construed solely as the army's response to the agony of unsuccessful war and revolution, in fact began in St. Petersburg in 1899; the men listed above helped lead that renaissance. The most important officers who became politicized in the post-1905 period, whether they drifted to the left or to the right, had all been involved with the society from its inception. As we will see in chapter seven, both groups of "young turks" came from the society, as did the editorial board of the paper *Voennyi golos*, as did those officers like Rittikh and Skugarevskii who were to adhere to neo-Panslavism. As we shall see later, there was a distinct connection in the Russian army between military professionalism and politics.

Were these officer-educators successful in their mission? To an extent they were, but their achievement fell short of the desired goal: the complete transformation, the thorough intellectualizing of the entire officer corps. The Society of the Zealots of Military Knowledge was a moderate success: it did enjoy a respectable growth. In a sense to belong to it was to be a card-carrying military professional. Yet, although

---

[104] *Godovoi otchet za 1-i god deiatel'nosti obshchestva revnitelei voennykh znanii* (St. Petersburg, 1900), pp. 5-8, 12; *vtoroi godovoi otchet* . . . (St. Petersburg, 1901), pp. 4-6, 22-23; *tret'ii godovoi otchet* . . . (St. Petersburg, 1902), pp. 5, 8-11; *chertvertyi godovoi otchet* . . . (St. Petersburg, 1903), pp. 1, 6-7, 10-13; . . . *za shestoi god* . . . (St. Petersburg, 1905), pp. 4-5; *deviatoi godovoi otchet* . . . (St. Petersburg, 1908), pp. 2, 10-14; Novitskii, *Na puti*, p. 153.

[105] *Vestnik obshchestva revnitelei voennykh znanii za 1898-1903* (St. Petersburg, 1898-1903), passim.

[106] Novitskii, *Na puti*, pp. 148-149.

branches were founded in Vil'na, Riga, and Minsk, and although it was possible to take out a corresponding membership in other places, the society was too rooted in St. Petersburg, too much a phenomenon of the General Staff to capture the imaginations or raise the tone of the entire officer corps. As late as 1905 over one-half of all the members in the society still served in St. Petersburg District.[107]

Razvedchik, however, was both widely disseminated and popular. It probably did have some effect on raising the professional consciousness of the officer corps, but this effect was slow-working. A study conducted by *Razvedchik* itself concluded that in 1909 almost 38 percent of Russian officers still never read military books. In the same year, a commentator writing in the War Ministry's official journal, *Voennyi sbornik*, angrily berated the officers for their gutter tastes in literature: a certain infantry division had recently published a list of the books most requested by officers, and over 90 percent of them were either frivolous or frankly pornographic.[108]

The chief problem, of course, with this professionalizing activity lay in the naive faith which the professional officers had in the uplifting power of the printed word. Yet, if officers did not read they were effectively isolated from the professional message. Officers had to read regularly to be persuaded of the necessity of reading. One might suspect that all too often the professionalizing officers were preaching to the converted. Further, unlike professionals in other occupational groups, the professional officers could offer no tangible material benefits to those of their compatriots who joined the "professional movement"—no monopolistic control over a market, no higher fees, and little in the way of improved career prospects.

MILITARY PROFESSIONALISM: THE WAR MINISTRY

The Russian army, then, did contain a leaven of self-conscious military professionals. But the War Ministry itself became imbued with the new professional spirit from 1880 to 1905. It was in this period that graduates of Miliutin's reformed academies came to dominate key institutions within the Ministry, such as the Chancellery, the Main Staff, and important posts in the staffs of the military districts. These officers came from the same milieu which produced the Society of Zealots and *Razvedchik*. They read the new military literature sympathetically, and some of them actually wrote it. An example would be future War Minister

---

[107] *Godovoi otchet za shestoi god*, pp. 4-5.
[108] L. V. Evdokimov, "Bol'shoe delo mol(1)govo ofitsera," *VS*, no. 9 (Sep. 1909): 111.

A. F. Rediger, who by the late eighties, although both a professor at the Staff Academy and a major functionary within the War Ministry Chancellery, also pursued an active career as a military journalist and scholar, contributing articles and lectures to *Razvedchik* and *Vestnik*, and to *Russkii invalid* and *Voennyi sbornik* (the official military newspaper and journal, respectively).[109] Such officers did not initially run the Main Administrations or the Military Inspectorates, but, as important second- and third-level bureaucrats, in a sense they set the War Ministry's agenda, and represented the collective embodiment of its institutional point of view.

That institutional point of view increasingly came to be preoccupied with the fact that the Russian army was faced with two great challenges, challenges which had to be met squarely. The first of these was the military danger to the Russian Empire in the West posed by a vigorous German Reich. Russia's humiliation at the Berlin Congress of 1878, the Boulanger crisis with the imminent threat of a preemptive German attack, the strident warnings of the French—all tended to bolster the Ministry's anxiety about the Germans. Second, there was a growing appreciation in the Ministry that the technological revolution in rifles, explosives, and artillery had substantively transformed warfare. Failure to adopt new military inventions (and to adapt to them) could only condemn the Empire to a parlous condition of military weakness.

The War Ministry's devotion to its own vested interests deepened in response to its conflicts with the other governmental ministries. And the number of such conflicts increased in the late nineteenth century as the political power of the War Ministry declined. The War Ministry had enjoyed favored status under Alexander II. Dmitrii Miliutin managed to defeat most of his political foes and by the 1870s even extruded his Ministry's influence into a broad range of state affairs only indirectly connected with the army. But the War Ministry weakened in the 1880s and 1890s as the autocracy realized that fiscal problems and internal unrest jeopardized its continued existence. Preoccupation with short-term survival began to take precedence over planning for long-term security. As a result, the Ministries of Finance and Interior accrued advantages in their struggles with the Ministry of War. All of this only served to sharpen the War Ministry's self-perception as a distinct interest group; its commitment to the special interests of the army hardened as the satisfaction of those interests became more difficult.

The following two chapters detail the War Ministry's conflicts with the Ministries of Finance and the Interior and also consider the insti-

---

[109] See TsGVIA, f. 409, op. 1, d. p/sp, 155-433, ll. 2-4.

tutional reasons for its sagging influence within the Empire. But we should pause here to discuss one of the other factors instrumental in the decline of the War Ministry: the attitudes and values of Russia's last two autocrats. It is no endorsement of the Cleopatra's nose interpretation of history to observe that autocratic politics are at least in part the politics of the autocrat. And the Imperial Russian army was unfortunate in the last two reigning Romanovs.

Whatever one thinks of the intelligence of Alexander III (and the depiction of this corpulent toper as a man of limited intelligence has become a cliché in the historical literature), he doubtless possessed a masterful and intimidating personality.[110] He was also extremely willful with regard to his personal tastes. One of the things for which he had great distaste was military life, perhaps because of his close association with it. Unlike most Russian emperors, who had merely undergone a military education, Alexander III was one of the few who had actually held field command in time of war. In 1877 he had served as nominal general in command of the Rushchuk, or Eastern Detachment. Alexander's detachment saw considerable action and acquitted itself splendidly during the sieges of Elena, Osman-Zasar, and Rushchuk. At one point the detachment, some seventy thousand men strong, held off double their number of Turkish troops for several days.[111] Most of the credit for the achievements of the detachment has gone not to Alexander but to his Chief of Staff and subsequent War Minister, P. S. Vannovskii. Still, Alexander developed at the front a profound disgust with organized slaughter which contributed to his reputation as the "Peacegiver." As he once observed to Finance Minister Sergei Witte: "I am glad that I was at war and saw for myself all the horrors which are inevitably connected with warfare. I think that no person with a heart can wish for war and that any ruler whom God has entrusted with a nation ought to take all measures to escape the horrors of war."[112]

But if this abhorrence for war lowered Alexander's esteem for the Russian army, there were other components as well. One was his longstanding suspicion of D. A. Miliutin and, by extension, the entire Miliutin military system. To Alexander, his father's liberal policies had

[110] P. A. Zaionchkovskii, *Rossiiskoe samoderzhavie v kontse XIX stoletiia* (Moscow, 1970), pp. 39, 44.

[111] L. G. Beskrovnyi, *Russkoe voennoe iskusstvo XIX v.* (Moscow, 1974), pp. 322-323, 328; V. A. Zolotarev, *Russko-turetskaia voina 1877/78 g.g. vo otechestvennoi istoriografii* (Moscow, 1978), p. 99; Alexander's military dispatches were all printed in *Sbornik materialov po russko-turetskoi voine 1877/78 g.g. na Balkanskom poluostrove*, vol. 16, pt. 1 (St. Petersburg, 1900), pp. 3-102.

[112] S. Iu. Vitte, *Vospominaniia*, ed. A. L. Sidorov, vol. 1 (Moscow, 1960), p. 411.

created a climate which facilitated the rise of radicalism and terrorism. Chief among the liberals who had urged the former Emperor to pursue the rash course of reform had been War Minister Miliutin. Regardless of Alexander's statement that Russia "really has only two trustworthy allies—her army and her fleet," Alexander never totally trusted his military men.[113] In the first year of his reign he witnessed the collapse of the military organization of the People's Will terrorist conspiracy (which contained over two hundred serving officers). In the same year Vannovskii forced him to accept N. N. Obruchev as Chief of the Main Staff. And Obruchev was compromised in Alexander's eyes not only by association with Miliutin but indiscreet revolutionary activity in the early 1860s.[114]

Another feature of Alexander's character which affected his relationship with the military was his famed intolerance for ceremonial and ritual. He definitely preferred family life to the world of the parade ground and avoided the latter regularly. Although Alexander's impatience with the vestiges of the *platz-parad* tradition led to desirable simplifications in army drill, his absence from the principal military reviews was often noted by his officers.[115]

To be sure, Alexander was personally devoted to P. S. Vannovskii. He was warm towards the besotted companion of his drinking bouts, Adjutant General P. A. Cheverin. He felt attachment to those officers who had been under his direct command in the Turkish war. We find him, for example, (characteristically) drinking to the glory of the Rushchuk detachment at a ceremonial dinner in 1889.[116] It was also true that Alexander did appoint some military men to civilian posts. In 1890, 13 of the 50 governors (26 percent) of Russia's European provinces bore military rank.[117] But one good way of comparing the degree to which Alexander II and Alexander III relied on the army is to examine the Council of State. In 1863, that august body comprised 20 civilian and 35 military members, if members of the Romanov dynasty are excluded. In 1895 there were 47 civilians and only 19 generals, while only 4 of the 25 members of the three legislatively important Departments of the

[113] Kersnovskii, *Istoriia*, p. 498.

[114] Zaionchkovskii, *Samoderzhavie*, pp. 61-62; Kersnovskii, *Istoriia*, p. 509; Vitte, *Vospominaniia*, vol. 1, pp. 35, 304; for some stimulating remarks on Alexander III's personality, see Richard Wortman, "The Russian Empress as Mother," in *The Family in Imperial Russia*, ed. David L. Ransel (Urbana, 1976), pp. 69-70, 72.

[115] Ignatyev, *Subaltern in Old Russia*, pp. 16-17; [V. P. Obninskii]. *Nikolai II, Poslednii samoderzhets* (Petrograd and Moscow, 1917), pp. 5, 15.

[116] Zaionchkovskii, *Rossiiskoe*, p. 44; TsGVIA, f. 278, op. 1, d. 14, ll. 15, 37.

[117] *Spisok vysshim chinam gosudarstvennogo, gubernskogo i eparkhial'nogo upravleniia. Ispravelen po 15 marta 1890* (St. Petersburg, 1890), passim.

Council were Russian soldiers. On the average 54 percent of Council members were soldiers during the reign of Alexander II; 36 percent were soldiers during the reign of Alexander III.[118] In the next chapter we shall see how Alexander III's redoubtable fiscal conservatism and parsimony affected the Russian army.

Where Alexander III was cool to the army, Nicholas II was a military enthusiast. Given the education, in Witte's words, of a Guards colonel of good family, tutored by such eminent military academics as Leer, Dragomirov, and Puzyrevskii, Nicholas II wholeheartedly embraced the military milieu.[119] While heir to the throne, Nicholas served in several Guards regiments and participated in military maneuvers. To judge by his writings, military service was one of the most beloved of Nicholas's activities in his early years. He wrote to the Empress Maria in the summer of 1887: "I am now happier than I can say to have joined the army"; similar statements enliven the otherwise laconic entries in his diaries.[120] Even after his coronation Nicholas took pains to preserve his cordial connections to military life. When in residence at Krasnoe selo, he religiously attended the monthly regimental dinners of the Life Guard Hussars, drinking port and champagne with his old co-officers until four in the morning.[121] He enlarged the Imperial suite and appointed military men to the highest of posts. When he named former War Minister P. S. Vannovskii Minister of Education in 1901, he would inform Grand Duke Sergei Aleksandrovich that "what I need now is a military man."[122] He expressed great solicitude for the lot of his peasant soldiers; his forty-kilometer march to test the new infantryman's equipment could be entered in evidence.[123] Nor were his officers neglected. He proclaimed to Kuropatkin in 1898 that "the interests of the regular army officers— the captains—are dear to me."[124] As Mosolov declared, the "Tsar re-

---

[118] N. M. Korkunov, *Russkoe gosudarstvennoe pravo*, 6th ed., vol. 2 (St. Petersburg, 1909), p. 54. I am indebted to Professor T. Taranovsky of the University of Puget Sound for calling my attention to this reference. See also W. E. Mosse, "Aspects of Tsarist Bureaucracy: Recruitment to the Imperial State Council, 1855-1914," *SEER* 57, no. 2 (April 1979): 241.

[119] L. G. Zakharova, quoting Witte in "Krizis samoderzhaviia nakanune revoliutsii 1905 goda," *Voprosy istorii*, no. 8, 1972, p. 121; *Dnevnik Imperatora Nikolaia II 1890-1906 g.g.* (Berlin, 1923), p. 12.

[120] Edward J. Bing, ed., *The Letters of Tsar Nicholas II and Empress Marie* (London, 1934), p. 33.

[121] V. N. Voeikov, *S tsarem i bez tsaria* (Helsingfors, 1936), p. 44.

[122] TsGVIA, f. 648, op. 1, d. 71, l. 160.

[123] Mossolov, *Court of the Last Tsar*, pp. 21-22.

[124] TsGVIA, f. 165, op. 1, d. 1868, l. 7.

garded himself as a soldier—the first soldier in his Empire."[125] On the face of it Nicholas II should have been the logical champion of army interests in Russia. But he was not, and to understand why, it is first necessary to appraise his concept of the military world.

Witte's description of Nicholas's education was quite apposite. For Nicholas's military world was neither that of the officers of the technical services, whose specialties were incomprehensible to him, nor that of the officers of the General Staff Academy, which he had never attended. His military world was that peopled by the officers of the Guards cavalry; his ideal the madcap hussar, rather than the cold-blooded military *Fachmann*. His real passion was the outward form of military life—romance, color, reckless heroics, and pageantry—rather than its content—competence grounded on countless hours of training and study. Nicholas consequently displayed little understanding of the military realities of his Empire. He actually believed, for instance, that the regimental orders of the Preobrazhenskii Guards (the most elite infantry unit in Russia) furnished him with insights into the typical infantry regiment, and he conned these orders every day on that presumption.[126]

From the vantage point of the General Staff building, Nicholas's notorious vacillation and weakness of will were just as detrimental to military interests as his defective understanding of the army. To the despair of his ministers, Nicholas II was quite capable of changing his mind and his policy from year to year, month to month, week to week. In her trenchant article on the nature of Nicholas's autocracy, Soviet historian L. G. Zakharova finds proof for these directional shifts in Nicholas's frequent changes of ministers. From 1894 to 1904 there were five Ministers of Interior, five Ministers of Education, four Ministers of Foreign Affairs, and three Ministers of Finance.[127] Thus although Nicholas vowed in January of 1898 to back his new War Minister A. N. Kuropatkin and to defend him from the other ministers and "even . . . from other persons close to me," Kuropatkin soon discovered that Nicholas's deeds belied his words.[128] Indubitably, Nicholas was more interested in the Russian army than his father had been; but the army was not his principal concern. Nicholas could be convinced, he could be coaxed, he could be bullied. The other ministers had plenty of opportunity to sell their programs and viewpoints.

The War Ministry accordingly was obliged to wrestle with the other ministries in order to propagate its ideas and interests. As it did so, those

---

[125] Mossolov, *Court of the Last Tsar*, p. 23.
[126] TsGVIA, f. 280, op. 1, d. 5, p. 546.
[127] Zakharova, "Krizis samoderzhaviia," p. 139.
[128] TsGVIA, f. 165, op. 1, d. 1868, l. 6.

professional departments within the Ministry which bore major responsibility both for the elaboration of ministerial goals and for contact
with other ministries of state became more prominent. The Main Staff,
for example, the nexus of war planning, military training, and personnel
affairs, gained operations and statistical sections in 1900 and more employees under its new charter of April 1903.[129] The Chancellery of the
War Ministry, the channel for correspondence with the all-important
Ministry of Finance, took on more officials in 1900 as well.[130]

But War Ministry professionalism manifested itself in other ways.
We can discern a whole complex of new measures emanating from the
Ministry in the eighties which reflect the self-critical professional spirit.
Just as officer-professionals promoted education, so the War Ministry
itself came to value education and training as one of its prime functions.
This logically meant that the Ministry placed increasing emphasis on
field maneuvers and training exercises. The most important of these
took place during the summer. Every year each military district prepared
a schedule of exercises for its troops. "Special camps" for cavalry, artillery, and engineers were held in June and July and were followed by
"general camps" with the participation of troops from every arm of the
service.[131] After 1885 the War Ministry organized mobile exercises (pod-
viznye sbory) in August, which were actually large-scale maneuvers
(division level and above) designed to introduce the soldier to combined
operations. The infantryman would be better prepared for the battlefield
if he had learned what it was like to oppose a mock army equipped with
cavalry and field guns. Sometimes, when the Ministry could afford them,
massive war games involving units from several military districts supplemented this summer training.

N. N. Obruchev provided the intellectual underpinning for the remarkable expansion in field maneuvers. Shortly after he became Chief
of the Main Staff, he began energetically to promote field training. In
1892, for instance, Obruchev commended General Gurko of Warsaw
District for his imaginative conduct of mobile maneuvers there and
begged Alexander III to endorse an order urging other military districts
to devote more attention to their maneuvers.[132] Indeed, extension of
summer maneuvers so as to include greater and greater numbers of
Russia's active duty troops became an essential element of War Ministry
policy in the eighties and nineties. Doubt has recently been cast on the

[129] Kavtaradze, "Iz istorii," p. 78.
[130] TsGVIA, f. 970, op. 3, d. 600, l. 1.
[131] TsGVIA, f. 1, op. 2, d. 163, l. 15.
[132] Vsepoddaneishii doklad po voennomu ministerstvu 1892 goda (St. Petersburg, 1892),
pp. 39-40.

effectiveness of these maneuvers in imparting useful military skills; supposedly the maneuvers were conducted as inane parade ground exercises, in which formal precision, rather than initiative and problem solving, were rewarded.[133] But such charges could be (and have been) made about maneuvers held by almost any other army at this time. For instance, the German General Staff routinely rigged the Kaisermanöver—the largest military exercises in the country—every year from 1895 to 1905 to ensure that Kaiser William II would win.[134] Even at German maneuvers the artillery ordinarily did not fire from covered positions before 1911.[135] Austro-Hungarian maneuvers were linguistic nightmares, rendered less than realistic due to the interference of members of the Imperial house.[136] The important thing is that the Russian Ministry of War believed firmly in the efficacy of maneuvers and took great pains to expand them. This was at least in part due to the fact that the Ministry understood that the economic duties which lay on the field army were so heavy that the summer was the only practicable time for training.[137] In 1881, 71 percent of all infantry, 64 percent of all cavalry, and 74 percent of all artillery units participated in "general camps." For 1894, the proportions were 91 percent, 92 percent, and 95 percent.[138] Table 1 shows the percentages of Russian troops taking part in general camps and mobile exercises from 1899 to 1903. By contrast, no more than one-third of the French army could expect to visit a training camp in any given year.[139]

The War Ministry's concern for training and education was also reflected in its increased demands on officers and men. At the beginning of the nineties, for example, an officer was obliged to be familiar with some 40 military codes, service orders, and regulations; by 1901, he was responsible for 61.[140] Similarly, in 1902 the War Ministry restructured

[133] John Bushnell, "Peasants in Uniform," p. 568; John Bushnell, "Tsarist Officer Corps," pp. 763-765. However, we should note that even parade ground training may have had its uses. According to some veterans of World War I such apparently pointless exercises helped to build the esprit de corps and sense of comradeship which actually prepared men for the trenches. One (surprising) expression of this point of view occurs in Erich Maria Remarque, *All Quiet on the Western Front* (New York, 1929), p. 21.

[134] Kitchen, *German Officer Corps, 1890-1914*, pp. 17-20; Michael Balfour, *The Kaiser and His Times* (London, 1964), p. 150.

[135] *Articles on the German Army Maneuvers reprinted from The Times* (London, 1911), p. 60.

[136] Gunther E. Rothenberg, *The Army of Francis Joseph* (West Lafayette, Ind., 1976), p. 149.

[137] Bushnell, "Tsarist Officer Corps," pp. 766-768.

[138] *Obzor deiatel'nosti*, pp. 81-82, TsGVIA, f. 400, op. 3, d. 4125, l. 52.

[139] Porch, *March to the Marne*, p. 201.

[140] Skugarevskii, *Ocherki*, vol. 2 (Vil'na, 1901), pp. 185-190.

TABLE 1
Percentages of Russian Troops Participating
in Summer Exercises, 1899-1903

Year	General			Mobile		
	Inf.	Cav.	Art.	Inf.	Cav.	Art.
1899	87	89	97	55	61	61
1900	88	92	97	40	50	45
1901	60	71	73	89	94	98
1902	87	92	97	64	67	67
1903	88	92	99	60	70	68

SOURCE: TsGVIA, f. 400, op. 3, d. 4365, ll. 36-37

the junker schools. Three-year courses of training replaced the previous two-years ones, while the curriculum was rendered more approximate to that of the elite military schools.[141] And the Russian soldier was affected by the Ministry's attempt to reintroduce compulsory primary education for the illiterate draftee in 1902. This Miliutin program of the seventies had been scrapped for financial and ideological consider-ations in the early years of the Vannovskii administration.[142]

An equally significant indicator of War Ministry professionalism was the Ministry's foredoomed scheme to secure more autonomy at the dynasty's expense. In February 1903, the Main Administration of Mil-itary Justice prepared a plan for the creation of a Higher Disciplinary Council to have jurisdiction over staff officers above the rank of colonel. In the past, a special ad hoc application to the Emperor had been necessary to punish high-ranking officers. Under the terms of the proposal, how-ever, the Council, acting as a sort of super-regimental court, would have allowed the Ministry to discipline and even remove unsuitable higher officers while downgrading the Emperor's role in this process. Thus the Ministry was trying to take charge of its own house, insinuating the principle that military expertise should be the paramount consideration in judging appointments and service.

Kuropatkin, who backed the proposal, nonetheless ordered that all military district commanders, Cossack atamans, and corps commanders be polled for their reactions. Opinions were divided. Some district com-

[141] TsGVIA, f. 1, op. 2, d. 163, l. 17.
[142] Denikin, *Tsarist Officer*, p. 83.

manders, such as Dragomirov of Kiev, held that such a council would limit their own personal power. Some corps commanders believed with the commander of the 15th corps in Warsaw that such a council would discredit higher army officers and would open the path towards a proliferation of invidious complaints and denunciations. Yet when the Military Justice Administration reviewed the 52 responses it had received, it reported that a full 38 of those responses endorsed the establishment of the Council. At this stage, however, Nicholas II aborted the project. While willing to tolerate a few minor changes in the Disciplinary Code, he adamantly refused to relinquish his power as sole agent for the removal of higher officers. Quite obviously, the proposal was exactly predicated on Nicholas's renunciation of this power.[143]

One final important feature of War Ministry professionalism was the outgrowth of the tendency to view its friends and enemies in purely functional terms. A man who worked for a rival ministry could hence be regarded as an adversary even if he was an officer and wore the military uniform. His officer's epaulettes connoted nothing to the War Ministry if he placed the interests of another department of state before those of the army.

The number of persons in this position was not in fact negligible. Although Alexander II's edict of March 1, 1872 had forbidden officers to occupy a variety of civilian posts without special Imperial exemption, the list of positions which officers could occupy grew longer with every passing year.[144] In 1890 there were 669 officers on active duty who were actually employed by the Ministries of the Interior, Finance, Foreign Affairs, and the Imperial Court. In 1895 there were 674; in 1899, 740; in 1900, 763; in 1901, 799; and in 1902, 740.[145] The War Ministry's attitude towards these officers was conditioned entirely by the role they played. This fact, incidentally, explains the War Ministry's eagerness to unify the civilian and military powers in the border regions by having one general serve simultaneously as governor-general and military district commander. The Ministry knew that it could usually rely on its district commander to support army interests over those of the Ministry of the Interior. The Interior Ministry understood this very well and vigorously and sometimes successfully strove to keep such offices as the Governor-General of Kiev-Podol'ia-Volynia out of military hands. But

---

[143] TsGVIA, f. 801, op. 39, d. 9, ll. 1-2, 17, 45, 87, 138, 153.

[144] SZ, vol. 3, *Ustav o sluzhbe 1896 g.*, bk. 1, arts. 154-155.

[145] *Vsepoddanneishii otchet o deistviiakh voennogo ministerstva za 1890 god po glavnomy shtabu* (St. Petersburg, 1982), p. 1; . . . *za 1895* (St. Petersburg, 1897), p. 1; . . . *za 1900* (St. Petersburg, 1902), p. 1; . . . *za 1901* (St. Petersburg, 1903), p. 1; . . . *za 1902* (St. Petersburg, 1904), p. 1.

the Interior Ministry often failed. In 1897, for example, the friction between Governor-General A. P. Ignat'ev and the Kiev district commander assumed the proportions of a crisis. Despite Ignat'ev's support from his ministry, he was recalled to Petersburg, while Dragomirov was left in control of his military district and the governor-generalship.[146] Ignat'ev, by the way, was also an army general. The War Ministry's treatment of officers serving in the the police, and the Ministries of Finance and the Interior as outsiders or enemies testifies to the sharpening definition and increasing parochialism of military interests.

There were two styles of civil-military confrontation in late Imperial Russia—the negative corporatist and the professional. The first is best typified by clashes between officers and civilians over questions of "honor" or perceived antimilitary bias. The second, by contrast, is best illustrated by conflicts between military officials and civilian bureaucrats or courtiers over the interests and purposes of the army. To a great extent negative corporativism was the antithesis of pure military professionalism. But ideal military professionalism did not exist in Russia at this time. Professionalism and negative corporatism could and did coexist in the minds of Russian officers. While the majority of officers were thoroughly unprofessional in terms of our definition as late as 1910, not even the most professional was a total stranger to negative corporatist sentiments. Both professionalism and negative corporatism became more intense in the tsarist officer corps from 1881 to 1914. Both stimulated civil-military conflict, which also grew more serious during this period. Yet those conflicts which were most important in the history of Imperial Russia were those engendered by military professionalism, since military professionalism was the greatest source of challenge both to the traditional practices of the autocracy on the one hand and to the professional program of Russia's civil bureaucrats on the other. In subsequent chapters we shall pursue the evolution of these conflicts—in the chancelleries, in the courts, and on the streets.

[146] Lukomskii "Ocherki," pp. 465-469; Vitte, *Vospominaniia*, vol. 2, pp. 130-131.

TWO

Financing the Russian Army, 1881-1903

THE RUSSIAN ARMY BUDGET

AFTER the ignominious termination of the Russo-Japanese War, Gen. A. N. Kuropatkin composed a lengthy monograph while living in forced retirement on his Pskov estate. Entitled *The Results of the War (Itogi voiny)*, these volumes represented a self-justification by the commander who had led the Russian land forces in the Far East to disastrous defeat at Shakhe, Liao-yang, and Mukden. With an aggressiveness conspicuously absent from his conduct of the campaign of 1904, Kuropatkin boldly rebuked nearly every branch of the Russian civil administration for inadequately supporting the war effort. But Kuropatkin reserved the bulk of his wrath for the Ministry of Finance, concluding that "the main reason for our military inefficiency was the inadequate funds granted by the treasury."[1]

Kuropatkin's work was suppressed in Russia. Indeed, Nicholas II had expressly forbidden the disgraced general to write on any subject. Yet the book circulated widely in manuscript, and various sections of it were translated and printed abroad.[2] It was this phenomenon which prompted former Finance Minister S. Iu. Witte to prepare a formal reply to Kuropatkin's charges. Dated June 1909, Witte's *Vynuzhdennyia raz"iasneniia* (Obligatory Explanations) was his final accounting of his fiscal stewardship, at least as far as the Russian army was concerned. The statistics in this pamphlet all purported to illustrate that, as Witte expressed it, the "state gave much," that the Russian army was not starved for revenues, and that the responsibility for the correct management of the resources placed at the army's disposal rested with the Ministry of War.

Witte demonstrated that Russia had spent more than any European state on her army in 1902; he also proved that Russia's percent of increase in military spending from 1892 to 1902 outstripped that of any other

---

[1] A. B. Lindsay, trans., *The Russian Army and the Japanese War by General Kuropatkin*, vol. 1 (London, 1909), p. 143.

[2] *Knizhnyi vestnik*, no. 2 (Jan. 14, 1907): 53; TsGVIA, f. 280, op. 1, d. 5, p. 563.

great power.[3] It thus appeared that Witte had rebutted Kuropatkin with an impregnable array of evidence. Since Kuropatkin had been War Minister from 1898 to 1904, Witte was obviously parrying Kuropatkin's accusations by turning them back against him, a sort of argumentative equivalent of the fencer's *prise de fer*.

However, fatuous as Kuropatkin's charge had been (the only reason for defeat could not have been merely a lack of funds—sorry generalship played a part), Witte had nevertheless begged the question. For Kuropatkin's complaint was not that the state did not give much, but that it did not give what was necessary. To be sure, the Russian Imperial state devoted huge sums to the maintenance of its army towards the end of the nineteenth century. From 1881 to 1902 over 6.2 billion rubles were expended, varying from 200 to 395 million rubles a year. But considerable as these allocations were, the annual percentage share of the Russian army in the total expenditures of the state nevertheless declined, a point which can be verified by an examination of Table 2. Yet, on the basis of this table, it is impossible to evaluate one important feature of Witte's argument: Russia's relative defense spending vis-à-vis Europe, a gap which is partly filled by the following charts.

There is, of course, an essential caveat to be made when adducing the army budgetary figures for any of these countries. As Mikhail Kashkarov pointed out in 1903, the Russian War Ministry budget paid for such nonmilitary activities as the civil administration of Eastern Siberia and Turkestan, not to mention geodesic and astronomical surveys; at the same time, the army received services rendered by other ministries and funded from their budgets. The state charged the costs of conscription, for example, partly to the Ministry of the Interior and partly to the Treasury. Again, from 1889 to 1898, 1,433 versts of strategic roads were built in the western portion of the Empire at a cost of 24.8 million rubles to the Ministry of Transport and Communications.[4] Similar observations could be made about the army appropriations in France and Germany. Although the practice of concealing defense spending under misleading budgetary rubrics was not as common before 1914 as it was to become afterwards, France and possibly several other powers indulged in it. During the 1890s the French War Ministry was able to secrete 300 million francs for the development of the 75-mm field gun in allocations for the improvement of the municipality of Paris.[5] The foregoing charts

[3] S. Iu. Vitte, *Vynuzhdennyia raz"iasneniia po povodu otcheta Generala-ad"iutanta Kuropatkina o voine s Iaponiei* (Moscow, 1911), pp. 11, 15, 18-19.

[4] Mikhail Kashkarov, *Finansovye itogi poslednego desiatiletiia 1892-1901 gg.*, vol. 2 (St. Petersburg, 1903), pp. 21-31; TsGVIA, f. 1, op. 2, d. 158, l. 37.

[5] Lt. Col. Rimailho, *Artillerie de campagne* (Paris, 1924), pp. 59-63.

TABLE 2
Army Share in Russian Imperial Expenditure, 1881-1902

Year	(1) Total Army expenditures	(2) Total State expenditures	(1) as % of (2)
1881	255,627,000	840,284,657	30
1882	206,378,886	788,371,173	26
1883	203,445,927	804,065,115	25
1884	199,967,339	815,832,703	22
1885	206,651,930	913,138,168	23
1886	211,994,690	945,023,261	22
1887	210,952,762	930,942,613	22
1888	212,095,763	927,267,329	22
1889	225,989,252	962,838,859	23-24
1890	240,610,000	1,056,511,678	22-23
1891	252,761,471	1,115,646,704	22
1892	159,054,000	1,125,455,707	23
1893	267,283,000	1,060,535,852	25
1894	284,686,451	1,155,141,662	23
1895	285,444,000	1,520,819,000	19
1896	294,359,000	1,484,353,000	19-20
1897	293,789,000	1,494,598,000	19
1898	303,277,000	1,772,211,000	17
1899	333,579,000	1,785,112,000	18-19
1900	389,755,000	1,889,216,000	20.6
1901	344,602,000	1,844,216,000	18.6
1902	325,639,000	1,946,572,111	18

NOTE: 1881-1886 in credit rubles, 1.5 credit rubles = 1 gold ruble; 1897-1902 in rubles = ⅟₁₅ of an Imperial. Columns 1 and 2 show summary figures derived from adding "ordinary" and "extraordinary" expenditures.

SOURCES: Compiled on the basis of *Otchet Gosudarstvennogo kontrolia za 1881-1902 gg.* (St. Petersburg, 1882-1903) and *Ob''iasnitelnaia zapiska k otcheta Gosudarstvennogo kontrolia 1881-1902 gg.* (St. Petersburg, 1882-1903), passim

do not, and indeed cannot, take all such episodes of budgetary deceit into account. The records which would permit an absolutely faithful reconstruction of the balance sheets of these European nations were unavailable to me. Yet Tables 2, 3, and 4 do display the majority of the funds which the war ministries of Russia, France, and Germany directly

TABLE 3
Army Share in French State Expenditure, 1881-1902

Year	(1) Total French Army expenditures (without pensions), millions of francs	(2) (1) as % of total French State expenditures	(3) Russian Army budget, millions of francs
1881	739.1	20	679.7
1882	754.1	20	598.96
1883	739	19	508.6
1884	694.8	19.6	515.9
1885	696.6	19.6	529
1886	591.7	17.6	519.4
1887	710.2	21	485.2
1888	694.3	21	500
1889	753.2	23	598.9
1890	727.2	22	719.4
1891	709	21.7	701.4
1892	677.9	20	658
1893	649.5	19.2	707.4
1894	647.6	18.7	771.8
1895	637	18.5	775.3
1896	645.5	18.7	785
1897	683.6	19	783.4
1898	658.6	18.6	808.8
1899	664.1	18.5	889.6
1900	673.3	17.9	1,039.4
1901	726.8	19.6	919
1902	737.2	19.9	868.4

SOURCES: French ordinary and extraordinary budgets combined for 1880-1890; thereafter summary budget. Sources for French budgets: Alfred Neymarck, *Finances contemporaines*, vol. II, *Les Budgets 1872-1903* (Paris, 1904); *Ministère des finances. Bureau de statistique et de legislation comparée. La France financière et économique* (Paris, 1919), vol. I; *Compte géneral de L'administration des finances rendu pour l'année 1881 par le Ministre des Finances* (Paris, 1883); . . . *pour l'année 1883* (Paris, 1885); . . . *pour l'année 1885* (Paris, 1887); . . . *pour l'année 1887* (Paris, 1889); . . . *pour l'année 1889* (Paris, 1890); . . . *pour l'année 1891* (Paris, 1892)

The Russian credit ruble fluctuated rather considerably in value until Witte's stabilization of 1894-1895. The franc value of Russian army spending has therefore been calculated on the basis of the average selling price of the ruble in Paris. Sources: 1881-1894: Arthur Raffalovich, *Le Marché financier en 1895-1896* (Paris, 1896), p. 299; 1894-1902: Arthur Raffalovich, *Le Marché financier en 1896-1897* (Paris, 1897), p. 667

TABLE 4

Army Share in German State Expenditure, 1881-1902

Year	(1) Total German Army expenditures (without pensions), millions of marks	(2) (1) as % of total German State expenditures	Russian Army budget, millions of marks
1880/81	369.8	67	544.5
1885/86	421.6	66	417.6
1886/87	396	57	381.8
1887/88	528.6	60	400.8
1888/89	550.5	53	483.6
1889/90	541.3	48	565.4
1890/91	719.5	53	568.7
1891/92	566.5	45	531.0
1892/93	576.6	46	569.3
1893/94	645.9	48	626.3
1894/95	611.1	47	628
1895/96	562.7	43	635.8
1896/97	549.6	43	634.6
1897/98	540	41	655
1898	632.7	34	655
1899	644.7	32	720.5
1900	656.1	29	841.9
1901	673.1	28	744.3
1902	653.7	28	703.3

SOURCE: Total summary budgets for the German Empire, including both ordinary and extraordinary expenses, have been employed. Sources for German budgets: *Statistisches Jahrbuch für das Deutche Reich, herausgegeben vom Kaiserlichen Statistischen Amt* (Berlin, 1894; 1897; 1902). Until 1898, the German budget did not run in accordance with the calendar year. Russian figures which reflect the later year have therefore been given. The Russian credit ruble fluctuated considerably until Witte's stabilization of 1894-1895. The mark value of the Russian army budget has therefore been calculated on the basis of the annual average selling price of the ruble in Berlin. Sources: 1881-1895: *Ministerstvo Finansov. Osobennaia kantseliariia po kreditnoi chasti. otdelenie II. stol. I. N°16000 "Ob ispravlenii denezhnogo obrashcheniia"* (St. Petersburg, n.d.), p. 55; 1895-1902: Arthur Raffalovich, *Le Marché financier en 1896-1897* (Paris, 1897), p. 667

controlled; there can be little doubt that these figures represent the core of army expenditures in each state.

In comparing the tables it is immediately evident that, in contrast to Russia, the share of the army in France's financial outlay remained relatively constant and that in Germany, although the share of the army in state revenues declined, it never declined below 28 percent. At the same time, *total* expenditures in Germany grew much more dramatically than in either Russia or France. Yet an examination of the absolute amounts involved is perhaps more meaningful. From 1881 to 1902 France spent at least 15,200.3 million francs on her army. Russia spent 15,306.9 million francs, or just .7 percent more. Similarly, from 1881 to 1902, Germany spent 10,470.2 million marks and Russia 10,762.9 million, or 2.79 percent more. Military spending is certainly cumulative, but Russia spent more at the *end* of that period than at the *beginning*. Thus, since the small amounts of Russian expenditure over and above that of France and Germany resulted largely from outlays clustered after the mid-nineties, the Russian "advantage" was actually less than it appears at first sight. Yet Witte was certainly correct when he stated that the Russian army enjoyed the highest growth rate in appropriations of any European army in the 1890s. In 1884 the army received 199.96 million rubles; in 1900, 389.75 million, or 94 percent more. Russia consistently outspent France on her army after 1892, and outspent Germany after 1894.

A shallow concentration on quantities of rubles, francs, and marks, however, ought not to substitute for an analysis of what these numbers really meant: how much security was Russia purchasing with her defense outlay compared to that of France and Germany? Or, to phrase the question differently, why was Russia spending more on her army in the 1890s than the other great European powers? The question is especially important since Russia was poorer than either France or Germany, and one might expect that she could afford to spend less than either of these states. The answer is simply that Russia spent more because she had to spend more—her peacetime army was larger than that of any other state. The single greatest cost of Russia's army was its size. In 1893, Russia had 992,000 men under arms, compared to 573,000 in France and 521,000 in Germany. And Russia's military forces were larger than those of the other European powers for three reasons at least. The first of these was the defense of the Empire's frontiers, more gigantic in their extent than those of any state. Although the chief potential threat to Russia lay along her borders with Austria-Hungary and Germany, Russia still regarded Turkey as a menace, and towards the end of this period was rightly uneasy about the security of the Maritime Provinces and Manchuria in the East.[6]

A second reason why Russia's army was larger than those of the West inhered in the Russian conscription system. After 1874, the average Russian conscript was required to serve from four to five years in the ranks before being discharged into the reserves; in Germany, after 1893, a drafted soldier served only two years, and in France, after 1889, three. France and Germany, blessed with highly educated populations, could fulfill all of the objectives of their training programs in periods of time which were thought to be inadequate for training the Russian peasant recruit. This circumstance obliged the Russian army to retain lengthy periods of basic service, which in turn meant a larger army than in France or Germany, where any given cohort of conscripts could work their way into the reserves more quickly.[7]

The third reason for Russia's army of almost one million men was allied to the second, in that both directly originated in Russia's backwardness. This was the issue of mobilization. Due to the superlative development of transportation in Germany, the German High Command could call up reserves, equip them, and transport them to the frontier more rapidly than could Russia. The Russian military therefore believed that they had to support a greater number of men on active duty than Germany, and additionally had to place a great number of them in the West in order to compensate for Germany's mobilization superiority.

A large army inevitably needs more of everything—food, arms, fodder—than a smaller one. Yet Russia was funding an army almost twice the size of those of France and Germany with military appropriations which were hardly twice the approprations of these countries. Table 5, based on data for 1893, demonstrates the consequences of this fact in terms of expenditures per soldier.

Russia was therefore spending 75.3 percent less on each of her soldiers than Germany and 58.9 percent less than France. These statistics might imply that prices for certain crucial stores (such as cereals, for example) were higher in Western Europe than in Russia, which was indeed the case. But they also imply that the Russian army was much less well paid, equipped, and fed than the armies of the West, which was also true. Indeed, the comparative poverty of the tsarist army helps account

[6] Zolotarev, *Zapiski*, p. 415; on the Turkish threat, see Kuropatkin's diary for 1899: TsGVIA, f. 165, op. 1, d. 1868, l. 55; on the Far East, see TsGVIA, f. 1, op. 2, d. 158, l. 3 (War Ministry report for 1898).

[7] Craig, *Prussian Army*, pp. 243-245; Theodore Zeldin, *France, 1848-1945*, vol. 1 (Oxford, 1973), p. 638; *Vsepoddanneishii doklad po voennomu ministerstvu 1882 goda* (St. Petersburg, 1882), p. 41.

TABLE 5
Comparative Military Expenditures, 1893

Country	Expenditure	No. of troops in peacetime	Amount per soldier
Germany	576.6 million marks	521,000	1,106.7 marks
Russia	626.3 million marks	992,000	631.4 marks
France	649.5 million francs	573,000	1,133.5 francs
Russia	707.4 million francs	992,000	713.1 francs

SOURCE: A. M. Zolotarev, *Zapiski voennoi statistiki Rossii*, vol. 1 (St. Petersburg, 1894), p. 443

for the persistence of what John Bushnell has described as the "regimental economy": that system whereby the Intendancy issued grain, leather, and cloth to military units, which then baked their own bread, cobbled their own boots, and tailored their own uniforms.[8] The increase in Russian army spending in the nineties should accordingly be viewed against the background provided by all of this information. In outspending France and Germany, Russia was not marching to the drumbeat of militarism, but was rather attempting merely to catch up. And the most important area in which she was behind was that of arms. Technological innovations towards the end of the nineteenth century were revolutionizing warfare, making all previous weapons obsolete. The magazine rifle, for example, was unquestionably superior to single-shot rifles, and most European powers had started to adopt some sort of magazine weapon in the 1880s. France introduced the 8-mm Lebel rifle in 1886, and Germany began large purchases of Mauser-made 7.91-mm Gewehr rifles in 1888.[9] The Russian War Ministry was finally able to order its own magazine rifles (the Mosin 3-line rifle patent 1891) in 1892, but did not acquire all of the over three million pieces it needed until 1902.[10] In this case, the Russian army was able to procure an adequate supply of necessary weapons, although slightly later than the other powers. But the army's record with regard to other vital arms was much poorer. By 1902, Russia had only 2,650 three-inch quick-firing field pieces, as

[8] Bushnell, "Tsarist Officer Corps," pp. 765-768.

[9] James E. Hicks, *French Military Weapons, 1717 to 1930* (New Milford, Conn., 1964), p. 29.

[10] TsGAOR, f. 601, op. 1, d. 441, ll. 1, 4, 29-30; L. G. Beskrovnyi, *Russkaia armiia i flot v XIX veke* (Moscow, 1973), p. 315.

compared to over 3,000 each in France and Germany.[11] It is important to note that Russia never initiated any great armament innovations on her own account during this period. Rather she responded, belatedly, to the military improvements which had been adopted abroad. The Russian army did not amass stockpiles of modern weapons and materiel comparable to those in Western arsenals both because of its share of the national budget and because of the high cost of industrial production in the Empire (it was more expensive to manufacture a Mosin rifle in Russia than it was to order one made in France).[12] Thus, on the eve of the war with Japan, Russia still lacked an adequate supply of heavy field guns and howitzers, her fortress artillery was outmoded, and many of her fortresses themselves were in disrepair. In 1903, Russia was short by 1,274 pieces of fortress artillery. Barracks, communications equipment, and the strategic railroad network were all substandard. Over 400 battalions of infantry, 311 squadrons or sotnia of cavalry, and 153 artillery batteries were not housed in state barracks. Such modern equipment as Russia did buy entailed enormous expenditure. The Mosin rifles had cost the War Ministry almost 180 million rubles from 1890 to 1896, while about 40 million had been spent on quick-firing guns by January 1, 1904. Part of the increases in army spending after the eighties is therefore traceable to investment in these modern arms.[13]

But if arms acquisition helped to inflate the army budget, other factors contributed. One such factor was the changing price levels of food and cloth. These costs naturally affected the appropriations which the army would request in any given year, a circumstance which had been appreciated and allowed for when Russia first acquired her modern budget in the early 1860s. Tatarinov's budgetary rules of 1862 had prescribed definite deadlines for the preparation of ministerial estimates. These were to be submitted to the Ministry of Finance for review every September 1, before being sent to the Economic Department of the Council of State on November 1. Yet Tatarinov excused the War Ministry from his arrangement, permitting it an extra thirty to forty days to deliver its estimates to Finance. The State Controller made this exception not only because of the complexity of the Ministry's budget but also because it was impossible for the Ministry to compile any meaningful figures without information about the abundance of the harvest, information which was unavailable until early October. Although, because of the world agricultural depression, the prices of most cereals declined in the

[11] Ibid., p. 358.

[12] TsGAOR, f. 601, op. 1, d. 441, ll. 29-30.

[13] TsGVIA, f. 1, op. 2, d. 163, ll. 36, 51; TsGVIA, f. 1, op. 1, d. 61605, l. 10; TsGVIA, f. 601, op. 1, d. 441, l. 29; TsGVIA, f. 1/L, op. 2, d. 1140, ll. 87, 126.

late nineteenth century, Russia was not interested in purchasing grain abroad. The essence of Vyshnegradskii's strategy as Finance Minister, after all, had been to force a high volume of grain exports even in periods of relative domestic scarcity. Therefore, bad harvests had the effect of driving up domestic prices, thus squeezing the budget of the Russian military Intendancy, which was the largest single purchaser of grain in the Empire. Grain prices shot up by 19 percent from 1890 to 1891; the higher cost of foodstuffs also resulted in army budgetary increases in 1892, 1898, and 1902 (1891-1892 and 1902 were years of poor harvests). The acquisition of special food reserves occasioned larger appropriations in 1893 and 1894. The price of cloth, moving up in 1893 and 1894, and again sharply at the end of the century, also added a significant number of rubles to the military budget.[14]

But the army estimates of the 1890s concealed still other costs which were unrelated to any military improvement. Leaving aside the 2.5 million rubles which the War Ministry spent on the coronation of Nicholas II, and the expenses of running the Transcaspian railroad and quartering the Gendarmes in Poland (charged to the War Ministry after 1899), the most important of these costs evolved from Russia's fatal involvement in the East. As the power closest to the disturbance, Russia bore the greatest part of the burden of suppressing the Chinese Boxer Rebellion of 1900. Military operations in that year cost over 56 million rubles, and another 18 million in 1901. Yet the problem of Manchuria was even more serious for the War Ministry. The seizure of the Kwantung peninsula and the defense of Dalnyi, Port Arthur, and Vladivostok drained millions away from the army. This meddling in the Far East, part of the general upsurge of European imperialism at the turn of the century, had never been desired by responsible officials at the War Ministry. To Kuropatkin, the Eastern expansion was a potentially dangerous liability, which added an unwelcome burden to the already overstrained military budget. The War Ministry was able to secure money for the East, some 24 million rubles from 1899 to 1903 (although the sums granted were never really adequate for its defense), while

[14] *Ministerstvo finansov 1802-1902*, pt. 1 (St. Petersburg, n.d.), p. 317; *Gosudarstvennyi kontrol' 1811-1911* (St. Petersburg, n.d.), p. 144; Jacob Metzer, "Railway Development and Market Integration: The Case of Tsarist Russia," *The Journal of Economic History* 34, no. 2 (Sept. 1974): 536, 548; Robbins, *Famine in Russia*, pp. 6-8; M. P. Kokhn, *Russkie indeksy tsen* (Moscow, 1926), p. 158; *Ob"iasnitel'naia zapiska k otchetu Gosudarstvennogo Kontrolia 1892 goda* (St. Petersburg, 1893), p. 53; . . . *1893 goda* (St. Petersburg, 1894), p. 60; . . . *1894 goda* (St. Petersburg, 1895), p. 63; . . . *1898 goda* (St. Petersburg, 1899), p. 63; TsGVIA, f. 1, op. 2, d. 162, l. 48; A. Koniaev, *Finansovyi kontrol' v dorevoliutsionnoi Rossii* (Moscow, 1959), p. 68.

knowing all the time that the millions squandered there should have been devoted to strengthening the Western frontier. As Kuropatkin wrote in 1903: "This diversion of War Ministry funds to the East is now a great obstacle to the satisfaction of many essential needs of our army and [also hinders] our taking measures towards the further strengthening of our military position on the Western front, which is most important to us."[15]

Thus, S. Iu. Witte was correct when he announced that Russia had outspent the West on her army in the 1890s. But this fact did not mean, as Witte implied, that the Russian army was satisfied in all of its needs, let alone well prepared. As we have seen, some of the increased expenditure of the army resulted from higher costs, others from such new national priorities as an imperialist policy in the Far East. Money spent under either of these categories cannot be considered as contributing to the increased military efficiency of the Empire. Another group of expenditures can be ascribed to a manic attempt to catch up with the aggressive rearmament of Western Europe after the fiscal neglect of the Russian army in the 1880s. Yet this attempt was unsuccessful: the state never furnished the army with the requisite money. To be sure, the national expenditures of Russia increased enormously in the 1880s and 1890s, which obviously explains why the Russian army could receive a greater absolute amount of money while its share in Imperial outlay declined. National wealth also increased, but Russia remained a poor nation by comparison with France or Germany.

Today it is customary to measure defense spending as a percentage of the gross national product of any state, a procedure which is difficult to apply to the army budgets at the turn of the century because of the unreliable statistical base at the historian's disposal.[16] If, however, we accept S. N. Prokopovich's figure of 6,579.6 million rubles for the gross domestic product (GDP) of the fifty provinces of European Russia in 1900, we find that Russia's army appropriations equalled 5.9 percent of this total.[17] W. G. Hoffman's computations for Germany would indicate that the German army received 2 percent of the net national product in the same year; if France's GDP for 1900 was approximately 29,095

[15] *Ob"iasnitel'naia zapiska k otchetu Gosudarstvennogo Kontrolia 1896 goda* (St. Petersburg, 1897), p. 59; . . . *1899 goda* (St. Petersburg, 1900), p. 67; . . . *1900 goda* (St. Petersburg, 1901), p. 52; . . . *1901 goda* (St. Petersburg, 1902), pp. 50-51; TsGVIA, f. 1/L, op. 2, d. 1140, l. 126; TsGVIA, f. 1, op. 2, d. 162, l. 3.

[16] See, for example, Davis B. Bobrow, "Bread, Guns and Uncle Sam's International Realities," in *New Civil-Military Relations*, ed. John P. Lovell and Phillip S. Kronenberg (New Brunswick, N.J., 1974), p. 305.

[17] A. L. Vainshtein, *Narodnyi dokhod Rossii i SSSR* (Moscow, 1969), p. 63.

million francs, as T. J. Markovitch has suggested, then the French army was supported by 2 percent of that sum.[18] Although all three of these estimates were made on the basis of contemporary market prices, they are of course not strictly comparable. Prokopovich's figure is clearly too small: it comprises, after all, only European Russia and also excludes, in line with Marxist statistical practice, "unproductive" government expenditures. Net national product, which Hoffman has calculated for Germany, excludes depreciation and capital outlays, which are included in Markovitch's GDP: the sum for Germany should accordingly be increased as well. Yet crude as these measurements are, they provide a rough index of Russia's economic difficulties in military competition with the prosperous West. In 1900, Russia spent 54 percent more than France and 28.3 percent more than Germany on an army which was by no means as well trained or equipped as the armies of these two powers. Yet to maintain her army even at the unsteady preparedness level of 1900, Russia had to pay out two to three times the proportion of national income which France and Germany were spending. Russia could not simply withdraw from international military competition. In the judgment of her military leaders, Russia had to compete with the West, for they believed that an aggressive war, launched by Germany, was right around the corner. In view of this, and in view of the fact that Russia was already lagging behind the West, the sagging share of the army in state expenditures could only be regarded with alarm.

REASONS FOR THE ARMY'S DECLINING SHARE OF STATE REVENUE

How, then, did this bizarre situation come to pass? At least one scholar—P. A. Zaionchkovskii—has taken note of the strange phenomenon of the army's declining share of state revenue. Essentially demonstrating the same point as Table 2 by comparing the rate of increase in appropriations granted to each ministry and department of state from 1882 to 1903, he nonetheless chose not to investigate the motives which informed Imperial budgetary decision making. Instead of such an analysis, he blamed the relative poverty of the army in this period on "financial difficulties" (*finansovye trudnosti*).[19]

Another explanation which has been advanced in both Soviet and non-Soviet studies is that the Russian army itself was to blame for its declining share. Scholars who adopt this position depict the period 1881-

[18] B. R. Mitchell, comp., *European Historical Statistics, 1750-1950* (London, 1975), pp. 785, 797.

[19] Zaionchkovskii, *Samoderzhavie*, p. 82.

1903 as an "epoch of military stagnation." The War Ministry was led by officials who were too insouciant, ignorant, or stupid to appreciate the technological transformation of modern war. As a result, they did not fight hard enough for the interests of the army, or for military modernization.[20] War Ministry reports, however, confute this view. War Minister P. S. Vannovskii filled each of his annual reports to the Emperor with dire warnings about technological backwardness. He tenaciously and continually appealed for the appropriations necessary to purchase the latest weapons. The historiographical representation of Vannovskii as a military ignoramus hardly squares with the man who emerges from the sources as a fiery advocate of quick-firing artillery, smokeless powder, magazine rifles, telegraphs, strategic railways, electrified artillery parks, etc.[21]

There is another explanation for the erosion of the army's fiscal status within the Empire which is much more obvious and convincing than the explanation of ineptitude: the state was deliberately preferring other types of expenditure to military expenditure. And the most important reason for this preference was the rise of the Ministry of Finance to preeminence within the Imperial government.

Various scholars of Russian history have developed the concept of the triumph of "institutional points of view" within the Russian ministries by the second half of the nineteenth century. In the opinion of one scholar, these viewpoints "tended to be independent of the personality and convictions of any given minister."[22] Nowhere was this trend toward impersonal professionalism more evident than in the so-called technical ministries, such as the Ministry of Finance, which had been actively recruiting academically trained economists, accountants, and other specialists since the early days of the Great Reforms. Since the institutional goal of the Ministry of Finance was austerity, fiscal health, and later economic expansion, it inevitably came into conflict with every other ministry of state. Indeed, George Yaney has made the well-documented struggle between the Ministry of Finance and the Ministry of the Interior

[20] Kersnovskii, *Istoriia*, pp. 499-500, 507-509; N. P. Eroshkin, *Ocherki istorii gosudarstvennykh uchrezhdenii dorevoliutsionnoi Rossii* (Moscow, 1960), p. 285; Wildman, *Russian Imperial Army*, p. 17.

[21] *Vsepoddanneishii doklad po voennomu ministerstvu 1882 goda* (St. Petersburg, 1882), pp. 6-7; . . . *1883 goda* (St. Petersburg, 1883), p. 243; . . . *1885 goda* (St. Petersburg, 1885), p. 5; . . . *1888 goda* (St. Petersburg, 1888), pp. 1-2, 11; . . . *1892 goda* (St. Petersburg, 1892), p. 7; . . . *1893 goda* (St. Petersburg, 1893), p. 3.

[22] N. I. Lazarevskii, *Lektsii po russkomu gosudarstvennomu pravu*, vol. 2, pt. 1 (St. Petersburg, 1910), p. 178; Theodore Taranovsky, *The Politics of Counter-Reform. Autocracy and Bureaucracy in the Reign of Alexander III, 1881-1894*, Ph.D. diss., Harvard University, 1976, p. 95.

the centerpiece of his interpretation of the Imperial government from the emancipation of the serfs to the outbreak of the revolution of 1905.[23]

Yet the Finance Ministry's conflicts with the War Ministry were in fact no less bitter; not only did the War Ministry consume such a prodigious proportion of the state revenues, it also managed to circumvent every budgetary control which the Finance Ministry could devise until 1881. For example, from 1874 on, the Finance Ministry had theoretically capped the growth of the army budget through the imposition of absolute, maximum appropriations which could be granted in any year. The Turkish War, of course, caused a breakdown in the application of this principle, and after the war, in December 1878, the War Ministry secured the right to appeal for additional credits above any maximum appropriation which might be approved.[24]

Finance Minister Reutern had violently opposed hostilities with Turkey. As he had foreseen, the war, which began in April 1877, severely damaged Russia's financial position. The value of the credit ruble in relation to gold declined by 7.8 percent from September to November 1876 alone. Expenditure on war preparations and the war itself from 1876 to 1877 totalled a shocking 888 million rubles. In 1881, three years after the Congress of Berlin, Russia still found herself straining to service a national debt of some 4.9 billion. The economic depression which partly grew out of the postwar slump was to endure until 1887.[25]

The gravity of this postwar fiscal crisis put strong cards into the hands of the Ministry of Finance. The Ministry's proposals for economic recovery won respectful support from some of the most influential statesmen in the government, including most importantly, the new autocrat himself. Although the Ministers of Finance subsequent to Reutern—Bunge (1881-1886), Vyshnegradskii (1887-1892), and Witte (1892-1902)—entertained similar long-term objectives, each undertook his own individual programs. The academically trained Bunge, for example, primarily concerned himself with redesigning the tax system and with stablizing the ruble. Vyshnegradskii added state railway investment, massive grain exports (to secure a favorable balance of trade), and the protectionist tariff of 1891 to this package of measures. Witte amplified

[23] George L. Yaney, *The Systematization of the Russian Government. Social Evolution in the Domestic Administration of Imperial Russia, 1711-1905* (Urbana, 1973), chap. 8, esp. pp. 305-316.

[24] *Vsepoddanneishii doklad po voennomu ministerstvu 1880 goda* (St. Petersburg, 1880), pp. 200-201; Jean de Block [Ivan Bliokh], *Les finances de la Russie au XIXe siècle*, vol. 2 (Paris, 1899), p. 245.

[25] A. F. Iakovlev, *Ekonomicheskie krizisy v Rossii* (Moscow, 1955), pp. 144-148; *Obzor deiatel'nosti ministerstva finansov v tsarstvovanie Imperatora Aleksandra III (1881-1894)* (St. Petersburg, 1902), p. 130.

state railway construction, put Russia on the gold standard, and actively pursued foreign capital in order to give an even greater stimulus to Russia's growing industrial capacity. What clearly united these men and their associates was an obvious appreciation that Russia's chief problem inhered in her poverty. To solve this problem, they therefore had to redirect Russia's existing wealth into the most productive channels, and they further had to create new sources of wealth altogether. As early as 1880, Bunge had suggested to Alexander II that industrialization be fostered "as the chief source of state revenues."[26]

Several obstacles nevertheless choked the road to prosperity which the Ministry of Finance envisioned for Russia. One of the chief of these, from the Ministry's point of view, was the Russian army's insatiable appetite for money. In his report to Alexander II on the 1881 budget, Finance Minister A. A. Abaza had cautioned that

> the natural increase of state revenues has certain limits. In the course of the last twenty years, total revenue has more than doubled, yet it has invariably been swallowed up by expenses. Even though our foreign policy has resumed its peaceable directions, about a third of the budget is still put at the disposal of the Minister of War. In these conditions, the Minister of Finance believes himself obliged to express his conviction that it is urgent to take measures to reduce the sacrifices of the country for her armed forces.[27]

That this opinion was widely shared within the financial chancellery is confirmed by the official histories of the Finance Ministry during the reigns of Alexander III and Nicholas II. As one of these publications bluntly expressed it:

> A special danger to the successful application of measures to reduce deficits threatened from size of expenses generated by the demands of state defense. Expenses of this kind attained such huge sums that even a comparatively insignificant increase in them, occasioned by an increase in the number of troops, the perfection of armaments, or higher food prices, might immediately render nugatory all efforts directed to the attainment of parity between revenues and expenses.[28]

This statement was less than candid. For although the immediate goal of the Ministry of Finance after 1881 was the reduction of deficits, its long-term mission was the creation and taxation of wealth. Any

[26] I. Gindin, *Gosudarstvennyi bank i ekonomicheskaia politika tsarskogo pravitel'stva* (Moscow, 1960), p. 57.

[27] Block, *Finances de la Russie*, p. 299.

[28] *Obzor ministerstva finansov*, p. 118.

method—including deficit spending—was permissible to achieve this goal. Indeed, the railway boom of the 1880s and 1890s was expedited by deficit financing accomplished through the deft manipulation of the Russian Empire's divided budget. Since 1864, the budget of the state had been separated into two sections, an ordinary section and an extraordinary section. Ordinary expenditures were supposed to be balanced by ordinary revenues, extraordinary expenses by extraordinary revenues. But extraordinary revenues consisted almost entirely of the proceeds of domestic and foreign loans, and in this period the gigantic sums poured into the railway system were classified as extraordinary expenditures. This meant that Russia could preserve the appearance of a balanced budget; in fact, as critics of the regime never tired of pointing out, the summary budget was never balanced in the eighties or nineties.[29]

Why then was the Finance Ministry so eager to spend money on railways, so reluctant to give it to the army? Simply because the Ministry did not regard military expenditures as productive, but instead as absolutely wasteful. This was of course not necessarily true. In a recent series of articles, Clive Trebilcock has ingeniously argued in support of the economic utility of state investment in domestically produced armaments in the period before World War I. And even in Russia, Professor N. P. Iasnopol'skii, writing in 1894, was not prepared to discount the salutary regional economic impact of army spending.[30] But such thinking was foreign to the Russian Ministry of Finance. There it was held that each kopeck added to the army budget cheated the national industrialization program, a program which was apparently crowned by astounding success. By reorganizing the tax system, by going onto the gold standard, by creating effective tariff barriers, and by pumping as much domestic and foreign money as possible into the Russian economy, the Ministry of Finance found itself presiding over one of the most rapid expansions of industrial capacity in the history of the world.[31]

[29] Peter I. Lyashchenko, *History of the National Economy of Russia to the 1917 Revolution*, trans. L. M. Herman (New York, 1949), pp. 554-555.

[30] See, for example, Clive Trebilcock, "The British Armaments Industry 1890-1914: False Legend and True Utility," in *War, Economy and the Modern Mind*, ed. Geoffrey Best and Andrew Wheatcraft (London, 1976), pp. 89-107; N. P. Iasnopol'skii, *O geograficheskom raspredelenii gosudarstvennykh raskhodov Rossii* (Kiev, 1894), p. 226.

[31] Since the early 1970s, an ever growing number of practitioners of the "new economic history" have challenged the traditional explanatory model of Russia's economic boom. Thus, McKay has argued that foreign capital, not domestic forced savings, was the "critical mass" necessary for economic takeoff. Drummond has stressed the huge economic costs of the gold standard to Russia, as has H. Barkai, etc. The best summary of these new interpretations is to be found in Paul R. Gregory, "Russian Industrialization and Economic Growth: Results and Perspectives of Western Research," *Jahrbücher für Geschichte*

Gerschenkron and Falkus have both stated that a major motive behind Russia's state-inspired industrialization was government fear about Russia's military decline vis-à-vis the other great powers of Europe. Gerschenkron writes: "Clearly a good deal of the Government's interest in industrialization was predicated upon its military policies," and Falkus insists that the Minstry of Finance's drive for prosperity was founded on strategic considerations.[32] If this had been so, it would have been logical for the Ministry of Finance to have served both the economy and the army by vigorously constructing a network of strategic railways. But in fact, although any railroad may conceivably be "strategic," the Minister of Finance purposely evaded sponsoring purely strategic railways. Of the 20,500 versts of rail laid down from 1893 to 1900, 10,500, or 55 percent, were built by private companies (although financially aided by the government). These roads were not chiefly strategic. Of the 9,500 versts which the government itself added to the railway network in these eight years, only 3,000 versts, or 14.6 percent, were constructed in European Russia, the strategic theater of most importance to the Russian Ministry of War.[33] Not all of this 14.6 percent could have been strategic by any means—at least in terms of the war the Russian General Staff foresaw.

A nonstrategic interpretation of Russian railroad construction is supported by other evidence. If the testimony of Witte is any guide, the Ministry of Finance only agreed to strategic railways when pressured to do so—as, for example, in 1900, when the government of France made a loan to Russia contingent on the construction of the Orenburg to Tashkent line.[34] To be sure, the 2,000-odd versts of the Transcaspian railroad were built under War Ministry authority during the nineties;

Osteuropas, neue folge, 25, no. 2 (1977): 200-218. Dr. Gregory implicitly and explicitly (pp. 209, 214) disagrees with those historians, like Kahan, who would argue that the Witte system was economically counterproductive and that "private investors" could have accomplished a much smoother and speedier industrialization. He concludes that, although the effects of state intervention in the Russian economy of the nineties are less clear than was first supposed, the industrial boom would have been inconceivable without state action. In any event, the Ministry of Finance obviously thought that its economic policies were responsible for industrialization: T. H. von Laue, "A Secret Memorandum of Sergei Witte on the Industrialization of Imperial Russia," *Journal of Modern History* 26, no. 1 (Mar. 1954): 64-74.

[32] Alexander Gerschenkron, *Economic Backwardness in Historical Perspective* (Cambridge, Mass., 1966), p. 20; M. E. Falkus, *The Industrialization of Russia, 1700-1914* (London, 1977), p. 62.

[33] A. M. Solov'eva, *Zhelezno-dorozhnyi transport Rossii vo vtoroi polovine XIX v* (Moscow, 1975), pp. 252-254.

[34] D. N. Collins, "The Franco-Russian Alliance and Russian Railways, 1891-1914," *The Historical Journal* 16, no. 4 (Dec. 1973): 779.

still, the motive for this line was at least as much commercial as military. The state further took the management of the road away from the army in 1899.[35] Perhaps the most telling detail of all is the fact that as late as 1902, despite its repeated efforts, the Ministry of War had been unable to place a representative on the Ministry of Transport's Railway Construction Committee.[36] Thus throughout the eighties and nineties the War Ministry had little input into railway construction decisions.

The Ministry of Finance undertook railway construction and industrialization for the sake of industrialization itself. This circumstance explains why the Finance Ministry tended to undervalue the needs of national security, absorbed as it was by economic problems. The lack of unity in the Russian government, which was practically a principle of autocratic administration, naturally enhanced the tendencies of each ministry to assume that its own objectives were the same as the general interests of the state. As Vyshnegradskii wrote Alexander III in 1888: "I consider it my duty as a subject to truly express to your Imperial Majesty my firm, clear and deep conviction that the well-being of the people, even given a certain imperfection in the military establishment, will render more use in a period of armed conflict than the most complete military preparedness of the army."[37] Vyshnegradskii was not alluding here to the advantages of a strong industrial base in wartime, but rather to the higher morale which a prosperous soldier would presumably bring to the battlefield. As these words suggest, Vyshnegradskii felt that the economy took precedence over any other field of state activity. And Witte very probably would have denied that his industrialization policies were framed as contributions to the military might of the Imperial regime, had he felt free to do so. Certainly the irreconcilability of massive military spending with successful economic development was always uppermost in his mind. To be sure, in his published lectures on the national economy Witte did pay lip service to the importance of railroads in military mobilization, but he placed much more stress on the positive impact of improved transport on agriculture and manufacturing.[38] This distribution of emphasis accurately reflected Witte's thinking: as von Laue writes, "obviously the economy rather than the defense was the

---

[35] *Ministerstvo voennoe. Otchet po postroike krasnovodskogo uchastka zakaspiiskoi voennoi zhelezhnoi dorogi* (St. Petersburg, 1898), p. 1; *Glavneishie statisticheskie vyvody o razvitii i deiatelnosti zheleznykh i vodnykh putei Rossii za poslednie 15-t' let (1880-1894 g.g.)* (St. Petersburg, 1896), p. v; TsGVIA, f. 1, op. 2, d. 1141, l. 103.

[36] TsGVIA, f. 1, op. 2, d. 1141, l. 103.

[37] *Obzor ministersva finansov*, p. 308.

[38] S. J. Witte, *Vorlesungen über Volks- und Staatswirtschaft*, trans. Josef Melnik, vol. 2 (Stuttgart, 1913), pp. 61-95.

chief beneficiary of Witte's financial management." Nowhere in Witte's famous secret memorandum to Nicholas II of 1899, that formal justification of his policies, does he speak of the military advantages accruing to Russia as the result of industrialization. Although he mentions the benefit of economic and hence political independence from the West, and although he speaks of strength, he clearly construes strength in economic terms.[39]

The Russian War Ministry did not perceive the strategic significance of Russia's rapid industrialization either. In the first place, the received wisdom at the War Ministry held that the coming war would be short and would have to be fought with material *already* stockpiled. Were a war to be over in a matter of weeks, national industrial potential would never come into play. Second, as we have seen, Russian tactical doctrine emphasized the superiority of man to machine in warfare. While first-rate equipment was important, the staunchness of the individual soldier under fire determined the success or failure of a campaign. And the military establishment of Russia believed that the peasant, not the industrial laborer, possessed the best military qualities. This belief lent a peculiar ideological coloration to the dispute between the Ministries of War and Finance; for not only did industrialization, inspired by the Finance Ministry, beggar the Russian army, it also threatened the very nerve of Russian military strength—rural society. This is why in 1892 Chief of Staff N. N. Obruchev denounced Finance Minister Vyshnegradskii as a thief who was ruining all the productive forces of Russia, and why Kuropatkin wrote in his diary for 1903 that

> to us, the military establishment, this result [industrialization] is very disturbing, since exactly this part of the population [the peasantry] of Russia gives her the army, which until this time with relation to its common soldiers was above all the armies in the world. If this part of the population is impoverished, becomes discontented, loses its faith in authority . . . then this will of course reflect on the moral temper of the future soldier.[40]

That there was hostility and mistrust between the Ministries of Finance and War, then, needs little additional confirmation. Yet we must still examine how Bunge, Vyshnegradskii, and Witte were all so successful in their duels with the Ministry of War.

One reason, of course, was the Finance Ministry's cohesion and tight

[39] A. L. Sidorov, ed., *Materialy po istorii SSSR*, vol. 7 (Moscow, 1959), pp. 173-195; von Laue, *Sergei Witte and the Industrialization of Russia*, pp. 100-102.

[40] V. N. Lamzdorff, *Dnevik, 1891-1892*, p. 278, "Dnevnik A. N. Kuropatkina s 17 noiabria 1902 g. po 6 marta 1903 g.," *Krasnyi arkhiv* (Moscow) 2 (1922): 25-26.

central organization, which lent it superiority in bureaucratic maneuver. To be sure, the War Ministry was hierarchically organized under a single minister. But the existence of powerful, semi-independent Main Administrations within the War Ministry, and the de facto independence of the Military Inspectorates outside the Ministry, undercut the authority of the War Minister as the prime initiator of military policy and occasionally embroiled him in painful internecine intrigues. The Minister of Finance was, by contrast, spared such challenges to his control as these independent entities, which were essentially built into the structure of the War Ministry by its organizing statutes, contained in the second volume of the *Svod zakonov* and the first volume of the Military Code of 1869. Untroubled by competition or mutiny from within his own ministry, the Minister of Finance was free to conclude strong alliances with the State Control, the Ministry of Transport, and the Economic Department of the State Council. But models such as the foregoing, which purport to explain the victory of this or that policy through a consideration of institutional dynamics alone, are never sufficient in themselves. Personalities deserve consideration. For instance, the physical weakness of War Minister P. S. Vannovskii and the bureaucratic inexperience of his successor, A. N. Kuropatkin, also weakened the War Ministry in its struggle with the technical ministries. Vannovskii suffered from recurring bouts of ill health. His service record reveals that he was abroad or visiting Russian spas for treatment for two or three months every year from 1883 to 1887, for four months in 1889, three in 1890 and 1893, and six months in 1895. Since the second-in-command of the Ministry, the Chief of the Main Staff, possessed no real power in the absence of the Minister, Vannovskii's broken health and consequent frequent departures from the capital left the War Ministry defenseless before its adversaries. As for Kuropatkin, even A. F. Rediger, who admired him, noted that he was all too often psychologically mesmerized by the brilliant Witte.[41]

Yet clearly the most important reason for the triumph of the Finance Ministry over the War Ministry from 1881 to 1902 was the support of the autocrats Alexander III and Nicholas II, support which was especially decisive in view of the lack of a united Russian ministry.[42] The Emperor was the final arbiter of interministerial disputes. Because they were reasonably confident of his favor, Ministers of Finance could judiciously threaten their opponents with direct appeals to the highest power. Of-

---

[41] TsGVIA, f. 409, op. 1, d. p/s 79-176, l. 10; TsGVIA, f. 280, op. 1, d. 3, pp. 333, 382.

[42] On the lack of a united ministry, see V. G. Chernukha, *Vnutrenniaia politika tsarizma s serediny 50-kh do nachala 80-kh g.g. XIX v.* (Leningrad, 1978), pp. 179-198.

ficials of the Finance Ministry made no secret of this maneuver. A. Morskoi, a prominent bureaucrat in the Finance Ministry, observed that because of the backing of the two emperors, the Ministry of Finance

> succeeded in holding departmental appropriations within the limits of resources, not exceeding the means of the state treasury, and, with regard to increasing assignments of money for military needs, received approval, over and above this principle, that the magnitude of the increased appropriations ought not to be determined exclusively on the basis of proposals arising in the Army and Navy Ministries . . . but also through a consideration of both the possible growth of state resources and of other urgent state needs.[43]

Witte himself declared that Alexander III's parsimony, isolationism, and trust in his Ministers of Finance represented the foundation of Russian economic progress.[44] With regard to Nicholas II, during the early years of his reign, the memory of his redoubtable father so cowed him that he meekly submitted to Witte. At least at first, Witte found it easy to frighten his Imperial master with the bugaboo of fiscal collapse. In June 1895, for instance, Witte sternly lectured Nicholas that any increased military spending would automatically cause deficits.[45] Eventually Nicholas came to supplement Witte's already considerable powers with others even more broad-ranging. Thanks to this carte blanche, Witte made himself the most influential Imperial minister and built up, in the words of one of his colleagues, "a State within the State."[46]

The first symptom of Alexander III's favoritism for the Ministry of Finance came almost immediately after his accession. By pointing out that the deficit for 1881 was likely to amount to over fifty million rubles, Finance Minister Bunge, Controller General Sol'skii, and Chief of the Department of State Economy Baranov were easily able to persuade the new Emperor to endorse immediate cutbacks in the budget for 1882. These cutbacks, which were approved in April 1881, dealt the War Ministry a punishing blow. Alexander ordered his new War Minister, P. S. Vannovskii, to make the reduction of military expenditures his top priority. The army appropriation was reduced by nearly 20 percent. The government summarily fired 1,200 army officers, discharged over 80,000 soldiers, and instituted a new policy which lowered the number of al-

---

[43] A. Morskoi, *Voennaia moshch' Rossii. Predskazaniia general-ad"iutanta A. N. Kuropatkina i ikh kritika grafom S. Iu. Vitte* (Petrograd, 1915), p. 103.

[44] Vitte, *Vospominaniia*, vol. 1, pp. 406, 408-409.

[45] *Ministerstvo finansov 1802-1902*, p. 623.

[46] Charles Louis Seeger, trans., *The Memoirs of Alexander Iswolsky*, (London, 1921), p. 148.

lowable yearly promotions, thus ruining the chances of thousands of officers to make a career in the service. Measures like these were hardly greeted with delight in the officers' bivouacs throughout the Empire. Criticism of the regime, in fact, became so audible in officers' circles that it even reached the ears of Konstantin Pobedonostsev, Alexander's old tutor and now Procurator of the Holy Synod, who wrote Alexander on November 27, 1884, advising that he make some small concessions to the officers to stifle the discontent.[47]

It was not enough, however, for the Ministry of Finance to secure temporary cuts in army spending. An instrument to contain future military allocations had to be found. The so-called maximum budget (*predel'nyi biudzhet*) became this instrument. In the wake of the Boulanger crisis in France and the consequent Russo-German war scare, an alarmed Vannovskii visited the Ministry of Finance in early May 1888 to demand an increase in army appropriations, and specifically money to purchase magazine rifles. Vyshnegradskii agreed to cooperate, but only on the condition that the Ministry of War accept a Faustian bargain: to accede to a five-year maximum budget to cover the years 1889 to 1894. Under the terms of this proposition, the total annual amount of revenue passed over to the War Ministry was to be predetermined as 211 million rubles per year for five years in advance. This sum would be increased only under special circumstances: declaration of war, certain weapon improvements, or increased food prices. Vannovskii acquiesced in this scheme, which passed via special conference to Alexander III, who duly approved it. It is an index of Alexander's adherence to the Finance Ministry's conception of Russia's interests that he wrote on this occasion that he condoned increased army spending, "But only to the degree permitted by the condition of the monetary resources of the treasury without incurring for this purpose special loans, or increasing taxes."[48]

Maximum budgets for the War Ministry were enacted to cover the years 1894-1898, 1899-1903, and 1904-1908. Although the Ministry of Finance later insisted in 1908 on the abolition of this institution (claiming that it was too beneficial to the army establishment, which knew that its appropriations could never be *reduced* relative to those of a previous

[47] *Ministerstvo finansov 1802-1902*, pp. 295-297; *Vsepoddanneishii doklad po voennomu ministerstvu 1882 goda* (St. Petersburg, 1882), pp. 1-2, 9-10, 14; TsGVIA, f. 280, op. 1, d. 3, p. 380; *Pis'ma Pobedonostseva k Aleksandru III*, vol. 2 (Moscow, 1926), p. 63.

[48] *Vsepoddanneishii doklad po voennomu ministerstvu 1889 goda* (St. Petersburg, 1889), pp. 1-4; *Sbornik tsirkularov izdannykh po gosudarstvennomu kontroliu v 1884-1889 g.g.* (Tambov, 1890), p. 270.

year), it is nonetheless true that the motive behind this special budget was not the defense of the country but rather the defense of the Treasury from any sudden raids by the military. Regardless of what Finance Ministry spokesmen were to say in later years, one effect of the maximum budget was to put the Ministry of War at a tremendous disadvantage in the financial negotiating process: because of the rules for the operation of the maximum budget, any army request for increased allocations was certain to be subject to the most intense scrutiny. No ministries in the state other than the War and Marine Ministries were afflicted with a maximum budget. This is not to suggest that the War Ministry inevitably lost all of its budgetary struggles from the accession of Alexander III to the Japanese attack on Port Arthur; it did win various increases in this period. But shackled as it was to the maximum budget, the War Ministry's freedom of maneuver was necessarily constrained. The Minister of Finance, the State Controller, and the Emperor himself could, if they chose, reject any army appeal for more money in the years covered by the budget as an insolent attempt to violate state law. This psychological pressure easily led the War Ministry to moderate its demands merely out of a sense of despair.[49]

The maximum budget, however, only applied to ordinary expenditures. It was still possible for the Ministry of War successfully to request larger appropriations for such items as rearmament through the extraordinary budget. Thus the War Ministry could also profit from deficit financing. The Finance Ministry, however, was not unaware of this loophole, and closed it with budgetary rules of June 4, 1894, which completely redefined ordinary and extraordinary revenues and expenditures.[50] According to these guidelines (first applied in 1895), the costs of rearmament were specifically excluded from the extraordinary budget, meaning, of course, that the state would not borrow to pay for new weapons.[51] These expenses were henceforth transferred to the ledger of the ordinary budget, which authentically had to be balanced. By deft manipulations of the budgetary regulations, then, the Finance Ministry prevented any large-scale crash rearmament program before the beginning of the war with Japan. When Vannovskii approached the Finance

[49] U. S. Plekhan, *Biudzhetnye zakony Rossiiskoi Imperii* (St. Petersburg, 1911), pp. 408-409; see TsGVIA, f. 280, op. 1, d. 3, p. 284 for Rediger's comments on the huge convenience of the "limited budget" for the Ministry of Finance. For an example of War Ministry budgetary self-censorship, see TsGVIA, f. 1, op. 1, d. 61605 (preparation of limited budget for 1904-1908), ll. 43, 49-51.

[50] *Otchet po deloproizvodstvu Gosudarstvennogo Soveta za sessiiu 1893-1894*, vol. 2 (St. Petersburg, 1894), pp. 555-570.

[51] Kashkarov, *Finansovye*, vol. 1, p. 12.

Ministry in 1897, requesting an additional 565 million rubles for improvements, including the rearming of the artillery in the upcoming five years, Witte effortlessly whittled this sum down to 160 million. The entire sum Vannovskii had wanted for field artillery (110 million) was deducted, as was over 100 million for strengthening military organization, 115 for stocks of material, and 59.5 million for engineering equipment.[52]

Even though he proved to be a better negotiator than the enfeebled Vannovskii, Kuropatkin experienced similar defeats at the hands of the Finance Ministry during his tenure as War Minister. Praised by military writers because of his solicitude for the soldier, the able Kuropatkin did indeed establish state-subsidized military libraries and foster officers' clubs, improve the quality of soldiers' food, and secure the army pay increase of 1899.[53] But Kuropatkin was unable to find the funds to expand the artillery parks, to improve Russia's defenses on her uneasy Western frontier, or to protect Russia's ill-advised territorial acquisitions in the East. In 1901, for instance, Witte invoked the limited budget to halve Kuropatkin's request for 16 million for quick-firing artillery.[54] Kuropatkin was likewise powerless to halt the bizarre practice, initiated by the Finance Ministry in the early nineties, of using the War Ministry's budget to subsidize domestic grain production. Witte had originally coaxed Vannovskii into the scheme of buying a proportion of army grain each year at inflated prices set by the Minister of Finance. The War Ministry lost over 1.5 million rubles from 1893 to 1903 as a result of these overpayments.[55]

The Far East posed a particularly vexatious dilemma for Kuropatkin. The de facto annexations there had to be defended, and Kuropatkin had to fight for the money to do so, even though he was far more concerned by security in the West. Further, the army had to compete with the imperialists at the Admiralty for such new Far Eastern appropriations as were permitted. Witte was even able to turn these military expenses in the East to his own advantage by using them as an excuse to plump for stricter supervision of the army budget. By the terms of an imperially endorsed State Council decision of June 10, 1900, before military estimates could be sent to the Ministry of Finance and the State Council, that is, before the War Ministry could even release them, they had to

[52] *Vsepoddanneishii doklad po voennomu ministerstvu 1893 goda* (St. Petersburg, 1894), p. 4.

[53] Kersnovskii, *Istoriia*, pp. 520-521.

[54] TsGVIA, f. 1, op. 1, d. 61587, l. 92.

[55] T. M. Kitanina, *Khlebnaia torgovlia Rossii 1875-1914 g.g.* (Leningrad, 1978), p. 260. I am indebted to Dr. Thomas Fallows for calling my attention to this reference.

be reviewed in special conferences at the War Ministry to which representatives of the Finance Ministry and State Control were to be invited. The Finance Ministry was thus empowered to insinuate its agents into the War Ministry's own internal budgetary process. Slightly later, Nicholas II was to invest Witte with the authority to approve or disapprove *any* one-time War Ministry expenditures in excess of 100,000 rubles.[56]

CONSEQUENCES

The consequences of the army's declining share of state revenue were far-reaching, both for the army and for the state. In the first place, as we have already illustrated, the Finance Ministry discerned an obvious connection between the amount of money disbursed to the army and the amount available for industrial development. From 1893 to 1902, the Imperial state spent roughly 15,952,785,100 rubles. Liashchenko has estimated that the state invested at least 3.5 billion rubles of this sum in its various economic programs. Arcadius Kahan has objected that much of this amount did not represent real productive economic investment and has declared that the Russian government directly expended no more than one billion rubles from 1880 to 1900 on railway construction.[57] Of course the railway system by no means comprised the entire economic stimulus afforded the economy by the government. And regardless of whether the 3.5 billion rubles were productively invested or not, there can be no doubt that they were spent, and spent under the guidance of the Ministry of Finance and its allied ministries. Now the share of the army in state expenditure from 1893 to 1902 averaged 19.57 percent annually, or 3,122,413,451 rubles for the ten years. If the army had enjoyed a 30 percent share, which had been customary before 1881, it would have received instead 4,785,530,000 rubles. The difference is 1,663,422,080 rubles, or 47 percent of the entire amount of money which the state spent on the economy in this decade, according to Liashchenko.

It is possible to take exception to the method we have used here. Surely the growth of state revenues (and consequently expenditures) in the nineties was partially conditioned by governmental investment. But we may dispense with this criticism if, assuming that state economic investment fed the growth of state expenditures, we calculate a hypothetical, lower total of state expenditures for the years 1893-1903, based

[56] TsGVIA, f. 1, op. 1, d. 61587, ll. 1, 12; TsGVIA, f. 280, op. 1, d. 3, p. 382.

[57] Lyashchenko, *History of the National Economy*, p. 556; Arcadius Kahan, "Commercial Policies and the Industrialization of Russia," *Journal of Economic History* 27, no. 4 (Dec. 1967): 466.

upon their annual average growth rate in the previous decade. If state expenditures from 1893 to 1902 had grown at this rate (3.06 percent), they would have amounted to 14,952,774,000 rubles. Thirty percent of this figure is 4,399,787,300; 19.5 percent is 2,926,257,872. The difference is 1,473,529,430, still 42 percent of Liashchenko's figure. Clearly, one opportunity cost of the great industrial boom of the nineties was the technological and material neglect of the Russian army. The Ministry of Finance understood that Russia's rapid economic progress depended on keeping the army poor; many supporters of the army within the War Ministry and the government at large understood the same thing.

In 1896, as a coronation present to the army, Nicholas II decreed that, starting in 1897, three million extra rubles were to be spent to improve soldiers' rations. War Minister Vannovskii dutifully applied to the State Council for this sum. As the Department of State Economy could not reach a unanimous decision, it referred Vannovskii's request to the General Assembly. Here a very interesting thing happened. While one might expect discussion to have revolved around the straightforward issue of army victuals, in fact a debate ensued on a much more important question—the wisdom and consequences of the entire edifice of budgetary regulations which the Finance Ministry had erected to fence the army in.

Thirty-five members of the State Council, adhering to the line taken by the Finance Ministry, maintained that if the War Ministry desired to satisfy the wishes of the Emperor (as it was bound to do), it had to find the funds to upgrade rations within its own existing budget. No help would be forthcoming from the Finance Ministry or the Council; army appropriations, as established by the five-year maximum budget, ought to be inviolate. Eighteen members (including Vannovskii and Chief of Staff Obruchev) rejected these arguments, pointing to the terrible inadequacies in the military establishment which had already resulted from low appropriations, and demanding that the Council vote the additional credits. In the report prepared on behalf of the eighteen, the following words appeared: "the rise in the economic power of Russia . . . of course is due in large measure to the fact that the expenditures on the army have never amounted to such a small percentage of the state budget in the course of the last fifty years, as now."[58] On this occasion, Nicholas II sided with the War Ministry against the Finance Ministry. He commanded that 2.5 million rubles, a compromise sum,

[58] *Otchet po deloproizvodstvu Gosudarstvennogo Soveta za sessiiu 1896-1897* (St. Petersburg, 1897), pp. 360-375, esp. pp. 367-368.

be spent on improving soldiers' food in 1897 and again in 1898, when the next maximum budget came up for review.

From the military point of view, the chief danger to Russia from the army's declining share of state revenue lay in her insufficient supply of modern arms. As Kuropatkin noted in a summary of his report to Nicholas II of September 23, 1898: "We have been left behind in the technical regard. . . . [What] will the situation be after five years? We will be even more backward."[59] It was Russia's meager stock of modern arms, as much as altruism and the love of peace, that induced Nicholas to summon the unsuccessful international disarmament conference of The Hague (1899).[60] The Russian army remained ill-equipped by comparison with those of the West. There is high irony here: the Russian government curtailed its arms expenditures at precisely the time when contemporary conditions mandated that they be increased. But arms were not the only thing which the Imperial army lacked. Although the War Ministry, especially under Kuropatkin, had made various improvements, the standard of living of officers and men was still depressed, and was to remain so. Thus state policy with respect to military finance provides both proof of the declining influence of the army in Russian society and government, and a further reason for it: proof, because the army's performance in the combat with the Ministry of Finance was so unsatisfactory; a reason, because with the need for arms, higher prices, and the obnoxious responsibility for the East chipping away at the army budget, the army lacked the resources to exert its influence in government or to shore up its crumbling prestige in society.

It is not our purpose here to offer Olympian judgments about what the Russian government should or should not have done with its revenues from 1881 to 1904. Even if the connection between industry and war potential had been perfectly understood by all, policy makers would still have been confronted with an almost insoluble dilemma. Industrialization might make the country strong, but such efforts would be wasted if sudden war caught the Russian army unprepared. Yet if the state chose guns over railroads, it was also choosing to perpetuate Russia's economic backwardness and military weakness.

Nor can we exonerate the Russian military establishment which, given the magnitude of the fiscal crisis, should have taken great pains to spend every kopeck with care. Yet there was notable incompetence and mismanagement in War Ministry spending. Certain Main Administrations

[59] "Novye materialy o Gaagskoi mirnoi konferentsii 1899 g," *Krasnyi arkhiv* (Moscow and Leningrad), 54-55 (1932): 60.

[60] Dan L. Morrill, "Nicholas II and the Call for the First Hague Conference," *Journal of Modern History* 46, no. 2 (June 1974): 313.

such as the Artillery and the Intendancy were notorious sinks of corruption.[61] Even taking all of this waste into account, however, Kuropatkin had been closer to the truth than Witte. The Finance Ministry's illiberality did hurt the Russian army and was to damage its performance in the war with Japan.

It was military professionalism, solicitude for the army, and anxiety over military weakness which underlay the conflict between the Finance and War Ministries. However, the military professionalism of the War Ministry also stimulated other conflicts. Chief among these were conflicts which arose over the army's performance of internal repressive service. It is to this subject that we will now turn.

[61] TsGVIA, f. 280, op. 1, d. 3, p. 273; also see material on the Senatorial revision of the War Ministry provided in chap. 8.

THREE

The Tsarist Army and Repression, 1881-1904

UPON HIS INDUCTION into the Imperial Russian army every soldier was required to swear a solemn oath to defend the sovereign and the fatherland from their foreign and internal enemies. Military commanders considered it exceptionally important to impress the significance of this oath on the draftees. A "detailed program for the training of recruits" devised in Kiev Military District and offered to the rest of the army as a model in 1890 contained the following lines: "The soldier's task: the soldier is the servant of the sovereign and the fatherland, their defender from enemies." Commentary on this piety followed immediately: "When the recruits are capable of giving an intelligent answer to the question 'What is the soldier's task?' then the company commander explains to them that enemies of the sovereign do not only have to be foreigners but also rebels, thieves and others who do not obey the laws, or who oppose the authorities."[1]

The army reinforced its explanation of the seriousness of the struggle with the "internal enemy" through the mass distribution of moralistic pamphlets and short stories. "The Soldiers' Library," a series of tales which exactly fit this description, enjoyed the official patronage of the Main Staff. Typical of the works included in the "Soldiers' Library" was K. Tkhorzhevskii's "The Reliable Soldiers" (1897). Set in a provincial town in 1878, the story concerned soldiers who were guarding a civilian prison. One evening prison guards discovered that seven convicts were unaccounted for. The governor of the province, assuming they had escaped by slipping through the military cordon outside the prison walls, upbraided the soldiers of the garrison for their carelessness. But the general in command of the division objected: his soldiers were so trustworthy that no fugitives could have eluded them. So sure was he of this that the general wagered the governor one thousand rubles that the seven prisoners were still hiding within the prison; when the escape attempt came, his soldiers were certain to foil it. As one might expect,

---

[1] *Razvedchik*, no. 25 (April 1890): 194. Compare with *Ustav vnutrennei sluzhby Vysochaishe utverzhden 23 marta, 1910 goda* (St. Petersburg, 1910), p. 1.

75

the end of the story proves the general correct. When the seven convicts do scale the prison walls the alert military sentries quickly recapture them, killing two in the process. "And thus," Tkhorzhevskii concludes, "the chief of the division won a thousand rubles from the governor, which he gave to the regiment for vodka then and there."[2] The moral of this fable, albeit crude, could not have been more clear: fidelity to duty could earn temporal as well as spiritual rewards.

The reason the army placed such emphasis on this sort of indoctrination is just as clear. It was quite likely that the average Russian soldier might find himself in the position of battling or thwarting internal enemies. These unpleasant and thankless duties often involved standing guard over rotting prisons in desolate Siberian towns, shootouts with gangs of bandits and smugglers in Transcaucasia, marching on insubordinate villages in the Ukraine, and dispersing crowds of Baltic workers with indiscriminately fired volleys. None of these activities was unprecedented in Russian history: the army had long fulfilled functions of internal defense within the state. In the eighteenth century, only the army had the power to crush the dangerous servile uprising of Emelyan Pugachev.[3] In the subsequent century the army suppressed the Polish rebellions of 1830 and 1863, marched out on unruly peasants over two hundred times between 1826 and 1854, and at Bezdna, in 1861, acted decisively to stifle peasant discontent with the terms of the emancipation.[4]

Of course, other more "advanced" Western European countries had recourse to their armies for similar purposes. In Britain, the government held eighteenth-century Ireland by military occupation and used the army in the post-Napoleonic period to back up the police in struggles with Luddites, Chartists, and rural laborers.[5] In 1848 and 1849 continental armies everywhere used violence to defeat revolution: Cavaignac unleashed his troops against Parisian workers; Windischgrätz bombarded Prague and Vienna into submission; Paskevich and Haynau reduced

---

[2] K. Tkhorzhevskii, *Nadezhnye soldaty*, 5th ed. (St. Petersburg, 1907).

[3] John T. Alexander, *Autocratic Politics in a National Crisis: The Imperial Government and Pugachev's Revolt, 1773-1775* (Bloomington, Ind., 1969), esp. pp. 253-254.

[4] John Sheldon Curtiss, *The Russian Army under Nicholas I, 1825-1855* (Durham, N.C., 1965), pp. 74-95; R. E. Leslie, *Reform and Insurrection in Russian Poland* (London, 1963), pp. 232-236; I. I. Ignatovich, *Pomeshchich'i krestiane nakanune osvobozhdeniia*, 3rd ed. (Leningrad 1925), p. 345; Daniel Field, *Rebels in the Name of the Tsar* (Boston, 1976), pp. 31-106.

[5] On the use of armies as instruments of internal security generally, see Corvisier, *Armies and Societies*, pp. 189-191; Eric Hobsbawm and George Rude, *Captain Swing: A History of the Great English Agricultural Uprising of 1830* (New York, 1968), pp. 253-256.

rebellious Hungary.[6] Later in the century, the French army suppressed the Paris Commune of 1871 and thereafter frequently broke up strikes in the factories and mines.[7] In May of 1898, the Italian army "restored order" in Milan, killing some eighty Milanese in the process.[8] And the list could go on.

In Russia, however, the army's employment for internal defense, especially as the nineteenth century progressed, grew to exceed, both in its special qualities and in its extent, any comparable uses in the West. In the West, as in Russia, armies were involved in guard duty, bandit chasing, and outright shooting and bayoneting of civilians. Yet in Russia, these activities became routinized features of army life, rather than transitory episodes. Further, the Russian Imperial State constantly widened the applicability of military judicial repression against the civilian population. We will explore some of the reasons for the tsarist government's growing readiness to respond to the people with naked military force somewhat later in this chapter. We must, however, note here that along with financial disputes, military internal repression was the basis for the most bitter civil-military conflicts in the Russian Empire. The next chapter will concern military justice and the subjection of civilians to it. This chapter will consider the soldier in his capacities as guard, helpmate to the police, gunman, and riot controller.

MILITARY REPRESSION: LEGISLATION

In nineteenth-century Russia, the duties and obligations of civilians and the military with regard to the internal use of troops were continuously refined and made more precise. Nicholas I's General Order (*Nakaz*) to all civil governors of June 1837 instructed them in the procedures to be followed in the event of banditry or revolt. If his own police resources were wanting, the governor was first to appeal to the provincial commander of the corps of internal defense. This corps, created in 1811, was organized in districts and was designated almost entirely for internal repressive duties. The governor could summon any quantity of troops

[6] William L. Langer, "The Pattern of Urban Revolution in 1848," in *French Society and Culture Since the Old Regime*, ed. E. M. Accomb (New York, 1966), pp. 90-118; Gunther A. Rotenberg, *The Army of Francis Joseph* (West Lafayette, Ind., 1976), pp. 19-20; Craig, *Prussian Army*, p. 91; Theodor Schiemann, *Geschichte Russlands unter Kaiser Nikolaus I*, vol. 4 (Berlin, 1919), pp. 199-206.

[7] Paul-Marie de la Gorce, *The French Army: A Military-Political History*, trans. Kenneth Douglas (New York, 1963), pp. 29-30; Theodore Zeldin, *France, 1848-1945*, vol. 1 (Oxford, 1973), pp. 475, 732.

[8] Whittam, *Italian Army*, p. 140; see also Charles Tilly, Louise Tilly, and Richard Tilly, *The Rebellious Century, 1830-1930* (Cambridge, Mass., 1975).

and in an emergency could issue his summons verbally instead of in writing. If the demand was pressing and less than one company of men was needed, even a local police chief (*zemskii ispravnik*) could ask for these troops. Yet occasions might arise in which the corps itself was unable to cope with internal security threats. In that event, the governor could apply to the commanders of the regular troops quartered nearby.[9] Laws of 1764 and 1775 (still in effect in 1860) required such commanders to subordinate themselves immediately to the governor and to fulfill all military measures he might prescribe in order to put down revolt or force compliance with government orders in the province.[10] Summoning the army, however, did not always mean that the soldiers loaded their muskets and fixed bayonets for immediate action, for if the unrest at issue was peasant disobedience, the provincial governor had to exhaust all means of persuasion (including personal visitation to the rebellious village) before weapons could be used. After 1830 the decision to fire on the peasants was never to be at the discretion of the military authority; only the civil power could make this determination.[11] Civil authorities were also allowed to use the army to break up gangs of bootleggers or smugglers, and even to fight locusts (although it is amusing to note that troops could be dispatched no further than seven versts from their barracks for this purpose).[12]

The first significant change in the system occurred when Miliutin established the military districts in 1864. As part of his program, Miliutin abolished the corps of internal defense and divided Russia's troops into two parts, "field" and "local." Field troops were those which would see combat in war. Local troops, comprising seventy infantry, nineteen rifle, and three sapper reserve battalions, plus certain other units, were under the control of a commander of local forces in each military district, who had underneath him provincial and uezd military chiefs.[13] Unlike the old internal defense corps, the local troops had some specific military duties, for their headquarters were to be the centers for inducting, equipping, and training recruits designated for "field" units.[14] Yet Miliutin's edict also made the local troops the first line of defense against internal disorder. Civilians confronted with unrest or brigandage had to appeal

---

[9] *PSZ*, no. 10303 (1837), arts. 55 and 56.

[10] *Svod voennykh postanovlenii, chast' tret'ia. Nakaz voiskam* (St. Petersburg 1859), art. 465.

[11] Ibid., arts. 473 and 474.

[12] Ibid., arts. 476, 477, 478. See also Curtiss, *Russian Army under Nicholas I*, pp. 273-284.

[13] *Imennoi ukaz, 6 Avgusta 1864, PSZ*, no. 4166 (1864), arts. 1. 1 and 3. *Polozhenie ob upravlenii mestnymi voiskami voennovo okruga*, arts. 1, 3, 8, 50 and 51; *PSZ*, no. 4166 (1864), Zaionchkovskii, *Voennye reformy*, pp. 84, 87 and 99.

[14] *Imennoi ukaz*, art. 3.a.

to the local troop commanders; if the local troops, because of their small numbers, were unequal to the disorders, the provincial local troop commander, not the governor, was to negotiate with the staff of a field troop unit for extra help.[15]

Miliutin obviously recognized that the civilian government had legitimate demands on the army for internal security; yet he also wanted to squeeze as much military preparedness as possible out of the resources at his disposal. What he had done in fact was to interpose the local troops between the civilian power and the more highly prized combat forces, gambling that the local troops could discharge their obligations to the bureaucracy while simultaneously educating new military cadres. Within less than a year he realized that he had miscalculated; an Imperial decree of June 17, 1865 exempted all reserve troops, which constituted the overwhelming bulk of local troops in the first place, from service in the interests of the local civilian government.[16] Training of recruits outweighed inconvenience to combat troops, on whom the central responsibility of aiding the civilians now reposed.

But Miliutin was still interested in regulating such aid, and a law for this purpose passed through the Council of State and was confirmed by Alexander II on October 3, 1877. The "Rules Determining the Method for the Call of Troops to aid the Civil Power" endured until 1906. If only because of their persistence, the rules of 1877 are worth reviewing at some length.[17]

If the civil authorities were short of police they could summon troops
1. to keep order during church services, fairs, and public assemblies;
2. to protect state property;
3. to extinguish forest fires, help during floods, and assist in the destruction of harmful animals and insects;
4. to hold or transport convicts;
5. to capture bandits and robbers when they were numerous, or when armed resistance was anticipated;
6. to prevent or stop popular disorders;
7. to prevent smuggling;
8. to serve as guards;
9. to be present during the execution of judicial sentences;
10. in general, to assist judicial authorities.

This catalogue was extensive, but the list of persons entitled to call for military aid was somewhat more circumscribed. Governors-general, governors, *gradonachal'niki* (city officials with the rank of governor),

---

[15] *Polozhenie*, arts. 96, 97, and 99.
[16] *PSZ*, no. 42217 (1865).
[17] *PSZ*, no. 37748 (1877).

ispravniki (rural colonels of police), and *politseimeistery* (urban colonels of police) possessed this right, as did senators conducting a full-scale investigation (*reviziia*) in a particular province. *Ispravniki* and *politseimeistery* could summon troops on their own authority only if help in the execution of a judicial sentence was required.

Although Miliutin had attempted to include careful controls over civilian power to call out the troops, the decree of 1877, as was characteristic of much tsarist legislation in this period, contained many ambiguities and allowances for "exceptional circumstances." All civilian officers were, for example, to appeal for troops to the commander of the appropriate military district, or if he was unavailable, to the provincial military chief. But if neither could be reached, the civilians were permitted to contact the closest military commander. Again, requests for aid were supposed to be made in writing, but in "extreme emergency" could be made orally. At any rate, requests were to contain a precise description of the reason for calling out the troops, accompanied by a statement detailing the number of troops required. Civil officials were not themselves to command the troops, but were to transmit their instructions concerning the placement of guard posts and pickets through the military officers present. If, all else having failed, the civil official decided that weapons had to be used, he was to inform the military commander, who was to order armed action entirely in his own manner, but only after the riotous or disobedient crowd had been warned three times by drumbeat or trumpet. The army could, however, resort to force without civilian instruction in self-defense or to protect human life. When the senior army officer on the spot terminated armed action, all authority for the preservation of public order was to revert exclusively to the civilian power. The civilian power was, further, to decide itself when the troops summoned could be released to return to their quarters.

Another feature of the rules was a prohibition against dispatching less than an infantry company, a cavalry squadron, a sotnia (basically a Cossack squadron), or an artillery crew with less than two guns to aid the civil power. The intent of this was to prevent the division of a military unit into minuscule groups, bereft of the controlling supervision of officers, while setting a rather stiff lower limit of the numbers of troops called. If civilians could not theoretically demand military support unless they faced a situation so ugly that at least eighty soldiers were necessary, the number of civilian appeals might be kept in check. Yet this safeguard against civil abuse of its military prerogative was undermined by the existence of an elastic clause in the rules, article B 3, which stated that troops could be summoned for purposes other than those numerous ones already iterated in the law; in such cases, the civilian officials were to direct the military to supply the quantity of troops (and it could be any quantity) that they required.[18]

But if the rules applied to what were supposed to be extraordinary circumstances—riots, plagues, famines—the army also had responsibilities to the civilians which remained constant in normal as well as abnormal times. By law, the army had to provide escort parties for all convicts being transported to Siberia. Soldiers, not policemen, were to man the guard boxes at the most important civil prisons. Any prison, for example, which confined criminals sentenced to forced labor (*katorga*) was to be ringed with military, not civilian guards. Local troops were, moreover, obliged to protect provincial and uezd treasuries.[19]

These then were the decrees which governed the common soldier's involvement in internal defense and repression. Miliutin's plan had been to satisfy the reasonable security needs of the civilians while shielding the army from unwarranted and burdensome civilian requisitions. How did his plan work out in practice? How often were soldiers called to aid the civilians or to protect institutions?

MILITARY REPRESSION IN PRACTICE

To answer this question we must turn to the statistics compiled in the Main Staff. These statistics are problematical, not so much because indolent colonels in the provinces omitted to file reports on their aid to civilians (though this sometimes happened), but more because the various formats for these reports were so complex and ambiguous that they could be interpreted in a variety of ways. By way of illustration, suppose there are street demonstrations in Warsaw. A company of troops is called out by the civilian officials, and spends the entire day in the streets, returning to its barracks at night. The disorders are presumed over, but this presumption is incorrect—the next day they break out again and the same company returns to police duty. Even though the regimental duty officer sends out the troops on the basis of the same order, the same piece of paper he has received from the staff of Warsaw Military District, is this one summons, or two? Are the soldiers participating to be counted twice, or once? The Main Staff naturally tried to relieve the confusion with reporting formats. But the law concerning reports of the first and second order of urgency (*polozhenie o srochnykh i vnesrochnykh doneseniiakh*—Main Staff Circular number 30 for 1888) was itself

---

[18] Ibid., passim.

[19] TsGVIA, f. 400, op. 3, d. 2533, l. 17. The role of soldiers as convoy escorts is well described by George Kennan, *Siberia and the Exile System*, vol. 1 (London, 1891), pp. 369-386.

ambiguous. And when the Main Staff completely overhauled the system of reporting assistance to civilians with the still ambiguous but more emphatic regulations of 1901, it harvested such quantities of reports that it came to suspect its own statistics.[20] At least the Staff confessed to this problem, but there was another problem to which it did not confess. Reports were assembled on the basis of the number of times "companies," "squadrons," or "sotnias," were employed. But were those really comparable units? An infantry company in the eighties and nineties could consist of anywhere from 90 to 160 men. Since the same was true for sotnias, and squadrons, these were exceedingly crude units of measure.

In Table 6, it is the alleged number of times a military command was sent out, not the identity of the unit itself which is significant. In other words, if the same company acted twice, it is counted twice. The statistics therefore reveal nothing about the proportion of companies, squadrons, or sotnias, in the army which participated in the prevention or suppression of disorders. Thus the following statistics cannot be embraced as absolutely definitive. Still, they remain the only centrally tabulated statistics we have on military repression and provide some gauge, even if rough, of the use of military as an internal police force.

Statistics for the period after 1889, shown in Table 7, contain more information. There are new categories: numbers of soldiers sent out

TABLE 6
Troops Called in the Aid of the Civil Power, 1885-1889

Year	No. of companies	No of squadrons/ sotnia	No. of places where troops were used
1885	85⁷⁄₁₂	24½	45
1886	116	3¾	35
1887	50	11	20
1888	25	11	19
1889	32½	7	14

SOURCES: *Otchet po Glavnomu Shtabu za 1885 god* (St. Petersburg, 1887), p. 55; . . . *za 1886 god* (St. Petersburg, 1888), p. 51; . . . *za 1887 god* (St. Petersburg, 1889), p. 53; . . . *za 1888 god* (St. Petersburg, 1890), p. 56; . . . *za 1889 god* (St. Petersburg, 1891), p. 58

[20] *Otchet po Glavnomu Shtabu za 1901 goda* (St. Petersburg, 1902), p. 35.

TABLE 7

Troops Called in the Aid of the Civil Power, 1890-1895

Year	No. of times	Companies	Squadron or sotnia	Separately deployed soldiers	Uses of weapons	Military Casualties		Civilian Casualties	
						Killed	Wounded	Killed	Wounded
1890	57	59½ + 2 o.k.*	43½	368	10	7	5	18	3
1891	57	64	52	461	8		22	18	4
1892	135	178¼ + 2 o.k.	112	1,099	18	7	33	48	97
1893	88	98½ + 8 o.k.	71	312	13	4	13	41	7
1894	77	24¾ + 8 o.k.	59¾	411	13		3	10	36
1895	93	103	55	405	16	2	25	12	13

SOURCE: TsGVIA, f. 400, op. 3, d. 2560, ll. 214-229. See also TsGVIA, f. 400, op. 3, d. 2465, l. 378

* Okhotnichyi kommand, or "scouting command."

who were deployed separately, i.e., not as part of a company or a squadron; data on the use of arms by troops; and civil and military casualties. The civilian casualty statistics are especially suspect, as evidence suggests that there was significant underreporting here, both because it is evident that many wounded civilians ran away to avoid arrest and hence went uncounted and because some military commanders may have preferred to file lower figures to minimize the seriousness of the disorder.[21] The number of places to which troops have been sent is replaced by figures on the number of times civilians in the Empire required military aid.

As for guard duty, the War Ministry furnished guards for both civil and military buildings. The army protected its own artillery warehouses, divisional storerooms, courts, and prisons, but, as we have seen, also guarded civilian prisons and treasuries. As of September 1, 1880, there were 13,285 guard duty posts in the Russian Empire—of which 4,541 were for the benefit of the civil administration.[22] I have used the somewhat cumbersome term "duty posts" to denote one full twenty-four hour stint of guard duty; since the Ordinance of Internal Service mandated shifts of no more than eight hours, at least three soldiers per post were needed on any given day. At the end of 1891, there were 13,104 duty posts, 4,620 maintained for civilians. Of these, 3,194 involved guarding civilian prisons; 399, escorting convicts; 539, protecting treasuries, branches of the State Bank, and telegraph offices; and 488 for direct assistance to the police patrols. Interestingly enough, only 11.5 percent of the guard posts manned by soldiers for civilians was located in European Russia.[23]

These figures would tend to indicate that the burden borne by the army at the behest of the civil authorities was not excessive. In 1894 there were over 860,000 soldiers on active duty in the Russian Empire—10,000 or so involved each day in civil guard duty would not seem to make much of a difference. In the same year the army boasted over 885 line infantry battalions—that is, over 3,500 companies.[24] This was indeed the case. At least until 1894, the demands of civilians for military aid did not absorb significant numbers of troops. Further, when troops were called, the disorders which they marched to avert or suppress were on almost all occasions rural disorders, which appear to have been rituals in which government and peasants abided by mutually understood rules,

[21] For a discussion, see John Bushnell, *Mutineers and Revolutionaries: Military Revolution in Russia, 1905-1907*, chap. 2 (forthcoming, Indiana University Press).

[22] TsGVIA, f. 400, op. 21, d. 1850, l. 28.

[23] *Vsepoddanneishii otchet o deistviiakh voennogo ministerstva za 1891 god* (St. Petersburg, 1893), p. 14.

[24] Zolotarev, *Zapiski*, pp. 388, 395.

rather than unpredictable confrontations. According to materials collected by the Department of Police, of the 271 disorders of all types in the Russian Empire from 1887 to 1890, only 13 percent were traceable to factory conditions, 3 percent were caused by religious disputes, and a further 3 percent were so-called Jewish disorders (that is, pogroms against Jews).[25] Peasants, generally Great Russian peasants, were responsible for most of the rest.

Peasant Disorders

What was a peasant disorder? In the main it was not an orgy of arson, property destruction, and mayhem, but rather a refusal by peasants to obey governmental laws or decrees, a reaction which was not uncommon in the countryside whenever the government attempted to tamper with the status of the peasant. In 1889, for instance, the state instituted a new system of rural administration—land captains—throughout the districts of the Empire. These land captains, selected from local nobles, were given extensive administrative and especially juridical authority over the peasants. Since peasants widely interpreted the land captains decree as an attempt to reintroduce serfdom, they naturally enough resented it and refused to comply with its provisions. The peasants of the village of Dolzhik, Khar'kov Province, were not atypical when they ignored the decree's instructions to choose *volost'* judges. This act of disobedience occasioned the dispatch by the 10th army corps of two *sotnias* of Cossacks, and later four hundred infantrymen.[26]

Peasants might similarly passively resist decrees which were more benign in intent than the land captains edict. The act of January 1, 1888 which mandated the obligatory destruction of diseased livestock had to be enforced under the guns of the army in the village of Mikhailovskii (near Stavropol') in 1890.[27] Resistance to land surveying or disputes with landlords over access to water or woodlands lay behind still other "disorders."[28] At times, the government might employ the threat of military force to convince the peasants to pay up their tax arrears.[29]

[25] "Krest'ianskoe dvizhenie v kontse XIX v. 1881-1894," *Krasnyi arkhiv* (Moscow and Leningrad) 89/90 (1938): 249. On ritual trials of strength between peasants and authority, see Eric Hobsbawm, "Peasants and Politics," *The Journal of Peasant Studies*, vol. 1, no. 1 (Oct. 1973), p. 15.

[26] TsGVIA, f. 400, op. 3, d. 2221, l. 38, also A. V. Shapkarin, ed., *Krest'ianskoe dvizhenie v Rossii v 1890-1900 g.g. Sbornik dokumentov* (Moscow, 1959), pp. 102-107.

[27] TsGVIA, f. 400, op. 3, d. 2221, l. 51, and Shapkarin, *Krest'ianskoe*, pp. 93-97.

[28] Shapkarin, *Krest'ianskoe dvizhenie v Rossii*, pp. 128, 551, 497-500; TsGVIA, f. 400, op. 3, d. 2221, l. 11.

[29] TsGVIA, f. 400, op. 15, d. 1345, ll. 1-13.

Especially in the Caucasus, the civil government might call on the army to ferret out gangs of bandits and thieves.[30]

As a general rule, at least until the mid-nineties, the arrival of the army in a recalcitrant village was immediately followed by peasant capitulation. Thus a fistfight between several drunken peasants at a fair in Podol'ia Province in 1890 terminated at once with the appearance of the sixth company of the 75th Sevastopol infantry.[31] Sometimes disobedient peasants actually greeted the incoming soliders with bread and salt, as the Old Believers of Kapustino did in 1892.[32] A report for Warsaw Military District declared that the peasants submitted at once without demur as soon as soldiers arrived during all peasant "disorders" in the region from 1883 to 1893.[33] Even if peasants did make a show of resistance it usually came to nothing. When, in 1891, one thousand Saratov peasants armed with stakes, stones, and pitchforks took possession of a landlord's mill, encirclement by a mere two companies of infantry plus the administration of some exemplary floggings led them to kneel in repentance.[34]

Indeed, peasants were far more likely to attack local civilian officials— mounted policemen or zemstva surveyors–than to dare a showdown with the regular army. This was not only because the peasants understood the consequences of massed volleys fired into their midst from Berdan or Mosin rifles, but because even if the army did not act with lethal consequences, its mere presence could entail severe economic disruption, if not ruin for a village. Even though a law of May 1886 specified that the costs of moving and supporting troops called in aid of the civilians were to be borne by the Treasury through the War Ministry's budget, it was not unheard of for civil and military officials to extract punitive damages from a village occupied by the army, damages which went to

[30] TsGVIA, f. 400, op. 3, d. 2442, ll. 20, 52.

[31] TsGVIA, f. 400, op. 3, 2221, l. 3.

[32] TsGVIA, f. 400, op. 15, d. 1345, l. 6.

[33] *Varshavskii voennyi okrug pod komandoi general-ad''iunta generala-ot-kavalerii I. V. Gurko, 1883-1893 gg.* (Warsaw, 1893), p. 43.

[34] Shapkarin, *Krest'ianskoe dvizhenie v Rossii*, pp. 81-85. Soviet historian V. A. Petrov has charged that the army deliberately lied about the lack of violence in the countryside; armed clashes between soldiers and peasants were in his opinion much more frequent than army reports indicated. Yet Petrov provides little evidence for his view, and indeed fails to adduce a plausible reason for the presumed mendaciousness of army commanders. "Tsarskaia armiia v bor'be s massovym revoliutsionnym dvizheniem v nachale XX v.," *Istoricheskie zapiski* (Moscow) 34 (1950): 330-331. These beatings were carried out by the police, not the army. Shortly after corporal punishment for rebellious peasants was reinstituted in 1885, an Interior Ministry circular issued under *War Ministry* pressure forbade civilian officials from ordering soldiers to wield the whip. Zaionchkovskii, *Rossiiskoe*, pp. 170-171.

defray the cost of the occupation.[35] Three companies of the first regiment of the 41st infantry division, quartered in Cherikovskii and Klimovichii uezdy (Mogilev Province) from April 19 to May 28, 1890 spent over one thousand rubles from commune funds and slaughtered twenty-six cows and nineteen pigs owned by the peasants.[36] In 1893 the governor of Tambov ordered the uezd *ispravnik* to seize a cow from the village elder in order to feed the troops sent to uphold the law in the village of Tafino.[37] A similar command of the Podol'ia governor supplied animals taken from the peasants as the meat ration for the 160 Cossacks billeted a week in the village of Tissakh, Litinskii uezd.[38] That the confiscation of peasant livestock in this indiscriminate and arbitrary fashion was interdicted by law seemed not to have worried Russian governors; but for many peasants the ownership of a domestic animal could be the margin between relative prosperity and destitution.

In the overwhelming majority of cases, up to the mid-nineties the management of disorders was well within the unassisted powers of the police; there was simply no need to drag the army in. The army was summoned by civilians for about 15 percent of all disorders, rural and urban, in 1887, 18 percent in 1888, 14 percent in 1889, and 20 percent in 1890.[39] This situation was to change. As shown in Table 8, disorders multiplied in number and seriousness after 1895. And the civilian authorities responded by stepping up their demands on soldiers for repressive service. To be sure, there were still numerous examples of unconditional capitulation of peasants cowed by the mere sight of a fixed bayonet. Thus, one June day in 1900, the inhabitants of the settlement of Vodopeianovsk (Saratov Province) peaceably subordinated themselves to the authority of the provincial governor while a company of the 228th reserve battalion looked on.[40] In the same year, the determination of the peasants of Zhil'kovo, Kaluga Province, to defy the government by felling wood in a forest belonging to a local landlord collapsed at the news of the approach of the 10th Novoingermandland regiment.[41] And in 1902, a battalion of the 27th Vitebsk regiment only had to march from village to village in Radom Province for the recalcitrant peasants to pay their school tax.[42]

[35] *PSZ*, no. 3715 (May 20, 1886).
[36] Shapkarin, *Krest'ianskoe dvizhenie v Rossii*, p. 55.
[37] Ibid., p. 244.
[38] TsGVIA, f. 400, op. 3, d. 2221, l. 18.
[39] "Krest'ianskoe dvizhenie," p. 249.
[40] TsGVIA, f. 400, op. 3, d. 2442, l. 56.
[41] Ibid., l. 80.
[42] TsGVIA, f. 400, op. 3, d. 2471, l. 41.

TABLE 8

Troops Called in the Aid of the Civil Power, 1896-1900

Year	No. of times	Companies	Squadrons or sotnias	Guns	Separately deployed soldiers	Uses of force	Military Casualties		Civilian	
							Killed	Wounded	Killed	Wounded
1896	96	91½	43¾		408	12		1	8	6
1897	147	148½	76½		1,652	14		2	7	14
1898	165	198¼	46¼		2,608	31	4	7	15	11
1899	235	337½ + 21 o.k.	105	1	2,308	21	5	60	35	44
1900	117	116 + 13 o.k.	74		932	21	1	21	15	37
1901	271	314 + 4 o.k.	144¼	98	3,813	17	8	9	4	20
1902	522	578	312		5,701	14		55	28	84
1903	427	1,163 + 22 o.k.	280		4,885	28		162	80	174
1904	222	212¾	66		1,466	10	4	19	4	26

SOURCE: TsGVIA, f. 400, op. 3, d. 2560, ll. 214-229

Yet even the character of peasant disorders was perceptibly changing. Peasants began to ignore admonitions to disperse, occasionally resisting troops. Lieutenant Colonel Pereima of the 33rd Eletsk infantry regiment ordered a volley fired on some four hundred mutinous peasants from the village of Kovalenki, Poltava Province, during the celebrated turmoil there in 1902.[43] In the following year, the peasants of Strakholes'e, Kiev Province, resisted the attempts of the landlord to divide his land from theirs with a ditch by beating up his hired laborers and occupying the trench in force. Neither threats nor promises had any weight with the peasants; a company of infantry finally dislodged them with gunbutts.[44]

GROWING UNREST

Disturbing as these manifestations of peasant spunk might be, the army was far more perturbed by the rising tide of unrest in the borderlands and in the cities of Russia. When military officials tried to account for the increasing involvement of the troops in repressive duties at the turn of the century they laid stress on two points—first, the veritable epidemic of "banditry" in the Caucasus (there were seven calls for this in 1890 and fifty-three in 1899); second, and most important, the unanticipated explosion of strikes among the Empire's industrial laborers.[45] Russia's great industrial upsurge of the nineties had borne fruit in an ever-growing and ever more militant working class. By the end of the nineties, strikes numbered over a hundred every year; in the first four years of the twentieth century over one hundred thousand workers went out on strike at some point in each year. During the 1890s, factory and urban disorders amounted to 30 percent of the occasions in which the army

[43] M. P. Ardusheva, ed., *Krest'ianskoe dvizhenie v poltavskoi i kharkovskoi guberniiakh v 1902 g. Sbornik dokumentov* (Khar'kov, 1961), pp. 61-64.

[44] TsGVIA, f. 400, op. 3, d. 2493, l. 234.

[45] TsGVIA, f. 400, op. 3, d. 2465, l. 378. Almost nothing has been written on the explosion of "banditry" in the Caucasus and Transcaucasia in this period. Standard works, such as Louise Nalbandian, *The Armenian Revolutionary Movement* (Berkeley, 1963), David Marshall Lang, *A History of Georgia* (New York, 1962), Alexandre Bennigsen and Chantel Quelquejay, *Les mouvements nationaux chez les Mussulmans de Russie* (Paris, 1960), concentrate on the activities of intellectuals and political parties. On the upsurge of strikes and violence among the Empire's industrial work force after 1894, there is a large and varied literature. See, for example, Lionel Kochan, *Russia in Revolution, 1890-1918* (London, 1966), pp. 30ff; Allan K. Wildman, *The Making of a Workers' Revolution: Russian Social Democracy, 1891-1903* (Chicago, 1967), pp. 216-217; Jeremiah Schneiderman, *Sergei Zubatov and Revolutionary Marxism* (Ithaca, N.Y., 1976), pp. 17ff; A. G. Rashin, *Formirovanie rabochego klassa Rossii* (Moscow, 1958); L. M. Ivanov, ed., *Istoriia rabochego klassa Rossii, 1861-1900* (Moscow, 1972); A. S. Trofimov, *Proletariat Rossii i ego bor'ba protiv tsarizma, 1861-1904* (Moscow, 1979).

helped the civilians but accounted for over 50 percent of the infantry companies dispatched for repressive service.[46] But more alarming even than this from the army's point of view was the fact that strikes and urban protests of all kinds entailed more violence than typical agrarian disorders. There were several reasons for this. In rural communities, where everyone was known to everyone else, including the local estate manager and police chief, the identity of an "instigator" of a peasant riot could not long remain a secret, a fact which might itelf dampen the rebellious spirit. A peasant with nowhere to hide might think twice about throwing a rock at a mounted Cossack. Conditions were, of course, different in the cities, where it was simplicity itself for a radical or a hothead to discharge an armful of bottles or even a magazine of bullets into the closely packed soldiery and then disappear into the anonymity of the slums. In urban areas, as well, the army was hamstrung by the rules of 1877. Even a perfunctory examination of that document reveals that the only role foreseen for the army in popular disturbances was that of crowd control and forcible crowd dispersion—a role which suited the condition of rural, not urban Russia. The framers of the rules, never dreaming of the ferment which would breed in the Empire's cities and towns at the turn of the century, failed to take into account the most elementary features of urban geography. To be sure, a crowd of strikers, as well as a crowd of peasants, could be intimidated by bullet and bayonet, but what if the disorder was not the work of a crowd? The rules contained no prescription for dealing with snipers or with instances of looting and vandalism spread over scores of city blocks, as the army was shortly to discover and at the cost of much blood.

The rise in violent assaults on soldiers doing repressive duty in the Empire's cities at the turn of the century was sudden and dramatic. In April 1900, stones thrown by workers in Warsaw pitched *pod"esaul* Kozhevnikov from his horse and shattered his leg.[47] In July 1903, striking railway workers at Kiev station in Moscow rained stones on infantry and cavalry sent to disperse them.[48] But workers and urbanites often met troops with more dangerous missiles than stones and bricks. In August 1902 anti-Semitic riots broke out among the workers in the town of Czestochowa in Poland. Major General Baumgarten, the head of the garrison, later deposed that his troops had to battle the rioters street by street. The most serious confrontation occurred in the New Market,

[46] A. P. Korelin and S. V. Tiutiukin, "Revoliutsionnaia situatsiia nachala XX v. v Rossii," *Voprosy istorii* 55, no. 10 (Oct., 1980): 17. Statistics on the number of occasions involving workers calculated from TsGVIA, f. 400, op. 3, d. 2465, ll. 393-406.

[47] TsGVIA, f. 400, op. 3, d. 2442, l. 28.

[48] TsGVIA, f. 400, op. 3, d. 2493, l. 175.

where workers fired on the troops from revolvers, and where the cry "don't fear the soldiers—they've got blank cartridges" stimulated the misguided workers to throw themselves on the military command deployed there. The soldiers retaliated with gunfire, killing two and wounding eight.[49] As this episode illustrates, the insistence of the workers on standing up to the army, their occasional inability to understand that the soldiers would in fact shoot them down if so ordered, and the army's inability to do anything but fire volleys inevitably led to violence and tragedies.

Of these, one of the most horrible was the so-called Zlatoust massacre of March 1903, in which forty-five workers died and eighty-three were wounded. The railway and iron laborers in this small town in Ufa Province protested the issuance of new "worker's books." This protest led to arrests and the arrests to demonstrations for the release of jailed comrades. When the demonstrations failed, the workers smashed windows, fired on policemen, and finally besieged the house of the unpopular *gornyi nachal'nik*. The timorous governor of Ufa Province, later assassinated for his part in this incident, then signalled to the commander of the 214th Morshansk battalion to open fire. The latter did so, and the soldiers under his command raked the crowd with fire from two separate directions. While three companies massed near the cathedral fired, other soldiers crouching in the vestibule of the engineer's house opened up on the crowd through plate glass doors and windows. The crowd, astonishingly, endured three distinct volleys before dissolving in panic. The news of the massacre reached War Minister A. N. Kuropatkin as he was en route to Japan, and shocked him into ordering a complete (although inconclusive) investigation.[50]

Thus it was partly the violence of the "disorders" at the turn of the century which distinguished them from earlier confrontations. In the nineties, the only soldiers ever killed in the course of their repressive duties were killed by bandits. After 1900 the soldier called out into the streets or to the factory assumed more risk of injury. Even during the nineties, on the six occasions in which an army command involved in repressive action sustained more than ten casualties, five of these occasions were clashes between the army and the industrial workers.[51] This was a grim portent for the future.

But the difference between the disorders of the early nineties and those which were to break out at the end of the century can be measured

[49] TsGVIA, f. 400, op. 3, d. 2471, l. 67.
[50] TsGVIA, f. 400, op. 3, d. 2496, ll. 60-80; TsGVIA, f. 400, op. 3, d. 2494, l. 5.
[51] TsGVIA, f. 400, op. 3, d. 2465, l. 374.

in more than increased frequency and increased bloodshed. There was in fact a crucial change in the scale of disorders, perhaps best described by the Commander of Odessa Military District, who wrote in 1904:

> Formerly outbreaks of disorders usually took place in some factory, or in a village [but didn't] go beyond the bounds of a determined region of small size. . . . They were localized. . . . Now we see something entirely different; disorders swiftly possess significant regions, grow stronger, burn out, and again break out in entirely new places. Instead of concentrating a small force in one place, it is now necessary to disperse comparatively large detachments over significant distances.[52]

One most striking example of this qualitative difference in peasant disorders was the large-scale unrest in the provinces of Poltava and Khar'kov in March and April of 1902, in which trouble blazed up across the entire uezdy, and which required several battalions of infantry and squadrons of cavalry to crush. A note prepared by the Main Staff for the perusal of Nicholas II gives an idea of the extent of military activity in these areas: elements of no less than five regiments were involved in marches from village to village.[53] But factory, student, and urban unrest generated a similar frenetic pace of military repressive activity. The great strikes in Batum from January to March 1903 provide examples, as do the Baku riots which began later that May and extended into the summer.[54] Large strikes such as these could require the army to take actions which far exceeded the framework of mere crowd control. The employment of 150 members of the Caucasus sapper brigade as scab labor in August and September of 1900 helped to break the strike on the Transcaucasian railroad.[55] Police requests for military aid became more ambitious and extensive as well. The use of over one thousand soldiers to cordon off the area while the St. Petersburg police rounded up hundreds of felons and vagrants from the doss houses of the capital, as occurred on the night of March 26, 1903, would have been inconceivable ten years before.[56] The Nikolaev pogrom of 1899, the Gomel pogrom of 1903, the

[52] TsGVIA, f. 400, op. 3, d. 2534, l. 3.

[53] TsGVIA, f. 400, op. 3, d. 2471, ll. 125, 107. We should note, however, that the army continued to downplay the seriousness of peasant unrest. A. S. Lukomskii, for instance, wrote that the Khar'kov/Poltava troubles were "easily liquidated." Lukomskii, "Ocherki," p. 688.

[54] TsGVIA, f. 400, op. 3, d. 2494, ll. 41-42, 54, 57, 61, 83.

[55] TsGVIA, f. 400, op. 3, d. 2442, ll. 64, 66.

[56] TsGVIA, f. 400, op. 3, d. 2493, l. 5.

sporadic battles between Armenians and Tatars in the Caucasus, all represented novel challenges to the repressive force of the Russian army.

REPRESSION: THE MILITARY REACTION

How then did the officers of the Russian army feel about their repressive role? In public statements, of course, the government could rely on its generals to endorse policies of repression. M. I. Dragomirov's letter of commendation to the units involved in crushing the 1902 Poltava-Khar'-kov disorders was printed in the May 25 issue of *Kievlianin*.[57] Yet to judge by the private reports submitted to the Main Staff, significant numbers of important officers had reservations about repression, for complaints about it surfaced regularly. As might be expected, some officers railed against the frequency with which civilians summoned out the troops. In 1904, with the Russian and Japanese empires locked in combat, commanders of such military districts as Moscow and Kiev, which were already weakened by the policy of partial mobilization, might well have protested further drains on their military resources.[58] Yet district commanders and officials of the Main Staff were decrying repression long before the Japanese attack on Port Arthur. In studying these complaints, one must distinguish between those which concern the conditions under which repressive service was performed and those which concern the very principle of repressive service.

Complaints of the former variety were endemic to every corner of the Empire, and invariably consisted of condemnations of civil government behavior and practice with respect to the army. For instance, a typical complaint was that civil governors often chose to prolong the army's stay in a village or town indefinitely, even after disorders had stopped, just out of uneasiness that unrest might flare up again. By filing weekly reports to the Ministry of the Interior and the military district showing "cause" to hold the troops in place, the governors were thus able to circumvent an 1889 amendment to the rules designed to prevent the needless detention of the troops.[59] Since only a governor-general, the Minister of the Interior, or the Emperor could overrule a stubborn governor, the army often had to content itself with criticism as empty as that which the Staff of Moscow Military District levelled against the governor of Voronezh for detaining two companies in the already pacified village of Kurlak for the entire month of March 1902.[60]

[57] Ardusheva, *Krest'ianskoe dvizhenie v poltavskoi*, p. 180.
[58] TsGVIA, f. 400, op. 3, d. 2621, ll. 50, 55.
[59] For the amendment, see *Russkii Invalid*, no. 55 (Mar. 7, 1889): 1.
[60] TsGVIA, f. 400, op. 3, d. 2471, l. 298.

The army also frequently accused the governors of calling out troops without even the flimsiest justification. In his report for 1896, Adjutant General A. I. Musin-Pushkin, Commander of Odessa District, described the boundless proliferation of civilian demands for soldiers, noting that the majority of these requests were seated in the wish of the civil authorities to preserve order at fairs, processions, and the like, or in the desire to forestall potential disorders through an ostentatious display of military force. In Pushkin's opinion, civilian anxiety was baseless on almost all occasions.[61] High military officers further rebuked the civilians for summoning ridiculously large numbers of troops for the problem at hand. A typical example of this sort of redundancy occurred in June of 1902, when a policeman's telephone call from the Italian Hotel in Vil'na resulted in the dispatch of an entire company of armed men to capture a single pitiful thief who had taken refuge in the city cathedral. This incident provoked the ire of Nicholas II himself, who angrily penciled on the report sent him about it: "Outrageous! To summon an entire company to catch one thief!"[62] In a parallel case, the Main Staff condemned the governor of Tambov's appeal for five battalions and two sotnias to control the crowds of pilgrims and mendicants he expected to turn up for the ceremonial opening of the reliquary of St. Serafim in the Saravsk hermitage.[63]

In most of the above instances of friction, the civilians were entirely within the rights assigned them by the rules of 1877. Yet the civilians did not always comply with the rules so faithfully. In emergencies (real or imagined) the civilians sometimes simply ignored the rules; and emergencies became more and more prevalent at the turn of the century. From 1899 to 1904 the army excoriated the civilians for such rule violations as the summoning of troops by officials who were not entitled to do so, appeals for troops which bypassed the military district commander, and the fragmentation of half companies into tiny commands of a few men each.[64]

All of the military objections we have discussed to this point concerned only the terms of repressive service. There was, however, an entirely different register of complaints in which there was an implicit questioning of the very principle of the military's repressive role. Such complaints depicted repression as somehow "dishonorable" or unworthy of the army, while highlighting the ruinous damage to the army from

[61] TsGVIA, f. 400, op. 3, d. 2387, l. 22.

[62] TsGVIA, f. 400, op. 3, d. 2471, l. 24.

[63] TsGVIA, f. 400, op. 3, d. 2496, l. 4.

[64] TsGVIA, f. 400, op. 3, d. 2427, l. 28; TsGVIA, f. 400, op. 3, d. 2471, l. 24; TsGVIA, f. 400, op. 3, d. 2496, l. 127.

this service. And the Russian military leadership, both central and local, voiced complaints with almost monotonous regularity about one specific sort of repressive duty: police service, i.e., the use of troops to supplement the police or to stand guard at civil institutions. Even when the army was called ostensibly to suppress a disorder, often what the governor had in mind was rather policing or controlling a crowd. The annual report of Odessa Military District for 1901 observed:

> in threatening a peaceable crowd, the troops play a police role completely unsuitable to them. The task of the army is to pacify a riotous mob with an iron hand, and therefore it is wrong to accustom it [i.e., the mob] to the frequent appearance of threatening troops, who however do not act with armed force. The masses must learn that the appearance of troops results in inevitably serious consequences, that is, the use of arms.[65]

This was merely a recapitulation of the War Ministry's position on the police question, a position which was consistent during the administrations of Vannovskii, Kuropatkin, and Sakharov. As Vannovskii wrote: "While I recognize the necessity of using troops to suppress disorders, I will never agree to their use in a police capacity or to their subordination to policemen." Sakharov later insisted that "the troops should have no . . . tasks with relation to the public which were the specialties of the police or the Separate Corps of Gendarmes."[66]

Of all species of police duty, none was more hotly detested than guard service. Throughout the nineties, every district headquarters in the Empire dispatched protests against guard duty to St. Petersburg. In a sense this is somewhat surprising, because the number of guard duty posts actually fell in this decade from roughly 4,600 in 1891 to 3,600 in 1900.[67] One partial explanation for the protests is that they were founded in frustrated institutional imperialism: the belief that the soldiers belonged to the army and that the army should therefore fully control what was done with them. As it was inarguably incumbent on the army to stop street riots, it was natural for army officers to attack guard duty—the most vulnerable sort of civilian-imposed internal service. But some of these military protests did in fact result from a "pinching shoe." To be sure the number of duty positions did decrease, but in the borderland military districts of the Caucasus, Turkestan, Omsk, and Amur, where troops were scattered thinly throughout gigantic territories, and where

[65] TsGVIA, f. 400, op. 3, d. 2475, l. 57.

[66] TsGAOR, f. 102 DP, 3rd deloproizvodstvo, d. 145 (1904), l. 10; TsGVIA, f. 400, op. 3, d. 2112, l. 62.

[67] TsGVIA, f. 1, op. 2, d. 159, l. 13.

civilian demand for guards was high anyway, even the reduced quantity of guard posts constituted a hardship. For example, when Caucasus District condemned guard duty in 1896, it provided a vivid illustration of what such duty could mean for a typical military unit, the Mikhailov fortress infantry battalion. This battalion might, at first glance, have enough soldiers for guarding service. But as the Caucasus staff was quick to point out, this battalion expanded in wartime into a five-battalion regiment. The soldiers of the peacetime battalion had therefore to maintain all the regimental equipment. Over 100 men were involved each day in such tasks as cobbling, sewing, servicing the reserves of the Intendancy, and cleaning 3,890 rifles. The battalion had 56 duty posts to fill each day, requiring over 160 soldiers. But the battalion could only spare 70 soldiers for guard duty: barely more than one shift, in view of the multitude of soldiers tied up with regimental housekeeping.[68]

But even if a military unit had enough soldiers to go around, guard duty could still be onerous. To break a strike or scatter a demonstration was one thing; at the most a few days might be lost. However, guard details were another thing altogether, since by their very nature they extended over long periods of time and were a constant drain on military resources. In the opinion of most military district commanders, civilians piggishly insisted on military guards because it was cheap and convenient for them and because they were maddeningly indifferent to the true purpose of the army: the protection of the state from the external foe. Thus civilians did not care that guard duty ruined the health of the soldiers, lowered their prestige and their morale and, most importantly, kept them away from the summer training exercises, which were so vital to the Russian High Command. As the Ministry of War and its military districts were doing all in their power to expand participation in these training camps, the countervailing civilian pressure for guard duty and ancilliary police services could only be regarded with distaste, since it contradicted the army's professional interests.

Writing in 1891, the Commander of Kiev Military District called for fewer military guards at civil prisons, pointing out that "in present circumstances, when there are no pressing reasons for cutting back on these details, the civil authorities frequently preserve them only because they represent no inconvenience. These completely useless details cost the civilians nothing."[69] The staff of the Caucasus District denounced police service in 1896, charging that the Cossacks sent each summer to reinforce the Frontier Guard were constantly denied the opportunity for

[68] TsGVIA, f. 400, op. 3, d. 2376, l. 65.
[69] TsGVIA, f. 400, op. 3, d. 4037, l. 19.

summer training.[70] In the same year, Odessa District condemned police duty because "the troops are diverted from their exercises in vain, frequently for entire weeks."[71]

Omsk District reported in 1897 that it was nearly impossible to train reserve battalions properly because of the inflated civil guard and convoy details in Tomsk and Tobol'sk Provinces. The Omsk Staff even complained of the participation of local troops in guard duty, heedless of the fact that such duty was the legal rationale for local troops.[72] In 1898, the Military Districts of Kazan', Siberia, Caucasus, Odessa, and Omsk all had harsh words for guard duty in their reports.[73] The Caucasus District underscored the particular burden of this duty for reserve units, a burden so crippling that they were frankly incapable of discharging their "chief task during mobilization," the training and processing of recruits.[74] And Musin-Pushkin wrote Nicholas II from Odessa in 1899: "Concerning the placing of troops at the disposal of the civil authorities, I consider it my duty to inform Your Imperial Majesty of the evil which it does to the field training of the army."[75] A document prepared by the Main Staff for the War Minister noted that the civil authorities in Odessa District were only extracting those services from the troops which the law permitted, yet the strain of these services "on the normal course of troop training remains obvious."[76]

The Caucausus District protested guard duty in reports for 1901 as did Kazan' and Kiev. Dragomirov, writing from Kiev, buttressed his argument by inserting a letter written to him by the commander of the 10th Army Corps: "frequent details of troops to stop and prevent street disorders in help of the police hinder the correct course of troop training in significant measure . . . the division of companies from regiments, and likewise the details of troops in the event of disorders . . . cannot but react negatively on the success of training."[77] Lieutenant General Sakharov, summarizing the opinions of Russia's district commanders in a memorandum to the Emperor (June 1901), stressed the burden of police duty on the army and the disastrous consequences for the army's training program, concluding that "aid rendered to the police, frequently

---

[70] TsGVIA, f. 400, op. 3, d. 2376, l. 42.
[71] TsGVIA, f. 400, op. 3, d. 2387, l. 22.
[72] TsGVIA, f. 400, op. 3, d. 2387, ll. 50, 66.
[73] TsGVIA, f. 400, op. 3, d. 2427, ll. 1, 4, 13.
[74] Ibid., l. 14.
[75] Ibid., l. 28.
[76] Ibid., l. 67.
[77] TsGVIA, f. 400, op. 3, d. 2475, ll. 4, 6, 24.

without extreme need, nourishes the bitterness of the population against the army, and pollutes the army's worth in the eyes of the people."[78]

Complaints were unceasing. Explicit linkage between police duty and poor training was made by the commanders of Kazan', Kiev, St. Petersburg, Siberia, and Turkestan in reports for 1903.[79] In the following year Generals Kaul'bars (Odessa), Golitsyn (Caucasus), Freze (Vil'na), and Bobrikov (Finland) added their voices to this chorus. While Golitsyn inveighed against the boredom, bad morale, and general unhealthiness engendered among the troops by this duty, Freze warned that it was the nursery of political discontent in the ranks of the army. All of these generals, as well as those in charge in Moscow, Kiev, and Warsaw, deplored the time lost from summer training as a result of internal service.[80]

MILITARY PROPOSALS FOR CHANGE IN REPRESSIVE SERVICE

These grievances resulted in a host of proposals for their redress. To correct those problems which inhered in the conditions of military repression and guard duty (too frequent calls, calls without need, bad treatment, and so forth), military men demanded a thorough revision in the existing legislation. And those officers who objected to police duty in principle felt that the division between the job of the army and the job of the police ought to be rendered absolutely distinct, a process which would mandate increasing the Empire's police forces.

Proposals of both kinds, drafted in the provincial military districts, were warmly embraced by the central War Ministry itself, where there was a powerful office committed to the training of the troops. This was the Main Staff's administration of the first *General-Kvartirmeister*, especially the second of its five sections. This department (officially called the "Troop Training and Organization Section") was charged with the task of overseeing the army's internal police duty. Yet as its name implies, it also organized and promoted maneuvers and training exercises. Thus the *one* office in the Ministry which oversaw military repression was *precisely the one* which had the greatest functional reason to resent it. The heads of this section, from Col. V. A. Avramov in 1890 to Lieutenant Colonel Iuon in 1905, unswervingly held that summer training, not police service, best served the interests of the army.[81]

[78] TsGVIA, f. 400, op. 3, d. 2465, l. 592.

[79] TsGVIA, f. 400, op. 3, d. 2534, ll. 26-27, 29, 49, 67, 59. See also TsGVIA, f. 400, op. 3, d. 2496, ll. 58, 160.

[80] TsGVIA, f. 400, op. 3, d. 2621, ll. 12, 43, 46, 48, 66.

[81] On the organization of the Main Staff, see *Obshchii sostav chinov Glavnogo Shtaba*

REVISION OF THE RULES OF 1877

Undesirable features of the rules of 1877 from the military point of view became manifest within a few years of their enactment. In January 1882, General Albedinskii of Warsaw Military District wrote the Staff asking for changes in the articles of the rules which gave civilians exclusive control over troops used in internal repression. Albedinskii wanted two substantive amendments here. First, he argued that the civilians should not be allowed to splinter such military entities as companies and platoons into nondescript, officerless groups of two or three men. Second, he noted that since only civilians could order the troops into action but did not always accompany them into the streets, the troops were often helpless witnesses to urban criminality. In order to prevent this, he wanted military officers to be less dependent on the instructions of the civilians.[82] The Main Staff submitted a copy of Albedinskii's proposition to each of the military district commanders. Those of Kiev, Vil'na, Khar'kov, and St. Petersburg immediately endorsed it.[83] Gurko (Odessa) went even further than Albedinskii and urged the total abolition of civilian power to direct the action of the troops once summoned.[84]

Impressed by the very favorable response to Albedinskii's suggestions and by the lucidity of Gurko's arguments, the War Ministry incorporated the ideas of both in a bill submitted to the Council of State.[85] Yet fierce political struggles in the Council emasculated the Ministry's bill; the law which the Council issued on December 28, 1882 was a rout for the military interest. Although it eliminated civilian control over such minutiae of military life as bivouacking and picketing, the decree did not give the army authority for independent action, and it concluded by lamely enjoining the civilians and the military to cooperate.[86]

The second important push to rewrite the rules was prompted in 1901 when the Ministry of the Interior published a circular advising governors to summon the cavalry instantly at the first whisper of disorder, even if they knew that armed force would not have to be used. To the Main Staff this circular was an intolerable insult, since it proved that, far from heeding the military's plea to cut back on needless appeals for assistance, the Ministry of the Interior was rather seeking to increase them. In the

---

po 1 fevralia 1905 goda (St. Petersburg, 1905). On Avramov, see TsGVIA, f. 400, op. 21, d. 1826, ll. 2, 5, 9; also see *Voennoe ministerstvo. Alfavitnyi ukazatel po ofitsialnym dannym* (St. Petersburg, 1904), p. 16.

[82] TsGVIA, f. 400, op. 3, d. 2112, l. 1.
[83] Ibid., ll. 19, 20, 26, 49.
[84] Ibid., l. 27.
[85] Ibid., ll. 40, 44.
[86] Ibid., l. 168.

opinion of the Main Staff it was essential to bung up the loopholes in the 1877 law which permitted the unjustifiable diversion of military resources for civilian purposes. When Nicholas II himself endorsed a revision of the rules, the Staff polled the district commanders about the changes in the rules they desired.[87] The consensus of opinion favored six major emendations:[88]

1. The elastic clause in the rules should be eliminated. Civilians should be able to summon troops, but only in a limited number of prescribed cases.
2. Troops should never in the future be used in a purely police capacity.
3. Troops should be called only to stop serious disorders. The practice of calling them to prevent or avert disorders should be proscribed.
4. Military officers, not civilians, should decide what sort of troops to send, and how many of them.
5. Military officers, not civilians, should decide whether the soldiers should use their rifles.
6. The military power, not the civilian, should decide when the troops were to return to their place of quartering.

Guided by these recommendations, War Minister Kuropatkin prepared a draft bill early in 1903 which at once encountered resistance—in the form of foot-dragging—from the Ministry of Internal Affairs. Plehve and his successor Mirskii delayed legislative action on Kuropatkin's bill until April of 1904, when the Ministry of the Interior conceded that a special interdepartmental commission should be appointed to study it. But the commission did not meet until 1905, and it was not until 1906 that the rules of 1877 were finally modified. By that time the pressure of the revolution had forced the excision of the most radical provisions of the War Ministry's bill; even in its diluted form, the new law would be almost impossible to implement until 1908, since the revolution led to a breakdown in military hierarchies and the almost total dominance of the civilian power over the military.[89]

Excluding the Army From Police Service

The War Ministry's efforts to achieve timely and meaningful revisions in the rules were thus not particularly successful. No more successful

---

[87] TsGVIA, f. 400, op. 3, d. 2560, ll. 1, 236.

[88] Ibid., ll. 1-3. For a thorough discussion of the evils of the system established by the rules, see TsGVIA, f. 400, op. 3, d. 2534 (report of the Kiev District Commander, ll. 2-3).

[89] TsGVIA, f. 400, op. 3, d. 2560, ll. 56, 58, 68, 71, 72, 245.

were its attempts to separate the army from the police. Even what at first sight appeared to be great legislative victories in this regard proved to be resounding defeats. The Shuvalov Commission of 1882, for example, produced a law which emphatically forbade the employment of soldiers in nocturnal police patrols except in those provinces subject to the "exceptional laws" of 1881. The pleasure of the officers in the General Staff building would have been diminished had they known the speed with which "extraordinary safeguard" and "reinforced safeguard" spread to more and more provinces and indeed became a regular instrument of government.[90]

Generally, however, the army tried to cut back on the military performance of police duty by admonishing the other ministries, especially those of the Interior and Justice, to hire more policemen, or to create their own special police forces. That such a measure was essential to the emancipation of the army from police service is demonstrable through an analysis of Russia's police resources.

All police forces in Russia, except for the Separate Corps of Gendarmes, the Frontier Guard, and the Customs Guard, came under the sway of the Ministry of the Interior. The Ministry's Department of Police (created in 1880) consequently had authority over the urban, rural (uezd), river, and factory police commands. In addition, the Department possessed several sections exclusively devoted to the struggle with sedition and revolutionary activity. The Corps of Gendarmes assisted the Department in the latter struggle. Although technically part of the army (and paid for by the Ministry of War), the Corps was only really integrated with the military command in the event of war. In peacetime the direction of the three Gendarme divisions (Petersburg, Moscow, and Warsaw) and the Gendarme administration in each province fell to the Department of Police. The Assistant Minister of the Interior was usually the head of the Police Department and Commander of the Gendarme Corps, while the Minister himself enjoyed the title of Chief of Gendarmes. To combat propaganda in large cities which were plagued with revolutionary organizations, the Police Department organized special "protective sections" which emerged by the mid-nineties as the infamous Okhrana, with its pool of secret agents and provocateurs.[91]

In view of all these police forces, one might think that the Russian

---

[90] TsGVIA, f. 400, op. 3, d. 2112, ll. 134a, 134b, 134v, 135. See Richard Pipes, *Russia under the Old Regime* (New York, 1974), pp. 305-307, on the persistence of the laws of August 14, 1881.

[91] G. B. Sliozberg, *Dorevoliutsionnyi stroi Rossii* (Paris, 1933), p. 185, 188; A. A. Lopukhin, *Nastoiashee i budushchee russkoi politsii* (Moscow, 1907), pp. 10-11, 15, 34-36.

101

government could rest secure. Yet in fact the Russian Empire was under-policed; the police were simply too few to execute all of their functions, even in times of civil peace, let alone in times of burgeoning unrest within the Empire. As the French expert Leroy-Beaulieu wrote of the Russian police: "To do justice to all the duties prescribed to them a member of the force should be at once a health officer, a chemist, an architect, a censor, an usher, an assistant at inquests, an excise inspector, an overseer of recruits and soldiers . . . and over and above all of this, the ever-ready executor of orders issued by any authority."[92] To be sure, in some major urban centers, the ratio of police to people was far in excess of that which obtained in comparable Western European capitals. According to data from the census of 1897, in that year Moscow's ratio of police to population was 1 to 234. In Paris, Berlin, and Vienna circa 1908, the ratios were 1 to 352, 1 to 400, and 1 to 436.[93] Yet the latter cities were not beset, as was Moscow, by the very real threat of revolutionary violence. In the countryside, however, the situation was much worse. Outside the cities and towns, the state had less than nine thousand policemen for a peasant population of ninety million.[94] As for the Okhrana, it never employed more than a few thousand surveillance agents during its entire existence.[95]

The call for larger police forces by the Ministry of War became more strident as applications for soldiers to perform police services—especially in industrial regions—increased. In his report for 1896, the Commander of Moscow Military District asked that two separate sotnias of Don Cossacks be raised for police duty in the factory territories of Vladimir Province; these units, which were not to have a military organization, were to be paid for by the Ministry of the Interior.[96] If this could not be done, one possibility suggested by Grand Duke Sergei Aleksandrovich was to transfer one or two of the five separate sotnias doing police duty in the Donets factory region to Moscow. The War Ministry, unhappy with both of these suggestions, saw the solution to Moscow's problem

[92] Anatole Leroy-Beaulieu, *The Empire of the Tsars and the Russians*, 3rd ed., trans. Zenaide A. Rogozin, vol. 2 (New York, 1898), pp. 121-122.

[93] *Pervaia vseobshchaia perepis' naseleniia Rossiiskoi Imperii 1897 g. Raspredelenie naseleniia*, vol. 2 (St. Petersburg, 1905), p. 149; "Police," *Encyclopedia Britannica*, 11th ed., vol. 21 (Cambridge, 1910-1911), p. 980.

[94] Weisman, *Reform in Tsarist Russia*, p. 62.

[95] Frederic Scott Zuckerman, "The Russian Political Police at Home and Abroad (1880-1917)," Ph.D. diss., New York University, 1973, p. 131; on the weakness of the rural police, see also Neil B. Weisman, "Rural Crime in Tsarist Russia: The Question of Hooliganism, 1905-14," *SR* 37, no. 2 (June 1978): 236.

[96] TsGVIA, f. 1, op. 2, d. 157, l. 11; TsGVIA, f. 400, op. 3, d. 2387, l. 14.

in the expansion of the civilian police force there.[97] Regardless of whether new sotnias were to be paid for by the Ministry of the Interior, as would occur if they were mobilized for Moscow police purposes solely, or by the War Ministry, as would happen if they were called up to replace those in the Donets region transferred to Moscow, the War Ministry felt that the army of Don Cossacks quite simply was already overstrained. The preference of civilian officials for Cossack troops in police duty, based on the awesome effect their ferocious appearance and reputation for ruthlessness had on crowds, had led to the call-up of so many Cossacks that the economy of the Don region was imperiled. Over 67 per cent of all male Don Cossacks were on service in 1897, a further 20 percent were unfit for duty, and 13 percent were excused on the basis of their family or property responsibilities. "Calling up persons of the latter categories would completely ruin their families, as they would be left incapable of [farm] work." Yet Nicholas II did not agree, and the army was compelled to raise a sixth separate sotnia, which was sent to Moscow Province in 1898.[98]

Military districts in the Empire other than Moscow carried the burden of inadequate civilian police establishments. Odessa's comments about this situation stimulated War Minister Vannovskii to send a letter to the Interior Ministry (April 1897) demanding more police generally in industrial areas. The Interior Ministry responded that it would in fact hire more police—at the expense of the industrialists themselves. In practice, this measure proved to be inadequate, and as the Main Staff observed in a note of February 1900: "As formerly, such centers as Nikolaev, Odessa, Ekaterinoslav, Elisavetgrad and Mariupol' need troops to strengthen the police. . . . numbers of police in centers with unruly populations are obviously inadequate."[99] A decree from the Council of State in December 1898 enhanced the Empire's police by a mere 160 rural sergeants and 2,320 urban policemen.[100] In his report for 1901, the Odessa District commander again called for more police, even if industrialists were forced to support them, and reiterated this demand the following year.[101] The creation of the rural guard in 1903 did not solve Imperial Russia's police problem, for this new and expanded guard, strongly backed by Plehve at the Interior Ministry, was phased in only gradually and was, moreover, still too small for its duties. Indeed, the areas of the Empire in which the police were strengthened the most were

[97] TsGVIA, f. 400, op. 3, d. 2387, l. 19.
[98] TsGVIA, f. 1, op. 2, d. 157, ll. 11-12.
[99] TsGVIA, f. 400, op. 3, d. 2427, l. 68.
[100] Ibid., l. 74.
[101] TsGVIA, f. 400, op. 3, d. 2475, l. 57; TsGVIA, f. 400, op. 3, d. 2534. l. 2.

Kuban and Tersk *oblasty* where the army *was* the civil administration, and paid for more civilian policemen out of its own pocket.[102] In 1904 the War Ministry would still be importuning the Ministry of the Interior to increase the police establishment.[103]

The Interior Ministry was not the only ministry to which the War Ministry appealed. In the opinion of the military leaders, too many troops were sent every year to reinforce the Frontier Guard in the Caucasus; this meant negotiations with the Ministry of Finance, which controlled the Frontier Guard. But this problem paled in significance when compared with the problem of guarding civil prisons, prisons administered by the Main Prison Administration, after 1895 a part of the Ministry of Justice.

In 1887, the Council of State had declared that as of March 1888, the army was no longer to guard most civilian prisons in European Russia, except for those in Astrakhan', Orenburg, Perm', Ufa, Viatka, Olonets, and Vologda. Instead, the Ministry of Justice was to hire and train its own special prison and convoy guard.[104] As was so often true in Imperial Russia, however, the implementation of this law dragged on for years. There were still significant numbers of soldiers at prison guard boxes in European Russia in 1898; further, military officials in Asia and the Caucasus had started to appeal for relief. But the Ministry of Justice indicated that it did not have the funds to apply the law of 1887 even in European Russia, and if the War Ministry wanted a civilian prison guard in the provinces of the Far East, or in the Caucasus, it would have to foot the bill, not the Ministry of Justice.[105] When the War Ministry inquired how much the bill would be, the Ministry of Justice made no reply for over four years.[106] Grumbling about prison duty meanwhile continued in Russia's district headquarters. In 1902, the War Ministry resolved to seek Imperial consent for the total freeing of troops from guarding prisons in all regions of the Empire.[107] This consent was obtained, but the Ministry of Justice stalled a further two years, by which time the challenges of war and then revolution caused the dispute to be shelved. Nicholas II's order of June 12 1904 on the fiscal austerity of wartime proved an air-tight defense for the Ministries of Finance, In-

[102] TsGVIA, f. 330, op. 46, d. 842, l. 142; on the rural guard, see Weisman, *Reform in Tsarist Russia*, pp. 64-65.
[103] TsGVIA, f. 400, op. 3, d. 2621, l. 24.
[104] TsGVIA, f. 400, op. 3, d. 2387, l. 58.
[105] Ibid., l. 85.
[106] TsGVIA, f. 400, op. 3, d. 2475, l. 10.
[107] Ibid., l. 10.

terior, and Justice. More civilian police and guards were obviously out of the question.[108]

REASONS FOR CIVIL-MILITARY CONFLICT OVER REPRESSION

For the War Ministry, and for many commanders in the field, the nexus of opposition to civilian demands for repressive measures lay in military professionalism and, most specifically, in the idea that the human resources of the army ought to be husbanded and trained. The great obstacle to military internal repression was the army's interest—and the army's interest demanded a schedule of prompt and regular training exercises.

But if the concept of the army's interest stiffened the resistance of the generals to unwarranted civilian requests for troops and aid, it could also blind them to the very real needs of the civilians. Civilian finances and powers were in fact limited, and tsarist bureaucrats did encounter authentic security crises far beyond their strength to overcome; at times the army was unwilling to recognize this. In 1904, for instance, Military District Commander V. A. Sukhomlinov tried to pull the 12th company of the 122d Tambov infantry out of Andreevko and the 11th company of the 121st Penza infantry out of Khar'kov Province. These units had been sent into these places to guard civilian prisons in 1901. Three years had now elapsed and they had neither been relieved nor withdrawn. But the Ministry of Justice retorted that the chronic rioting at the Andreevko correctional institution necessitated the constant vigilance of troops. In 1903 the inmates became so violent that only the timely intervention of the soldiers prevented the demolition of the entire prison. The budget of the Ministry of Justice supported one hundred guards at this prison; if the army were withdrawn, ninety-eight new guard jobs would have to be created at a cost of twenty-five thousand rubles a year, an extra expenditure the Ministry simply could not afford.[109]

The army did not, after all, bear the final responsibility for order and lawfulness in the Russian provinces. This was the duty of the civilians, and the civilians were swift to remind the military of this fact. When Colonel Kokunskii of the 1st Urupsk Cossacks fell into a dispute in November 1903 with the acting governor of Chernigov about military repressive action, the governor informed the colonel that he, not Ko-

---

[108] TsGVIA, f. 400, op. 3, d. 1621, l. 38. As late as 1905, Main Prison Administration officials would publicly request abrogation of the law of 1887 and a return to military external prison guarding everywhere in the Empire. Nikolai Luchinskii, "Voprosy mestnoi praktiki," *Tiuremnyi vestnik*, no. 8 (Oct. 1905): 653-656.

[109] TsGVIA, f. 400, op. 3, d. 2533, ll. 20, 22.

kunskii or even Kokunskii's superior, Sukhomlinov, was responsible for security in the province.[110]

Yet the civilians did not, in the opinion of the War Ministry, make enough of an effort to understand the military point of view. Military officers were highly suspicious of civilians who seemed to believe that the primary function of the army was to prop up internal order in the Empire. An incident which tended to confirm these suspicions had already occurred at the beginning of the eighties.

The 1882 pogroms against the Jews in the Pale of Settlement so enraged Emperor Alexander III that he ordered all measures be taken to prevent their recurrence. Minister of the Interior D. A. Tolstoi wrote the War Ministry a letter on this subject. Noting that there were too few troops in those southern and southwestern territories of the Empire which comprised the Pale, Tolstoi insisted that more soldiers be sent there, that all soldiers there be subordinated to the police, and that the deployment of the army be entirely revamped to better suit the needs of internal security. Predictably, Tolstoi's letter elicited sharp criticism from the army. The Commander of the Kiev District wrote that the deployment of the army was, and had to be, based solely on strategic considerations—e.g., the threat of war. Further, Tolstoi's proposals, if executed, would mean that troop training in these territories would be effectively eliminated. "To abstain from training troops in peacetime, on the mere supposition that disorders might occur [cannot be agreed to] by any state which is concerned with the military readiness of its forces in the event of a clash with an enemy."[111]

Civilians did not again seriously urge plans as drastic as this one— the essential transformation of the regular army into a sort of super police force—until the revolution of 1905. Still, throughout the period 1880 to 1904, civilians did summon troops without regard to disruption in training and military preparedness. In 1902 one particularly zealous prison official even summoned troopers of the Imperial convoy, the Emperor's personal guard, to assist the police in suppressing a riot at the St. Petersburg house of preliminary detention. On this occasion, however, Nicholas II sternly rebuked both the prison official and Baron Meierdorf, head of the convoy, who acceded to the request.[112]

Unending civilian demands for troops, dispatched heedless of the consequences to the army, were not the only aspect of civilian military policy which vexed the generals towards the end of the nineteenth cen-

---

[110] TsGVIA, f. 400, op. 3, d. 2496, l. 230.
[111] TsGVIA, f. 400, op. 3, d. 2112, ll. 58, 59, 118.
[112] TsGVIA, f. 970, op. 3, d. 692, ll. 6, 11.

tury. There were other features of that policy, promoted by some of the most eminent civilians within the councils of the Imperial state, which betrayed a narrowly civilian conception of the army and its purpose. After all, no responsible military officer in the nineties would have denied that military repression, albeit strictly controlled, was a legitimate duty of the army. But the civilian bureaucracy also used the army as an agent of indirect repression, damaging it without adequate justification or recompense as in the cases of the Finnish conscription plan and the "temporary rules" of 1899.

The idea of extending the Russian conscription system of 1874 uniformly throughout the Empire, including Finland, had originally been Miliutin's. Vannovskii had supported it, as did Kuropatkin. There were sound military reasons, principally a shortage of skilled manpower, which underpinned proposals to make the Finns share equally in the burden of national defense.[113] To Kuropatkin's horror, however, the Ministry of the Interior attempted to use the plan as a bludgeon directed against Finnish autonomy. A crisis in the relationship between the Grand Duchy of Finland and the rest of the Empire ensued; and the War Ministry, which had desired the cooperation of the Finns, instead became an object of hatred among them.[114]

The attempt of the government to cope with the great student unrest of 1899 also put the army in an awkward position. On July 26 (apparently at Witte's instigation) the government promulgated the "temporary rules," legislation for impressing troublesome students into military service.[115] The rules backfired, however, for they radicalized the students instead of cowing them into docility.[116] They were unpopular in the universities, and just as unpopular in the army, as even the Department of Police admitted in 1901.[117] And they provoked an acid confrontation between Kuropatkin and Nicholas II in July 1899. While Nicholas main-

---

[113] *Ministerstvo voennoe. Doklad po glavnomu shtabu. Otdelenie v. stol 1. 22 Maia 1898 goda. no. 6. Istoriia sostaveleniia i utverzhdeniia Finliandskogo ustava o voinskoi povinnosti* (St. Petersburg, 1898), pp. 2-27, passim. On the Finnish response, see Eino Tutikalla and Kauka Pirinen, *A History of Finland*, trans. Paul Sjöllom, rev. ed. (New York, 1974), pp. 229-232.

[114] TsGVIA, f. 165, op. 6, d. 1868, ll. 69-70.

[115] A. S. Suvorin, *Dnevnik A. S. Suvorina*, ed. Mikhail Krichevskii (Moscow and Petrograd, 1923), p. 230. In a forthcoming monograph, Samuel Kassow of Trinity College will make a stronger case for Witte's instigation of the rules than Suvorin's passing reference, cited above. The army had managed to ward off an earlier version of the "temporary rules" in 1882. Zaionchkovskii, *Rossiiskoe*, pp. 314-315.

[116] *Materialy po istorii studencheskogo dvizheniia v Rossii*, vol. 1 (London and St. Petersburg, 1906), pp. 21, 57.

[117] TsGAOR, f. DP OO, d. 3, ch./25 MI/1898g., l. 140.

tained that the duty of correcting these obstreperous youths was innately
an honorable one, Kuropatkin countered that the rules were turning the
army into a penal institution and cheapening military honor to boot. In
addition there was the danger that student propagandists might try their
hands at spreading sedition in the ranks. Kuropatkin closed by warning
the Emperor that the army could endure the rules only if they truly
were temporary.[118] In June 1901 Nicholas discharged those students who
had been forcibly inducted and allowed the temporary rules to lapse.[119]

Civil-military conflict over military repression, then, grew worse as
the problem of the internal security in the Empire grew worse. Interdepartmental conflicts were not a novelty in Imperial Russia. They had
occurred frequently in the early nineteenth and even eighteenth centuries, but then, as often as not, they were based on personalities. The
change at the turn of the century was that the central dynamic of the
conflict was the clash of civilian traditionalism and military professionalism.

It was in the traditional interest of civilians to use as many troops as
necessary, even more than necessary, to stabilize the Empire, just as it
was in the professional interest of the army to extricate the troops,
insofar as possible, from this very kind of service. The conflicts which
resulted from this tug of war were not unimportant episodes in a history
of civil-military cooperation and mutual respect, for the conflicts subtly
changed the way in which civilians and soldiers related to each other in
tsarist Russia. Especially after 1902, military district commanders were
increasingly prone to dismiss governors' requests for military aid. Governors would then appeal to the Ministry of the Interior, which would
then have to apply pressure on the central administration of the War
Ministry. Provincial antagonism hence fueled cyclical antagonism in St.
Petersburg, while the security problem identified by the governor,
whether real or not, had to await interministerial resolution.[120]

Further, the military's perception that civilians were prone to "cry
wolf" sometimes made the army almost reflexively discount rational
civilian pleas for the troops necessary to suppress large-scale disorders.
At the end of June 1903, for instance, the Interior Ministry informed
the War Ministry that since major trouble could be expected in the port

[118] TsGVIA, f. 165. op. 1, d. 1868, ll. 43-44.

[119] A. V. Bogdanovich, *Tri poslednikh samoderzhtsa. Dnevnik A. V. Bogdanovich* (Moscow and Leningrad, 1924), p. 260. On the degree to which the army tried to limit the
applicability of the rules, see V. Orlov, "Studencheskoe dvizhenie v 1901g.," *Krasnyi
arkhiv* 2 (75) (1938): 82-112.

[120] The Main Staff stressed this in July of 1903. TsGVIA, f. 400, op. 3, d. 2496, ll. 192-
193.

of Nikolaev, two sotnias of the 7th Don Cossacks should forsake maneuvers and remain in the city all summer. But the army refused to part with more than one sotnia and serious riots did erupt less than a month later, requiring the commitment of many more troops than the two sotnias originally requested.[121] Had the Ministry of War been more trusting, the Nikolaev violence might have been averted, or at least more easily checked.

On still other occasions, military contempt for civilian incompetence or arbitrariness led the army to eschew taking the initiative, to wait irresponsibly for the civil power to request military aid in accord with proper and legal form. The most appalling example of such behavior occurred during the great Kishinev pogrom of April 1903.[122] There can be no doubt that the pogrom was planned long in advance and extremely well organized: disciplined commands of ten to twenty men attacked Jews and destroyed their property, melting away when boys on bicycles alerted them to the approach of troops. And, as Major General Shostak wrote in the War Ministry's postmortem about the Kishinev events, there was also reason to suspect that the anti-Semitic governor of Bessarabia, R. Von Raaben, had prior knowledge of the pogrom yet did nothing to forestall it.[123] Although the pogrom began on the morning of the 6th, the governor did not call out the troops until later that afternoon. Even after he had the troops, Raaben made poor use of them. On the 7th, Raaben sat in the comfort of his office, dispatching troops pell-mell from one district of the city to another without giving them any instructions as to what they were to do when they got there, or without sending with them a civilian official empowered to order them to fire. Starting at 11:30 a.m. Lieutenant General Bekman, the head of the garrison, tried to persuade Raaben to put full authority into the hands of the army, but Raaben waited until 4:00 that afternoon to decide to do this. As soon as Bekman had Raaben's written authorization he divided the city into four sections and systematically swept the rioters from the streets. During these two days of mob violence, six hundred apartments and seven hundred shops and stores were destroyed; 46 died and over 300 were wounded. Of the 800 taken into custody, 494 were arrested directly by the army.[124] Besides amply illustrating the obvious inadequacy of the rules of 1877, the Kishinev pogrom serves as a sorry indictment of the state of civil-military relations in a Russia poised on

[121] Ibid., ll. 179-180, 184.

[122] For the report of Lieutenant General Bekman, head of the Kishinev garrison, see TsGVIA, f. 400, op. 3, d. 2493, ll. 313-314.

[123] TsGVIA, f. 400, op. 3, d. 2496, ll. 103-106.

[124] Ibid., ll. 107-108.

the verge of war with Japan. It also helps substantiate the view that the civilians and military men in late Imperial Russia were functionally distinct from each other. Raaben, after all, had been a general in the army and a war hero of 1877. Yet to the serving officers in the Kishinev garrison he was no more than the local representative of the civilian power.[125]

The willingness of the army to bend the rules at the behest of the civilian power had eroded; the army was now willing to assume all the responsibility, or none of it. After all, Raaben had urged the army to take whatever action it deemed necessary (including firing on the crowd) but the head of the garrison refused to operate under these unlawful orders, and would only act expeditiously if Raaben surrendered all of his powers, including control of the police, to the army.

On the eve of war and revolution, the army and the civilian bureaucracy entertained fundamentally different concepts of military repression. To the civilian officials, repression was one of the chief purposes (if not *the* chief purpose) of the army, since the internal security of the state was preeminent. This being so, the military ought not to criticize the bureaucrats but obey them. For military officials, however, repression was burdensome, for it distracted the army from its authentic task of upholding the external security of the Empire. Matters were to deteriorate further in the coming years when war and revolution sharply aggravated the preexisting crisis in civil-military relations. But conflicts over repression were not solely confined to arguments over the employ of combat troops. The civilians placed heavy repressive demands on the military judicial system as well.

[125] Prince Serge Dmitriyevich Urussov, *Memoirs of a Russian Governor*, trans. Herman Rosenthal (London, 1908), pp. 57-60. Urussov points out that the rules gave the army much opportunity to be idle during the pogrom. He also states that in his opinion most of the officers of the Kishinev garrison were anti-Semitic. Yet S. M. Dubnov, *Evrei v Rossii i zapadnoi Evrope v epokhu antisemitskoi reaktsii*, vol. 2 (Moscow, 1923), pp. 39-44, largely absolves the army of responsibility for what happened at Kishinev, placing it on the civilian government.

FOUR

Civilians in Russian
Military Courts,
1881-1904

CLEMENCEAU is once supposed to have remarked that "military justice is to justice as military music is to music." These words expressed the most prevalent civilian conception of military courts: that they were arbitrary, that they did not respect due process of law, that the accused had little opportunity to clear himself, and that the punishments meted out by them were severe. For civilians in Imperial Russia, and many civilians today, military trials could be described in Hobbesian adjectives—nasty, brutish, and short.

In early nineteenth-century Russia the subjugation of civilians to military justice was a relatively common phenomenon. Nicholas I had characteristically expanded the list of crimes for which a civilian became liable to military justice. After 1833, all convicts serving terms of hard labor who committed additional offenses, and all civilians who perpetrated crimes along with soldiers fell into this category, as did peasants who rioted against military cordons after 1826, and arsonists after 1842.[1] But Russia's judicial reform of 1864 sharply reduced the number of cases in which civilian suspects were handed over to the army for trial.[2]

This civilian judicial reform provoked a parallel reform of military justice in 1867. The reform established a three-level hierarchy of military courts. At the base were regimental courts, summoned at the discretion of the regimental commanders. They handled cases of such triviality that we can pass over them here. More important were the middle-level military district courts, one for each of Russia's military districts. Military district commanders could supplement these courts, if occasion demanded it, with temporary military courts appointed for a specific locality removed from district headquarters. It was in the district courts

---

[1] John P. Le Donne, "Civilians under Military Justice during the Reign of Nicholas I," *Canadian-American Slavic Studies* 7, no. 2 (Summer 1973): passim.

[2] On this reform, see Friedhelm Berthold Kaiser, *Die Russische Justizreform von 1864* (Leiden, 1972) and Richard J. Wortman, *The Development of a Russian Legal Consciousness* (Chicago, 1976). On the reduction of civilian cases in military courts after 1864, see D. F. Ognev, *Voennaia podsudnost': sravnitel'nyi ocherk* (St. Petersburg, 1896), p. 177.

and the temporary courts that all principal cases were heard. At the apex of the military judicial system stood the Chief Military Court, which had numerous duties, including the review of cases submitted by the district courts on the basis of cassation. The Chief Military Court was in turn subordinate to the Chief Military Procurator, who was at the same time the head of the entire Main Administration of Military Justice (Glavnoe voenno-sudnoe upravlenie or GVSU). As conceived by War Minister D. A. Miliutin, the military judicial system was clearly designed to try cases involving military personnel, not civilians.[3]

But after 1878, and especially after the enactment of the "safeguard" law of 1881 and certain subsequent pieces of legislation which we will consider more fully below, the government forged instruments which made it possible for civilians indicted for a whole range of crimes to find themselves in the presence of military judges. Although the provisions of the law of 1881 that dealt with military justice were seldom invoked in the eighties or nineties, they were invoked in growing numbers of instances starting at the turn of the century. From 1905 to 1910, literally thousands of civilians would pass through military courts. It was in these latter years that the military court became a true theater of civil-military conflict. But the basic pattern of conflict had already emerged in the quarter century before the revolution of 1905. The government extended the application of military justice to civilians in this period as part of its repressive program. In political cases, the regime further desired the courts to punish the "guilty" regardless of due process of law. The military jurists, however, resented these encroachments, in part because of the traditional army hostility to bumptious civilian interference and in part because of their highly articulated legal ethos. The professionalism of the military judiciary in short led to friction between the military lawyers and the administration.

In the last two decades of the nineteenth century the most typical legal foundation for the prosecution of civilians in military courts was not "safeguard" legislation but rather provisions of the judicial reform of 1864. Article 1246 of the 1864 Code of Criminal Procedure declared that civilians who committed crimes in the company of soldiers which affected military discipline or military service were to be tried by the army. In 1898 the Council of State amplified article 1246: in the military districts of the Caucasus, Turkestan, Irkutsk, Omsk, and the Amur, civilians who abetted soldiers in the theft of arms, cartridges, or powder were similarly to be subject to military justice. In such cases, however, civilians who were convicted were not to receive military punishments;

[3] Zaionchkovskii, *Voennye reformy*, pp. 108-115.

112

rather, the military court was to award them the penalties fixed by civilian law for their offenses.[4] From 1881 to 1903 military courts tried between two hundred and one thousand civilians a year in accordance with these laws. Table 9 separates the military defendants from the civilian cases heard in military district court (cases tried under "exceptional" legislation are excluded). The military category comprises both soldiers and civilian employees of the War Ministry, who were already subject to military law by statute.

With seventeen or eighteen thousand defendants appearing before military district courts every year, the few hundred civilians included in this tally hardly overtaxed the military judicial system. Further, most civilians were involved in simple cases that were susceptible to speedy resolution, such as petty larceny or the receipt of stolen goods. Such were the cases of the peasant Ivan Golikov, who bought a cabbage from two soldiers even though he knew it had been stolen from the military mess, and the *meshchanin* Leiba Eidel'man, who knowingly purchased fifteen horseshoes from Iakov Kuznetsnov, senior blacksmith of the 7th battery of the 25th artillery brigade.[5] In both these matters, military courts convicted and punished the civilians, but did so on the basis of the statute of civilian justices of the peace. Although it might seem ridiculous to call an entire military court into session merely to stand in for a local justice of the peace or land captain, the rationale was that military justice should try such cases as a courtesy to the army.

But if cases like the above were the typical cases of civilians in military courts for the last twenty years of the nineteenth century, there were a variety of atypical cases, resulting from the application of the notorious law of August 14, 1881. This measure, drafted by a state driven to desperation in its attempts to extirpate the revolutionary People's Will Movement, prescribed rules by which provinces and entire regions of the Empire could be placed under exceptional states of emergency. In that event, the police and the Ministry of the Interior had greatly enhanced authority to take steps to defend public order. The law defined two degrees of emergency status: reinforced safeguard and extraordinary safeguard. The Minister of the Interior could proclaim the first if agitation or conspiracy against governmental or private security seemed so ominous in a region that the preservation of order by means of regular

---

[4] *Ustav ugolovnogo sudoproizvodstva, Prodolzhenie svoda zakonov 1906 g.* (St. Petersburg, 1907), vol. 16, pt. 1, arts. 1246, 1248.

[5] *Resheniia glavnogo voennogo suda 1903-1908 gg.* (St. Petersburg, 1903-1909), pp. 94, 135-136. Both of these cases were heard on cassation in the Chief Military Court. Civilian lawyers argued that these two defendants were wrongly tried by the army. The Chief Military Court rejected these pleas on the basis of numerous precedents.

TABLE 9
Military District Court Cases

Year	Total number of defendants	Military		Civilians	
		Convicted	Acquitted or released	Convicted	Acquitted or released
1881	18,872	811	9,142	531	1,088
1882	18,532	7,644	9,766	564	564
1883	17,311	6,841	9,652	520	298
1884	18,785	7,260	10,268	584	673
1885	17,240	6,746	9,279	448	767
1886	16,307	5,979	9,408	476	448
1887	17,076			291	773
1888	15,989	5,632	9,627	216	514
1889	16,104	5,390	10,275	111	329
1890	15,942	4,738	10,904	198	102
1891	15,571	15,140—total Military		531—total Civilians	
1892	17,749	4,412	11,852	740	745
1895	15,010	4,230	10,492	154	134
1899	18,002	3,927	13,848	68	159
1900	17,197	3,661	13,365	56	115
1902	18,833	3,630	14,889	74	240
1903	18,711	3,842	14,626	87	156

SOURCES: *Otchet po glavnomu voenno-sudnomu upravleniiu za 1881* (St. Petersburg, 1883), p. 10; . . . *za 1882* (St. Petersburg, 1884), pp. 10-11; . . . *za 1883* (St. Petersburg, 1885), p. 11; . . . *za 1884* (St. Petersburg, 1886), pp. 10-11; . . . *za 1885* (St. Petersburg, 1887), p. 11; . . . *za 1886* (St. Petersburg, 1888), p. 11; . . . *za 1887* (St. Petersburg, 1889), p. 10; . . . *za 1888* (St. Petersburg, 1890), p. 10; . . . *za 1889* (St. Petersburg, 1891), p. 12; . . . *za 1890* (St. Petersburg, 1892), p. 11; . . . *za 1891* (St. Petersburg, 1893), p. 14; . . . *za 1892* (St. Petersburg, 1895), p. 11; . . . *za 1895* (St. Petersburg, 1897), p. 11; . . . *za 1899* (St. Petersburg, 1901), p. 11; . . . *za 1900* (St. Petersburg, 1902), p. 11; . . . *za 1901* (St. Petersburg, 1903), pp. 10-11; . . . *za 1902* (St. Petersburg, 1904), p. 11; . . . *za 1903* (St. Petersburg, 1905), p. 11

laws was impossible. An Imperially approved decision of the Committee of Ministers was required to introduce extraordinary safeguard—designed for situations in which propaganda or conspiracies had "seriously spread" among the population. Reinforced safeguard expired automatically after a year; extraordinary, after six months. If the Minister of the Interior wanted to prolong safeguard he had to make a special representation on this subject to the Committee of Ministers. In areas under reinforced safeguard, the governor-general (or governor or *gradonachal'nik*) arbitrarily could imprison any citizen for three months, impose fines of up to 500 rubles, prohibit meetings, and expel individuals from the territory. If extraordinary safeguard was in effect, the governor-general or other official designated by the sovereign was to assume the powers of a commander in chief in wartime. He enjoyed all rights granted the civilian administration under the rules for reinforced safeguard and could, in addition, sequester property used for criminal purposes, impose 3,000-ruble fines, remove even elected officials from zemstvo or gentry institutions, suspend any publication, and close any school for a period of up to one month. Provisions for military trials were appended to these awesome administrative powers in both states of safeguard. If a province was under reinforced safeguard, the governor-general or the Ministry of the Interior could transfer any case to military courts if it was "essential" to do so to preserve public order and peace. If a governor-general possessed the additional powers of extraordinary safeguard he could send any case to a military court without any justification whatsoever. Trials conducted on the basis of safeguard could be closed to the public. Most important, not only were the accused to be tried by military law, but by the military law of wartime, which mandated more severe punishments than the military law of peace. In addition, civilians convicted of armed resistance or attacks on soldiers or officials on duty were to receive the punishment prescribed by article 279 of the Military Code of Punishments—that is, the death penalty.[6]

All of this meant that in safeguarded areas it was possible to try civilians under laws that were harsher than those that applied to the army itself. After all, civilians were to be tried by the military laws of war, soldiers by the military laws of peace. Thus, if safeguard were in effect and a soldier murdered his commanding officer, the most he could receive from a military court was a lifetime of hard labor; however, if a civilian drew a knife on a policeman, the same military court would be constrained to put him to death.

[6] *Prilozhenie 1 k st. 1 (prim. 2) Svoda ustavov o preduprazhdenii i presechenii prestuplenii. Polozhenie o merakh okhraneniiu gosudarstvennago poriadka i obshchestvennago spokoistviia 14 avg. 1881 g.* (St. Petersburg n.d.), arts. 4, 6, 9, 12, 14, 15, 16, 17, 18, 19, 24, 25, and 26.

When enacted, the law of 1881 was intended as a temporary measure. Writing to the Ministry of the Interior in 1882, the Ministry of Justice envisioned a time when the voiding of the law would cause "the immediate reestablishment of the full force of laws valid in ordinary situations."[7] Yet the government never relinquished safeguard, which, as the years passed, became more and more a standard means of administration. Indeed, the regime continuously issued decrees which either enhanced safeguard or were analogous to it. For example, in 1887, the Committee of Ministers appended a series of rules for places *not* under safeguard to the original law. These rules, activated anywhere in the Empire at the discretion of the Committee of Ministers, empowered the police to detain any person suspected of state crimes for a week. The Minister of the Interior and the Minister of Justice could, moreover, send any cases they desired to military courts to be tried by the laws of war. Now there was no corner in the Empire in which a civilian could hide from the rigors of military justice.[8]

Still later the government promulgated yet another set of laws which would send civilians to the gallows as a result of military court decisions. Laws of July 29, 1891 and January 25, 1893 prescribed military courts and death sentences for damage to the Transcaucasian or Vladikavkaz railways or for armed assault on their officials or passengers. On September 13, 1893, the same legal arrangements were instituted for tribesmen of the Caucasus or Stavropol' Province found guilty of banditry, murder, arson, or rebellion.[9] In 1892, the administration unveiled a further decree on martial law. Framed with a view to an actual future state of war, the law placed all civil administration within the theater of military operations in the hands of military officials. Those sections of the act which discussed the subordination of civilians to military justice were merely rearrangements of the articles of the law of 1881.[10] Even if foreign enemies were to invade the country, the Russian government could contrive no harsher penalties for its civilian criminals than those legislated in 1881.

MILITARY JUDICIAL REPRESSION IN PRACTICE

How many civilians found themselves at the bar of military courts as a result of these "emergency laws"? Table 10 provides some sense of how the laws were used.

[7] TsGAOR, f. 102, op. 136, d. 27, 153, 1881 g., l. 20.

[8] *Polozhenie*, art. 31.

[9] K[uz'min]-K[aravaev]. [V.D.], "Smertnaia kazn' po voenno-ugolovnym zakonam," *BE*, vol. 30a (St. Petersburg, 1895), p. 500.

[10] *Obshchee uchrezhdenie gubernskoe, SZ* (St. Petersburg) 2 (1892), st. 23 Prilozhenie.

TABLE 10

Civilians Tried by Military Courts on the Basis of
Exceptional Legislation

Year	No. & (if known) types of cases	No. of defendants	Penalties imposed (if known)
1881	66: 11 state crimes	25	
	50 pogroms	287	
1882	40: 31 pogroms	239	111 acquitted
	5 prison guard murders	30	4 katorga
	1 resistance to rural police	3	4 exile
1883	5	40	17 katorga
			4 exile
1884	10	206	2 to hang
			34 acquitted
1885	9	118	7 to hang
			36 acquitted
1886	7	74	4 to hang
			13 acquitted
1887	9	55	2 to hang
			53 acquitted
1888	0		
1892	12: cholera riots	638	239 acquitted
			81 to hang*
1898	3: 1 espionage	9	23 to hang
	1 Fergai rebellion-Turkestan (martial law)	420	374 katorga
	1 banditry-Turkestan (martial law)	34	
1899	1: Fergai rebellion	5	5 to hang†
1902		15	13 to hang
1903		30	4 to hang
1904		18	6 to hang†

Sources: *Vsepoddanneishii doklad po voennomu ministerstvu, 1882 goda* (St. Petersburg, 1882), p. 65; *1883 goda*, pp. 99-100; *1884 goda*, p. 105; *1885 goda*, p. 111; *... za 1886*, p. 100; *... za 1888*, p. 76; *... za 1889*, pp. 76-77; *... za 1892*, p. 65; *... za 1893*, p. 83; TsGVIA, f. 1, op. 3, d. 158, l. 18; TsGVIA, f. 1, op. 2, d. 159, l. 19; TsGVIA, f. 1, op. 2, d. 162, ll. 20, 34; TsGVIA, f. 1, op. 2, d. 163, ll. 23, 40; TsGVIA, f. 801, op. 56/79, d. 27, ll. 184-185.

Note: Data are incomplete; some years are not represented.

* 78 of these commuted to hard labor.

† All commuted to hard labor.

The original purpose of the law of 1881 had been to unleash the military courts against criminals of state. This is precisely what occurred at first. Forty-two of the seventy-three People's Will trials of the 1880s were heard in military courts. But revolutionary populism of the terrorist variety was largely handled by the military courts in the first years of the decade. Thereafter, and up to 1903, there were in fact very few cases of state crimes tried in military courts. The archives of the Police Department reveal that from 1885 to 1903 there were only seventeen cases of state crimes tried in this fashion. Yet the majority of even these cases did not concern the exposure of underground socialist plots. The category of state crimes naturally included treason as well as conspiracies against the government. A full eleven of these seventeen cases were espionage cases, and in eight of these, the chief defendants were foreigners—Austrian or Prussian subjects.[11] The rest of the civilians tried by the army in the period before 1905 were generally common criminals—rapists, murderers, and bandits. Governors, especially governors in the Empire's more remote and wilder provinces, often stretched the phrase in the 1881 act about crimes which endangered the public order to include felons of this type. In any event, governors in "safeguarded" provinces were *required* to send cases involving armed resistance to the police to the army. And it was just as easy for a burglar to take a shot at a policeman in hot pursuit as it was for a revolutionary, working over his clandestine printing press, to reach for his revolver when the gendarmes surprised him. Thus Biaram Ogly, who robbed and then stabbed a Cossack on a road in Krasnovodsk uezd one summer day in 1891, found himself in the Turkestan Military District Court.[12] In the same fashion, when in 1899 Ivan Bonaskik and Anton Patsuk ambushed some Yenesei peasants returning home from work in the goldfields, shot one, and covered another with kerosene and burned him alive, making off with sixty rubles, the Siberian Military District Court sentenced them to death.[13] The Amur Military Court, likewise, tried exile Ustin Sharenov and his son Dmitrii for slaughtering an entire family in the course of a 1904 robbery.[14] The Amur Court also sat in judgment over settlers R. Skidlovskii and Ia. Steblianskii, accused of murdering a local priest and his entire family in an exceptionally "bestial" fashion.[15]

---

[11] N. A. Troitskii, *Tsarskie sudy protiv revoliutsionnoi Rossii. Politicheskie protsessy 1871-1880 g.g.* (Saratov, 1976), pp. 335-336; N. A. Troitskii, *"Narodnaia volia" pered tsarskim sudom 1880-1901 g.g.* (Saratov, 1971), pp. 106-107. TsGAOR, f. DP, 7th deloproizvodstvo, d. 450, t. III, 1882 g. (sic), ll. 17-22.

[12] *Otchet po glavnomu voenno-sudnomu upravleniiu za 1891* (St. Petersburg), p. 25.

[13] TsGAOR, f. 102, op. 136, d. 27, 153, 1881 g., ll. 36, 42.

[14] TsGVIA, f. 801, op. 56-49, d. 26, 1905 g., l. 14.

[15] "Khronika," *Pravo*, no. 11 (Mar. 9, 1903): 803-804.

Yet even if the largest contingents of civilians sentenced by military courts on the basis of the "exceptional" laws were spies, traitors, and vicious felons, the law entered the statute books as a weapon against the revolutionaries. Why did the government prefer military justice in its attempt to grapple with the problems of revolutionary activity and public disorder?

THE BENEFITS OF MILITARY JUDICIAL REPRESSION

It is one of the ironies of Russian history that the liberalization of society during the reform era was coterminous with the appearance of violent opposition to the regime, as was represented by the Karakozov assassination attempt of 1866 and the Nechaev circle of the late sixties. The government was frankly apprehensive about dispatching cases of state crime to its newly reformed civilian courts. In order to try Karakozov, for instance, the government created a special tribunal outside the regular judicial system.[16] Yet the ambivalence of the government is illustrated by the fact that it continued at times to rely on the ordinary courts of the Ministry of Justice to prosecute state criminals, albeit on such non-political charges as murder. But after "light sentences" were handed down in the case of the Nechaevists in 1872, the government resolved to invent a mechanism for exempting certain sorts of state criminal trials from the regular judicial process as a matter of course. In June of 1872 a decree made it possible to try political cases without a jury in a special office of the Governing Senate (Osoboe prisutsvie pravitel'stvuiushchego senata or OPPS). Here the judges were senators chosen by the Emperor and representatives of certain estate organizations chosen by the Minister of the Interior. Departures from the criminal code of 1864 were permitted in the OPPS, including the closing of trials to the public. Between 1873 and 1878, thirty-seven of the fifty-two political cases in Russia were tried by the OPPS. Regular courts did still hear some political cases; however, after the celebrated acquittal of Vera Zasulich in 1878 for the attempted assassination of General Trepov, the government recognized that public jury trials for terrorists were decidedly risky. Even the OPPS was not entirely satisfactory: in the first place, the judges occasionally displayed too much mercy for the government's taste; in the second place, OPPS trials all had to occur in St. Petersburg itself, which entailed delays, high costs, and excessive publicity.[17] Accordingly, in August of 1878 the regime enacted the first in a series of laws on the transfer to military courts of cases involving persons who resisted the authorities

[16] Adam B. Ulam, *In the Name of the People: Prophets and Conspirators in Prerevolutionary Russia* (New York, 1977), p. 165.
[17] Troitskii, *Tsarskie sudy*, pp. 101-104, 207.

with force, laws which were later superseded by the "safeguard" legislation of 1881. Highly placed civilian officials deemed the military courts to be much more suitable for repression than either the courts of the Ministry of Justice or the OPPS. Trials in military courts were faster than in civilian tribunals. And the decentralized military judicial system was obviously more convenient for the government than the central OPPs. Further, it was more difficult in a military court for a revolutionary to turn the proceedings into a carnival or to make inflammatory speeches from the dock than it was in civilian courts. When Pobedonostsev wrote Alexander III about the would-be regicides apprehended in 1887, he urged that they be consigned to a military court "where the procedure is swifter and simpler" than in the OPPS.[18] Under civilian law defendants were either tried by juries in courts presided over by irremovable judges or tried in the OPPS where the majority of the judges were irremovable senators.[19] In military trials, cases were not heard by juries but by panels of military justices who could be removed or transferred by the Chief Military Procurator. Yet there was another reason to favor military courts in political cases: such courts were more likely to hand down harsh sentences, including the death penalty.[20]

In decrees of 1753 and 1754 Elizabeth Petrovna had abolished the death penalty in all civilian courts within the Russian Empire. Catherine the Great had resurrected it for state crimes. The code of 1832 had added that it could be used against those who violated quarantine regulations (a response to the recent epidemic of cholera in the Empire). By the terms of the third and fourth editions of the Code of Punishments (1866 and 1885), then, the only capital crimes in civilian law were breaking quarantine, conspiring against the person or rights of the Emperor, and plotting to overthrow the government.[21] After the new Criminal Code was introduced in 1903, conspiring against Russia's fundamental laws and system of succession as well as attempts to separate any section of the Empire from the rest also became punishable by death.[22]

In peacetime, military law generally recognized only two applications of the death penalty: against a criminal who attacked a sentry who was

[18] *Pis'ma Pobedonostseva k Aleksandru III*, vol. 2 (Moscow, 1926), p. 140.

[19] Samuel Kucherov, *Courts, Trials and Lawyers under the Last Three Tsars* (New York, 1953), pp. 93-94.

[20] N. A Troitskii, *Tsarizm pod sudom progressivnoi obshchestvennosti 1866-1895 g.g.* (Moscow, 1979), p. 60 for Durnovo's views on this subject.

[21] Mikhail Gubskii, "Smertnaia kazn'," *BE*, vol. 30a (St. Petersburg, 1895), p. 497.

[22] TsGVIA, f. 801, op. 39/45, d. 31, l. 5. Also see N. S. Tagantsev, ed., *Ugolovnoe ulozhenie 22 marta 1903 g.* (St. Petersburg, 1904), pp. 181, 188, 195 (arts. 99, 100, 101, 102 and 108).

guarding the person of the Emperor and against a spy. But, as we have seen, civilians who were ushered into military district courts on the basis of the safeguard law were tried under the military laws of war, and these prescribed some thirty cases in which hanging or shooting were permitted. Although civilians hardly could lose the regimental colors, surrender an army to the enemy without resistance, or desert the battlefield, they were capable of premeditated murder, banditry, robbery, and rape. And the military courts were empowered to try cases on bases other than military law. The safeguard decree with its mandatory death sentences for armed resistance to the authorities is a case in point.[23] Further, the government was often willing to have military courts rather than civilian ones hear cases of revolutionary conspiracy punishable by death under civilian judicial statutes.

From the foregoing, one might entertain the misconception that military judges in Imperial Russia were the servile and bloodthirsty Slavic equivalents of such hanging judges as George Jeffreys or Isaac C. Parker. To be sure, the military laws of the war contained obligatory death sentences for a range of offenses. To be sure, the military judiciary was less independent and more susceptible to outside pressure than the civilian. Indictments were also easier in military courts where they were frequently handed down on the sole basis of policy inquiry rather than preliminary judicial investigation. Procedural irregularities did occur: Soviet historian N. A. Troitskii has assembled numerous examples of them in the military courts which tried members of the People's Will in the early eighties.[24] And military courts did indeed pass death sentences, some ninety-three against soldiers and civilians from 1901 to 1904 alone.[25] But military courts were not merely kangaroo tribunals from which the government could always squeeze any sentence it desired. The structure of Russian military justice, the legal education of military judicial personnel, and the attitudes and practices of that personnel all buttressed due process of law.

MILITARY JUSTICE AND THE LEGAL ETHOS

After the military judicial reform of 1867 the majority of military trials were public, and the adversary system obtained in military as well as

[23] TsGVIA, f. 801, op. 39/45, d. 31, ll. 3-5.

[24] Troitskii, *Tsarizm*, pp. 66-67; N. A. Troitskii, *Bezumstvo khrabykh. Russkie revoliutsionery i karatel'naia politika tsarisma 1866-1882 g.* (Moscow, 1978), pp. 189-190.

[25] Ia. L. Berman, "Deiatel'nost' voenno-okruzhnykh i polkovykh sudov," *Pravo*, no. 13 (Sept. 8, 1913), p. 2063.

civilian courtrooms.[26] In fact, save for the absence of jurors, military and civilian criminal procedure were identical; the procedural articles of the military judicial code were transcribed word for word from the corresponding articles of the civilian legal statutes.[27] When a soldier was prosecuted, the court appointed a defense attorney from among the young military jurists (called candidates) attached to it. This was disadvantageous to the accused, since the military prosecutor often had more service seniority than the president of the court himself. A contest between an experienced prosecutor with the rank of major general and a fledgling defense attorney who was a captain might well be unequal. Pobedonostsev obviously supposed that this system of assigning court-appointed attorneys was retained when civilians were in the dock. Writing of the assassination conspiracy of 1887, in the letter quoted above, he declared that "it is difficult to prevent the participation of defense attorneys, as they are required by law in military courts, too, and also an interdiction of defense attorneys would require a special imperial order which in the present case is undesirable. But in this regard the military court is more convenient, because it itself appoints a defense attorney for the accused from its candidates, and in the special office of the senate the accused may choose anyone they wish from the outside."[28] Pobedonostsev was mistaken, however. Military courts often permitted civilians to select the civilian attorneys of their choice, and in prerevolutionary Russia gifted radical lawyers willing to represent clients in military as well as civilian courts were not lacking, even though in military courts legal erudition and guile counted for more than the mealy-mouthed eloquence which was presumed so notoriously effective with Russian juries. A War Ministry circular of 1882 had forbidden both prosecutors and defense attorneys in military courts to employ "insulting remarks, inappropriate criticism, metaphor, allegory or any other oratorical tricks."[29] A further right all defendants in district military courts enjoyed was that of appeal to the Supreme Military Court in Petersburg. This right was not inviolate since governors-general, or, in their absence, military district commanders who confirmed the sentences of the courts, also had the power to quash appeals. Yet in significant numbers of cases,

---

[26] Kucherov, *Courts, Trials and Lawyers*, p. 50. See also *Svod voennykh postanovlenii,* 3rd prodolzhenie, bks. 22 and 24, 1868.

[27] M. V. Dukhovskii, *Russkii ugolovnyi protsess* (Moscow, 1910), pp. 426-428.

[28] *Pis'ma Pobedonostseva,* p. 140.

[29] "Voenny sudy," *BE,* vol. 6a (St. Petersburg, 1891), p. 858. "Iz obshchestvennoi khroniki," *Vestnik Evropy* 17, no. 6 (June 1882): 901-903. For examples of civilian legal "eloquence," see A. B. Bobrishchev-Pushkin, *Sudebnye rechi,* vol. 1 (St. Petersburg, 1909), passim.

and especially in those where civilians had been tried on capital charges, appeals were allowed to go through. Frunze, among other noted revolutionaries, was to owe his life to this right of appeal.[30]

The caliber of the officials of the Main Administration of Military Justice was in itself a guarantee of due process. In 1900 there were eleven military district courts of the Empire (eight in European Russia, plus those of Turkestan, Siberia, and the Amur). Each of these courts had a chief justice or president, in addition to a prosecutor and a directorate of prosecutions, which included a team of military investigators. Fifty-one officers held the position of military judge in Europe and fourteen in the Asiatic territories of the Empire.[31] To be sure, both regular military district courts and special temporary courts had so-called temporary as well as permanent members. The district commander appointed the former to six-month terms from among the field officers of his district headquarters. They sat on the courts with the right of military judges. Although these temporary members were theoretically the equal of permanent members, it was in fact the permanent members—the court president and the military judges—who dominated the court.[32] And after 1883 all permanent members had received advanced juridical training, in most cases at the Military Judicial Academy, which after 1898, was called the Alexander Academy of Military Justice.

The Alexander Academy was founded shortly after Miliutin's comprehensive military judicial reform of 1867, but it was Lt. Gen. P. O. Bobrovskii's reform of the Academy itself in 1878 which stamped it with its final character.[33] As was true of the Nicholas Staff Academy, admissions were highly competitive. In 1884, eighty officers applied for fifteen places at the school.[34] The difficult entrance examination stressed literature (familiarity with the works of Nekrasov, Dostoevsky, and Tolstoi was required as early as 1886), history, physics, chemistry, military administration, French, and German.[35] Again, just as at the Staff Academy, only the students who had most distinguished themselves in the first two years of study were permitted to enroll in the third and final year of the course. Students in the first and second year attended

[30] TsGVIA, f. 801, op. 7, d. 10/28, 1909 g., l. 100; see also A. Skobennikov, "M. V. Frunze (Arsenii) na kartoge i v ssylke," *Katorga i ssylka* (Moscow) 20 (1925): 250-254.

[31] TsGVIA, f. 970, op. 3, d. 600, ll. 149-150.

[32] Zaionchkovskii, *Voennye reformy*, pp. 103-115; F. Kon, "Voennye sudy v Tsarstve Pol'skom," *Katorga i ssylka* (Moscow) 19 (1925): 148.

[33] *Tret'e dopolnenie k zhurnalam konferentsii voenno-iuridicheskoi akademii gody 1893-1896* (St. Petersburg, 1896), p. 53.

[34] TsGVIA, f. 348, op. 1, d. 375, ll. 18-42.

[35] TsGVIA, f. 1, op. 2, d. 1140, l. 60.

lectures which were exclusively devoted to legal theory, languages, and civilian legal practice.[36] The study of military law did not begin until the third year.

There are three salient points to be made about the training and atmosphere of the Alexander Academy from 1880 until 1914. Like any modern law school, the Academy was more interested in inculcating abstract principles of legal reasoning ("learning how to think like a lawyer") than it was in rearing legal functionaries and technicians. But in doing this, the Academy placed considerable emphasis on the comparative approach, and more specifically, the study of Western law. Students in first- and second-year courses sat through lectures on the laws of constitutional states. Volodimirov's course on criminal procedure, taught from 1881 to the mid-nineties, devoted as much attention to France and Britain as it did to Russia, at least to judge by his lecture outline. Even the course on police law offered at the Academy included frequent references to what was happening abroad—in this case, the solicitude of Western governments for public welfare, health, and disease prevention.[37] The bias toward Europe was also evident in the holdings of the Academy's library. In 1899 the library contained 1,313 volumes in Russian on general law, including treatments of the law of Russia. Yet it also possessed 1,044 copies of books on the law of foreign countries.[38]

Of course the Alexander Academy did furnish its students with training in the techniques and procedures of military justice, but such training was concentrated in the third year of the course. Lectures on military criminal procedure, forensic medicine, military administrative law and the rest were supplemented by frequent field trips to prisons, courtrooms, and interestingly, by the constant reenactment of actual military judicial cases in moot courts. These cases, selected from the archives of the St. Petersburg Military District Court, were retried by groups of five or six officers who worked together throughout the year.[39] The Academy organized the moot courts in such a fashion that each officer had the opportunity to play each of the important court actors at least once in

[36] On the course of study in the Academy before the 1878-1879 reform, see TsGVIA, f. 348, op. 1, d. 202; f. 348, op. 1, d. 200; for the course introduced after the reform, see TsGVIA, f. 348, op. 1, d. 236, ll. 28-29; f. 348, op. 1, d. 241, d. 360, d. 332, ll. 6, 13-14, d. 345, d. 283, d. 260.

[37] TsGVIA, f. 348, op. 1, d. 220, ll. 8, 64-71.

[38] Calculated on the basis of *Biblioteka Aleksandrovskoi voenno-iuridicheskoi akademii. Sistematicheskii katalog*, Parts 1-3 (St. Petersburg, 1899). I have subtracted from the total of books on Russian laws 369 copies of Russian statutes, 46 books on Roman law, and 46 books on international law.

[39] TsGVIA, f. 348, op. 1, d. 345, l. 24; TsGVIA, f. 348, op. 1, d. 715, l. 2.

the year. Every officer consequently served as prosecutor, defending attorney, chairman of the court, clerk, and military judge.[40] This system of training had obvious heuristic advantages of which the most important was its exact correspondence to the reality of the military judicial administration. Any jurist who put in thirty years of service would at one time or another occupy all of these posts in real courts.

The last significant feature of the Alexander Academy was that it boasted a faculty of famous and highly respected scholars, many of them with reputations for "liberalism." As we have seen earlier, P. S. Vannovskii's counterreform of military education had resulted in the expulsion of civilian teachers from military classrooms. The Alexander Academy represented a vivid exception to this trend, and indeed, in the nineties and in the early years of the twentieth century, the majority of teachers at the Academy were civilians. Thirteen of the eighteen professors and lecturers at the Academy in 1890/1891 were civilians, as were thirteen of the nineteen in 1901/1902.[41] Such learned and revered civilian jurists as K. D. Kavelin, N. M. Korkunov, S. A. Bershadskii, N. D. Sergeevskii, and N. A. Nekliudov held Academy professorships.[42]

In terms of its curriculum, educational philosophy, and faculty, the Alexander Academy of Military Justice closely resembled a civilian law school.[43] Since the civilian law schools and the lawyers who graduated from them were among the strongest supporters of the *Rechtsstaat* concept in late nineteenth-century Russia, it is not surprising that military jurists, like their civilian colleagues, were unhappy with extralegal problem solving on the part of the government, including the subjection of civilians to military courts on the basis of the 1881 law. Volodimirov, among other Academy professors, publicly condemned this practice on technical grounds.[44]

Some military jurists trod the path of "liberalism" still farther. V. D. Kuz'min-Karavaev, first in his class at the Alexander Academy in 1883, taught all the courses in military criminal procedure in the Academy during the nineties. In 1901, as a major general and professor, he was placed in charge of the Academy's entire moot court program.[45] Yet

[40] On rules for moot courts, see *Pervoe dopolnenie k zhurnalam konferentsii voenno-iuridicheskoi akademii (gody 1889-91)* (St. Petersburg), 1891, pp. 85-88.

[41] TsGVIA, f. 348, op. 1, d. 360, ll. 15-16; TsGVIA, f. 348. op. 1, d. 505, ll. 1-2.

[42] *Pervoe dopolnenie*, pp. 144-145.

[43] "Aleksandrovskaia voenno-iuridicheskaia akademiia," *BE*, vol. 1 (St. Petersburg, 1890), p. 251.

[44] K. Shavrov, "Predanie voennomu sudu grazhdanskikh lits dlia suzhdeniia po zakonam voennogo vremeni'," *Pravo*, no. 10 (Mar. 4, 1901): 534-535. Also see Ognev, *Voennaia podsudnost'*, pp. 189-190; Wortman, *Russian Legal Consciousness*, pp. 279-281, 288.

[45] TsGVIA, f. 348, op. 1, d. 360, l. 5; d. 5-5, l. 64.

he was one of the most implacable foes of capital punishment in the Russian Empire. In 1900 he wrote a piece for the Brockhaus/Efron encyclopedia which denounced executions even under martial law.[46] And as a delegate in both of the first two Dumas, he was a sponsor of the bills to abolish the death penalty.

To state that the Academy enjoyed a modest success in inculcating respect for the law and abhorred administrative arbitrariness (*proizvol*), is not the same as arguing that all Academy graduates were bubbling over with enthusiasm for these ideals. Legal-mindedness could be compared to a vaccination performed by the Academy, and in some rather spectacular cases the vaccination did not take. The repulsive P. G. Kurlov, who eventually as assistant head of the Police Department was responsible for numerous political provocations, was third in his Academy class in 1888. One of his instructors in that year praised his talent, his intellectual capacities, his knowledge and legal oratory.[47] Still, the Academy embodied the idea of a professional, military-legal ethos. However respectful of the powers of the state they were, the Academy's professors were all deeply devoted to the concept of legality (*zakonnost'*). When Nicholas II in 1910 called three of the Academy's professors leftists, this presumably is what he had in mind.[48]

The majority of the 902 military jurists who graduated from the Academy from 1878 to 1910 took away with them a highly developed legal ethos. This ethos found expression both in regular cases and in those cases in which civilian defendants were indicted under "exceptional" legislation. Absolute scrupulousness and fairness in these latter cases was the avowed policy of the Main Administration of Military Justice. As the Supreme Military Court declared in March 1903: "The handing over to military courts of persons who are not indicted under the ordinary order of procedure, with the application to the convicted of punishments established by the laws of war, is an extreme measure and is obviously called for by extreme necessity. Therefore military courts are obligated to take appropriate pains to establish those circumstances which mitigate the guilt of the accused."[49] Of course, in specific cases governmental pressure could and did influence military court decisions. But in bending to the wishes of civilian authorities, subverting

[46] *BE*, vol. 30a (St. Petersburg, 1895), p. 500.

[47] TsGVIA, f. 348, op. 1, d. 320, l. 105.

[48] A. A. Polivanov, *Iz dnevnikov i vospominanii po dolzhnosti voennogo ministra i ego pomoshchnika 1907-1916 gg.*, ed. A. M. Zaionchkovskii, vol. 1 (Moscow, 1924), p. 100.

[49] *Resheniia glavnogo voennogo suda 1903-1908 gg.* (St. Petersburg, 1908-1909), p. 66.

the law in the interests of repression, military judges were acting against their training and instincts.

Generally, military courts strove to respect due process in the trials of civilians. Thus, improperly prepared indictments were frequently dismissed.[50] Further, on occasion military courts handed down sentences in strict accord with the law regardless of whether this was vexatious to the civil government or to the Emperor himself. High governmental officials were stunned, for example, by the "leniency" of the Kiev District Court in the trial of the twelve in 1884. And Alexander III was appalled in 1886 when the Military Court of the Caucasus failed to order the execution of the underage murderer of rector Chudetskii.[51] G. Filat'ev, reviewing the history of civilian crimes of state in military courts for the entire period 1902-1912, observed that the courts acquitted a larger proportion of defendants in such cases than in any other variety of case.[52] This evidence might imply that at least some military judges sought to shirk the responsibility of passing harsh sentences, including the sentence of death. In any event, there is no doubt that the Military Justice Administration (GVSU) itself regarded the presence of civilians in military courtrooms as a heavy drain on its judicial resources, and the trying of such persons as extraneous to its primary responsibilities.[53] The annual military judicial reports always listed cases tried on the basis of exceptional laws separately from those cases which justly came within military judicial provenance. Statistics on exceptional trials of civilians were never included in calculations of total number of cases or defendants. The rough draft of an internal memorandum prepared within the GVSU in September of 1907 pointed out that military courts had originally been created with the interests of the army in mind. Now, however, the courts had assumed the "honorable burden and heavy duty" of trying civilians. A GVSU official, perhaps even the recipient of the memo, Chief Military Procurator Ryl'ke, crossed out the word honorable.[54]

Almost as if embarrassed by the role of hangman to the autocracy,

---

[50] TsGVIA, f. 801, op. 56/79, d. 26, l. 14 contains a typical example from Vil'na Military District court in 1904.

[51] Troitskii, *Tsarizm*, p. 70; *Pis'ma Pobedonostseva*, p. 114.

[52] G. Filat'ev, "Dorevoliutsionnye voennye sudy v tsifrakh," *Katorga i ssylka* (Moscow), 7, no. 68 (1930): 1551.

[53] For example, see the report for 1898 in TsGVIA, f. 1, op. 2, d. 158, l. 18, where the author is careful to distinguish between cases undertaken as a result of "primary responsibilities" of the Military Justice Administration, and those "exceptional" cases which were not.

[54] TsGVIA, f. 1, op. 1, d. 7087, l. 44. I make the assumption that the crossing out was done at the time the memo was received based on the similarity of pencilled marginalia with the lines drawn through the word "honorable."

the Military Justice Administration ignored the problems created by its civilian trials. No special educational efforts were *ever made* to train officers to deal with them. At no time from 1880 to 1914 did any of the moot court cases studied at the Alexander Academy feature a civilian defendant tried as a result of the law of 1881, martial law, or the law on banditry in the Caucasus. Such cases were not included in the academy curriculum even during the years 1906-1908, when a full one-third to one-half of all cases the army tried were exactly of this type, so that the newly graduated military jurist confronted cases like this as soon as he took up his duties in any military court of the Empire from the Far East to Poland.[55]

The pressure on the Military Justice Administration was to increase geometrically with the huge influx of civilian cases during the first Russian revolution. Military judges severally adapted to the conditions of the revolution. Some stepped into the forefront of the reaction, eagerly participating in the counterrevolutionary bloodbath. Others, probably the majority, continued to observe the traditions of legality and fairness, refusing to subvert the law at the whim of the government. At least a few did everything in their power, including twisting the law, to avoid passing sentences of death. When Ministry of Justice official Khrulev urged the abolition of the trials of civilians in military courts in 1905, he did so not because he regarded them as inhumane, but because he deemed them a failure as a deterrent. Since in a significant number of cases, persons who were obviously guilty were eluding capital punishment in these courts, the prospective criminal might hope that he might be equally lucky. This hope undercut the deterrent emotions of fear and terror which the military courts were supposed to inspire.[56]

---

[55] TsGVIA, f. 348, op. 1, d. 360, ll. 35-37; TsGVIA, f. 348, op. 1, d. 505, ll. 3-63; TsGVIA, f. 348, op. 1, d. 320, passim; TsGVIA, f. 348, op. 1, d. 345, l. 40; TsGVIA, f. 348, op. 1, d. 587, ll. 48-49; TsGVIA, f. 348, op. 1, d. 683, ll. 13-14; TsGVIA, f. 348, op. 1, d. 715, l. 2.

[56] *Materialy po peresmotru ustanovlennykh dlia okhrany gosudarstvennoga poriadka iskliuchitel'nykh zakonopolozhenii. XI. Zapiska Prokurora khar'kovskoi sudebnoi palaty S. S. Khruleva ob iskliuchitel'nykh zakonopolozheniiakh* (St. Petersburg, 1906), p. 8.

FIVE

Civil-Military Conflict in the Russian Revolution, 1905-1907

L'Armée est aveugle et muette. Elle frappe devant
elle du lieu où on la met. Elle ne veut rien et agit
par ressort. C'est une grand chose que l'on meut et
qui tue; mais aussi c'est une chose qui souffre.

Alfred de Vigny,
Servitude et Grandeur militaires, 1835

IN THE REVOLUTIONARY YEARS 1905-1907, a period of hysteria and bloodshed that provided the greatest challenge the Russian Empire was to know until the First World War, the army did in fact save the Imperial government from collapse. However, far from playing the part of enthusiastic helpmate to the repressive autocracy, the War Ministry discharged many of its obligations with reluctance. To what did the Ministry object? Generally it did not oppose supplying troops to civilians beleaguered by riot or open revolt. In thinking of the revolution one tends to recall the most dramatic episodes of military intervention: the army shelling the slums and barricades of Moscow, gunning down rebels in Lithuania, or reducing the mutinous towns of Siberia. However, such actions were neither typical of the army's experience in the Russian revolution nor the only important features of its involvement. According to official statistics, on only 7.9 percent of all occasions in which the army undertook repressive service in the year 1905 did the troops in fact have recourse to weapons. For 1906 the percentage was 6.4 and for 1907 (until November 1) an even lower 4.5.[1] Besides actually applying

[1] The tension between the War Ministry and the civilian government has never before received thorough treatment, in part because of efforts made by the government to prevent news of the disputes from leaking. See TsGVIA, f. 400, op. 3, d. 2862, ll. 252, 255; a recent article by Michael Perrins, "Russian Military Policy in the Far East and the 1905 Revolution in the Russian Army," *European Studies Review* 9 (1979): 331-349 makes some reference to the tension. TsGVIA, f. 1, op. 1, d. 70264, l. 23; TsGVIA, f. 400, op. 3, d. 2913, passim.

force, the other main contribution of the army to the preservation of state power during the revolution inhered in its dispersal throughout the Russian countryside, in its undertaking of guard duty—in short, in its *deterrence* of insurrection. It was precisely this deterrent role which the War Ministry could not abide.

Indeed, the army had become increasingly unhappy with this role after 1881. Since that date the War Ministry had generally argued that it was inappropriate to arm troops for any internal purpose other than the forcible suppression of unrest, which, moreover, was only justifiable if the police and gendarmes had already tried and failed. As we have seen, the army's prime objective in agitating for revision of the rules of 1887 had been to outlaw the employment of troops in a deterrent capacity. Of course, civilian ministries had long maintained that it was impossible to dispense with military deterrence and clung to that view with even more tenacity after 1905 than before.

Yet the War Ministry beginning at the end of 1905 and continuing into 1906 and 1907, pursued a policy of resistance to civilian requests for deterrent military force. In part the resistance was based on the War Ministry's mistrust of the Empire's provincial governors: these men had been notorious for exaggerating threats to civil peace in the prerevolutionary period and there were those at the War Ministry who held that the governors were no more credible now. But this policy was also informed by the belief that repressive service, especially prevention of disorder, took such a heavy toll on the stability and efficiency of the army that its continued existence as a professional force was put in doubt. Wedded to its own self-interest, the War Ministry at times tended to behave as if the preservation (and improvement) of the army outweighed all other considerations—even the most serious challenges to the tsarist regime. There was a third consideration allied to the second in the minds of War Ministry officials: a sense that the army's discharge of repressive duties reduced its prestige among the population—an extraordinarily dangerous phenomenon since public support was the nerve of military strength.

1905	3,893 actions	311 weapon uses	7.9%
1906	2,559 actions	164 weapon uses	6.4%
1907	1,058 actions	48 weapon uses	4.5% (to 1 November)

These 1905 and 1906 statistics for the number of actions and weapons uses are too low, both because of variances in reporting styles in the districts and because information from the punitive detachments was most likely incomplete. However, the percentage relationship between actions and uses is probably roughly correct.

The War Ministry's attitude towards prevention of disorder led to seemingly endless disputes with the civil ministries—Justice, Finance, Roads and Communications. Yet the civilian government, under Witte and later Stolypin, prevailed in the most significant of these disputes, in large measure because of a civilian-sponsored decentralization of the army. The civil power thus prevented the War Ministry from advertently or inadvertently hamstringing the state's repressive effort. By early 1908, frustrated professional ambition, concern for the deterioration of the army, and hatred for the shabby treatment meted out by the civilians had combined to produce in the War Ministry an opinion of its civilian counterparts so low and venomous that it transcends explanation in the terms of mere institutional rivalries. The legacy of the revolution would deeply scar civil-military relations in Russia; the gap between military and civilian programs and goals would grow still wider and both sides would become even less amenable to compromise.

The Russo-Japanese War

To understand the revolution of 1905 we must begin with a brief consideration of the Russo-Japanese War. The leadership of the army had not desired conflict in the East. In fact it was Witte's Ministry of Finance which in 1895 initiated the economic penetration of Manchuria, thus souring Russo-Japanese relations. Tokyo's ill-will toward Petersburg deepened when in 1897 Russia not only colluded with other powers to cheat Japan of some of the fruits of her victory over China, but occupied Kwantung herself. Thereafter, Japan began to prepare for armed conflict with Russia, while Russia, whipped on at first by Witte and later by such sinister figures as Abaza and Bezobrazov, consolidated her control in Manchuria and intrigued in Korea while blithely underestimating the seriousness of the Japanese threat.[2] War Minister Kuropatkin, preoccupied with Russia's weakness in the West, regarded the defense of Russia's new Far Eastern territories as an unwarranted drain on the army's resources.[3] If the army was to bear this burden, Kuropatkin demanded that the Ministry of Finance at least provide the appropriate sum of money. But the Ministry of Finance deliberately chose to underfund Russia's military effort in the East.[4] By January 27, 1904—the

[2] John Albert White, *The Diplomacy of the Russo-Japanese War* (Princeton, N.J., 1964), pp. 19-110, passim. Shumpei Okamoto, *The Japanese Oligarchy and the Russo-Japanese War* (New York, 1970), pp. 47-49, 71.

[3] TsGVIA, f. 1, op. 2, d. 162, l. 3 (War Ministry report for 1902 written in 1903).

[4] White, *Russo-Japanese War*, p. 143.

date of Japan's surprise attack on Port Arthur—Russia possessed a mere 98,000 soldiers, 168 field guns, and 8 machine guns in her Far Eastern military districts.[5]

Although innocent of provoking the war, the Russian army and Kuropatkin were clearly accountable for its horrendously poor conduct. If Kuropatkin had spoken with the voice of a Cassandra about the dangers of war, he was nevertheless supremely overconfident about Russia's military power. In 1903 he had boasted of the martial qualities of Russia's small force in the Far East.[6] Shortly after assuming command of Russia's land army in the war, Kuropatkin again evinced his overconfidence when he prophesied the rapid capture of Tokyo.[7] On the fields of Manchuria itself, Kuropatkin pursued a defensive strategy, waiting for the accumulation of overwhelming numerical superiority before decisively confronting the Japanese. When the Japanese forced battle on Kuropatkin, his constant disengagement and retreat, plus his wasteful policy of holding excessively large tactical reserves of up to one-half of his troops, put the Russian army at a considerable disadvantage in the conflict. Linevich, who relieved Kuropatkin as commander in chief in March 1905, proved less formidable than his nickname, "the Siberian Wolf" might have implied.[8] The quality of Russian leadership at a less exalted level was no better. Contemporary accounts abound with vignettes of the careless, nonfeasant, and malfeasant behavior of Russia's generals in the Far East: Stackelberg ordering soldiers to drench his private railway carriage with cooling water, Sakharov spending more time with his mistress than his maps, Stoianov, cheating at cards, Rennenkampf and Kaul'bars pursuing their pointless feud, scores of Russian officers carousing in the bar of the International Hotel in Mukden on the very eve of battle.[9]

From the first major conflict at Tiurenchensk (April 1904) through

[5] B. Frolov, "Russko-iaponskaia voina 1904-05 gg. Nekotorye voprosy voennogo iskusstva," *Voenno-istoricheskii zhurnal* 16, no. 2 (Feb. 1974): 84.

[6] *Otchet voennogo ministra po poezdke na Dal'nyi Vostok, chast' 1: osmotr voisk, voennykh uchrezhdenii i zavedenii* (St. Petersburg, 1903), pp. 151-154.

[7] A. S. Lukomskii, *Vospominaniia*, vol. 1 (Berlin, 1922), p. 17.

[8] Frolov, "Russko-iaponskaia", p. 85; M. Kazakov, "Ispol'zovanie rezervov v russko-iaponskoi voine, 1904-1905 gg.," *Voenno-istoricheskii zhurnal* 13, no. 4 (April 1971): 46; V. Veresaev, *In the War. Memoirs*, trans. Leo Wiener (New York, 1917), pp. 278, 283.

[9] Carl Joubert, *The Truth about the Tsar and the Present State of Russia* (London, 1905), p. 77; TsGVIA, f. 400, op. 393, d. 4, ll. 47-50; TsGVIA, f. 330, op. 51, d. 1086, l. 4; Frederick McCormick, *The Tragedy of Russia in Pacific Asia*, vol. 1 (New York, 1907), pp. 180-181; M. Menshikov, "Oblomovshchina v armii," *Novoe Vremia*, no. 10749 (Feb. 16, 1906): 3; A. Kvitka, *Dnevnik Zabaikal'skogo kazach'ego ofitsera. Russko-iaponskaia voina 1904-1905 gg.* (St. Petersburg, 1908), pp. 52-53.

the battles of Liaoyang, Shakhe River, the siege of Port Arthur, and the final bloodbath at Mukden (February/March, 1905) the Russian army did not win a single significant victory in the war.[10] Although foreign observers commended the heroism of the Russian private soldier, and although the stupendous logistical achievement of supplying an army several thousand miles away by means of the single-track Trans-Siberian railroad earned deserved acclaim, in the main Russian military performance in the war presented a picture of unrelieved gloom.

THE RUSSIAN REVOLUTION: INITIAL STAGE

Back in European Russia, the news of unending defeats for tsarist forces in Manchuria considerably increased discontent.[11] Beginning in the spring of 1904, Socialist revolutionaries and radical minority nationalists unleashed campaigns of terrorism against governmental officials. In the fall liberals, working through the Union of Liberation, sponsored a series of loosely veiled political banquets at which speakers denounced the policies of the government. In the industrial areas, workers became more restive.[12]

The revolution began in St. Petersburg with the events of January 9, 1905. On this day ("Bloody Sunday"), a detachment of police and soldiers opened fire on a pacific workers' march, slaughtering several hundred people in the process. Sympathy demonstrations elsewhere soon engulfed urban Russia in mass unrest. February saw the first outbursts of agrarian disorders, which spread even more widely in the summer. Meanwhile, liberal and radical parties and associations mobilized themselves to extract the maximum political capital from the turbulence. In August, Nicholas II proclaimed the so-called Bulygin Duma, a consultative institution to be elected by limited suffrage. This concession did not pacify the country, however, and the great October general strike pressured a timorous government into the promulgation of the October Manifesto, with its attendant promises for a considerably more demo-

[10] The military history of the Russo-Japanese War can be studied in hundreds of publications. V. Luchinin, *Russko-iaponskaia voina 1904-1905 gg. Bibliograficheskii ukazatel'knizhnoi literatury* (Moscow, 1940) contains a good guide to contemporary Russian writing on the war. See also I. I. Rostunov, ed., *Istoriia russko-iaponskoi voiny 1904-1905 gg.* (Moscow, 1977), pp. 370-381.

[11] Sidney Harcave, *First Blood: The Russian Revolution of 1905* (New York, 1964), p. 42; Leon Trotsky, *1905*, trans. Anya Bostock (New York, 1972), pp. 61-62; Lukomskii, *Vospominaniia*, p. 19.

[12] Shmuel Galai, *The Liberation Movement in Russia, 1900-1905* (Cambridge, Mass., 1973), pp. 207-209; Harcave, *First Blood*, p. 59.

cratic Duma. Yet these reforms also backfired, for although they detached conservatives and some moderates from the revolution, workers and peasants widely interpreted them as signs of weakness. Violence and insurgency became more intense after October 17 than before. Still, for most of this year, the civilian government had no overarching strategy of repression. With a significant part of the army tied up in a war with Japan at the other end of the Eurasian land mass, the government cautiously vacillated between concession and punishment.[13] At least until the fall of 1905, when the government did resort to force, it defended itself with the same battery of police and military measures it had employed in the prewar years.

"Conventional" use of the army elicited the conventional military complaints against the civilians. Thus field commanders frequently criticized the use of armed detachments as a prophylaxis against disorders. The commander of the 3rd Grenadier division, for instance, reported in May 1905 that the reputed "unrest" among the striking factory workers of Ivanovo-Voznesensk had in fact been a peaceful demonstration.[14] A September letter to the War Ministry from the Inspector General of the Cavalry alleged that civilian summons for cavalry were frequently unfounded, in the sense that disorders were over before the horsemen arrived.[15] And in a memorandum sent to the Ministry of the Interior, the Main Staff noted that although the army had responded to 1,390 civilian requests for aid from January 1 to June 11, on only 240 occasions did the troops actually take part in suppressing rebellion.[16]

Yet these familiar charges concerned what were, after all, perfectly legal actions of the civilian power. The War Ministry was on firmer ground when upbraiding the civilians for violations of the 1877 rules. In May, Moscow District pointed to the frequent "clashes between military and civilian officials" which resulted from this, as did Odessa in June.[17] A letter from the War Ministry to the Ministry of the Interior in June summarized the army's grievances. Instead of demanding troops from the military district commanders as the law prescribed, governors were appealing to the Minister of the Interior, who was badgering the War Ministry directly. Further, governors often assigned the direction of military repressive action to such low-ranking civilian officials as district police captains. Other governors had ordered the troops to march a circuit of their provinces to impress the peasants by an exhibit of force.

[13] TsGVIA, f. 1, op. 2, d. 165, l. 42.
[14] TsGVIA, f. 400, op. 3, d. 2749, l. 24.
[15] Ibid., l. 29.
[16] TsGVIA, f. 400, op. 3, d. 2618, l. 135.
[17] TsGVIA, f. 400, op. 3, d. 2749, l. 25.

This was yet another violation, since the rules declared that troops were to be summoned for duty at specific points only.[18]

Of course, such transgressions stemmed from the radically dangerous challenge of the revolution to the state, a challenge to which civilian officials were more sensitive than military men. One early and notable feature of the military reaction to 1905 was a reluctance to accede to changes in the instrumentalities of repression. Military district commanders and the bureaucrats of the War Ministry were wary of condoning innovations which would alter the established character of military repression or disrupt the chain of command.

To be sure, in February 1905, when the Ministry of the Interior proposed the creation of "flying detachments" in the countryside, anticipating as it did large-scale peasant unrest in fifteen provinces, only two military districts (Kiev and Odessa) rejected the scheme outright. But the War Ministry quite clearly interpreted the term "flying detachment" differently than did K. N. Rudzevskii at the Interior Ministry. To War Minister Sakharov, rather than consisting of migratory punitive columns, "flying detachments" were rather to be units assembled at their headquarters, available for hasty dispatch to a specific trouble spot. Although in Sakharov's thinking certain companies, squadrons, and batteries would be entirely detailed to repressive service, many military units were already exclusively given over to it. The "flying detachment," then, represented little novelty since it was a fancy title describing what the army was already doing. To Sakharov "flying detachment" implied a concentration of troops; to the Ministry of the Interior, it connoted their dispersal.[19]

But when the War Ministry understood that a suggestion by the Interior Ministry involved more than a change in nomenclature, the generals stoutly resisted. One such proposal matured in the mind of D. F. Trepov. In early June 1905 he wrote Sakharov that the government's practice of defraying all the costs of military repressive activities had come to vex him. Not only was the policy too merciful, it might even benefit a rebellious district, for the mutinous peasants might well realize tidy profits from purveying food and drink to the army. Why not make the peasants bear the expense of crushing their own unrest, or at least why not have the army pay for its provisions with special notes, redeemable in cash by the Treasury only after the peasants had discharged their debts and arrears? As was standard, the War Ministry invited comment from the districts on Trepov's plan. By October, the

[18] TsGVIA, f. 400, op. 3, d. 2618, l. 83.
[19] Ibid., ll. 1, 54-56.

overwhelming majority of district commanders as well as the central organs of the Ministry itself had repudiated Trepov's idea. The Main Administration of the Intendancy, that venal institution charged with supplying the army, showed remarkable common sense on this occasion. Trepov's basic assumption—that the peasants were somehow making money from the troops quartered on them—was fatuous: "The population acquires no material advantages or profits from the deployment of troops, as the Ministry of the Interior supposes. Rather, the reverse. Under conditions of general impoverishment [the peasants] nearly always encounter difficulties in securing their own extremely meager victuals."

The Intendancy's opposition to the Trepov scheme was not entirely founded on compassion; it noted that such forcible exactions might well inflame a village to further revolt rather than pacify it.[20]

The army was, of course, less squeamish in those regions of the Caucasus, Turkestan, and Siberia where it simultaneously controlled the civil administration. Punitive exactions such as Trepov supported had long been common there. In December of 1904, for instance, the temporary Commander of the Caucasus Military District, enraged by the murder of the local tax collector in Shushi, billeted one battalion of grenadiers and one sotnia of Cossacks on this town in punishment. These units were to be supplied at the town's expense for two months, or until the assassins were apprehended.[21] But the army was in the last analysis responsible for public order in the Caucasus and countenanced repressive measures there that it would not knowingly tolerate elsewhere. In those central territories of the Empire with a clearly articulated civilian administration, the War Ministry did not desire novelties that might blacken the army's reputation.

Certain district commanders similarly balked at another Interior Ministry proposal later in the year. In October, Trepov advised the War Ministry that disorders were becoming so serious martial law might have to be imposed throughout the Empire. He therefore requested that the War Ministry supply him with a list of officers who might be suitable candidates for the office of temporary governor-general in each of the provinces of the country. The Main Staff dutifully polled the district commanders, and most of them replied with rosters of reliable generals. After all, this was merely a contingency plan; Trepov did not propose instituting martial law at once but just wanted to hold these data in reserve. Yet even Trepov's contingency planning was sufficient to irritate

[20] TsGVIA, f. 400, op. 7, d. 1997, ll. 41, 92, 253.
[21] TsGVIA, f. 400, op. 3, d. 2609, l. 8.

certain commanders. Lieutenant General Sukhotin, for instance, telegraphed from Omsk that because of the small number of troops in his Siberian district and because of the promulgation of the October Manifesto, the introduction of martial law was "hardly desirable." He therefore declined to nominate any generals to oblige Trepov.[22] Sukhotin's reaction was of course explained in part by his uncertainty about the precise meaning of the manifesto, a trait he shared with many other state officials; however, his intractability also derived from his distaste for repressive innovations.

Phase Two: The Witte System

But innovation seemed necessary if the government was to survive. As we have already seen, the October Manifesto fueled rather than extinguished the various different revolutionary conflagrations—nationalist, urban, and rural. By late October 1905 the Baltic provinces were in a state of full-blown rebellion; the Caucasus was afire with ethnic and nationalistic violence; and the peasants of the central agricultural provinces were looting and burning the estates of the hated landlords. Soon parts of the Siberian railway would fall into the hands of revolutionaries. The response of the government was to intensify repressive operations. In October Nicholas II placed the forts of Vyborg, Sveaborg, and Kronshtadt under martial law and appointed Lt. Gen. V. U. Sollugub governor-general of the Baltic territories, most of which were already under martial law. Around the same time Nicholas ordered several members of his suite to investigate sedition in specific provinces and empowered them to take all measures necessary to uproot it. Sakharov (and later Maksimovich) operated in Saratov and Penza; Dubasov went to Kursk, Chernigov, and Poltava; Strukov was assigned to Voronezh and Tambov; Count Ignat'ev to Kherson; and Prince Englychev to Stavropol'.[23] Just as Nicholas had turned to Trepov, another suite member, to reestablish order in Petersburg the preceding January, he now entrusted similar repressive tasks to other members of the suite, both because of the psychological impact this had (the Emperor himself, in the person of a member of his own entourage, commands obedience) and presumably because he and his chancellery had especial trust in their fidelity. In December, as well, urban workers' risings, of which the most famous was in Moscow, were crushed by armed force. In the same month, Nicholas proclaimed martial law for the Siberian railroad. In early Jan-

[22] TsGVIA, f. 400, op. 3, d. 2665, ll. 1, 12.
[23] TsGVIA, f. 1, op. 2, d. 165, l. 43.

uary 1906 the sadistic General Meller-Zakomel'skii moved down the railway east from Moscow, crushing revolutionary activity with fiendish brutality. Rennenkampf, advancing up the railroad from the Pacific, exhibited more restraint. Other punitive columns would shortly march in the Caucasus and southern Russia.

Still, the government was applying martial law and authorizing punitive detachments on a case-by-case basis. A consistent strategy for military repression was still lacking. This gap was filled by S. Iu. Witte, who developed exactly such a strategy in late 1905 and early 1906. Witte, who had been elevated to the chairmanship of the Council of Ministers on October 17, devised a three-part program for the military, a program which might be summarized by the words *ruthlessness, decentralization,* and *frequency.*

On December 13, 1905 Witte engineered a resolution of the Council of Ministers which sternly censured the army for the "indecisiveness" of its repressive work and stated that "the spread of disorder and the limited success in the struggle with it results to a significant degree from the fact that the troops are not acting sufficiently energetically." Although in normal times troops might try to avoid using their arms against the people, these were not normal times. In the future, troops were to respond with force at the slightest sign of armed resistance.[24] The resolution received a powerful endorsement from a not unexpected quarter—the Emperor. In the Ukrainian city of Nikolaev, on December 14, some five thousand persons demonstrated in violation of the police chief's prohibition of mass meetings. When the crowd fired on men of the 7th Don Cossack regiment, their colonel, Zamchalov, ordered them to withdraw. Nicholas' intense irritation guided his pen when he wrote of this that "the troops are obliged to answer fire with fire and are to smash the feeblest appearance of armed resistance." The Emperor commanded that all military district leaders be informed of his resolution about the Nikolaev affair. The War Ministry accordingly sent telegram 684 over the wires: "In stopping disorders, any crowd using arms ought to be fired on without mercy."[25]

Ruthlessness was all very well, but what if there were no troops on the spot? The decentralization of the army and its dispersal throughout the Empire would facilitate the accumulation of adequate forces in any particular location. With this in mind, Witte convened a special conference in two sittings of January 28 and March 1, 1906. In addition to Witte, Durnovo attended from the Interior Ministry, Rediger and Po-

[24] TsGVIA, f. 400, op. 3, d. 2609, l. 8.
[25] TsGVIA, f. 400, op. 3, d. 2671, ll. 17, 35.

livanov from the War Ministry, Palitsyn from the General Staff, and Nikolai Nikolaevich from the Council of State Defense. At the first meeting of the conference Durnovo unveiled a plan for the total redeployment of the army to satisfy the security needs of forty-nine provinces. There *were* enough troops in European Russia to carry out the Durnovo plan: Durnovo required 584¼ battalions, 442½ squadrons and sotnias, and 216 batteries for use in the military districts of St. Petersburg, Vil'na, Warsaw, Kiev, Odessa, Moscow, and Kazan'; the War Ministry disposed of 688, 506, and 291 respectively in these districts. But what Durnovo proposed was to juggle the distribution of these forces so as to protect the heartland by denuding the western periphery. For example, he wished to remove 194 battalions from Warsaw District, leaving a scant 15 behind.[26] Rediger and Palitsyn were simply aghast: such an arrangement was not only impractical but it would thoroughly disorganize Russia's defenses. But Count Witte ridiculed the idea that there could be any threat to Russia from Germany or Austria-Hungary in the foreseeable future. At the meeting of March 1, Witte wrangled the assent of the conference to a modified version of the Durnovo plan. Although a complete redeployment of the army was abandoned, the commanders of the military districts which included Durnovo's forty-nine provinces were to divide their districts into "regions" and in some cases were to subdivide them further into "sections." In each region or section the district commander was to appoint a military chief to act for him. When civilians in these districts wanted troops they were to apply to this local military chief, not the district commander. In addition, more troops were to be rushed to the eighteen southern provinces which the Interior Ministry had identified as the most unruly.[27] As a sop to the army, the conference formally resolved in addition that the military was to "avoid" quartering troops in units of less than a regiment, separate battalion, or separate battery. Thus the bête noir of the Russian governor with a riot on his hands—the remote, skeptical, and stiff-necked district commander—was to be replaced by a military official who was much more available, and presumably much more tractable and sympathetic to boot.[28] On March 12, 1906 Nicholas II promulgated Witte's measures by special decree.

[26] TsGVIA, f. 400, op. 3, d. 2749, l. 111.

[27] Mogilev, Kiev, Kursk, Poltava, Khar'kov, Chernigov, Ekaterinoslav, Voronezh, Nizhegorod, Orel, Tambov, Tula, Penza, Perm', Samara, Saratov, Simbirsk, Kherson, Tauride (Dnepr uezd).

[28] TsGVIA, f. 400, op. 3, d. 2749, ll. 99-102, 274-279. The journals of the conference, minus War Ministry working papers, have been printed in "Bor'ba S. Iu. Vitte s agrarnoi revoliutsiei," *Krasnyi arkhiv* (Moscow) 6, no. 31 (1928): 81-108.

The third aim of Witte's plan for the army was a dramatic increase in the frequency of its use. Witte hoped this would be easy to accomplish, since with the conclusion of peace with Japan, troops would shortly be returning from the fields of Manchuria to reinforce the under-strength European garrisons. But in any event, expansion in use would be essential whether easy or not, as Witte argued in a note to the Emperor of January 10, owing to the relative weakness of the rural police. Although 14.3 million rubles were budgeted for them in 1906, and although the Ministry of the Interior was now requesting an additional 3.6 million (which it was likely to receive), the police could never supplant the army.[29] Witte seems to have been thinking here both of the prevention of disorder and of the execution of police functions by the army. He did, however, send out contradictory signals on this latter point. On January 28, he wrote to A. F. Rediger (War Ministry, 1905-1909) with official news of the decisions of the Council of Ministers fifteen days before. At that meeting, the Council had resolved that police duty and passive guard duty were inappropriate for the army. Responsibility for preventing disorders reposed with civilian provincial and uezd officials. The army's task was simply to carry out civilians' directives and then return to its barracks.

Yet Rediger must have been dismayed by the conclusion of the letter, for here Witte stated that the Council did envision certain duties for the troops after a disorder was over—e.g., the apprehending of revolutionary instigators, the recovery of stolen property—or other police duties. Thus, Witte was both deploring the discharge by the army of police duty and ordering it to discharge police duty.[30] Witte's disparaging references to police service for the army were all the more insincere and valueless since the commission on reviewing the rules of 1877 had by now completed its long-awaited work. And the outcome was not to the army's liking: the revised rules of February 1906 contained legal justification for military police service and the military prevention of disorders. The punitive requisition of food and supplies (the very thing that the Intendancy had condemned in June) was, moreover, legalized.[31]

The last two aims of Witte's program were in direct contravention of

[29] B. B. Veselovskii, V. I. Pichet, and V. M. Friche, eds., *Materialy po istorii krest'ianskikh dvizhenii v Rossii. Agrarnyi vopros v sovete ministrov (1906 g.)* (Moscow and Leningrad, 1924), pp. 72-73.

[30] TsGVIA, f. 400, op. 3, d. 2732, l. 1. Howard D. Mehlinger and John M. Thompson, *Count Witte and the Tsarist Government in the 1905 Revolution* (Bloomington, Ind., 1972), p. 165; also note Witte's ambiguous pronouncements on the role of the army in late January 1906.

[31] TsGVIA, f. 400, op. 3, d. 2560, l. 245.

the policy of the Ministry of War. Witte's decentralization of army authority, with the resulting breakdown in the chain of command, was naturally odious to a hierarchical institution such as the Russian army. Rediger had insisted at the first meeting of Witte's special conference that "the state of the army results in the unconditional necessity for concentrating the troops," not dispersing them.[32] The Ministry surmised (correctly, as it subsequently proved) that it would soon lose control over the activities of the quasi-independent local military chiefs.

War Ministry Concern over Decentralization

As the months passed, it became increasingly apparent that the War Ministry had not only lost control over its army in the Russian hinterland, but was also largely ignorant of what was happening out there. On July 1, 1906 the Ministry sent a sharply worded circular to all districts. It was clear that in their ignorance of the rules the local military chiefs were supinely acquiescing to even the most extravagant civilian demands.[33] Fourteen days later the Main Staff would have to confess that it did not even possess a complete list of the names of these regional chiefs.[34] All it could be reasonably sure of was that there were seventy-two of them.[35] At the end of the year, the Ministry abashedly confessed to the Department of Police that it did not know precisely which regions of the Empire were under martial law and hence under the sway of temporary military governors-general.[36]

In another circular to the district staffs in August 1906, the Ministry once again inveighed against rule violations perpetrated with the complicity of the local chiefs. The chiefs were unfamiliar with the rules and displayed an overly "passive attitude . . . to the attempts of the civil administration to exceed the authority granted it by the rules."[37] In this connection, the circular cited 22 violations in Vil'na District from June 27 to July 16, 6 in Odessa from July 1 to July 15, 23 in Kiev for the same period, 14 in Moscow from June 22 to July 19, 9 in Kazan' for the same period, and 13 in the Caucasus for the first seventeen days of July.[38] And these were only the violations the Ministry knew about. Channels of communication between the Ministry and "regions" via the

[32] "Bor'ba S. Iu Vitte," pp. 89-90.
[33] TsGVIA, f. 400, op. 3, d. 2731, l. 122.
[34] TsGVIA, f. 400, op. 3, d. 2752, l. 45.
[35] TsGVIA, f. 400, op. 3, d. 2862, l. 2.
[36] TsGVIA, f. 400, op. 3, d. 2752, l. 168.
[37] TsGVIA, f. 400, op. 3, d. 2731, l. 346.
[38] Ibid., ll. 347-356.

military districts were breaking down. Reports were slow in being written, sent, and filed. An official memorandum of the Main Staff, prepared as late as February 1908, would roundly condemn rule violations in the following terms: "the civilian power abuses its power to call troops and calls them even in those cases when it is unjustified, while the military leaders unconditionally fulfill the demands of the civilian authority, even though these demands contravene the IMPERIALLY approved rules."[39]

The inability of the Ministry to secure strict compliance with the regulations by its subordinates and the manifest impossibility of supervising repression (often entrusted to green and ambitious young officers) combined to make the Ministry realize that the situation in the provinces was completely out of hand. Uncontrolled repressive missions were often resulting at best in excesses, and at worst in atrocities which were turning the army into an object of contempt and derision.

A typical example occurred in June 1906, when a Podol'ia landlord by the name of Demenchuk telephoned the police captain of Vinnitsa uezd to declare that the peasants of Sal'niki were cutting his wood and burning his ricks. The policeman called for military aid, and cornet Orel and one-half sotnia of the 36th Akhtyrka dragoons duly arrived. Demenchuk greeted Orel and the police captain with yet another charge: the peasants were illegally pasturing their cattle in his field. At Demenchuk's insistence, Orel ordered his troopers into action; fifteen head of cattle were gunned down.

The incident, up to this point absurd, now turned ugly. The village elder of Sal'niki assembled the peasants in front of the schoolhouse to meet with Orel and Demenchuk to request compensation. But before they could do so, Orel ordered two volleys fired into the peaceable crowd. Not content with this, he gave his dragoons free rein, and the latter threw themselves, drawn sabres in their hands, upon the terrified peasants. Three peasants were murdered in this massacre, and twelve others suffered serious injuries. Investigation later established that Demenchuk had been lying from the beginning: none of the Sal'niki peasants had ever damaged his property. In fact, he himself was illegally felling trees and craved an excuse with which to hoodwink the Wood Preservation Committee. As for the mendacious landlord's field—the peasants had long enjoyed legal pasturage rights there. This entire episode ended in the State Duma, which issued an interpellation about it.[40] A sordid affair like this (and this one was hardly unique) could only debase the army in the eyes of the people and sully the soldier's reputation.

[39] TsGVIA, f. 400, op. 3, d. 2897, l. 364.
[40] TsGVIA, f. 400, op. 15, d. 2879, ll. 1, 5, 8.

The soldier's reputation was indeed taking a drubbing in the public press. Military performance in the war with Japan had not been of the caliber to inspire ovations, as numerous articles, pamphlets, and books of 1905 and 1906 tirelessly pointed out. In addition, major literary figures were increasingly turning to the army for material and composing novels and stories set against a background of military life. This was a somewhat unusual phenomenon, since there had been no author of "military" tales of any literary stature since Garshin. Regrettably, from the army's point of view, the majority of these new works were informed by an overt bias against everything military. Many of these works were productions of members of Gorkii's *Znanie* group, for whom the publication of at least one antimilitary story seems to have been de rigueur. Because of the relative freedom of the press during the revolutionary period, the Russian public was able to read works by Gusev-Orenburgskii, Teleshov, and Muizhel which savagely condemned war and the military way of life.[41] L. N. Andreev's powerful fable of pacifism, *The Red Laugh*, which was set during the Russo-Japanese War, appeared in *Znanie*'s third literary miscellany (1905) and sold an astounding sixty thousand copies.[42] A. I. Kuprin acquired notoriety when his novella *The Duel* was published in *Znanie*'s sixth collection (also 1905). This popular work depicted military service in a small town on the Western frontier, leaving the reader with the impression that the Russian officer corps consisted chiefly of fools, braggarts, sadists, and madmen.[43] It was difficult to dismiss Kuprin's story as the delirious fantasy of a civilian who had never even visited a military bivouac, since he had in fact served four years as an officer with the 46th infantry regiment in Podol'ia.[44]

In 1906 the populist author V. G. Korolenko made his contribution to the growing pile of antimilitary works with his pamphlet "The Tragedy of General Kovalev and the Customs of the Military Environment," a republication of articles originally written for *Russkoe bogatstvo*. Korolenko's discussion of Kovalev's torture of Dr. Zabusov in 1904 served as an introduction to a rogues' gallery of violent, spiteful officers. Arguing that such officers were not exceptional, but rather typical, he concluded that: "soldiers ought to be citizens of their countries. . . .

---

[41] B. V. Mikhailovskii, *Russkaia literatura XX veka* (Moscow, 1939), p. 38. Only one treatment of the military theme in early twentieth century Russian literature exists in English, to my knowledge. This is Richard Luckett's cursory "Pre-Revolutionary Army Life in Russian Literature," in *War, Economy, and the Military Mind*, ed. Geoffrey Best and Andrew Wheatcraft (London, 1967), pp. 19-31.

[42] James B. Woodward, *Leonid Andreyev. A Study* (Oxford, 1969), p. 98.

[43] V. Afanas'ev, *Aleksandr Ivanovich Kuprin*, 2d ed. (Moscow, 1972), pp. 52-53.

[44] V. Afanas'ev, "Sovremennitsa 'Poedinka'," *Ogonek*, no. 36 (1960): 19.

the law ought to be the same for all, professional customs ought not to stand in opposition to the principles recognized by all society. Only then will we see the disappearance of Kovalev tragedies, Kursk horrors and much, much more."[45]

Nor was Korolenko the only collector and purveyor of military atrocity stories: accounts of military torture, rape, illegal political activities, massacre, and the like regularly appeared in the papers. Colonel Stashevskii's assassination of the editor of the newspaper *Russian Turkestan* early in 1905 had considerably (and not unnaturally) stimulated antimilitary journalism. The Press Bureau of the Main Staff, which the War Ministry established in mid-1906 to monitor (and if possible shore up) the decline of army prestige, recorded the publication of 242 military atrocity stories in the St. Petersburg press for the month of December 1906 alone.[46]

MILITARY REACTION TO EXPANSION OF ARMY REPRESSIVE ACTIVITY AND RUTHLESSNESS

As we have seen, in early 1906 Witte desired to supplement military decentralization with an expansion of the army's internal repressive role. Final figures for 1905 indicated that civilians had made 3,894 requests for troops, involving 25,283¼ companies, 5,354 squadrons or sotnias, 32 training commands, 19 convoy commands, 18 local commands, 7 scouting commands, 410 field guns, 770 machine guns, and 120,476 soldiers deployed separately from all of these. Such prodigious quantities of military men and firepower would never be marshalled for repression again. However, the figures for 1906 were sufficient to alarm the Ministry of War: 2559 occasions, 3,142⅜ companies, 1,057¾ squadrons or sotnias, 22 training commands, 20 scouting commands, 9 local commands, 4 convoy commands, 278 field guns, 71 machine guns, and 29,332 separately deployed soldiers.[47] Even if civilian calls for troops slackened off in 1906, the civilian demand for military guards was unabated. In January 1905 there were already 9,000 military guards at civilian prisons, banks, treasuries, and the like. One year later there were almost 10,000, and on January 1, 1907 the number had risen to the ominous total of over 19,000.[48] Yet the Ministry of War was committed not only to oppose expansion but even to curtail the preexisting incidence of detachments and guards in the aid of the civilian power. A Main Staff memorandum of January 27, 1906 described the War Ministry as attempting "with

---

[45] Korolenko, *Tragediia*, p. 24.
[46] TsGVIA, f. 400, op. 15, d. 2916a, ll. 449-472.
[47] TsGVIA, f. 1, op. 1, d. 70264, l. 232.
[48] Ibid., l. 21.

great effort to extricate itself from this position . . . that is, to gather together the remnants of its forces for the possible reestablishment of the discipline and firm spirit of the army."[49]

As for the first part of Witte's system, ruthlessness, there is no doubt that there were officers who advocated savage military violence in the countryside. Witte himself made much of the suggestions advanced by Major General Kryzhanovskii, head of the 2d cavalry division. In a letter of December 21, 1905 that general had denounced reliance on "falsely humane half measures" in combatting peasant unrest. Kryzhanovskii recommended that villages be shelled or burned to the ground at the first breath of disorder. But, pertinently, Kryzhanovskii's letter was not a modest presentation of the option most likely to prove successful in crushing the revolution; rather, he was endorsing these bestial policies as the best method for preserving the army. His plan called for the *concentration* of troops in provincial and district capitals, and their concomitant release from all police service. Troops were to be ordered out into the countryside exclusively to punish, burn, and shoot. If the civilians demanded succor, this was the way in which the army could help them that was least dangerous to military interests. "A few villages filled with rebels and a half wild population are not dear to Russia, her army is dear to her. . . . Therefore, it is important above all to isolate the army from the ruinous influence of the revolution. This system provides that isolation." Palitsyn at the General Staff, who originally brought Kryzhanovskii's ideas to the attention of Witte and Durnovo, wrote that "we all agree" with them, adding that "our chief enemy is incompetence and its chief representative is the local civilian authority."[50] In other words, Kryzhanovskii's ardor for ruthless punitive measures was explained by his *opposition* to the repressive policy of the civilian government—decentralization—rather than any spontaneous agreement with it. The same characteristic habit of thinking first of the army, second of the government, accounted for War Minister Rediger's disapproval of Kryzhanovskii's plan: "I had no desire at all to turn the troops into executioners or punitive commands as I calculated that this was not their job at all, and, moreover, thought that it was very dangerous; under such conditions the troops would easily run amok and would simply turn into bandits, while the population would come to hate the army and would refuse the funds for the satisfaction of its needs."[51] Kryzhanovskii's "harshness" and Rediger's "mercifulness"

[49] TsGVIA, f. 400, op. 3, d. 2749, l. 87.
[50] Ibid., ll. 39-42.
[51] TsGVIA, f. 280, op. 1, d. 4, p. 550.

145

then both derived from the same source: a fixation on the interests of the army. But Kryzhanovskii, closer to the firing line, was especially concerned with the integrity of his command, while Rediger, directing the entire War Ministry, had to be mindful of public relations with the convocation of the Duma in the offing. It is worth noting that in August 1906 Rediger would himself urge ruthless measures to bring rebellion in the Caucasus to heel. For example, he ordered that houses where explosives had been hidden be put to the torch. And the reasons he adduced for such a course were identical to Kryzhanovskii's: that the protracted use of soldiers in police capacities would soon spoil even the best of troops.[52]

War Ministry Concern for Discipline, Hardship, and Health

One of the most disquieting developments of all, however, was the steady erosion of military discipline. The Ministry of War ascribed this phenomenon to the fact that civilians in the provinces were fragmenting and dispersing the units sent to succor them. Throughout the entire revolutionary period, it was Gen. V. A. Sukhomlinov in Kiev who was the keenest opponent of this practice. For instance, in December 1905 he wrote Rediger that the governor's predilection for splitting army units down into less than one-half company, squadron, or sotnia was both obnoxious and dangerous. In illustration of his point, Sukhomlinov enclosed correspondence from Kursk, where Colonel Mazan had led the 2d Eisk regiment of Kuban Cossacks on a temporary mission. Mazan stated that in October the Kursk governor had shattered his regiment into minuscule parties of three to ten men. The governor had employed these soldiers as police patrols and had even quartered some of them for lengthy periods of time in various points around the province, including private estates. All regimental training exercises had ceased. And without their officers, isolated among an obstreperous and hostile population, ill-housed and badly fed, the Cossacks were beginning to succumb to the blandishments of revolutionary propaganda. Cossacks had already authored three anonymous letters to the governor, requesting that they be sent home. Pointing out that the Cossacks in his regiment had been mustered for war duty, but then had been commandeered for internal service instead, Mazan declared that despite all efforts it was practically impossible to explain the concept of the internal enemy to the "uneducated Cossack." "Internal discipline can only be maintained when there

[52] TsGVIA, f. 400, op. 3, d. 2739, l. 398.

is constant contact between Cossacks and their officers." The Ministry of War thereupon persuaded the Ministry of the Interior to issue a December circular to all governors, forbidding the division of troops into quantities of less than one-half company or squadron.[53] But this instruction, like so many others, was honored in the breach.

Indiscipline did however find much more ominous expression than the mere dispatch of anonymous notes. October, November, and December of 1905 saw at least 195 instances of mutiny in military units, involving elements of one-third of the army in European Russia. Stimulated by the soldiers' belief that the October Manifesto meant that the regime had lost its nerve, the army disorders were chiefly nonviolent presentations of "illegal demands" for the betterment of living and working conditions. And on most of these occasions, the soldiers rather quickly returned to duty.[54] But sometimes the mutinies were quite grave. In mid-December 1905, for instance, five sotnias of the 2d Urupsk regiment of Don Cossacks rebelled in Ekaterinodar, demobilized themselves, and started for home. General Dukmasov, who investigated this embarrassing transgression on behalf of the War Ministry, reported that the Cossacks had lost faith in their leaders. The prestige of the impoverished Cossack officer was at its nadir. In their own manifesto, the Urupsk Cossacks declared that internal repressive service had touched off their rebellion: "We guarded hospitals and public houses, we were given into the authority of common policemen who exploited us for their own gain."[55]

Incidents as serious as this were few. However, the naked panic that mutinies like this engendered in the government gave War Minister Rediger the psychological edge to force through an entire program of improvements in the common soldiers' conditions of service. These included appropriations for tastier, more plentiful, and more wholesome food; increased pay (the private now received twelve rubles a year); and the issuance of blankets and linen, which until this point soldiers had had to provide for themselves.[56]

[53] TsGVIA, f. 330, op. 49, d. 814, ll. 1-4, 6, 14.

[54] TsGVIA, f. 400, op. 3, d. 91, ll. 5-9; Bushnell, "Mutineers and Revolutionaries," Ph.D. diss., pp. 45-46, 70, 72-74, 81, 84-92, 99-100, 114. We should note, however, that if *elements* of one third of the army mutinied, this does not mean that one third of the army mutinied. It would seem that Bushnell's study, though superb in other respects, overemphasizes the seriousness of mutiny by counting as thoroughly unreliable regiments, say, in which only companies actually rioted. See pp. 72, 435.

[55] TsGVIA, f. 330, op. 50, d. 1195, ll. 3, 118; TsGVIA, f. 330, op. 50, d. 1194, ll. 9-11.

[56] Denikin, *Staraia armiia*, vol. 1, p. 139; Bushnell, "Mutineers and Revolutionaries," Ph.D. diss., p. 116.

Whether because of the impact of these concessions on most of the soldiery, or other factors, the first wave of military mutinies was over by mid-December, 1906. However, the reforms of December and January were hardly the total antidote to the poison of indiscipline. Although Rediger (overoptimistically) predicted in April of 1906 that the danger of military mutiny was past, there were possibly more than 134 mutinies in the army in the months of May, June, and July 1906.[57] Kaul'bars wrote from Odessa in 1906 that "the insistence of civilian leaders and the truly unfortunate state of things in many areas of the district frequently force us to recoil from faithful adherence to the principle of concentrating the troops; we are sacrificing them for the preservation of the social order and peace."[58] Discipline was one chief component of that sacrifice. Even after the 1906 mutinies had burned themselves out (this happened by the fall), problems with discipline persisted. When, in late 1906, eight machine guns were purloined from the Tashkent arsenal (possibly with the connivance of soldiers in the machine gun company), the War Ministry had to attribute this shameful incident to slack discipline.[59] Even in 1907, the commanders of 7th and 8th army corps would still assert that the widespread use of the troops in repressive operations sapped their discipline and exposed them to criminal political propaganda.[60]

But the economic hardship of repressive service also disturbed the Ministry of War. In no case was this more pronounced than in that of the seventy thousand Cossacks of the second and third reserves. Although they had already fulfilled their initial obligation of active military service, these men in their twenties, thirties, and forties were recalled from their farms to the colors and plunged into the struggle with the revolution in late 1905. The families of these Cossacks often faced destitution since they were unable to afford the cost of hiring field hands in the Don and Kuban where labor was scarce and wages high. In January 1906 Rediger urged Nicholas II to bestow a grant of 100 rubles on each affected family. This sum, itself inadequate to relieve a family bereft of its breadwinner, was further reduced by the Ministry of Finance to 75 rubles.[61]

It was likewise becoming obvious that the army was paying another price for its repressive duty in terms of the impairment of the soldiers' health. Sukhomlinov was furious in early January 1906 when he dis-

[57] Ibid., p. 291; TsGVIA, f. 400, op. 15, d. 2617, l. 465.
[58] TsGVIA, f. 400, op. 3, d. 2862, l. 56.
[59] TsGVIA, f. 400, op. 15, d. 3090, l. 4, 7, 11.
[60] TsGVIA, f. 400, op. 3, d. 2897, l. 364.
[61] TsGVIA, f. 280, op. 1, d. 5, p. 554.

covered that soldiers were often forced to stand guard at civilian institutions for twelve-hour shifts without a break.[62] In his summary report for 1905 the commander of Kazan' District flatly declared that "the rise in the percentage of sickness and death (per thousand) is exclusively explained by the burdensome conditions of the service of the men in assisting the civilian authorities." The Moscow District Commander agreed.[63] Over a year later—in November 1907—Sukhomlinov was still railing against the poor accommodations provided the troops guarding the railways in Kiev District. The men had not enough air, light, or heat and in consequence were becoming sick.[64]

War Ministry Response

By the late winter of 1906 the Ministry's worries over declining discipline, erosion of prestige, and civilian interference all combined to implant the idea that ministerial control over the army had to be reestablished at all costs. Fewer detachments of troops were to be sent to civilian authorities; troops on long-term repressive assignment had to be brought back if possible. A vigorous campaign was to be waged to persuade civilian officials to create their own guard forces so that the pressure on the army for military guards might be relieved.

The regional military chiefs, of course, far beyond the reach of ministerial influence, continued to rubber stamp multitudes of civilian requests. But when a case was brought up to a district commander, the outcome might be different. Egged on by the War Ministry, district commanders now began to greet civilian requests for military assistance with intransigent refusals. Thus Vil'na refused the Kurland governor a regiment for the port city of Vindava.[65] In May 1906 Kazan' denied the Saratov governor a guard detail for Saratov city prison.[66] In June, Subbotich pulled all military guards off duty at state financial institutions throughout Turkestan.[67] And in August, when the governor of St. Petersburg Province asked that a regiment be posted to Schlüsselberg because there were five factories located there, St. Petersburg District declined. In an explanatory note to the War Ministry, the district chief of staff declared that the best reason for not sending the troops to

[62] TsGVIA, f. 400, op. 3, d. 2731, l. 11.
[63] TsGVIA, f. 400, op. 3, d. 2734, ll. 69, 140.
[64] TsGVIA, f. 400, op. 3, d. 2897, l. 418.
[65] TsGVIA, f. 400, op. 3, d. 1459, ll. 27, 34.
[66] TsGVIA, f. 400, op. 3, d. 2733, ll. 51, 53.
[67] Ibid., l. 75.

Schlüsselberg was exactly the presence of many workers there.[68] The danger of propaganda disseminated by the workers could not be over-emphasized. Thus, paradoxically, the very reason that the St. Petersburg governor needed troops in Schlüsselberg was the very reason that the army was not intending to send them. Clearly, the officials of St. Petersburg had resolved that the need for the political isolation of the army outweighed the need for state security.

At the same time, the War Ministry was pressuring other ministries in the state to raise their own forces of guards. By 1906 common soldiers everywhere in the Empire were standing guard in front of banks, hospitals, zemstvo buildings, prisons, even police stations. Support for the Ministry's plan emanated first from those territories where the army was responsible for civilian administration, largely since the troops were most thinly distributed there. In June 1906, Lieutenant General Prince Odoevskii-Maslov, ataman of the Don, wrote that he could not provide "military guards to the institutions of other departments."[69] In August, he proposed civilian guards as replacements for military ones, or at least the arming of civilian employees, since this measure was "more expedient" than burdening the army.[70]

In the same month, the War Ministry informed Sukhomlinov that if, as he reported, landlords in Kiev and Kursk were panicking at his attempts to reconcentrate his forces, they should be compelled to raise their own militia in defense of their property.[71] A week later Rediger demanded that the Ministries of Interior and Finance strengthen their police and guard forces, thus releasing the army from police and guard duty. Stolypin immediately dismissed the War Ministry's appeal.[72] And the Ministry of Finance followed suit, employing arguments which underscored the difficulties in which it found itself. Since 1885, the Finance Ministry had in fact maintained its own corps of bank guards. These reliable detectives could ordinarily cope with typical bankrobbers. They were not, however, equal to the task of defending banks from the onslaughts of organized gangs of bandits and revolutionaries armed with Mauser rifles and automatic pistols.

From the beginning of 1905 to mid-1906, the Finance Ministry calculated that revolutionary banditry had cost the Imperial banks over one million rubles. Much of the stolen money had in fact come from the army's own mobilization fund which, for self-evident reasons, was dis-

---

[68] TsGVIA, f. 400, op. 3, d. 1459, ll. 42, 45-46.
[69] TsGVIA, f. 330, op. 50, d. 1236, l. 1.
[70] TsGVIA, f. 400, op. 3, d. 2731, l. 204.
[71] Ibid., l. 400.
[72] Ibid., l. 249.

persed throughout the local branch banks of the Empire. The Finance Ministry therefore could not agree with the War Ministry: military details would have to remain in the banks and treasuries.[73] The audacious daytime robbery of the Tashkent treasury and the robbing of the Russo-Chinese bank in Kokand demonstrated forcefully that the Ministry of Finance was unable to protect the banks unaided.[74] Indeed, the Finance Ministry's case was so obviously sound that the army pledged itself to continue guarding the banks and treasuries.[75] But this promise only stiffened the War Ministry's resolve to remove military guards from all other civilian institutions.

At the end of October 1906 the War Ministry convened a special conference on releasing the troops from police and guard duty. Attending for the Ministry of the Interior was Zuev, from the Police Department, and Savvich, the Chief of Staff of the Gendarmes. The War Ministry pointed out that one excuse which the civilian bureaucrats often gave for the employment of troops as guards was that they lacked the funds to hire their own. Yet the Treasury was disbursing 3.5 million rubles a month to pay the costs of military repression. The Interior Ministry and the other ministries should therefore accept this sum with the army's compliments and use it to beef up the police and the civilian guards. Zuev and Savvich objected to this program, and submitted their own counterproposal: if the War Ministry was so concerned with the army's cohesion, with the shambles of its training program, let it detach a proportion of the army (at least four battalions of infantry, plus one squadron or sotnia from *every cavalry regiment* in the Empire) and hand it over to the Ministry of Interior. Dismayed by this suggestion for the dissolution of Russia's armed forces, the War Ministry broke off negotiations with the Interior Ministry and made preparations to bring this issue to the attention of the Council of State Defense (Sovet gosudarstvennoi oboroni or SGO).[76]

The War Ministry compiled a draft appeal to the SGO dated November 1906 which contained an indictment of Russia's entire civilian administration. The governors of the Empire were portrayed as the natural adversaries of the army, maliciously refusing to discharge unneeded troops, never tiring in their rapacious efforts to secure even more. When the army tried to relieve the four squadrons of the 31st Riga dragoons by exchanging them for four from the 34th, the governor of Kursk greedily retained them all. The War Ministry questioned the utility of

---

[73] TsGVIA, f. 400, op. 3, d. 2733, ll. 88-89.

[74] Ibid., ll. 127-128; also TsGVIA, f. 330, op. 50, d. 1236, l. 8.

[75] TsGVIA, f. 400, op. 3, d. 2733, l. 129.

[76] TsGVIA, f. 400, op. 3, 2862, ll. 152-154.

such civilian policies, and cited the host of evils which were visited on the troops as a result of them. The draft memorandum further noted that the reckless dispatch of troops to the countryside could exacerbate agrarian tensions rather than calm them. A young officer assigned to lead his troops on a protective mission to the estate of a private landlord often considered that landlord as his superior. In his eagerness to please, such an officer might well put the interests of the landlord above the interests of justice. What better incitement to peasant riot could there be? Guard duty was heavy, especially in view of the fact that as of October 1, 1906 there were 218½ battalions and 210 squadrons or sotnias deployed by civilians away from their general headquarters. Although the army agreed to guard state financial institutions, it had to give up the guarding of liquor stores, post offices, telegraph stations, and police stations.[77]

The issue of emancipating the army did not in fact reach the Council of State Defense. But Nicholas II was swayed by the War Ministry's plea and summoned several of the military district commanders to a special conference on the subject in St. Petersburg. At this meeting (November 18, 1906), Nicholas asked the commanders of Warsaw, Vil'na, Kiev, and Moscow Districts, all also governors-general, how they believed military detachments for civilian use could be pared down. Only Skalon from Warsaw argued against reducing the detachments. There were only 1,200 policemen in Warsaw and at least 580 more were urgently needed. To stimulate enlistment in the police, Skalon urged that police pay be raised. For the moment, however, he endorsed the Interior Ministry plan: 280,000 men should be detached from the army and enrolled in the police. Sukhomlinov (Kiev) and Krshivitskii (Vil'na) disagreed violently. They themselves were trying to diminish detachments, but emphasized that in view of the decentralized system of regional military chiefs, they were not always able to curb the governors subordinate to them. Nicholas II ended the conference with a weak declaration that he expected all governors-general to help in reducing detachments.[78]

However, the total size of the military details allocated for civilian use did not meaningfully decline in the course of 1907. Main Staff data revealed that from January to the end of October there were 1,058 civilian summons for aid; 997½ companies, 4 training commands, 7 local commands, 42 scouting commands, 340¼ squadrons or sotnias, 16 field guns, 4 machine guns, and 4,704 soldiers in separate commands took part.

[77] Ibid., ll. 205-211.
[78] Ibid., ll. 236-237.

The army used weapons at the civilian request 48 times.[79] But the staff suspected that its information was not complete and sent out letters to all districts ordering them to report every civilian demand for assistance, including daily guard duty. These instructions resulted in an appalling increase in the reported number of civilian uses—4,649 for November and 4,964 for December.[80]

Although Stolypin once again had asked all governors to refrain from subdividing military units in a circular of November 20, 1906, his words went unheeded.[81] There were grounds to assume that Stolypin and the Interior Ministry generally were insincere in their protestations of willingness to assist the army. War Ministry policy was that the army ought to guard only financial institutions, yet at the end of January 1907 the Police Department was still insisting that the army protect the post offices in the Don.[82] In July, Stolypin informed Rediger that due to "restlessness" among workers and peasants, a cutback in the number of troops scattered throughout the provinces of the Empire was out of the question.[83] In August, the Interior Ministry punctured the army plans to withdraw the 8th Ural Cossacks from Penza to Perm'[84] and prevented Sukhomlinov from bringing a division out of Kursk, Poltava, and Chernigov into Kiev.[85] A November 1907 staff report stated that the detachments of troops deployed for civilian, not military, purposes were still enormous, especially in the Caucasus and Warsaw Districts, "regardless of the fact that the higher civilian administration in them is in the hands of the military district commanders."[86] In December, Palitsyn, head of the General Staff, pointed out that the ten infantry regiments, five reserve battalions, four cavalry regiments, eight Cossack regiments, and one artillery brigade currently on missions outside their military districts represented a grave impediment to any mobilization occasioned by war in the West.[87]

The War Ministry continued to try to hold the dike against the flood of civilian demands. Even some local military chiefs began to display a surprising stiffness of will when dealing with the civilians in 1907. For instance, Major General Ponomarev, commander of the Morshansk gar-

[79] Data worked up on the basis of TsGVIA, f. 400, op. 3, d. 2913, ll. 71-72, 84-85, 96-97, 108-109, 121-122, 138-139, 158-159, 177-178, 192-193, 203-204.

[80] Ibid., ll. 218, 280, 334-335, 371-372.

[81] TsGVIA, f. 400, op. 3, d. 2731, l. 445.

[82] TsGVIA, f. 330, op. 50, d. 1236, l. 18.

[83] TsGVIA, f. 400, op. 3, d. 2897, l. 99.

[84] Ibid., l. 213.

[85] Ibid., l. 246.

[86] Ibid., l. 315.

[87] Ibid., l. 421.

rison, refused troops to the civilian authorities desperately coping with the March railway strike there, even though the civilian request was undeniably proper, for unrest had already begun.[88] The Vladimir garrison commander insisted that summer exercises for the 9th Siberian and 10th Little-Russian Grenadier regiments took precedence over Governor Sazonov's security requirements.[89] District commanders, of course, persisted in their obstinacy. In August, General of Infantry Karass defied War Ministry orders and relieved 22 Cossack sotnias in Kazan' District before replacements arrived.[90]

In mid-1907, the War Ministry scored one success when it secured the demobilization of some of the Cossack regiments of the second and third reserves originally called up in 1905. The Ministry also enjoyed some modest victories in interdicting new detachments. Rediger disregarded Stolypin's appeal for one more Cossack regiment for the troubled province of Perm' in midsummer,[91] just as Polivanov did with the Mogilev governor's request for renewed military guards at the Gomel' post and telegraph station later that autumn.[92] At the same time, the Interior Ministry was barraged with War Ministry demands for the strengthening of the civilian police.

RATIONALE FOR WAR MINISTRY POLICY: A REPRISE

Why was the War Ministry so obstructionist, so opposed to meeting the demands of the government for internal security? Clearly, the Ministry saw repressive service as burdensome, distracting, and ruinous. As far back as June 1905, Rediger had informed the Interior Ministry that the dispersal of the troops on police duty was "completely incompatible with the interests of the military," while in August Sukhomlinov had denounced the damage to army interests from "the uncontrolled summons of troops which exists now."[93] In a circular of May 10, 1906 to all districts, Rediger flatly declared that "detachments of troops to aid the civil power do not always correspond with the demands of reasonable economy, as they result in the excessive fatigue and frequently the total exhaustion of the troops." He urged all district commanders to halt detachments not mandated by "unconditional necessity."[94] A follow-up

[88] Ibid., ll. 17-18, 31, 36.
[89] Ibid., ll. 37, 38-40, 41.
[90] Ibid., ll. 230, 231.
[91] Ibid., l. 108, ll. 110-111.
[92] Ibid., l. 340.
[93] TsGVIA, f. 400, op. 3, d. 2618, l. 83; TsGVIA, f. 400, op. 3, d. 2749, l. 27.
[94] TsGVIA, f. 400, op. 3, d. 2739, l. 130.

circular of June 20 was even more forceful: "Continuation [of the policy of helping the civilians] will doubtless lead to the total disintegration of the army and the loss of it as an organized military force." Rediger enjoined the district commanders to pay special heed to the "full and systematic training" of the troops, for which purpose all detachments "ought to be reduced to the limit of necessity."[95]

On the deepest level, the quarrel between the War Ministry and the Interior Ministry arose from fundamentally opposing conceptions of the purpose of the army in the modern state. Rediger's remarkable August-September 1906 exchange of letters with P. A. Stolypin, Chairman of the Council of Ministers, reveals how widely the army and the government diverged in their assessments of the revolution and the military role in it. "I have the honor to inform Your Excellency," wrote Rediger on August 3, "that I deem my primary task to be the preservation of the troops in order that they might above all answer to their chief function"—i.e., *external* defense. Civilian authorities, requesting military support, never considered "how much these detachments are burdensome for the troops, how much they impede the War Ministry in the attainment of its main duty—the training and military preparation of the units subordinate to it." Governors' requests for troops were often founded on hysteria rather than the sober assessment of threats.[96] On August 17 Rediger wrote Stolypin once more; here he observed that the extraordinary credit to cover the costs of military repression was exhausted, and he demanded that the Interior Ministry relinquish its grip on the army.[97] But as Stolypin continued to maintain his silence, at the end of August Rediger petitioned him yet again. Pointing out that the army needed to curtail repressive operations in the interests of reform, training, and reconstruction, Rediger alluded to the spate of military mutinies in 1905 and the ongoing mutinies of 1906 and implied that such events could not be averted unless the army was relieved.[98]

Stolypin had not received Rediger's last communiqué when he wrote his bilious response to the first two. In a letter dated September 4, Stolypin emphasized that the Empire was in the midst of an extraordinary crisis which obviously required the War Ministry to deviate from its function of "exclusively" preparing the army for war. Resurrecting a civilian argument from previous years, he reminded Rediger that the governors and the Interior Ministry, not the army and the War Ministry, bore responsibility for order in the country. It was not the business of

[95] Ibid., ll. 399-400.
[96] TsGVIA, f. 400, op. 3, d. 2733, l. 81.
[97] TsGVIA, f. 400, op. 3, d. 2739, l. 240.
[98] Ibid., ll. 399-400.

the military to certify whether a particular civilian request was justified or not. The survival of the army as an army was important, true; but the survival of the governmental authority the army was sworn to uphold was even more important. For this reason, Stolypin argued, Rediger should be prepared to tolerate violations in the rules of February 1906 which governed military aid for the duration of the struggle. If Rediger could not in good conscience bend the regulations to accommodate the civilian power, in particular by permitting the dispatch of troops in small detachments, he had better ask Imperial permission to do so.[99]

Rediger's reply (September 13) once again invoked the specter of military insurrection. He opened his letter by repudiating his views on the necessity for training the army. The army was quite willing to forego training to "help calm the Empire." But the issue at hand now was the preservation of the army. As War Minister, Rediger was driven to "the extreme of anxiety" by the excessive use of troops and the subdivision of military units. At present "all organs which enjoy the support of the troops have completely forgotten that the army is not a machine but a living organism which can be threatened, and which acts as a real support [for the state] only if certain qualities are present, qualities inculcated by suitable education and the preservation of internal order and discipline." But the preservation of discipline was inconceivable when the army was fragmented, denied the leadership of officers, and assigned tasks which could only facilitate its corruption. He added that "without doubt . . . a chief task of state power ought to be a concern for preserving the army and protecting it from harmful ideas. . . ." All organs of state power ought to strive for this and ought "not to spoil the army, even unconsciously." Rediger therefore declined to seek Imperial approval for shelving the rules of 1906, since he deemed such a course disastrous.[100] Rediger's sketch of the dismal condition of the army is certainly worthy of notice. But another important feature of the letter is that it discloses Rediger's allegiance to the army above all else. In arguing for retrenchment in military repression regardless of the consequences for state power, Rediger ipso facto took the position that the interests of the army superseded those of the government. Nor was he alone. The higher functionaries of the War Ministry and the majority of district commanders, particularly those of Kiev, St. Petersburg, Kazan', Vil'na, Siberia, and Turkestan, also placed the welfare of the army before that of the regime.

Were these officers solely motivated by fear of impending revolution

[99] Ibid., ll. 242-244.
[100] TsGVIA, f. 400, op. 3, d. 2862, ll. 219-222.

in the ranks? This fear did have weight with them. Correspondence and memoranda from 1905-1907 are studded with blunt warnings about the potentially dire effect of indiscipline in the army. Logically enough, the evidence of greatest anxiety at the War Ministry dates from those months during and just after the largest clusters of military mutinies: November and December 1905 and May, June, and July 1906. To be sure, very few of these mutinies—only ten in 1905 and eight in 1906—involved any gunfire between loyal and disloyal military units.[101] However, even if the majority of mutinies were not full-scale rebellions, there were numerous instances known to Ministry officials in which mutinous soldiers had refused orders to disperse crowds or even to open fire.[102] It was this sort of behavior which Rediger had in mind when he spoke of the "disintegration" of the army and of the "loss of it as an organized military force" in his circular of July 20, 1906. Although military officials were aware that such things as poor food and ill-treatment laid the groundwork for military mutinies—Rediger once wrote that improvements in such areas as these would remove "justifiable reasons for dissatisfaction"—they also tended to see mutiny as the success of propaganda in the army, and the success of propaganda as the consequence of splintering the army into tiny detachments in aid of the civil power.[103] The War Ministry thus launched its campaign to free the army from repressive service in mid-1906 in part because it dreaded still more mutinies. Yet a parallel concern in the thinking of the War Ministry officials was the havoc repressive duty wreaked on training exercises. Affidavits from district commanders about spoiled training abound in 1905, 1906, and 1907.[104] There was a linkage between the training and indiscipline issues. If a soldier was attending summer training camps he was obviously not guarding a factory where seditious workers might propagandize him. But the War Ministry valued the summer training camp as more than a quarantine against the revolutionary bacillus. Just as in the past, the War Ministry promoted training because of its narrow, but all the same professional, aspiration for a powerful, combat-ready Russian army. In internal War Ministry documents references to the negative consequences of bad training for the army are *more common* than allusions to the danger of military rebellion. If the War Ministry put so much stress on the latter in its dealing with the Interior Ministry and the Council of Ministers, it was because the Ministry assumed that

[101] Bushnell, "Mutineers and Revolutionaries," Ph.D. diss., pp. 74, 292.

[102] Rediger made this point to Stolypin in a letter of August 27, 1906. TsGVIA, f. 400, op. 3, d. 2739, l. 400.

[103] Ibid., ll. 399-400.

[104] For some typical examples, see TsGVIA, f. 400, op. 3, d. 2749, ll. 27, 111.

this issue would impress the civilians the most. After all, Rediger's first letter to Stolypin in August 1906 had spoken of the disastrous effects of bad training, not indiscipline. Rediger reverted to the theme of mutiny only when he realized that Stolypin was unmoved by his initial argument. Indeed, in the minds of War Ministry officials there existed an almost maniacal obsession with the effects of revolutionary suppression on the military training program. The tension between training and assisting the civilians had, as we have seen, already emerged at the end of the nineties. However, the commitment to training was enormously amplified by the army's experience in the war with Japan and must be considered in that context.

It is fair to say that the Russo-Japanese War was an enormous trauma for the tsarist army. In the officer corps the loss of the war engendered despair, frustration, and a sense of betrayal. The War Ministry officially blamed the Finance Ministry for the inadequate state of Russia's war equipment.[105] But many Russian officers, with Kuropatkin at the head, also made much of the demoralization of the army by European Russia's defeatist press.[106] Still other officers perceived the cause of the defeat in a deeper and more general malaise of Russian society which had infected the army as well. Russian tactical doctrine, as enunciated by Dragomirov, stressed the importance of the element of morale in warfare: the better motivated army ought always to emerge victorious. In the Russo-Japanese War, there could be no doubt about which army was better motivated. In a very real sense, Russia's own military doctrine explained her defeat. The odious comparison of the enthusiastic Japanese recruit, eagerly rushing to his death in support of the national goals, and the illiterate Russian peasant soldier, ignorant of the purposes of the war, could only rankle in the hearts of Russian officers.[107]

[105] TsGVIA, f. 1, op. 2, d. 165, l. 6 (War Ministry report for 1905).

[106] Lindsay, *Japanese War by General Kuropatkin*, vol. 1, p. 299; Martynov, *Iz pechal'-nogo*, pp. 9-10, 165; D. Parskii, *Prichiny nashikh neudach v voine s Iaponiei. Neobkhodimye reformy v armii* (St. Petersburg, 1906), p. 8; on the press during the war, see B. I. Eisen, "Russkaia legal'naia pressa kontsa XIX-nachala XX veka," in *Iz istorii russkoi zhurnalistiki kontsa XIX-nachala XX v.*, ed. B. I. Eisen (Moscow, 1973), pp. 14-16. One veiled but surprisingly early expression of defeatist sentiment (barely two months into the war) appears in "Iz obshchestvennoi khroniki," *Vestnik Evropy* 1 (Mar. 1904): 420-423.

[107] Lindsay, *Japanese War by General Kuropatkin*, vol. 1, pp. 234-235; Martynov, *Iz pechal'nogo*, pp. 70-74. This argument was exploited by liberals and radicals who insisted that better morale for the army could only be achieved as the result of political and social reform. V. A. Apushkin, *Russko-iaponskaia voina 1904-1905 gg.*, 2d ed. (Moscow, 1911), p. 37, and Volonter [M. Pavlovich], *Russko-iaponskaia voina (prichiny, khod i posledstviia)* (St. Petersburg, 1905), pp. 70, 75, esp. 79-80, 88, 111.

The negotiations for the Peace of Portsmouth were still incomplete when Russian officers began to produce that rich and voluminous literature on the war which inaugurated Russia's so-called military renaissance, fueled by what military engineer A. V. von Schwarts would call "a burning desire" for military reform.[108] Both publicly, in the pages of magazines and newspapers, and privately, in secret memoranda, Russia's professional officers appealed for reform. These proposals spanned the political gamut from conservative to liberal, but generally shared a common concern for upgrading the quality and prestige of the Russian officer.[109] In reports for 1904 and 1905, the military district commanders of the Caucasus, Vil'na, Moscow, Warsaw, Odessa, and Turkestan demanded higher educational standards for officers and in some cases universal literacy for the soldiers.[110]

As it happened, the general who assumed the office of War Minister in June 1905 was also a zealous reformer. A. F. Rediger had successively served in the war with Turkey, in Bulgaria's War Ministry, as a professor at the Nicholas Staff Academy, and as head of the Chancellery of the Russian Ministry of War.[111] From 1905 to 1908, Rediger secured such substantive reforms as the establishment of the Higher Attestation Commission, a new and fairer officers' pension law, higher pay for Russian soldiers, a shortened term of service, and a vastly improved system for regimental purchasing.

Yet Rediger was unable to realize his entire package of reforms, for he confronted three formidable obstacles. The first of these was institutional. In June 1905, Nicholas II split the General Staff away from the War Ministry, raising it to equal ministerial status with the latter. The Council of State Defense (SGO) under Nikolai Nikolaevich was created to unify military and naval planning, while Nikolai's toady, General Palitsyn, was named Chief of Staff. The SGO was too unwieldy and cumbersome an institution to function properly. Not only did Rediger lose control over the Staff, but his lines of communication with it also broke down. Aping the German defense system—independent Staff and independent War Ministry—without establishing de facto suprem-

---

[108] Martynov, *Iz pechal'nogo*; Parskii, *Prichiny*; E. F. Novitskii, *Sandepu* (St. Petersburg, 1907); M. Galkin, *Novyi put' sovremennogo ofitsera* (St. Petersburg, 1907); D. N. Garlinskii, *Mysli ob armii*, vol. 3 (St. Petersburg, 1911). For a survey of General Staff opinion on the war, see A. Ageev, "Ofitsery russkogo general'nogo shtaba ob opyte russko-iaponskoi voiny 1904-1905 gg.," *Voenno-istoricheskii zhurnal* 17, no. 8 (Aug. 1975): 99-104. von Shwartz, *Vospominaniia*, p. 135.

[109] TsGVIA, f. 400, op. 3, d. 2785, ll. 1-8; *VG* (St. Petersburg, Jan. 3-Sept. 5, 1906).

[110] TsGVIA, f. 400, op. 3, d. 2734, ll. 29, 61, 140, 161, 169, 177, 180, 211, 231.

[111] TsGVIA, f. 409, op. 1, d. p/sp 155-483, ll. 1-8.

acy of either one over the other led to divided power and mutual ignorance, with Staff and Ministry unaware of each other's intentions and goals.[112]

A second constraint on the War Ministry was financial. Reorganizations cost money, as did the essential replenishment of Russia's stocks of war material, greatly depleted by the Japanese conflict. During the course of the war, the army had fired over 283 million bullets, not to speak of its consumption of tons of fodder, meat, and medicine.[113] In December of 1906 Rediger calculated that for total restocking, rearmament, and reform, the army required an immediate payment of 2.14 billion rubles, plus an extra 145 million a year. These were, of course, unthinkable sums. The 2.14 billion was almost equal to Russia's entire annual revenue.[114] The parlous state of the Russian fisc made Rediger's request all the more audacious. The war with Japan had soaked up nearly 2.5 billion rubles.[115] In Count Witte's opinion, only the famous 5 percent loan of April 1906 had saved the Empire from the ignominy of default and bankruptcy.[116] The pressure of Russia's huge war debt, the costs of suppressing revolutionary activity—neither augured well for major commitments of money to the Russian army.

The third constraint on army reform was the manpower drain resulting from the burden of internal repression. It may be true that the lessons of the Russo-Japanese War were less than clear, but every military district commander in Russia felt he understood the war and was eager to experiment with tactical innovations suggested by it. But the only opportunities for experimentation were military maneuvers which were severely curtailed in 1904, 1905, 1906, 1907, and even 1908 due to war, demobilization, and repression.[117]

The conditions of repressive service made training all the more difficult. At the end of 1906, district commanders reported from St. Petersburg, Moscow, Warsaw, Vil'na, Kiev, and the Caucasus that the troops were so broadly dispersed and so fragmented that troop training was inconceivable. Worse than this, the troops' command of basic military skills was fast deteriorating. The 63rd reserve infantry brigade, for

---

[112] Kersnovskii, *Istoriia*, pp. 599-601.

[113] TsGVIA, f. 1, op. 2, d. 165, p. 64.

[114] K. F. Shatsillo, *Rossiia pered pervoi mirovoi voinoi (vooruzhennye sily tsarisma v 1905-1914 gg.)* (Moscow, 1974), p. 39.

[115] Iu. N. Shebaldin, "Gosudarstvennyi biudzhet tsarskoi Rossii v nachale XX v. (do pervoi mirovoi voiny)," *Istoricheskie zapiski* (Moscow) 65 (1959): 180.

[116] B. V. Anan'ich, *Rossiia i mezhdunarodnyi kapital 1897-1914 gg.* (Leningrad, 1970), pp. 173-174.

[117] TsGVIA, f. 400, op. 3, d. 4559, ll. 4, 54-55; TsGVIA, f. 1, op. 2, d. 165, l. 41; TsGVIA, f. 1, op. 1, d. 70264, ll. 20-21.

example, had previously boasted a rating of "excellent" in marksmanship. A testing conducted in 1906, however, had produced scores so low that they could not even be measured on the scale.[118]

CIVILIAN MEDDLING: A NEW STAGE IN CIVIL-MILITARY HOSTILITY

So intensive an involvement in repression was bearing another evil fruit: civilians were manifesting an exasperating tendency to meddle in the internal procedure and life of the army. Civilian officials and elected bodies without the power to do so were petulantly demanding that troops be sent them, as did the Opochets city Duma in January of 1906 and the Yalta uezd noble marshal the following month.[119] But even when the troops were summoned lawfully, the army was defenseless against civilian interloping. In June 1906 the governor of Perm', already conspicuous for his gratuitous advice to the regimental colonel of Cossacks in his capital, filed an insulting report which rated the Cossacks for their rowdy, drunken behavior. Kazan' Military District indignantly rebutted these charges, claiming that the information for them had been supplied by low-ranking policemen and private spies hostile to the Cossacks.[120] Other governors wrote military leaders in their territories giving them opinions about promotions and the fitness of officers for service. Even Stolypin himself tried to interfere in promotion policy. All Gendarmes and many policemen in fact held military rank, and Stolypin, gratified by their arduous and faithful service, desired to reward them. More often than not, these rewards took the form of decorations or actual promotions in rank, accomplished by Stolypin and Nicholas II without the knowledge or approval of the Ministry of War. This discourtesy touched off a major feud in October 1906. Stolypin told Rediger that Nicholas had agreed to promote Colonel Baron Nol'ken, Gendarme officer and former governor of Tomsk, to the rank of major general. Yet Nol'ken had only been a colonel for two years. Rediger opposed Stolypin on the issue and Stolypin, who was clearly operating under considerable strain at this time, threatened to resign if Nol'ken's promotion did not go through. Rediger then "coolly" informed Stolypin that the question of the latter's resignation was not within his purview but that he could not permit "persons only wearing the military uniform to outstrip true soldiers serving in the armed forces."[121] Besides illustrating the degree to which a sense of unity between army and police had been sundered

[118] TsGVIA, f. 400, op. 3, d. 2862, ll. 50, 52, 53-54, 57, 64-65.
[119] TsGVIA, f. 400, op. 3, d. 1459, ll. 1, 3, 11.
[120] TsGVIA, f. 400, op. 3, d. 2739, ll. 86, 93.
[121] TsGVIA, f. 400, op. 3, d. 5, pp. 628-630.

by the tensions of the revolution, this quarrel also demonstrates Rediger's determination to preserve all vestiges of military authority insofar as possible.

Indeed, civilian intervention in military affairs intensified rather than abated throughout 1906. In the spring, the Tambov governor went even further. He demanded that the procedure for calling out the troops be simplified. But the procedure had already been simplified, since appeals for troops were now processed by the local military chiefs, not by the central office of the military district. Further "simplification" could only imply the complete civilian usurpation of all authority over the army.[122] Many governors were behaving as if they already possessed such authority. The Main Staff commented in September of 1906: "both the governors and the organs of local police subordinate to them regard the troops deployed within the borders of a given province or uezd as being under their authority. They therefore [think that they may] independently set tasks and indicate the goals of action; even rural policemen at times give orders about the movement of companies, squadrons and sotnias."[123] A pervasive suspicion that the other ministries of state were shirking their responsibilities grew in tandem with exasperation at civilian presumptuousness. "In the beginning the police were badly organized, and this explained their weakness, but it really ought to have been possible to organize them in two years that they might be in a condition to carry out their own functions," wrote Rediger in August of 1906.[124]

This latter concept—the idea that the Interior Ministry and the civilians were exploiting the army when they could and should have done otherwise—became a theme in War Ministry thinking at the end of 1906 and all throughout 1907. In September 1906, the War Ministry accused the Ministry of Finance of doing nothing to raise its own guard forces in Turkestan, even though it had had over one and a half months to act.[125] In the same month, alarmed by the costs of repression, the Council of Ministers handed down an ingenious ruling: all interest on the regimental economic capital funds of the Manchurian army were to be confiscated and devoted to paying the repression bill. The units which had fought the Japanese, often with signal valor, were to be bilked of eleven million rubles, part of the income they used for extra food and improvements.[126] This perfunctory decision incensed Rediger: he sub-

---

[122] TsGVIA, f. 400, op. 3, d. 2739, ll. 155, 157.
[123] TsGVIA, f. 400, op. 3, d. 2734, l. 74.
[124] Ibid., ll. 245, 221.
[125] TsGVIA, f. 400, op. 3, d. 2733, ll. 91-92.
[126] TsGVIA, f. 400, op. 3, d. 2739, ll. 432, 436.

sequently described the entire episode as "very characteristic" of the "attitude of the Council of Ministers to the army."[127]

Given all of these (and other) instances of confrontation, plus the widespread sentiment that the army was being ill-used, it is not entirely surprising that some officers began to act as if the true enemies of the army were neither workers, nor peasants, nor radicals, but rather the civilian bureaucrats of Russia. Beginning in late 1906 and continuing into 1907, case after case revealed the new behavior pattern. For instance, in November 1906, over six hundred peasants rioted in the village of Multan, Malmuzhsk uezd, Viatka Province. In the course of the riot, the mob stormed the police station and murdered two policemen. Yet Colonel Tiumenev, the uezd military chief, did not assist the beleaguered policemen, even though he had over two hundred reservists at his disposal. Tiumenev was "retired" from the army, but not so much for his criminal idleness as for what occurred the following day. The police captain accosted him and accused him of cowardice, but Tiumenev made no move to wipe out this insult with blood, as he should have done in the opinion of Lieutenant General Sandetskii, commander of Kazan' District.[128] Thus to Sandetskii it was not the unruly peasants whom Tiumenev should have shot and killed, but the district police captain. That peculiar and counterproductive cult of officers' honor, which had so often in the past resulted in violence against the doctor, the student, or the radical *intelligent*, was now being invoked against the Imperial police, presumably the army's ally in the struggle against disorder.

Again, in December 1906, another affair transpired, indicating the increasing anticivilian rancor in the army. In that month a police captain in Voronezh Province called for men of the 6th sotnia of the 29th Don Cossacks to assist him in sequestering the cattle of the peasants of the village of Berezovo for nonpayment of taxes. The police later reported that the Cossacks not only refused to help them, but allowed the peasants to take the cattle back, while urging them not to pay. The commander of the 3rd sotnia of the regiment wrote his colonel that the real focus of the Cossacks' grievances was the police captain's attempt to assume command over them. He darkly warned that such actions of policemen with respect to Cossacks were not only unhelpful but might elicit "undesirable consequences." Although the Cossack commander, Kosmachev, may have been misrepresenting the situation, in effect he was implying that civilian intervention in military affairs not only could lead to mutiny, but in a curious way, even excused mutiny. Rediger's response to

[127] TsGVIA, f. 280, op. 1, d. 5, pp. 632-633.
[128] TsGVIA, f. 400, op. 15, d. 3012, ll. 4, 132.

all of this was the quintessence of negative corporatism: in a draft letter to Stolypin he began by denying that the Cossacks had committed any wrongful acts, then argued that even if they had, they would only have been responding to civilian ineptitude.[129]

Anger at civilian behavior appeared again in a draft letter to the Interior Ministry in the Main Staff in September 1907. Shortly before, civilian authorities had called a company of the 11th Pakov infantry to Kotlynsk goldfield in Viatka Province. Arriving at 11:00 p.m., the troops were met by a policeman who escorted them to their quarters. When the company commander refused to accept the first building the policeman showed him, which was filthy, the policeman took them to another which, however, lacked windows and doors.

> This report graphically illustrates the attitude in several cases of the organs of the local civilian administration, resorting to the aid of troops, but not thinking of the necessity of satisfying their most essential demands. . . . repetition of such incidents in the future will doubtless lead to the gradual embitterment of the troops against the civilian administration and to the lowering, on their part, of energy during the suppression of disorders which will serve in its turn as the source of much evil.[130]

In short, key military leaders had begun to view the police as adversaries.

In May of 1907 General Selivanov filed a note from his general headquarters in Irkutsk. The civilians were now in charge of almost one-fifth of the infantry in his far-flung district, and Selivanov adduced several reasons for this sorry state of affairs. Civilians were dragging their feet in creating their own guard units and were taking no steps to enlarge prisons or fortify banks and treasuries. Obviously, the civilians wanted to slough off any responsibility they might have had for protecting their own property onto the shoulders of the army. Soldiers were now even guarding police stations. It was the "lack of courage of the civilian bureaucrats," said Selivanov, which was in the last analysis burdening the army.[131] By September 1907, the War Ministry had come to agree with Selivanov: if not cowardice, at least the incompetence or lassitude of the police explained the extent of guard and police duty borne by the Russian army. Accordingly, the Main Staff ordered local military leaders throughout the Empire secretly to accumulate material on the structure and the performance of the police. The military districts

---

[129] TsGVIA, f. 330, op. 51, d. 1104, ll. 1, 2, 25-26, 91.
[130] TsGVIA, f. 400, op. 3, d. 2897, l. 277.
[131] Ibid., ll. 42-43.

1. The personal pennant of the War Minister, adopted in 1892. The design beneath the cross represents the various branches of army service: rifles for the infantry, cannon for the artillery, sabers for the cavalry, spades for the engineers.

1. Ранецъ.
2. Сухарный мѣшокъ съ сухарями.
3. Шинель, закатанная въ полотнище походной
   палатки съ принадлежностями этой палатки.
4. Котелокъ.
5. Водоносная фляга въ чахлѣ.
6. Патронная сумка.
7. Шанцевый инструментъ.

2. A soldier of the engineers in full combat dress, 1898.

3. Repression. Cossack soldiers burning down a peasant hut in Georgia, 1906.

4. An infantry patrol, Warsaw, 1906. The tsarist government attempted to deter demonstrations by sending patrols like these into the streets of major cities during the 1905-1907 revolution.

5. Three soldiers to guard each policeman. The War Ministry's secret study of the Empire's police during the revolution concluded that "in the majority of cases the police try to avoid duty and even evince cowardice."

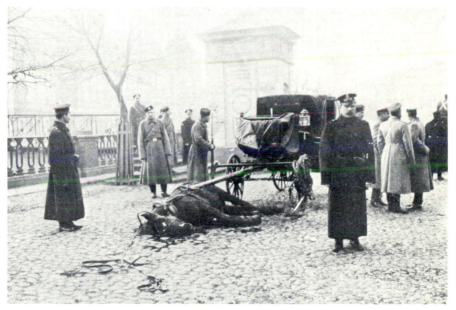

6. Revolutionary terrorism. A horse killed by a small bomb in the course of a politically motivated robbery.

7. The Russo-Japanese War. Entrenched Russian infantry during the battle of Liao-Yang, August, 1905.

8. Gen. A. N. Kuropatkin, former War Minister and commander in chief of Russia's forces in the east, awards a soldier a decoration during the battle of Liao-Yang.

9. The Ministry of War with St. Isaac's Cathedral in the background.

10. The lobby of the Chancellery of the Imperial War Ministry.

11. A training class for city policemen in turn-of-the-century St. Petersburg.

12. A mounted police patrol, St. Petersburg.

13. Police rounding up suspects, Moscow.

14. A cossack guard salutes Nicholas II, Emperor of Russia.

15. Russian war ministers:
(*top left*) D. A. Miliutin (1861-1881);
(*top right*) P. S. Vannovskii (1881-1898);
(*middle left*) A. N. Kuropatkin (1898-1904);
(*middle right*) V. V. Sakharov (1904-1905);
(*bottom left*) A. F. Rediger (1905-1911).

16. [We] Pacified [Them]. An antimilitary cartoon of 1906. A tsarist soldier surveys a ruined village with satisfaction.

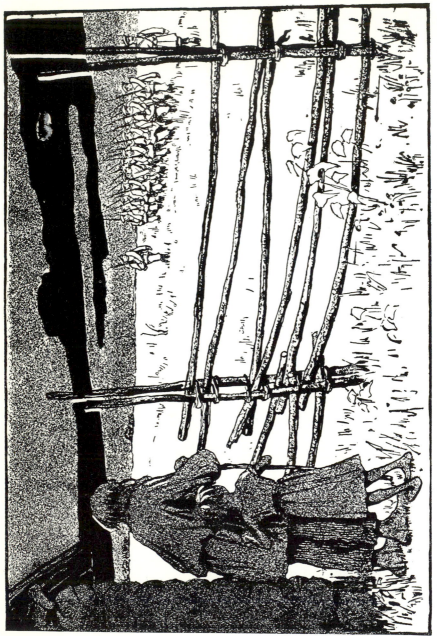

17. Antimilitary art. An untitled cartoon of 1906 depicts two peasants—an old man and a small girl—watching a military patrol pass by their village.

which replied damned the police for every possible abuse. The military chief of Dem'iansk uezd, for example, assailed the cowardice of the police. In 1906, ten policemen could not stop a prison riot, while nine soldiers could. In the fall of the same year, in the village of Pupov, the peasants disarmed the police and chased them away. Vil'na District's local military chiefs declared that the poor discipline and alcoholism of the police made them ineffective and discredited them in the eyes of the people. Warsaw reported that in the town of Ostrowiec, Radom Province, the police were so crazed with fear that they refused to show themselves in the streets without a military escort. Kiev District reports denounced the police for "hiding behind the troops" during rural disorders. Moscow District stressed the senseless abuse by the police of their privilege of military assistance. Kazan concluded that the police "did not always fulfill their function of stopping disorders among the population, for example, during the collection of taxes and arrears, and especially during the arrest of guilty or suspicious persons." N. Orlov, commander of the 3rd infantry division, wrote from Kaluga that "in the majority of cases" the police try to avoid duty and even "evince cowardice." Polivanov, Assistant War Minister, summed up the War Ministry's study of Russia's police in a letter to Stolypin of mid-January 1908: "The large amount of material we have by now received on this question gives us a basis to conclude that in many cases the troops are called out chiefly due to the incorrect use of the police, the incapacity of the police to fulfill its numerous obligations and the inability of senior police officials to put the issue of training the police on a correct footing."[132] By this point, however, the pressure on the Russian army was slackening. Already in December 1907, Makarov had written the War Ministry in the name of the Interior Ministry that the governors of eleven relatively "calm" provinces now at last agreed to release some of the troops they had summoned.[133] On March 4, 1908, Nicholas II ordered that military units be returned to their general headquarters insofar as possible. And as the general revolutionary ferment subsided, the number of troop uses for repressive service declined sharply.[134] The army was still, however, bedeviled with civilian guard duty, which persisted long after the revolution had died out. But for most units of the Russian army, save the Military Justice Administration, the Russian revolution was technically over. The Ministry now faced the task of reconstructing the army.

The training procedures and programs of the War Ministry were in

[132] TsGVIA, f. 400, op. 3, d. 2897, ll. 129, 158, 155, 160, 163, 165, 167, 168, 170, 189, 193, 195-202.
[133] Ibid., l. 369.
[134] TsGVIA, f. 400, op. 3, d. 3056, ll. 50-51.

ruins. There were no mobile training exercises in 1904, 1905, or 1906.[135] In 1907, only 504 battalions, 331 squadrons or sotnias and 306½ batteries were able to participate in summer exercises; in 1908, a more normal year, 751 battalions, 487 squadrons and sotnias, and 439 batteries would train.[136] Again, in 1907 only 37 percent of the troops in Odessa District would engage in "mobile" maneuvers, 30 percent in Moscow, and 52 percent in the Caucasus.[137] For budgetary, logistical, and organizational reasons, it was impossible for the troops to make up exercises which had been omitted in the years 1904-1907. Recruits who passed through the army in these years were denied an adequate measure of training. This no doubt impaired Russia's performance in the early days of the First World War, for the reservists who had been on active duty in each of these years were called to the colors on the very first day of mobilization (July 18, 1914). Regardless of the real damage it caused to Russia's defenses, lack of training seriously affected the army's *perception* of its relative weakness vis-à-vis the West in the years after the revolution.

The revolution's effect on the Russian officer corps also posed an unwelcome problem for the Ministry of War. Hundreds of officers showed their distaste for repression by sending in their resignations. In 1906 the district commander of Vil'na complained that he was lacking a full 20 percent of the officers he needed in his district.[138] By 1907 the Russian army as a whole lacked 20 percent of its legal complement of officers.[139] The army was short by 7.2 percent in October 1908, and still short by 5.5 percent in October of 1909.[140]

There were, in addition, attitudinal changes toward their civilian masters within the Russian officer corps as a result of the revolution, changes which could never be exorcised. Both the War Ministry and the civilian ministries displayed insensitivity to each other's difficulties in 1905-1907. The civilians did at times profess sympathy for the plight of the military, and at times issued circulars to the governors in the purported defense of the army's interests. But the circular was probably the most crafty bureaucratic device in Imperial Russia for evading the redress of grievances raised by other ministries. The civilian government's solicitude for the army was duplicitous. Witte, Durnovo, and Stolypin might forbid the governors to subdivide military units, but when the army made an issue of a particular governor's refusal to comply with these

[135] TsGVIA, f. 400, op. 3, d. 4527, l. 6.
[136] TsGVIA, f. 400, op. 3, d. 4559, l. 54.
[137] TsGVIA, f. 400, op. 3, d. 4527, l. 6.
[138] TsGVIA, f. 400, op. 3, d. 2734, l. 107.
[139] Denikin, *Staraia armiia*, vol. 1, p. 147.
[140] TsGVIA, f. 1, op. 2, d. 169, l. 8.

regulations, the Interior Ministry gave that official full backing from St. Petersburg.

On the other hand, did the civilians have any other choice? It was logical for the civilian state to rely as heavily as it did on the offices of the Russian army during the revolution, for financial reasons as well as considerations of efficacy. If a danger point required a guard, or a town needed more police, it was cheaper for the state to send in a soldier, paid from 6 to 12 rubles a year, than to hire a new policeman at an annual wage of 200-360 rubles. Similarly, in a moment of crisis a company of youthful soldiers, disciplined, motivated, and well-armed, was preferable to a handful of middle-aged policemen carrying rusty Berdan rifles from the 1870s. The War Ministry and key segments of the leadership of the Russian army refused to see the issue from this point of view.

To be sure, there were military men who backed the civilians in the internal security dispute. Generals Orlov and Meller-Zakomel'skii rarely allowed military interests to interfere with their zealous support of repression. Vorontsov-Dashkov was vitally concerned with the reestablishment of order in the Caucasus.[141] Malakhov and Gershel'man, Moscow District commanders in 1905 and 1906, routinely permitted Cossack units to be divided down to platoon level during patrols.[142] And Skalon of Warsaw was the most consistent supporter of the Interior Ministry, not War Ministry, policy among the military district commanders. At the 1907 conference of district commanders, as we have seen, his was the proposal that most closely paralleled Stolypin's. And in August 1906, to cite only one of many possible examples, he was dividing and subdividing his forces into even smaller units, in direct contravention of War Ministry orders.[143]

On various occasions governors and policemen sent letters of praise, not blame, about the activities of military commands in their territories to St. Petersburg—a fact which testifies to cooperation, not discord.[144] A good number of officers in the provinces strove to accommodate the civilians at every turn, some out of good will, some out of ignorance, and some out of greed for decorations and promotions. It should be noted, however, that the War Ministry strongly opposed granting such rewards, and tried to limit them to the statutory number of extraordinary awards permitted in each military district in time of peace.[145]

In understanding the antagonism between army and government in

---

[141] See his "situation report" of Feb. 16, 1906; TsGVIA, f. 400, op. 3, d. 2737, l. 25a.
[142] TsGVIA, f. 400, op. 3, d. 2731, l. 68.
[143] Ibid., l. 367.
[144] TsGVIA, f. 400, op. 15, d. 3090, l. 71; TsGVIA, f. 330, op. 50, d. 494, passim.
[145] TsGVIA, f. 400, op. 15, d. 3090, l. 86.

1905-1907, it is important to take the acute professional frustration of Russian officers into account. Ironically, at the very moment that a military consensus on the urgency of reform, increased army spending, and expansion of training had coalesced, the civilian government was denying the army the requisite money, manpower, and opportunity. This frustration, heaped on top of the fundamentally adversarial position of the War Ministry toward the civilian government with regard to internal repressive service, is the backdrop for the obstructionist conduct of the War Ministry during the revolution.

The War Ministry and significant segments of the military elite emerged from the revolution with scant trust in the civilian power which had put the army through such a harrowing ordeal, which was so oblivious to military interests, which had used the army so badly. Indeed, the Ministry's final verdict on the revolution was contained in its police study: the troops had *needlessly* been expended in the deterrence of disorders because of the defects, incompetence, and maladministration of the police. The War Ministry found the civilian power of the Empire culpable for its negligence, perhaps even maliciousness towards the military.

If Witte had not decentralized the army, if the War Ministry had had firm control over its local representatives, the Russian revolution of 1905-1907 might have taken a different course. At the very least, it would have been much harder to suppress. If the Ministry had had its way there would have been no scores of regiments dispatched away from headquarters, no military guards in the Russian provinces. At every turn in the revolution, we find the Ministry attempting to get its troops back, denying governors assistance, and expressing a distinct preference for military professionalism at the expense of internal security. The significance of the Russian revolution to the War Ministry is aptly summed up by a bitter remark made by Rediger to Stolypin on March 1, 1908: "The army does not train, but rather serves you."[146]

[146] Polivanov, *Iz dnevnikov*, p. 42.

SIX

The Russian Revolution
and Military Justice

IF THE GRADUAL DISENGAGEMENT of the Russian army in the country-side was contemplated with pleasure by the War Ministry Chancellery at the beginning of 1908, officials of the Main Administration of Military Justice (GVSU) had no cause to share in the rejoicing. The number of civilian defendants tried in military courts on the basis of the safeguard laws or martial law attained all-time high levels in 1908. In fact, there is a sense in which the revolution never ended for the military judicial network. Although the number of civilian defendants abated sharply in the years after 1908, that number never subsided to the normal level (less than fifty defendants) which had characterized the period before 1905.

It is important to note at the outset that the central institutions of the War Ministry were much more obliging when the civilians pressed for military court action than they were when the commitment of troops in a repressive capacity was at stake. Obsessed with the defense of the professional integrity of Russia's combat forces, such institutions as the Chancellery of the War Ministry and the Main Staff quite easily reconciled themselves to casting the GVSU to the civilian lions. The GVSU itself under the Chief Military Procurators in the years 1905-1909 (Pavlov, Ryl'ke, Osten-Saken) was amenable and in some cases even eager to extend all its help to the civilians in their battles with revolutionary contagion. At no point in the course of the revolution did the central GVSU ever overtly reject the repressive role which Russia's civilian leaders prescribed for it.

This latter fact makes the discernible responses to the revolution of the provincial officials of the GVSU—the military district court judges, the district prosecutors, district candidates—all the more interesting. Unfortunately, our analysis of these responses has to be confined to generalization. This is due both to the poverty of one section of the source base and the richness of another section of it.

Neither the Imperial government nor military superiors invited the comment of GVSU officials on the role of the military courts in the revolution. To the contrary, intimations of dissatisfaction, let alone opposition, were repaid with discharge, forced retirement, or undesirable transfer. In this atmosphere, GVSU officers who entertained doubts about civilian trials doubtless chose to keep them to themselves. Material on outspoken GVSU officers rarely surfaces in the records.

But there is a further point. For a group whose work was so closely allied to the written and spoken word, the officers of the Military Justice Administration were surprisingly reticent. Memoirs, autobiographies, even notes written by them are few: an exasperating gap for the historian of attitudes and perceptions. One can, of course, probe attitudes and perceptions by studying the activities of these men. But there are problems with the sources for this. The archival files of the Main Administration of Military Justice are in disarray. Yet while incomplete and difficult to obtain, the amount of extant material on the court cases in 1905-1909 is enormous. To analyze all of these data would require years, plus a grounding in prerevolutionary civilian and military law so extensive that the recognition of procedural quirks would be automatic.

Although the sheer volume of data precludes a systematic study of the entire collection a preliminary reading of the material can yield valuable insights. Statistics on cases, hirings and resignations, coupled with the laws enacted in this period and the remarks of civilian contemporaries, reveal the central dilemma which confronted GVSU officials: how, as professionals, could they cope with a situation which violated their canons of professionalism? This conflict was particularly intense. After all, unlike the Russian officer corps as a whole, membership in the GVSU was largely confined to professionals with higher juridical education.

MILITARY JUDICIAL REPRESSION

Table 11 puts the upsurge in military judicial actions against civilians into bold relief. The relationship between cases involving the extraordinary prosecution of civilians and regular cases increased ten-fold in 1905 by comparison with 1904. Still, the 165 cases tried in 1905 represented more a petty irritant than a crushing burden to the GVSU. In 1906 and 1907, however, there was a spectacular explosion of safeguard and martial law cases. By 1908 such cases comprised over half of all cases heard in military district courts. In subsequent years this load declined, although the quantity of cases (varying between three and five hundred from 1910 to 1912) was nonetheless several times greater than the number heard before 1905. That the court dockets were still bulging with civilian cases after 1907 does not necessarily indicate rampant criminality in these years. Rather these high figures were due to an over-

TABLE 11

Civilian Trials in Military District Courts on the Basis of Safeguard,
Martial Law, or Direct Action of the Interior Ministry

	1902	1903	1904	1905	1906	1907	1908	1909	1910	1911	1912
Number of cases (if known)	9	13		165	960	1,950	2,836		463	305	520
Number of defendants	15	43	18	308	4,698	4,335	7,016	5,400	2,045	733	960
Number of death sentences	13	6	6	41	254	486	1,135	441	116	74	129
Percentage of civilian defendants to total, civilian and military	.275	.788	.337	3.5	27.47	29.21	50.52	45.58	20.57	8.3	no infor.

SOURCES: Calculated on the basis of G. Filatev, "Dorevoliutsionnye voennye sudy v tsifrakh," *Katorga i ssylka* (Moscow), 7, no. 68 (1930), pp. 139-140. Checked against raw data on civilian court cases in TsGVIA, f. 801, op. 56/79, d. 47, 19059, ll. 12-389, passim; *Vsepoddanneishii otchet voennogo ministerstva za 1906, Otchet glavnogo voenno-sudnogo upravleniia* (St. Petersburg, 1908), p. 30. TsGVIA, f. 1, op. 1, d. 70240 (for 1906), ll. 2, 5-6, 13, 30-31; TsGVIA, f. 801, op. 56, d. 30 1907 g., ll. 13-62; TsGVIA, f. 1, op. 1, d. 72940, ll. 6, 26-194 (for 1908); TsGVIA, f. 801, op. 56, d. 47, 1908, ll. 7-66; TsGVIA, f. 801, op. 56, d. 7, 1909, ll. 8-63, passim; TsGVIA, f. 1, op. 1, d. 74243 (for 1909), ll. 25-139, passim

loading of the military judicial system during the revolution. Even after the revolution was over, the military courts were engaged in mop-up operations—i.e., attending to crimes committed during the revolutionary era itself. Statistics on cases involving crimes of state tried in 1909, for instance, reveal that there were 1,306 defendants (both civilians and soldiers). Sixty percent of these defendants were tried for crimes committed before 1908.[1]

How many civilians were brought to the bar of military justice from 1905 to 1912 because of strictly revolutionary deeds? Unfortunately, the boundaries between revolutionary and simply felonious activity are murky. To be sure, military courts indicted the overwhelming majority of civilians in this period on criminal rather than political charges. Leafing through the indictments one finds hundreds of instances of such crimes as premeditated murder, manslaughter, burglary, and robbery. In an era of revolution, however, a revolutionary act might well be the assassination of a policeman or a factory owner. Robberies were at times executed by bands of indigent revolutionaries, desperate to replenish the party funds. Some Soviet scholars would classify a broad spectrum of rural violence (attacks by poor peasants on richer ones, etc.) as "revolutionary," since class hatred presumably motivated such crimes. Conversely, astute criminals found it convenient to masquerade as revolutionaries when it suited their purposes. In 1908, for instance, one Sergei Skibenko (a graduate student in the natural sciences) sent a threatening letter to Professor Rennenkampf of Novorossisk University. Purportedly written by the "Odessa Group of Anarchist Communists," the note demanded money for the "needs of the prisons"; actually, Skibenko had his own personal plans for the cash.[2]

In the view of the Imperial Russian government, however, revolutionary unrest and common street crime were interwoven and self-supporting. It fell to the lot of the military courts to crush these allied phenomena with all possible energy. The government sought to justify its reliance on military justice and the military death penalty by pointing out that the average citizen as well as the authorities suffered as a result of the revolution. A GVSU report for 1906 contained the following official rationale:

> The significant increase in the criminal actions of the revolutionary organizations directed to overthrowing the existing state order and the principles of society has been marked by a whole series of

[1] Calculated on the basis of TsGVIA, f. 1, op. 1, d. 74273 (Military Justice Administration statistical data for 1909), ll. 25-139.
[2] Ibid., l. 72.

terrorist acts and an extraordinary increase of the most terrible crimes, directed not only against the government power but the lives, health, freedom and property of the peaceable population. In the struggle with these extremely dangerous phenomena . . . swift and correspondingly stern judicial repression has the greatest significance.[3]

The civilian government envisioned the military judicial system as the vanguard of this swift judicial repression and hence pressured the GVSU for speedier and "simpler" procedures in safeguard or martial law cases. By mid-1905, Nicholas II's insistence on celerity in such cases had led to the promulgation of a number of decrees. One commanded military prosecutors and military judges to take up cases of civilians *before* they handled soldiers' cases. Another instructed prosecutors to cut red tape by indicting civilians without the formal permission of the military district commanders, as was the usual rule. The district commanders themselves and the governors-general were told that they were to channel appeals in these cases to St. Petersburg only if they found them meritorious; a not too subtle hint to these officials that they were to quash more appeals.[4]

At first some bulwarks of due process held against the outcry for speed and simplification. In 1905, for example, the War Ministry, Interior Ministry, and Ministry of Justice agreed that the rules of the Code of Criminal Procedure were not to be abrogated in the military district courts: a police inquest was not enough to shunt a civilian case into a military court without an official preliminary investigation.[5] But in 1906 the government succumbed to panic and abandoned the vestiges of respect for legal niceties. An important step in this regard was the 1906 decision against preliminary investigation. The agreement between the Ministries of War, Justice, and the Interior was revoked; civilians could now be tried in the military courts on the flimsy basis of police inquest alone. In essence, then, the police themselves assumed the indicting power with respect to the military district courts.[6]

MILITARY FIELD COURTS-MARTIAL

This latter "simplification" was deemed insufficient, however. On August 19, 1906 the Emperor endorsed the notorious Council of Ministers'

[3] TsGVIA, f. 1, op. 1, d. 70270 (Military Justice Administration otchet data for 1906), l. 17.

[4] *Vsepoddanneishii otchet voennogo ministerstva za 1905* (St. Petersburg, 1907), p. 31.

[5] TsGVIA, f. 1, op. 2, d. 165 (War Ministry report for 1905), l. 50.

[6] TsGVIA, f. 1, op. 2, d. 70264 (War Ministry for 1906), l. 115.

decision on the creation of military field courts-martial. The inspiration for this drastic step appears to have come from Nicholas II personally. In early August his sense of alarm at widespread political murder and agrarian unrest in the Empire had moved him to summon the Council of Ministers to consider the issue; in a letter of August 12 addressed to Stolypin, Nicholas alluded to the need for an "exceptional law" which would give assurance that the government had "taken decisive measures."[7] The captious First Duma had already been prorogued, and Stolypin enacted the field courts-martial law in accord with Nicholas's request by employing the emergency clause (article 87) of the Fundamental Laws of the Empire, which allowed for ministerial legislation when the Duma was not in session.

In brief, the law on field courts-martial stated that they could be formed at the behest of governors-general or persons coequal in power in those areas of the Empire which were under extraordinary safeguard or martial law. They were to be used when the fact of criminal action by a civilian was "so obvious" that investigation was unnecessary. Courts were to be made up of five judges, selected by the governor-general from suitable military officers. Guilty parties were to be brought before the courts within twenty-four hours of arrest; trials, conducted under the military laws of war, were to last no longer than forty-eight hours; sentences were to be carried out within twenty-four hours of pronouncement.[8]

These courts were, of course, drumhead courts-martial, barely veiled excuses for official terrorism. If guilt was so obvious, why have a trial at all? Even Chief Military Procurator Pavlov, a man not noted for the quality of his mercy, objected to them.[9] In the country at large even some moderate political elements which sought a reconciliation with the government reviled the courts. The famed zemstvo leader D. N. Shipov, for instance, resigned from the Central Committee of the Octobrist Party when A. I. Guchkov, the party's nominal leader, approved of the courts in an interview he gave to the newspaper *Novoe vremia* at the end of August.[10]

---

[7] TsGAOR, f. 601, op. 1, d. 1125, l. 2; see also V. I. Diakin, *Samoderzhavie, burzhuaziia i dvorianstvo v 1907-1911 g.g.* (Leningrad, 1978), p. 26.

[8] *Sbornik postanovlenii izdannykh v poriadke stat'i 87 i osnovnykh gosudarstvennykh zakonov s ukazaniem otnosheniia etikh postanovlenii k pravilam deistvuiushchogo Svoda zakonov 1906-1907 g.g.* (St. Petersburg, 1907), p. 11.

[9] R. Zverev, ed., "Iz zapisok A. F. Redigera," *Krasnyi arkhiv* (Moscow), 5, no. 60 (1933): 126.

[10] D. N. Shipov, *Vospominaniia i dumy o perezhitom* (Moscow, 1918), p. 495. Shipov already had his disagreements with Guchov. The difference over the field courts was merely the last straw.

From the very beginning, Nicholas II left no doubt that he held military district commanders personally responsible for any laxness in enforcing this savage law.[11] But his fears were misplaced; leniency was not the hallmark of the military field court-martial. Although the records of these courts were never transmitted to Petersburg (and probably remain scattered in Soviet provincial archives), all evidence suggests that in the first six months of their existence these courts were responsible for the execution of at least 950 persons.[12] More importantly, this admittedly vague law was subject to widespread abuse. Certain governors-general compiled their own arbitrary roster of offenses which would render a civilian liable for trial in a field court, prompting the Council of Ministers to issue a "clarifying" circular of October 12, 1907. Only persons who committed murder, robbery, or banditry; resisted the authorities with force; attacked policemen or soldiers; or illegally prepared, secreted, or employed explosive substances were to face the retribution of the field court-martial.[13]

To be fair, many of those brought before these courts were apparently guilty of heinous crimes.[14] It is also true that not all of the judges who served on these courts were docile processors of sentences of death or hard labor. For instance, in early November 1906 a worker's funeral in Odessa occasioned a major demonstration and mêlée between police and laborers. A certain Isaakovich was arrested and turned over to a field court on the charge of firing at the police; objective witnesses confirmed his deed. Still, three of the members of the court found the text of the indictment inexact and declined to pass sentence. In the words of the governor-general and military district commander, General Kaul'bars, "the actions of this field court have produced an extremely terrible impression, especially on the police, who every day are subject to serious danger."[15]

Yet on balance, the military field court system was a travesty of military justice, a painful humiliation for members of the GVSU. The field court-martial was entirely outside the control of the military judicial authorities. Although directives on the law were often sent by the War Minister through the office of the Chief Military Procurator, the GVSU neither collected data on the trials nor participated in them. The latter

[11] Polianskii, *Tsarskie*, p. 196; M. N Gernet, *Istoriia tsarskoi tiur'my*, vol. 4 (Moscow 1954), p. 63.

[12] N. I. Faleev, "Shest' mesiatsev voenno-polevoi iustitsii," *Byloe* 2, no. 2114 (Feb. 1907): 80.

[13] Faleev, "Shest' mesiatsev," pp. 48-49; TsGVIA, f. 280, op. 1, d. 6, p. 694.

[14] Faleev, "Shest' mesiatsev," p. 52.

[15] TsGVIA, f. 400, op. 15, d. 2916a (Press Bureau), l. 51.

point deserves to be underscored; the field court-martial was a ploy to have military justice without the military judicial system, an attempt to circumvent the GVSU and the guarantees of due process institutionalized in its operations. A telegram from Chief Procurator Pavlov stated that the civilian government intended that judges for these courts be selected from among officers of the line, not officers of the Military Justice Administration, even if the latter *happened to be present*.[16] In other words, the government not only permitted officers without legal education to serve in the courts, but consciously preferred legal illiterates to professional jurists.

THE RETURN TO REGULAR MILITARY JUSTICE: CIVILIAN PRESSURE

The law on field courts was allowed to lapse on April 19, 1907, for Stolypin did not dare submit it to the newly convened Second Duma. However, Stolypin adopted this decision with reluctance. On May 15, 1907, Stolypin had a brief conversation with General Polivanov, who was representing Rediger at the Council of Ministers (Rediger had by this time abandoned attending meetings of the Council in view of his poor relations with its powerful chairman). Stolypin told Polivanov "that the military district courts, in the event of having to resort to them, would prove to be slow, and that it was necesary to strengthen them."[17]

Nicholas II shared Stolypin's concern. In 1907 the Emperor repeatedly expressed impatience at the delays in cases tried under the laws of war in military district courts.[18] The government predictably took steps to "hasten" and "simplify" the district court procedure. If the government could not have field courts-martial, it would try to twist the district courts into the closest possible approximation of them. A decree of June 27, 1907, in amendment of the military judicial code, slashed the period statutorily prescribed for preliminary investigation from three days to one.[19] A further modification of the code appeared on August 10. Military district courts had always included so-called temporary members, selected not from GVSU personnel but from among local officers of the line. In wistful imitation of the field courts-martial, the law of August 10 set new requirements for the selection of temporary members: no

---

[16] Faleev, "Shest' mesiatsev," pp. 47-48.

[17] Polivanov, *Iz dnevnikov*, p. 29.

[18] *Otchet glavnogo voenno-sudnogo upravleniia za 1907* (St. Petersburg, 1909), pp. 28-29.

[19] Nik. Stavrogin [pseud.], "Zakon 27 iiunia 1907 g.," *Pravo*, no. 28 (July 15, 1907): 1929.

officer with seniority less than that of a company or squadron commander of four years' experience was to become a temporary court member.[20] The purpose was to exclude young and impressionable officers since older men, seasoned by several years of line service, were deemed more likely to show firmness in their roles as judges. Again in 1907 and 1908, certain civilian cases not technically subject to military jurisdiction were transferred to it; this was because the Minister of the Interior had arrogated the power of making exceptions to the general rules on such transfers. For example, the military prosecutor of St. Petersburg district was perplexed by a September 1908 letter from the Interior Ministry which consigned to him the case of twelve peasants of Pskov Province. Allegedly, the peasants were members of a gang of robbers which had perpetrated numerous villainies in the province throughout 1907. Yet only three of the peasants were indicted for offenses which were within the competence of the St. Petersburg court; the other nine were charged with crimes not covered by safeguard law, such as belonging to a bandit gang. The Ministry of the Interior wanted all of the peasants tried in military district court and got its way by claiming the prerogative of making an exception to the law "when another direction of the case to court, to wit the division of the indictments into civilian and military judicial instances, is impossible."[21]

If blatant manipulation of the law was not irksome enough for officers of the military district courts, pressure from the higher civilian and military authorities further plagued them. Some pressure emanated from district commanders, especially those who were simultaneously governors-general. General Skalon in Warsaw was apt to force military prosecution of civilian cases which GVSU personnel had previously rejected.[22] And General Gershel'man in Moscow was conspicuous for his attempts to interfere with GVSU procedure. He frequently bellowed to St. Petersburg about the "soft" sentences handed down by the Moscow court and even managed to have Privy Councillor Bykov of the Supreme Military Court come and inspect it.[23]

Additional pressure was exerted by the Chief Military Procurator, across whose desk passed précis of all important civilian cases. If a defendant was convicted of a lesser charge than that in the indictment, or if he was acquitted without apparent cause, the Chief Procurator often demanded a justification from the chairman of the district court con-

---

[20] TsGVIA, f. 801, op. 56, d. 17, 1906-1907 g. (legal changes relating to Military Justice Administration), l. 43.

[21] TsGVIA, f. 801, op. 6166, d. 9/11 (St. Petersburg cases of 1908), ll. 773, 84.

[22] Lukomskii, *Vospominaniia*, p. 170.

[23] Ibid., p. 175; Polivanov, *Iz dnevnikov*, p. 32.

cerned.[24] Such unsettling admonitions or even reprimands from St. Petersburg at times distorted the judgement of a provincial GVSU official.

The highest civilian officials in the state also applied pressure on GVSU officers. In October, 1907 Stolypin informed the GVSU that he expected a swift and decisive military trial for the assassins of Masimovskii, head of the Prison Administration.[25] In another case, Polivanov reported Stolypin's observation in 1908 that it was necessary "to speed up the examination in military district court of the case of the terrorist arrested on February 7 for an attempt on the lives of Grand Duke Nikolai Nikolaevich and [Minister of Justice] Shcheglovitov."[26] Eventually, Stolypin's displeasure with the GVSU focused on Chief Military Procurator Ryl'ke (Ryl'ke's predecessor, the reclusive and morose Pavlov, had been assassinated in December 1906). Applying the unlikely term "Kadet" to Ryl'ke and believing that he was insufficiently stern, Stolypin badgered the Emperor and finally obtained Ryl'ke's dismissal in March of 1908.[27]

MILITARY DISTRICT COURTS AND THE LEGAL ETHOS

The military district courts were thus subject to formidable outside influences—from the Emperor, highly placed civilians, the Chief Military Procurator, the district commanders. Did the courts then yield and become mere rubber stamps for predecided repressive sentences? The answer to this question is a qualified no. To be sure, there were opportunists and careerists in the GVSU who found slavish accommodation to the government a small price to pay for advancement. But there were other military judicial officials who recoiled from this course and maintained high standards of fairness and decency, despite the obstacles strewn in their path. Indeed there were exemplars of this way of thinking in every military district court in the Empire. The very existence of pressure on the courts reflects great dissatisfaction with what the upper reaches of the Imperial government regarded as excessive, misplaced fastidiousness. The legal ethos absorbed in three years of intensive training at the Alexander Academy was difficult to shed.

Whereas the government viewed the courts as theaters of counter-revolutionary terror and exemplary punishment, the GVSU saw its courts as temples of justice. To the boundless irritation of the Interior Ministry, many district courts refused to countenance procedural irreg-

[24] For an example, see TsGVIA, f. 801, op. 5/65, d. 13/3, ll. 231-234.
[25] Polivanov, Iz dnevnikov, p. 34.
[26] Ibid., p. 41.
[27] Ibid., p. 29; TsGVIA, f. 280, op. 1, d. 6, p. 760.

ularities and extended to civilian defendants the same legal protections accorded defendants in the more placid prerevolutionary period. In Russian civilian criminal and military criminal law, for example, it was not difficult to make an insanity defense—certification by two doctors was usually sufficient. As an insane person could not stand trial, such cases either had to be postponed to await an improvement in the mental health of the accused or had to be dropped outright. No one would deny that many certifiably insane defendants appeared before the bar of Russian military justice from 1905 to 1910. The stresses produced by the revolution must not be discounted. Then, too, among the intelligentsia the decadent movement was in flower, a movement which encouraged fascination, both morbid and voluptuous, with the ideas of insanity, death, and suicide. Still, the number of insanity defenses in military court précis suggests that it was not uncommon for defendants to feign insanity, perhaps with the assistance of drugs.[28] Thus in the Petersburg trial of nine persons who purportedly conspired to murder railway engineer Rukhlov, the court decided in May of 1906 to continue the cases of three of the suspects in view of their insanity.[29] In April 1908, Petersburg court dropped the case against Tat'iana Safarova, a Socialist Revolutionary Maximalist, since it decided she had been insane at the beginning of 1907 when she was alleged to have committed her crime.[30] Again in 1907, Petersburg court acquitted A. I. Shelkova, a member of the Kronshtadt military-revolutionary organization, by reason of insanity.[31] Many other examples could be added.

Another feature of military court practice that exasperated repression-minded bureaucrats was rigorous attention to the evidence. If a material witness retracted in court a deposition previously given to the police, the court turned in a verdict of acquittal. Thus the Moscow court freed Vladimir Barmash and Aleksei Poliakov, on trial for robbing the office of Oil' and Company (1906), when the witnesses who had previously identified the pair recanted.[32] Ivan Romanov and Dmitrii Merkulov were discharged from custody for the same reason in November 1906, as was

---

[28] See A. N. Voznesenskii, *Teni proshlogo (po tsarskim sudam). Iz vospominanii politicheskogo zashchitnika* (Moscow, 1929), p. 44, for a description of a contrived insanity defense.

[29] TsGVIA, f. 801, op. 5, d. 577/5 (St. Petersburg cases 1906-1907), ll. 24, 39, 43.

[30] TsGVIA, f. 801, op. 6/60, d. 4/9, 1908 g. (St. Petersburg cases), l. 295.

[31] TsGVIA, f. 801, op. 5/65, d. 18/3 (St. Petersburg cases 1907). Also see TsGVIA, f. 801, op. 5/65, d. 13/3, l. 69.; TsGVIA, f. 801, op. 56/79, d. 26, 1905 g., ll. 39-40; TsGVIA, f. 801, op. 6, d. 4118, 1908 g., l. 181; TsGVIA, f. 801, op. 5, d. 12/3, 1907 g., ll. 124, 295, 468.

[32] TsGVIA, f. 801, op. 5/65, d. 579, 1906 g. (Moscow cases), ll. 213, 225.

Ivan Kuznetsov in the same month.[33] Once again, examples could be multiplied.

What about the interrogatory pressure of the Chief Military Procurator? The cases cited above were likely to attract his attention and prompt a request for explanations. The Chief Procurator's interrogatory was a much used device. However, in cases which featured insanity defenses, retraction of testimony, or the like, the Chief Military Procurator almost always accepted the justification offered by the district military court.

When the Petersburg court in September 1906 found three peasants guilty not of banditry (*razboi*), but the lesser charge of horse stealing, Procurator Ryl'ke wanted to know why. But Major General Birshert, who had presided in the case, responded that the charge of banditry had been based on the evidence of a single witness, who had declined to attend the trial. Ryl'ke washed his hands of the matter.[34] A parallel controversy between Ryl'ke and Petersburg court arose in February 1907 in the case of Ivan Vasil'ev, a burglar who allegedly took some shots at the police who were pursuing him. The attempted murder of a policeman in the line of duty was punishable by death; why had Vasil'ev received only fifteen years at hard labor? The assistant prosecutor of St. Petersburg District replied that although witnesses recalled the burglar holding a drawn revolver, all denied that he ever fired. The matter ended there.[35] Likewise, the Chief Procurator was satisfied with the explanation of a temporary military court in Orel: it had acquitted G. Borisenkov of the theft of one hundred rubles, because the chief eyewitnesses were not confident about identifying him during the trial (March 1908). In other words, the Chief Military Procurators themselves accepted the legal justifications that provincial courts offered in defense of their procedure.

But the courts were not only within their rights in adhering strictly to the law; they enjoyed other prerogatives as well. One of these was to appeal to the governor-general or district commander to show mercy in a particular case by reducing sentence. To judge from the archival material, these appeals were frequent and effective. Thus, the petition of the St. Petersburg District Court persuaded the St. Petersburg District Commander to commute the death sentence of the student Valentin Reztsov to three years in a fortress.[36] Similarly, three peasants would

[33] Ibid., ll. 303, 314. See also: TsGVIA, f. 801, op. 5, d. 22/35 otdel 1907, ll. 25-26, 47-48, 69-71; TsGVIA, f. 801, op. 7/67, d. 10/24, ll. 22, 24; TsGVIA, f. 801, op. 5, d. 8/31, 1910 g., ll. 129-130, 142; TsGVIA, f. 801, op. 6/66, d. 4/13, ll. 63-64, 121, 123, 364-368, 411-412.

[34] TsGVIA, f. 801, op. 5/65, d. 18/3, ll. 119, 123, 124, 125.

[35] Ibid., ll. 227, 231, 234-236.

[36] Ibid., ll. 156, 159, 161, 169.

have ascended the gallows in December 1905 but for the appeal of Colonel Adrianov, judge with the Temporary Military Court in Nizhnii Novgorod.[37]

But Stolypin and the Chief Military Procurator had good cause to rebuke military courts when they overstepped the law or bent it in the interests of the accused. In September 1905, the Warsaw District Court itself reduced the sentence of the peasant Papei, convicted of premeditated murder of an official, from death to twenty years' hard labor; this was a clear violation of the Imperial edict of August 11, 1887, which invested the district commander or governor-general alone with the power of commutation.[38] In September of 1906, Major General Tolubaev of the Simbirsk Temporary Military Court allowed the lawyers of P. Moshkin, accused of the premeditated murder of an official, to appeal to the first department of the Senate for a transfer of the case from military to civilian jurisdiction. Once again, this was a contravention of the military judicial code, which only tolerated appeals to the Supreme Military Court. When asked why he had permitted this illicit appeal, Tolubaev stated that in his understanding of the code the accused had the right to exhaust all means of defense, adding that "to halt examination of his [Moshkin's] case for one or two months, until the Senate resolved his appeal, cannot exert a substantive influence on the interests of speedy criminal repression." The Supreme Military Court thought otherwise and Tolubaev, who had been with the GVSU since 1883, was prematurely retired.[39]

Other courts simply ignored the law and handed down sentences lighter than those prescribed by the code. On March 10, 1907, the Temporary Military Court in Revel sentenced Ian Idol' to twelve years at hard labor, not the legal punishment of death for his attempt to disarm a military sentry.[40] Iakov Lasis, who had attempted to throttle a policeman, received three years in a corrective institution rather than death from the Revel Court in February 1907.[41] That such mismatched sentences were not mere abnormalities is shown by the report of the GVSU for 1907 (compiled in 1909), which commented that instances of illegally light sentences had been noted repeatedly (*neodnokratno*) and included a stern warning to the military judges of the Empire.[42]

It is not hard to understand why, for jurisprudential considerations,

[37] TsGVIA, f. 801, op. 5/65, d. 579, 1906 g., ll. 410, 419.
[38] TsGVIA, f. 400, op. 3, d. 2793, ll. 3-4.
[39] TsGVIA, f. 801, op. 5, d. 577/5, ll. 2-6, 12.
[40] TsGVIA, f. 801, op. 5, d. 577/5, ll. 10-11.
[41] TsGVIA, f. 801, op. 5/65, d. 18/3, ll. 226-227.
[42] *Otchet glavnogo voenno-sudnogo upravleniia za 1907* (St. Petersburg, 1909), p. 34.

Russian military judges were no happier with statutorily imposed sentences than American judges today. That dissatisfaction was manifest in the judges' reaction to their obligations to impose death penalties, in accordance with military laws of war, martial law, and the safeguard laws.

The great number of death sentences passed by the military courts in these years is often cited as evidence of the ferocity of Imperial repression. But, as Table 12 shows, many of these death sentences were in fact never carried out. Less than *one-third* of the civilians sentenced to death by military district courts were in fact executed from January 1, 1905 to April 20, 1907. That 225 persons were hanged or shot in this period is no trifle; yet the fact that 548 escaped death is not insignificant either, for it contravenes the popular image of Russian military judicial brutality.

Why were so few of these sentences carried out? Evidence exists that 2 civilians of the 548 (.36 percent) eluded the gallows by escaping from custody. A further 9 (1.64 percent) received Imperial commutations.

TABLE 12

Death Sentences on Civilians in the Russian Empire Passed by Military District Courts, January 1, 1905-April 20, 1907

Military District	(1) No. of cases	(2) No. of death sentences	(3) No. carried out	(3) as % of (2)
Warsaw	76	107	48	44.86
Moscow	9	17	11	64.7
Odessa	26	49	8	16.32
Kiev	36	61	8	13.11
Omsk	5	8	3	37.5
Caucasus	33	67	2	2.98
Turkestan	7	15	1	6.66
Vilna	72	163	91	55.82
Irkutsk	23	41	12	29.26
Kazan	13	21	0	0
St. Petersburg	53	111	17	15.31
Priamur	51	113	24	21.23
Total	404	773	225	29.107

SOURCE: TsGVIA, f. 801, op. 5/65, d. 8 1907 (military death sentences in Empire, January 1, 1905-April 20, 1907), calculated on the basis of ll. 1-110

The Supreme Military Court reviewed the cases of 19 others (3.46 percent) and reduced sentence, ordered a retrial, or transferred the case to civilian jurisdiction.[43] This still leaves the fate of 530 civilian defendants unaccounted for. These civilians all owed their lives to the reduced sentences given them by military district commanders or governors-general (usually military officers). Though the data are incomplete, it seems that the district commanders and governors-general often displayed leniency because of direct appeals for clemency by the district court that convicted the defendant. The Kazan' District Court, for example, never passed a single death sentence during the revolution without attaching such an appeal "in view of mitigating circumstances."[44] At civilian insistence, the central office of the GVSU repeatedly warned the judges about ill-founded appeals for mercy in 1906 and 1907, declaring that they would be held responsible. In 1907 the GVSU explained the scandalous number of these appeals as a reprehensible desire on the part of the courts to "place all [responsibility for] the severity of the sentences on the persons confirming the sentences."[45] That it was precisely the severity of the sentences and the obligatory death penalties in particular which bothered the military judges finds support in yet another source.

The murder of several police Cossacks at the Savva Morozov factory in Vladimir Province (November 1905) gave rise to military prosecution; Vladimir Province was under safeguard law. The offices of the Moscow Military District Court accordingly sent Maj. Gen. A. F. Pavlov (no relation to the Chief Military Procurator) to preside in the case. Before the Vladimir Temporary Military Court formally convened, however, War Minister Rediger received a letter in April 1906 from Minister of the Interior Durnovo, protesting the assignment of Pavlov. On the basis of secret police denunciations Durnovo charged that Pavlov "did not agree in general with the transfer of cases of a political character involving civilians to a military court and had openly expressed the opinion that military judges were burdened by the obligations placed on them by cases of this kind." Pavlov was also supposed to have remarked that as a result of this sense of burden, military judges systematically petitioned for the replacement of the death sentence by other penalties. Naturally,

---

[43] TsGVIA, f. 801, op. 5/65, d. 8, 1907 g. (military death sentences in Empire, Jan. 1, 1905-April 20, 1907), calculated on the basis of ll. 1-110.

[44] Ibid., ll. 72-73. And General Kossich, District Commander of Kazan' *always* commuted death sentences. See Mikhail L'vovich Mandel'shtam, *1905 v politicheskikh protsessakh* (Moscow, 1931), p. 64.

[45] *Otchet glavnogo voenno-sudnogo upravleniia za 1907* (St. Petersburg, 1909), p. 34.

the War Ministry commanded Pavlov to respond to these grievous allegations.

Pavlov's apologia, contained in a letter of May 7, 1906, is an extremely interesting and candid document. While understandably trying to cast his views in a more favorable light, this career officer of twenty-two years' service nonetheless blurted out some statements potentially more damaging than those of which the Interior Ministry had accused him. Pavlov did not deny that he had discussed the question of military trials of civilians with both the governor of Vladimir and with the chairman of the civilian circuit court. He remembered his statements on these occasions to have been roughly as follows: "In general it is burdensome to pronounce death sentences, and for us, the military judges, this burden is increased still more by the fact that we have to hear and read that the preservation of justice in military courts is sought in vain." If necessities of state call for death sentences, why should military judges alone be required to pass them? Why not give civilian judges this power? Were military judges supposed to have stronger nerves? Pavlov followed his rhetorical question with the comment, "Among us, the military judges, at the present time there are many with weak nerves, and there are many who are not foreign to the feeling of pity, and therefore, pronouncing sentences of death, we petition for the lives of the convicted." Pavlov was in effect claiming that his opinions were shared by great numbers of military judges. In deference to the Interior Ministry, the War Ministry removed Pavlov from the case.[46]

Respect for the law, "weak nerves," feelings of pity—all led military judges to frustrate that swift judicial repression sought by the civilians. Some military judges were so renowned for clemency and even judicial misconduct in favor of the accused that attorneys eagerly sought to have their clients' cases heard by them. Col. A. A. Adrianov, judge of the Moscow Military District Court from 1907 to 1909, especially distinguished himself in this regard. At various points in his astonishing career, he advised defendants to sham illness to delay trials and warned acquitted prisoners that the police intended to re-arrest them. A lawyer who defended terrorist I. I. Znamenskii before Adrianov later declared "he was not only a judge, he was a 'consultant' in the case, an advisor, suggesting the means and path to deliverance."[47] Adrianov was not isolated at the Moscow Court, for among his judicial colleagues Bulychevstev, Minin, Ivanenko, and Levashov were also noted for their clemency. These latter four judges were forced from the bench, but the "liberal" spirit persisted in the Moscow Court. General Baron von Osten

[46] TsGVIA, f. 801, op. 5/65, d. 579, 1906 g., ll. 101-120, 121, 123, 124, 127.
[47] Voznesenskii, *Teni proshlogo*, pp. 8-11.

Saken, Chief Military Procurator, saw fit to make Moscow one of the two military courts which he personally inspected in May of 1909.[48] The other court was Kazan', which was consistently lax in its sentencing. Moscow, Kazan', and Caucasus Courts may have been exceptionally merciful and Warsaw Court exceptionally harsh, but still, taken as a whole, the military district courts justified Stolypin's fear about their ineffectiveness as instruments of repression: military judges were frankly miserable about fulfilling their state-imposed repressive tasks. This fact, if not appreciated by the Russian public at large, was understood by the fraternity of Russian criminal lawyers. Indeed, one radical lawyer, A. N. Voznesenskii, declared that he and many other lawyers often *preferred* that their clients' cases be heard in military district courts rather than civilian criminal courts.[49]

No account of the military district court system in these years would be complete, however, without reference to the GVSU's striking difficulties in attracting and retaining personnel. As we have already seen, too much leniency on the part of a military judge might attract hostile notice in St. Petersburg, sometimes followed by "retirement" or discharge from service. Then, too, there existed a group of GVSU officers who were unable to stomach the state's demands and submitted their resignations. Almost one-fourth of the military district court judges in the Empire resigned in 1905, and almost one-sixth in 1906.[50] From January 1, 1905 to March 1906, 13.9 percent of GVSU employees left the service. From March 1906 to March 1907, 14.2 percent resigned.[51]

This was at a time when the GVSU was confronted with an unprecedented flood of court cases. Procurator Ryl'ke wrote Nicholas II at the end of September 1907 that the military district courts had originally been created to dispense military justice "and in this way, they served the interests of the military; at present, the activity of the military courts has exceeded the indicated limits by far; military cases have drowned (*potonuli*) in the mass of general criminal cases."[52] Ryl'ke's assertion is borne out by the statistical data in Table 13.

[48] TsGVIA, f. 801, op. 56/79, d. 28, 1909 g. (inspection of Osten-Saken), l. 1.

[49] Voznesenskii, *Teni proshlogo*, p. 5; two other radical defense attorneys, among others, stressed that at times "fairness," if not "mildness" could be found in the military-judicial system. Mandel'shtam, *1905*, p. 61; Anisimov, *Kak eto bylo*, pp. 7, 38, 42, 62, 67, 80-81.

[50] K. Oberuchev, "Voennyi sud," *Pravo*, no. 8 (Feb. 21, 1910): 437.

[51] Ibid., p. 436. See also *Otchet glavnogo voenno-sudnogo upravelniia za 1905* (St. Petersburg, 1907), p. 24. TsGVIA, f. 1, op. 1, d. 70270, l. 14, (1906 material); *Otchet glavnogo voenno-sudnogo upravleniia za 1906* (St. Petersburg, 1908), p. 23; *Otchet glavnogo voenno-sudnogo upravleniia za 1907* (St. Petersburg, 1909), p. 26.

[52] TsGVIA, f. 1, op. 1, d. 40807 (personnel changes in War Ministry administration), l. 45.

TABLE 13

Cases in Military District Courts

Year	Enter court	Resolved	Left over for following year
1903	3,936	3,840	603
1904	3,408	3,308	674
1905	5,403	4,278	1,297
1906	5,743	5,762	1,278

SOURCE: TsGVIA, f. 1, op. 1, d. 40807, ll. 54-55

NOTE: The reason the number of total cases under consideration in a given year (i.e., the number left over from the year before plus those started during the year) minus the number resolved does not equal the number left over for the following year is that some cases were dropped, or left without issue.

Because of this backlog of cases and the amplified workload generally, the GVSU made every effort to expand. Sixty-four jobs were added to the GVSU establishment in 1906, and a further 117 jobs were opened up (at a cost of over 142,000 rubles a year) in the beginning of 1908.[53] In July 1907, the GVSU established two new assistantships to the Chief Military Procurator.[54] In 1909, the government appropriated an additional 10,000 rubles for Chancellery expenses for the military district courts; in 1910, 49,140 rubles were assigned to these purposes.[55] At the same time, the number of students allowed to enroll in the Alexander Academy of Military Justice was increased and more of the Academy's graduates were received into the GVSU. The academic council of the Academy wanted to accept all 32 persons who passed its entrance examination in 1906, because of "insufficient personnel in the Military Justice Administration."[56] In 1908, although there were only 16 legal vacancies for army officers in the incoming class, the Academy accepted all 36 who passed the entrance examination.[57] Yet neither the creation

[53] Ibid., l. 71; also TsGVIA, f. 1, op. 1, d. 72970 (Military Justice Administration statistics for 1908), ll. 16-17.

[54] TsGVIA, f. 801, op. 56, d. 17, 1906-1907 gg. (laws relating to Military Justice Administration), l. 46.

[55] TsGVIA, f. 801, op. 56, d. 3, 1909 g. (laws relating to Military Justice Administration), l. 14.

[56] Aleksandrovskaia voenno-iuridicheskaia akademiia. Chetvertoe dopolnenie k zhurnalam konferentsii (s 18 sentiabria 1896 g. po 31 dekabria 1907 g.) (St. Petersburg, 1908), p. 349.

[57] Ibid., p. 438.

of new jobs nor increased enrollment at the Alexander Academy was an unqualified success; the GVSU continued to be embarrassed by difficulties in attracting and holding cadres.

At the very beginning of 1908 (before the 117 new positions had been officially registered) the legal number of jobs or *shtat* in the GVSU was still 758; yet there were only 692 employees, i.e., a shortage of 8.7 percent (66). By January 1, 1909, the *shtat* of the GVSU was 875, yet only 796 were in GVSU service—a shortage of 8.9 percent (79). And in 1910, there were still 71 jobs, or 8.1 percent of the total complement, unfilled. But these are aggregate figures. GVSU employees consisted of officers and bureaucrats, who acted as judges, prosecutors, and investigators (in other words, who occupied all important posts in the courts); and enlisted men, who served as janitors, court reporters, sergeants at arms, and the like. When these two categories are viewed separately, the personnel crisis of the GVSU assumes an aspect even more serious than that suggested by the statistics cited above.

Thus, if in 1909 the GVSU lacked 8.9 percent of its total number of employees, 12.7 percent of the most sensitive jobs in the court system went vacant. The Empire was still short of 9.3 percent of its military

TABLE 14
Vacancies in the Main Administration of Military Justice

	1907	1908	1909	1910
1. Jobs established by law:				
(a) Officers and bureaucrats	478	478	543	543
(b) Enlisted men	280	280	332	332
Total	758	758	875	875
2. Jobs actually filled:				
(a) Officers and bureaucrats	*	422	474	492
(b) Enlisted men	*	270	322	312
Total	643	692	796	804
3. Differences between 1(a) and 2(a) as percentage of 1(a)	*	11.7%	12.7%	9.3%

SOURCE: TsGVIA, f. 1, op. 1, d. 72970, ll. 6-7; TsGVIA, f. 1, op. 1, d. 74273, l. 15
* No information.

judges, prosecutors, and investigators at the beginning of 1910 (Table 14). In 1908, 1,334 military district court cases were left over from 1907; in 1909, 1,286 were left over from 1908; and in 1910, 982 were left over from 1909.

Those officers who remained with the GVSU and those tyros who joined it in these years found themselves trying to function with impossible caseloads. The judge, the prosecutor, and the investigator simply could not stay abreast of the cases flooding his office. When the Chief Military Court questioned the unseemly delays in the work of Moscow District investigator Nochev in May of 1907, that officer explained that he had been swamped with extra duties since September 1906. Nochev cited some examples. On August 15, 1906, he had started to take depositions in the cases of 3 generals, 20 officers, and 264 soldiers. He had been assigned this case while in Tambov (where he had been since the first of July and where he was to remain until the end of September) working on yet another case; it was hardly mysterious that he had been unable to attend to other cases in Voronezh, Kozlov, etc.[58] Captain Kondakov, who became military investigator of the 4th section (*uchastok*) of Warsaw Military District in June 1909, had 66 unfinished cases on his hands on January 19, 1910; he had not even been able to begin 33 of them.[59] In early 1909 the Amur Military District Court inquired into the inactivity of the investigator of the 1st section of Zaamur district of the Frontier Guard, Colonel Bulatovich. Bulatovich explained that from October 7, 1906, to September 19, 1907, he had in fact been entrusted with *two* sections of the district.[60]

But overwork could have more serious consequences than sloppy procedures or mere slowness. Chief Procurator Ryl'ke stressed this point as well in a letter of September 1907: "Daily, tense work of many hours results in extreme exhaustion, which has a sad outcome for many due to nervous disease."[61] Nor were these nervous disorders confined to the provincial officials of the GVSU. Rediger noted in his memoirs that the behavior of Chief Procurator Pavlov himself was characterized in 1906 by irritability and nervous stress.[62]

Irritability and overwork could also rob at least some GVSU officers of their tact, bringing them to make emotional outbursts in court which they doubtless regretted afterwards. In September 1906, a temporary military court heard the case of Onipko, a former Duma member, who

[58] TsGVIA, f. 801, op. 57/79, d. 18, 1907-1908 gg., ll. 39-41.
[59] TsGVIA, f. 801, op. 39, d. 19, l. 23.
[60] TsGVIA, f. 801, op. 56/79, d. 12, l. 12.
[61] TsGVIA, f. 1, op. 1, d. 70807, l. 44.
[62] TsGVIA, f. 280, op. 1, d. 6, p. 670.

was on trial for his revolutionary agitation among the Kronshtadt sailors. Onipko was represented by a candidate of the court, Staff Captain Popandopulo. Surveying the court and the audience with contempt, Popandopulo concluded his summation with the remark that "many [here] are already savoring the sentence and execution of former Duma member Onipko." Major General Tomashevich, who had presided in the trial, later apologized for Popandopulo to the military prosecutor of St. Petersburg District: Popandopulo had been overworked and overwrought, since he had been saddled with the defense of 708 persons in this case. Popandopulo received a reprimand and a transfer back to Warsaw Military District.[63]

In 1909, two soldiers of the 4th Turkestan rifle battalion, Kharin and Serov, plotted the murder of the former commander of Turkestan Military District, Lieutenant General Mishchenko. The plot had been foiled through the offices of yet another soldier in the battalion, one Korostelev, who was in fact a spy for the Askhabad Gendarmes.

In his speech for the defense, Captain Korsunovskii of the Military Justice Administration made much of Korostelev's police affiliations, rhetorically declaring at one point: "May God preserve the Russian army" from soldiers like Korostelev. Secret police denunciations forced the War Ministry to investigate Korsunovskii. Once again, Korsunovskii's judicial superiors attempted to intercede on his behalf. But no rationalization could expunge the fact that Korsunovskii had employed "inappropriate" expressions in relation to men of the *Okhrana* and the regular police. The hapless Korsunovskii was abruptly transferred to Amur Military District.[64]

Incidents like these were to be expected. GVSU personnel were functioning under enormous pressures. Gruelling work schedules combined with the uncomfortable sensation of being spied on by representatives of the higher civilian and military spheres might well bring a latent hostility toward the police to surface in court. But there was more than this: the repressive activities of military courts aroused public enmity towards the army, just as the punitive detachments of 1905-1906 had done. As Rediger wrote of the military courts during the revolution: "The [military courts] were supposed to hear the cases sent them and pronounce death sentences. To say nothing of how onerous this was from the standpoint of justice, the military courts were charged with enormous work, and against them, and indirectly against the entire

---

[63] TsGVIA, f. 801, op. 56/79, d. 18, 1905 g. [sic], ll. 62-71.
[64] TsGAOR, f. DP OO, d. 345, 1909 g., ll. 1-9.

army, the hatred of the population was aroused."[65] When the Committee of Ministers demanded that Rediger defend the death sentences before the First Duma, the War Minister refused, with the observation that "the War Ministry in judging cases of civilians according to the laws of war is only an executive agency." Answer to the Duma ought to be given by the power "which transferred these cases to the military courts."[66] Ultimately, Rediger was compelled to surrender, at least to the extent of deputing Chief Military Procurator Pavlov to address the Duma in his stead. Pavlov's speech (May 31, 1906) was an irretrievable fiasco. One auditor recollected that such indignation was stirred up in the Duma that "the debate took on the character of a real storm."[67] This episode provides yet another illustration of Rediger's commitment to the purely military interest. Perfectly willing to abandon the GVSU and hand it over unprotestingly as an instrument for civilian governmental repression, he became queasy only when the collapsing reputation of the GVSU threatened to pull down what was left of the rest of the army's reputation as well.

The response of the provincial officials of the Administration was quite different, for they—not Rediger, not the Main Staff, not the department heads of the War Ministry's Chancellery—were charged with the day-to-day management of Russia's judicial repression. In a sense, the experiences of the combat units of the Russian army and the military judiciary were curious inversions of each other. With regard to the combat units, it was the higher-ups, the Ministry of War itself, which sought to check, control, and rein in the repression, while the local military leaders—and especially the local military chiefs—were ready to participate in it. For the GVSU, it was precisely the leadership which promoted the repression, and the rank and file which had qualms. These qualms were expressed in varying ways: strictly adhering to the legal process, which gave the accused the benefit of technicalities; appealing for mercy without any grounds; tampering with cases and sentences; traducing the police; and abandoning judicial service altogether.

The leadership of the army and the War Ministry had elected to make concessions to the civilian power in the judicial regard, perhaps in hope of salvaging more in terms of the Empire's combat readiness. Hence the directors of the GVSU acted as they did. But the demand for "swift judicial repression" could only disturb great numbers of Russia's military jurists, since these men had partaken of a professionalism within the

[65] TsGVIA, f. 280, op. 1, d. 5, p. 598.

[66] Ibid., pp. 589-599.

[67] A. A. Kizevetter, *Na rubezhe dvukh stoletii. Vospominaniia 1881-1914* (Prague, 1929), p. 430.

walls of the Alexander Academy which was foreign to the mass of serving army officers. It was military professionalism which caused the jurists to question the wisdom of distorting the law in the interests of counterrevolutionary terror and which implanted the concepts of mercy and jurisprudence in them.

SEVEN

The Officers and Politics,
1906-1913

On December 16, 1905, the Emperor Nicholas II assented to a special decision of the Council of Ministers which three days later was published for the army as War Department Order number 804. Point one of the order read:

> It is forbidden for any persons in the army or navy service, including officers of all ranks, civilian bureaucrats . . . military clergy, and all enlisted men: (1) to join and take part in any unions, groups, organizations, societies, etc., of any kind whatsoever which have been formed with a political goal. It is equally forbidden to attend meetings of any kind at which political subjects are discussed; (2) to take direct part or participate in assemblies, gatherings or demonstrations of any kind.

Point two stated that any soldiers who violated this prescription faced discharge from the service; point three extended the prohibition against political activity to all reservists or retired officers who retained the right to wear military uniform.[1]

The decision to introduce this measure into the Council of Ministers had been the War Ministry's. And that Ministry had begun to consider the enactment of some sort of a law separating the military from politics in the immediate aftermath of the October Manifesto. A Main Staff memorandum dated October 25 contained a theoretical justification for the decree which was to emerge as Order number 804. The memorandum argued that to permit soldiers to engage in politics was potentially dangerous. The Staff worried that political parties might vie to win the army over to their positions. Hinting at the prospect of a military coup, the Staff cautioned that if a political party were to acquire military backing, an "element of force" would enter the national life. Freedom, the will of the people, and the will of the monarch would be subverted. The Staff also maintained that politics in the military milieu would breed

---

[1] *Prodolzhenie svoda zakonov rossiiskoi imperii 1906 goda*, pt. 5, vol. 14 (St. Petersburg, 1910), pp. 28-29.

an unwholesome antagonism between the Empire's soldiers. Unity of outlook and sense of common purpose would crumble. It therefore behooved the Russian Empire to follow the example of many other Western European states by isolating her army from politics.[2]

Aside from containing a misconception of the political role of the armies of the West, the Staff's memorandum is as interesting for what it omits as for what it includes. Political parties could strain to capture the army all they wished, but such exertions would be futile if the soldiers were deaf to political salesmanship. However, this document is *prima facie* evidence that the Staff dreaded lest the army become receptive to political messages. What sort of political activity did the War Ministry fear?

Was it simply the dissemination of radical ideas among the common soldiers? As we have seen, the Ministry was alarmed by seditious agitation in the barracks. The 1905-1907 revolution is notable for the army's maladroit, sometimes comic, attempts to counteract the influence of "harmful ideas." In December of 1905, for example, the Main Staff purchased and distributed several hundred copies of a patriotic tract entitled "What has Nicholas II Given to the Russian People?" Certain of the more ambitious military district staffs experimented with the publication of their own soldiers' newspapers and journals. The *Warsaw Military Herald* and the *Vil'na Military Leaflet* were both started in 1906. The political sophistication of the officers in charge of these programs was sometimes low. The Kazan' District Commander, reporting on the measures he had taken to combat propaganda among his troops, wrote on January 12, 1906 that he had urged all soldiers to make *Russkaia gazeta* their daily reading. Unfortunately, *Russkaia gazeta* was a virulently revolutionary paper; the general had confused it with *Russkoe chtenie*.[3]

To upgrade the political knowledge of Russian officers, the War Ministry devised a political science course to be taught in the school of pages, the military schools, and the junker schools. One of its goals was to inculcate an "acquaintance with Russian reality, and a critique of those conceptions about it which are introduced into the consciousness of the masses with the purpose of exciting them against the lawful power. . . ." Presumably, officers who took the course would graduate with the requisite knowledge to woo the common soldiers away from left-wing ideas by means of rational argument. Through study, these officers would

[2] TsGVIA, f. 400, op. 15, d. 26117, ll. 275-276.

[3] Ibid., ll. 37, 44, 74. On the press, see Z. P. Levasheva et al., comps., *Russkaia voennaia pechat' 1702-1916 gg.* (Moscow, 1959), nos. 137, 140, 142, 146, 166, 169.

become alive to the wiles of the socialists. But the tsarist government discontinued the course shortly after its inception in 1906 because of lack of money. The course was therefore far from being a plot to introduce "thought control" into the Russian army, as some Soviet historians have represented it.[4]

All the same, to hold that Order 804 was solely crafted as a defense against the revolutionaries is untenable. The strictest of laws already shielded the army against criminal propaganda and subversion.[5] The distribution of propaganda among the troops was a felony punishable by hard labor; for the soldier, as well as the civilian, adherence to a political party which advocated the violent overthrow of the state was a harshly punished offense.

Perhaps the War Ministry had the Russian officer corps at least partially in mind when it drafted Order 804. But there are difficulties to be overcome before this hypothesis merits acceptance. The main difficulty—and it is a striking one—is the avowed apolitical spirit of the Russian officers. Almost without exception, military memoirists writing about the empire period between 1880 and 1914 have noted, in some cases ruefully, that the majority of Russian officers were strangers to politics, if not outright political illiterates. The Staff did not know that the bovine indifference to politics so characteristic of the army officer at the turn of the century would survive the Japanese defeat and the revolution. The Staff and the War Ministry therefore may have feared that the real grievances of officers (of which there were many) might be translated into political action.

In any event, the War Ministry made a valiant attempt after 1906 to better the officer's standard of living. In December 1907 Nicholas II signed a decree increasing the pay of lower ranking army officers, effective January 1, 1909. An army second lieutenant previously earning 660 rubles a year would now receive 840 rubles. A captain's pay would rise from 1,200 to 1,740 rubles, a lieutenant colonel's from 1,740 to 2,400.[6] In 1909 the Ministry managed to extend its generous military pension law (the one which Rediger had wrested from a reluctant Min-

[4] L. E. Kritsman, ed., "Iz istorii ideologicheskoi bor'by samoderzhaviia s revoliutsionnym dvizheniem v armii," *Krasnyi arkhiv* 1, no. 44 (1931), pp. 167-170.

[5] L. T. Senchakova, *Revoliutsionnoe dvizhenie v russkoi armii i flote v kontse XIX—nachale XX v.* (Moscow, 1972), p. 129; A. Shebalor, "Vopros o smertnoi kazni za politicheskie prestupleniia nakanune Pervoi Dumy," *Katorga i ssylka* (Moscow), 17 (1925): 170.

[6] TsGVIA, f. 280, op. 1, d. 6, pp. 741-742. "Dovol'stvie voisk," *VE*, vol. 9 (St. Petersburg, 1912), p. 147.

istry of Finance in 1906) to 1911.[7] In 1911 the pension law was once again extended to 1912.[8] Coterminously, the Ministry was using the Higher Commission on Performance Reviews (Vyshaia attestatsionnaia kommissiia or VAK) to unseat superannuated or incompetent commanders, thus brightening career prospects for the young and talented. VAK operations paved the way for a surge in the number of appointments to high military positions. In 1906, for example, the Ministry of War distributed 185 new regimental commands, 6 cavalry brigade commands, 50 separate brigade commands, and 27 corps commands.[9] Stiffer reviews accounted for the pensioning off of 367 officers in 1907 and 1,402 in 1908.[10]

As a result of these measures, as well as the cooling down of public hostility to the army after 1907, the chronic shortage of officers that was the legacy of the 1904-1907 period was overcome. In 1907, the Russian army lacked 20 percent of its legal complement of officers; in 1908, 7.2; in 1909, 5.5 percent. By 1910, however, there was a surplus of officers.[11]

Despite these reforms, an officer's lot remained unenviable. Many of the drawbacks of officers' service persisted up to the outbreak of the First World War. The Vil'na District Commander observed in 1910 that officers were overworked and did not enjoy sufficient prestige in society.[12] Patronage was still necessary for advancement. Gen. P. N. Krasnov remembered his thrill in 1910 when he was appointed commander of the 1st Siberian Yermak Cossack regiment, even though that regiment maintained an isolated garrison on the frontier of China some 1,000 versts from the nearest railway. Krasnov confessed that protection and backstairs influence had been required to secure him even this not particularly dazzling command.[13] In addition, despite the 1909 pay increase, the Russian officer was still underpaid. Father Shavel'skii, the Empire's last Chief Military Chaplain, was referring to the years 1911-1914, when he wrote: "It is impossible to point to a class in old Russia worse provided for than the officer corps."[14] Shavel'skii's exaggeration nonetheless contained a kernel of truth. Bereft of society's esteem, ill-used by the tsarist

[7] TsGVIA, f. 1, op. 2, d. 169, l. 19.

[8] TsGVIA, f. 1, op. 2, d. 170, l. 16.

[9] TsGVIA, f. 1, op. 1, d. 70264, l. 7.

[10] TsGVIA, f. 1, op. 2, d. 170, l. 18.

[11] M. Grulev, *Zloby dnia v zhizni armii* (Brest-Litovsk, 1911), p. 32; TsGVIA, f. 1, op. 2, d. 169, l. 7; TsGVIA, f. 1, op. 2, d. 170, l. 4.

[12] TsGVIA, f. 400, op. 15, d. 3517, ll. 12, 32.

[13] P. N. Krasnov, *Na rubezhe Kitaia* (Paris, 1939), pp. 71, 11, 12-13.

[14] Georgii Shavel'skii, *Vospominaniia poslednego protopresvitera russkoi armii i flota* (New York, 1954), p. 94.

treasury, the officer equally had to suffer coarse treatment at the hands of his military superiors. Some district commanders were infamous for abusing their underlings. The motivation behind this crudeness was well expressed by Kazan' District Commander Sandetskii, who observed in 1910 that "our officers are worthless" (*drian'*).[15] In a confidential memorandum of 1912, the Department of Police discussed the "hidden discontent" among the officers due to slow promotions, bad pay, and ar-¹· ᵃʳᵛ treatment by military authorities. And N. A. Danilov, head of ᴜᵣ Ministry's Chancellery, made the same point in November 1913.[16]

Thus the War Ministry may have fretted over the possibility that officers would indulge in politics in order to air and redress their grievances. But this would be to credit the War Ministry with too much prescience. It was still only 1905, and the War Ministry was frankly sanguine about the success of the legislation it was initiating in aid of the officers' promotions, pay, and conditions of service. The composition and orientation of the Duma the Emperor had promised might be uncertain, but the Ministry already possessed the requisite authority to expel fractious officers from the army. In pursuing the stimulus that evoked the response of Order number 804, exclusive of the desire to mimic the advanced West, we must seek a group of officers who were already perceived as a danger in 1905, not merely regarded as potential troublemakers in the years ahead. And such a group of officers existed.

What is under consideration here is not that impotent handful of offiers who embraced the revolutionary movement through participation, for example, in the short-lived All-Russian Military Union or the conspiratorial nucleus of the All-Russian Officers Union, both unnatural births of the revolutionary years. The number of officers attracted by the far left would always remain small.[17] We must concentrate, then, on a different group: Russia's professional military intellectuals.

The Military Renaissance

As we have seen, the defeat in Manchuria created a "burning desire" for military reform among some Russian officers and inaugurated the "military renaissance." The "renaissance" inspired a veritable torrent

---

[15] Denikin, *Staraia armiia*, vol. 1, p. 123.

[16] TsGAOR, f. 102, op. 14, d. 291 (1913), DP OO, l. 2; TsGVIA, f. 165, op. 1, d. 5255, l. 113.

[17] On the All-Russian Officers Union, see S. Mstislavskii, "Otryvki o piatom gode," *Katorga i ssylka* (Moscow), 39 (1928): 7-36, esp. p. 36, which explains how many members promptly abandoned it after the promulgation of the October Manifesto.

of military books. In 1908, 462 separate titles on military subjects were published; in 1909, 432 appeared. In 1910, 1,075,000 copies of 572 different military books were issued, representing 1.9 percent of all titles and .97 percent of all copies appearing in the Empire that year. By way of comparison, in 1910, 1,580,661 copies of 304 separate books on law came to press.[18] Many of the military books contained appeals for reform.

There had been movements for military reform in the Russian Empire before—in the aftermath of the Crimean War, for instance. Some of the leaders of the latter movement had in fact connected an improvement in Russia's military strength with social transformation. It occurred to D. A. Miliutin, as well as to many civilians, that the institution of serfdom was a capital barrier to the Empire's military progress. However, this insight was not received wisdom within the army of Miliutin's time. What makes the reform movement after 1905 so striking by contrast is the fact that almost all of Russia's military intellectuals conceded that broad changes in the state and the country, changes that went beyond mere tinkering with military organization, were unarguably necessary if Russia planned to win the wars of the future.

It is not surprising that these ideas stirred the imaginations of professional officers previously associated with *Razvedchik*, and the Society of Zealots of Military Knowledge, since it was precisely these men who had the strongest commitment to a powerful, modern Russian military. In pamphlets, books, and articles, Russia's educated military elite stressed the interconnection between military effectiveness and thoroughgoing changes in the social and political life of the Empire. In his 1907 book on Russia's January 1905 defeat at the battle of San-de-pu, for example, E. F. Novitskii rejected the technique of singling out and blaming individuals; it was not individuals who were guilty, but the entire defective military system.[19] What was wrong with the system? Besides such retrograde features as patronage and low pay—the standard list of officers' complaints—the chief flaw of the system was that it failed to motivate the soldier. The patriotism, enthusiasm, and self-sacrifice of the Japanese private soldier had made an enormous impression on Russian officers. The Russian army, and by implication the Imperial Russian state, could not or would not inculcate these qualities. If Russia was to be victorious in the future, the mental outlook of her soldiers had to change; in a word, the nation and the Empire had to be morally regenerated in some way. Similarly, M. Grulev called for universal literacy as the first step

---

[18] *Ukazatel' novykh knig otmechennykh Knizhnim vestnikom za 1908* (St. Petersburg, 1908), pp. 149-153; . . . *za 1909* (St. Petersburg, 1909), pp. 169-173; *Statistika proizvedenii pechati vyshedshikh v Rossii v 1910 godu* (St. Petersburg, 1911), pp. 4, 8-9.

[19] Novitskii, *Sandepu*, pp. 68-69.

in overcoming the apathy of the soldiers.[20] The same concept underlay Gen. A. P. Skugarevskii's injunction that each soldier "should know the goal of action in a battle and should understand the task of the action of his company."[21] In a 1911 report to the Smolensk Province zemstvo board, Skugarevskii would call for the militarization of school children through the introduction of obligatory courses in gymnastics, marching, and shooting.[22] Similar endorsements of motivating and mobilizing the entire population for war were authored by Galkin, Martynov, and others.[23]

But how were these things to be done? As constituted, the moribund autocracy was clearly unwilling to take the requisite actions to benefit the country's military might. In the eyes of the military elite, the war with Japan had presumably proved this. Further, by unleashing the army against the rebellious civilian population, the autocracy was stripping the army of prestige and arousing the enmity of the population instead of promoting public respect for Russia's armed forces. It was an obvious deduction that either the physiognomy of the autocracy had to be altered, or at least popular attitudes towards the military had to be remolded. Hence elite Russian officers had to become involved in politics. What is interesting about the politics of Russian officers (either right- or left-wing) after 1905 is the process by which they assumed them. For the group of officers we have been discussing, the war and revolution engendered disappointment, and from this disappointment arose renewed patriotism and in some cases militarism, from which in turn political involvement emerged. In other words, a concern for the interests of the army pushed officers into politics. These were officers for whom army welfare took precedence over everything else, for whom "the reason for the existence of the army is war alone."[24] One of the first manifestations of this new political spirit was the newspaper *Voennyi golos (The Military Voice)*.

VOENNYI GOLOS

Voennyi golos was the first independent daily military newspaper in the history of the Russian Empire. As the first issue stated on January 2,

[20] Grulev, *Zloby*, pp. 76-77.

[21] Skugarevskii, *Ocherki*, vol. 3 (St. Petersburg, 1913), p. 74.

[22] *Doklad v Smolenskuiu gubernskuiu zemskuiu upravu gubersnkogo glasnogo A. P. Skugarevskogo* (Smolensk, 1911), p. 11.

[23] M. Galkin, *Novi put' sovremennogo ofitsera* (St. Petersburg, 1907), pp. 9, 31, 32; Martynov, *Iz pechal'nogo*, passim.

[24] Galkin, *Novyi put'*, p. 7.

1906, the paper was dedicated to the interests of the army and navy and military reorganization "on progressive principles corresponding to military duty and the new state structure of the Empire."[25] The editorial board was composed of a group of officers remarkable for their association with the General Staff, the Military Justice Administration, or the Society of Zealots of Military Knowledge: V. A. Apushkin, Lt. Col. N. P. Vishniakov, F. F. Novitskii, E. Shvarts, Col. R. I. Bashinskii, Col. N. E. Dukhanin, Col. Prince S. S. Drutskoi, A. N. Brianchaninov, V. N. Nechaev, P. A. Korovichenko, and S. K. Shneur, who also served as the paper's publisher.[26] Until its suppression eight months later (September 5, 1906), *Voennyi golos* provided a legal rostrum for appealing for military and political reform. Within a few months the paper had over three thousand subscribers; a further two thousand copies of each issue were sold to nonsubscribing officers and soldiers. So popular was *Voennyi golos* that serving officers in the field flooded the editorship with unsolicited letters and manuscripts.[27]

Discussions of military reform naturally filled the columns of the newspaper. But there was a political program as well, however ill-defined. In the main, *Voennyi golos* was constitutionalist, pro-Duma, latently hostile to autocratic privilege, and in favor of the participation of the army in politics. For example, the paper's response to Order number 804, an article entitled "The Incomprehensible Law" (January 12, 1906), averred that it was impossible and undesirable to isolate the officer corps from politics.[28] An article published three days later suggested that the interests of the throne and the nation could at times diverge. The army had to serve as "the national support of the constitutional and legal order."[29] In the middle of March the paper went on record as opposing any limitation on the Duma's budgetary authority over military expenditure: "The experience of Western European and other constitutional states has doubtless proved that the control of the peoples' representatives over the armed forces of the state is essential; it guarantees the troops the best conditions of life and removes bureaucratic routine."[30] In April 1906, *Voennyi golos* argued that while the constitutional monarch should be titular commander in chief of the army, the Duma should regulate the size of the army, enlistment, officers' service, mil-

[25] *VG* (St. Petersburg), no. 1 (Jan. 2, 1906): 1.

[26] von Shvartz, *Vospominaniia*, pp. 136-137. On lawyers' involvement with *Voennyi golos*, see N. S. "Armiia i narod," *VG*, no. 98 (May 4, 1906): 1.

[27] "Voennyi golos," *VE*, vol. 6 (St. Petersburg, 1911), p. 583.

[28] *VG*, no. 8 (Jan. 9, 1906): 3-4.

[29] "Armiia i konstitutsia," *VG*, no. 11 (Jan. 15, 1906): 2-3.

[30] "Biudzhetnoe pravo dumy," *VG*, no. 69 (Mar. 15, 1906): 1-2.

itary law, and the employment (if any) of troops in response to internal disturbances.[31] This latter point is one which *Voennyi golos* writers never tired of making. One of the slogans of the paper was "the troops are for war," not the suppression of internal unrest.[32] Thus *Voennyi golos* demanded a stop to the military trials of civilians for political offenses and an immediate halt to the practice of using the troops against civilians, in order to bolster public respect for the army.[33] The paper also condemned the dissolution of the First Duma, declaring that until a new Duma convened, the government of the country was in the hands of the same bureaucrats who were responsible for the pogroms, Mukden, the surrender of Port Arthur, the battle of Tsushima, and the "internal war."[34] The last issue contained an outraged assault on Stolypin's military field courts-martial, entitled "Why are Our Field Courts 'Military'?"[35]

There are at least two salient features of the politics of *Voennyi golos*. The first is that the paper always justified constitutionalism in terms of its alleged military advantages alone. Authors typically argued that untrammeled political participation of the Russian people in the government would reconcile them to the state and awaken their dormant patriotism. Second, it is clear that the army was uppermost in the minds of the editors and correspondents of *Voennyi golos*; these men created a cult of the army, almost worshipping it. When the word "army" appeared in a *Voennyi golos* article, it was almost invariably capitalized.

Even after the paper went out of existence, the *Voennyi golos* group continued operations, founding its own publishing company. Beginning in 1910, some former members of the group, including V. A. Apushkin, E. Shvarts, and E. F. Novitskii, collaborated in the editing and publication of the *Voennaia entsiklopediia* (Military Encyclopedia), a massive compendium of information on military technology, tactics, strategy, history, etc., of which seventeen volumes appeared by 1914. The encyclopedia rapidly established itself as the standard Russian work of reference on military subjects. In a way the encyclopedia might seem to be a reversion to the earlier military educational professionalism, almost the apotheosis of this trend. In fact, however, the articles in the encyclopedia

[31] "*Voennaia reforma*," *VG*, no. 87 (Apr. 20, 1906): 1-2.

[32] N. S. "Armiia i narod," p. 1.

[33] See V. Nechaev, "Novyia pravila o prizyve voisk," *VG*, no. 52 (Feb. 22, 1906): 2; Stroevoi, "Sodeistvie voisk grazhdanskim vlastiam," *VG*, no. 97 (May 3, 1906): 2; "Vospitanie obuchenie i vnutrenniaia sluzhba," *VG*, no. 110 (May 20, 1906): 1; A. Tolubeev, "Pochemu u nas ne liubiat armiiu?" *VG*, no. 118 (May 31, 1906): 2.

[34] "Mezhdu molotom i nakoval'nei," *VG*, no. 171 (Aug. 5, 1906): 1.

[35] "Pochemu polevye sudy 'voennie'?" *VG*, no. 195 (Sept. 5, 1906): 1.

were not ideologically neutral. Many of them contained barely veiled appeals for military reform, for the rebuilding of the army, and for the mass mobilization of the Russian population.[36]

Later various members of the group somewhat disingenuously denied that *Voennyi golos* had been a political paper. This was of course ridiculous, for the paper regularly pronounced on such political issues as the budget and the constitution of the Empire. But beyond this, believing as they did that the next war had to be national in character, the editors explicitly argued that military reform was senseless unless accompanied by social and political change. General Deniken later biliously dubbed *Voennyi golos* "a perverted reflection of the army's moods."[37] This may have been true in the sense that the majority of army officers were ill-educated, apathetic, and unlikely to possess coherent political ideologies. Still, the wide distribution of *Voennyi golos* and its seductive and articulate presentation of political affairs through the tinted lens of military interest rendered it powerful and dangerous.

The Young Turks

There were two discrete so-called Young Turks movements, a fact which has occasioned considerable confusion. One of these was purely academic, and as such of marginal political significance. This was the quarrel after 1910 at the Nicholas Academy of the General Staff between B. V. Gerua and N. N. Golovin (the Young Turks) and A. K. Baiov and M. D. Bonch-Bruevich. Golovin had returned from a year in France at Marshal Foch's *Ecole Superieure de Guerre*, full of enthusiasm for the "applied method" of teaching tactics. This method stressed practice and problem solving in the field over the study of military theory and military history in the classroom. Coupled with this view was a tendency to downplay the human element in warfare in favor of technology. As professor of Russian military art, Baiov quite naturally objected to a position so alien to the traditions of Russian military thought. Bonch-Bruevich played a nastier role in this spat, for he apparently started the rumor that the academic Young Turks were members of a seditious conspiracy. As Bonch-Bruevich was an intimate of War Minister Sukhomlinov (both were products of Kiev Military District), he encountered little difficulty in propagating this scurrilous falsehood throughout the War Ministry.

---

[36] von Shvartz, *Vospominaniia*, pp. 162-163. For examples of "political articles" see "Vol'nyia raboty," *VE*, vol. 7 (St. Petersburg, 1912), pp. 30-31; "Intendanstvo," *VE*, vol. 11 (St. Petersburg, 1912), pp. 14-15; "Lev L'vovich Lobko," *VE*, vol. 15 (St. Petersburg, 1914), p. 29; "Odinochnoe obuchenie," *VE*, vol. 17 (St. Petersburg, 1914), p. 105.

[37] Denikin, *Staraia armiia*, vol. 2, p. 141.

And Sukhomlinov, who was going through one of his paranoid phases at this time, apparently found the rumor credible enough to justify removing General Shcherbachev as head of the Academy in 1912. General Ianushkevich, who succeeded Shcherbachev, quickly purged the Academy of Young Turks.[38] Whatever the political aspirations of the academic Young Turks, they did not act on them.

The other Young Turk movement, chronologically earlier than that at the Academy, involved contacts between an amorphous group of officers and certain members of the State Duma. The idea for such contacts originated with the War Ministry. Scarcely a month after the Third Duma convened (November 1, 1907), War Minister A. F. Rediger invited selected members of the Commission on State Defense, including its chairman, Octobrist leader A. I. Guchkov, to his palace to discuss the army's requirements. The hearty support for the army evinced by the Commission on this occasion so delighted Rediger that he resolved to continue these helpful contacts.[39] He accordingly instructed Assistant War Minister A. A. Polivanov to meet privately with members of the Commission to lobby on behalf of the army. In his diary, Polivanov recorded meetings with Guchkov and others on February 6 and 12, 1908, March 25, 1908, December 15, 1908, November 17, 1909, and December 17, 1909. The site was often the apartment of Duma member P. N. Krupenskii.[40] As a supplement to these furtive discussions, Rediger gave permission at the end of 1908 for various military officials to meet with representatives of the Duma Commission on State Defense at the home of General V. I. Gurko. Among the officers who participated, in addition to Gurko, were Iu. Danilov, Col. Baron von Korf, and A. S. Lukomskii. These officers did more than cultivate Duma representatives: they had tacit permission to disclose military secrets deemed too important to entrust to the full Commission on State Defense, let alone the entire Duma. When he became War Minister in 1909, Sukhomlinov again sanctioned the meetings in the name of the War Ministry.[41]

These contacts had political significance. First, the conversations were clearly political, if only because by wooing the Duma the War Ministry was playing politics against the other ministries of state (especially the Ministry of Finance). There is also a sense in which the meetings were a political ploy against Nicholas himself, who did not know of the meetings and would have opposed them if he had. It is scarcely likely that

[38] Gerua, *Vospominaniia o moei zhizni*, vol. 1, pp. 251, 254-257. See also von Wahlde, "Military Thought," pp. 188, 192, 194.

[39] TsGVIA, f. 280, op. 1, d. 6, pp. 732-733.

[40] Polivanov, *Iz dnevnikov*, pp. 40, 41, 43, 55, 86, 90.

[41] Lukomskii, *Vospominaniia*, pp. 28-29; Denikin, *Tsarist Officer*, p. 182.

Rediger would have dared to inform him, in view of Nicholas's well-known repugnance to Guchkov in the wake of Guchkov's savage attack on the Grand Dukes in his famous Duma speech of May 27, 1908.[42] The War Ministry understood by 1908 that the Emperor was at best an erratic proponent of the army's interests. In view of this, friends in the Duma were not without value. But there is another sense in which the Guchkov meetings were political. War Minister Sukhomlinov correctly suspected that some of the officers who were fraternizing with the Duma representatives were sympathetic to the Octobrist political message, in fact so sympathetic that they might intrigue against the leadership of the War Ministry. Insofar as anything united the heterogeneous political groupings which styled themselves Octobrist in 1909, it was an unabashed imperialism, pride in Russia's status as a Great Power, and a desire for a large and strong Russian army.[43] And the latter attitude was especially attractive to elite military professionals like Gurko, Polivanov, and Lukomskii.

Under the leadership of Sukhomlinov, however, the War Ministry was drifting away from the principles of national military reform which Rediger had espoused, i.e., the idea that the army must be fully professional, consecrated to the task of defending the state against external enemies alone, while concomitantly striving to win the affection of the Empire's population. Sukhomlinov firmly believed in the existence of a Young Turk cabal and identified Polivanov, the Assistant War Minister, as its ringleader. While it generally required little evidence to convince Sukhomlinov of the existence of a plot, the fact that Polivanov intrigued against Sukhomlinov is beyond question. In July 1910, for example, Polivanov provided Finance Minister Kokovtsov with privileged information about Sukhomlinov's fortress demolition plan, in the obvious hope of forcing the War Minister to resign.[44] Polivanov also had some role in the newspaper campaign against Sukhomlinov which Guchkov orchestrated in April 1912.[45] On this occasion, Polivanov over-reached himself; that same month Sukhomlinov dismissed him from the War Ministry and shortly afterward disbanded the remaining Young Turks by dispatching them to distant field commands throughout the Empire.[46] In his explanation of this episode, Sukhomlinov accused Polivanov of

---

[42] Ben-Cion Pinchuk, *The Octobrists in the Third Duma* (Seattle, 1974), p. 67.

[43] J. F. Hutchinson, "The Octobrists and the Future of Imperial Russia as a Great Power," *SEER*, 50, no. 119 (Apr. 1972): 225-228, 234.

[44] H. H. Fisher, ed., and Laura Matreev, trans., *Out of My Past. The Memoirs of Count Kokovtsov* (Stanford, 1935), pp. 253-254.

[45] TsGAOR, f. DP OO, d. 144, 1913, ll. 150-151.

[46] Sukhomlinov, *Vospominaniia*, pp. 185-190.

self-serving careerism and unbridled ambition. Sukhomlinov declared, for example, that Polivanov had been the evil genius behind the ouster of War Minister Rediger; bitterly disappointed when his plot had not resulted in his own elevation to ministerial office, Polivanov was now bent on displacing Sukhomlinov.[47] Duplicitous and enigmatic as Polivanov was, however, there can be no doubt that his intrigues against Sukhomlinov were motivated by his belief that the interests of the army were in jeopardy. Looked at from this standpoint, Polivanov's baffling social and political contacts and his familiarity with everyone from the leaders of the Union of the Russian People to the chief figures in the Kadet Party make sense. As for his own political sympathies, they probably reposed with the Octobrists.

But Polivanov was not the only military officer with Octobrist sympathies. Other Young Turks, and indeed certain military men with no affiliation with that group, shared in this sympathy.[48] Certainly the supposition of political sympathy is more plausible than the theory advanced by V. Kobylin that the union between certain officers and the Octobrists was a consequence of their mutual participation in a secret military Masonic lodge.[49]

Guchkov regularly corresponded with both active and retired military officers. Such correspondence was perfectly legal. The Main Staff and the War Minister had ruled in early 1907 that there were no grounds for disciplining soldiers who only wrote letters to Duma representatives. Intensive police examination of Guchkov's mail in 1912 revealed that he was in touch with twenty-one army and navy officers, among them Lt. Gen. E. I. Martynov (previously associated with *Voennyi golos*), former War Ministers Rediger and Kuropatkin, Col. Kh. Ia. Oskanov of the Military Justice Administration, Major General Baturin, and Polivanov.[50] A letter of March 25, 1913 to Guchkov from Rotmistr N. Panteleev in Orel gives a sense of the epistles Guchkov regularly found in his mailbox: "We are familiar with your entire struggle for us and hope that you may be content with the blessings which all true soldiers who love the army send you. Know that the officers consider you the noblest son of our common motherland."[51]

[47] Ibid., p. 186.

[48] Mayzel, "Russian General Staff," p. 310 and n. 39, p. 320, correctly identifies the political goal of these officers as a desire for greater democracy, although he does not examine the reason behind this desire—i.e., that more democracy and hence greater patriotism was perceived as advantageous to the army.

[49] V. Kobylin, *Imperator Nilolai II i General Ad'iutant M. V. Alekseev* (New York, 1970), pp. 80-82.

[50] TsGAOR, f. DP OO, d. 144, 1913, l. 119; TsGVIA, f. 400, op. 15, d. 2999, ll. 5-6.

[51] Ibid., l. 21; on Kuropatkin's meetings with Guchkov, see TsGVIA, f. 165, op. 1, d. 5255, l. 127.

NEO-PANSLAVISM

In two influential volumes, Alfred Vagts charged that "Russian impe-rialism was officer imperialism." Scanning the period 1878 to 1914, Vagts claimed to detect the influence of imperialist Russian military officers behind each of the Russian Empire's aggressions. After the defeat in the Russo-Japanese War, Vagts argued, Russia's "imperialist military" re-discovered Panslavism, and applied pressure on the government for in-tervention in the Balkans.[52] Gerhard Ritter discredited Vagts's argument handily by demonstrating that imperialist officers actually had little influence on the formation of Russian policy.[53] However, there were imperialist officers, and Panslavist officers, especially after the Bosnian crisis of 1908 refocused the attention of Russian society on the Slavic problem.

A multitude of pro-Slavic societies existed in the Russian Empire, but the one most appealing to Russian army officers was the Slavic Phil-anthropic Society of St. Petersburg. A lineal descendant of the Slavic Philanthropic Committee (founded in Moscow in 1858), the Slavic Phil-anthropic Society greatly expanded its activities after 1907. Unlike the Society of Slavic Reciprocity, or the Moscow Society for Slavic Culture (associated with P. N. Miliukov), both of which stressed the equality of nations within the Slavic world (and hence demanded independence and justice for Poland), the Slavic Philanthropic Committee called for Russian domination of the Balkans and Slavic central Europe.[54] There were a healthy number of retired army generals among the Philanthropic So-ciety's members. Generals Bil'derling, Parenson, Sukhotin, Stavrovskii, Shcherbachev, and Pavlov, for example, attended a meeting of October 25, 1908 devoted to the question of Bosnia-Herzegovina. Retired Gen. (and former member of the *Voennyi sovet*) A. P. Skugarevskii joined the society in 1908, as did Col. M. Ia. Baliasnyi (on duty with the St. Petersburg Military Court), General of Artillery Onoprienko, Lt. Gen. K. I. Kurganovich, Lt. A. F. Pukovskii, and Staff Capt. N. N. Ionov.[55] In 1909, military statistician A. M. Zolotarev and Gen. A. I. Cherep-Spiridovich, among other prominent figures, took out memberships,

[52] Vagts, *History of Militarism*, pp. 386-389, 399; *Defense and Diplomacy: The Soldier and the Conduct of Foreign Relations* (New York, 1956), pp. 503-505.

[53] Gerhard Ritter, *The Sword and the Scepter: The Problem of Militarism in Germany*, vol. 2, trans. Heinz Norden (Coral Gables, Fla., 1970), pp. 80, 82, 84, 77.

[54] P. A. Kulakovskii, "Vozniknovenie slav'ianskikh obshchestv v Rossii i znachenie ikh pervogo s"ezda v Peterburge," *SI*, no. 5 (1909): 624, 633; "Slavianskie s"ezdy i pol'skii vopros," *SI*, no. 7 (1909): 870-872.

[55] "Deiatel'nost' S-Pb Slavianskogo blagotvoritel'nogo obshchestva," *SI*, no. 8 (1908): 464-465, 469.

while General Parenson was elected co-chairman of the society.[56] One noteworthy feature of the society is that it numbered several important Duma representatives among its members, including the ubiquitous A. I. Guchkov.

The goals of this society, avowedly political, were expressed not only in congresses and publicists' work but in the organization of Slavic demonstrations, such as the Slavic banquet campaign of 1913.[57] Why would Russian officers find the society interesting? We ought not to discount the possibility that there were officers who were also sincere Slavic idealists. But the neo-Panslavic ideology possessed certain practical advantages from the purely military point of view. We have already cited evidence that A. P. Skugarevskii, a prominent member of the society, was fascinated by techniques for the mass mobilization of Russian society for war. It was exactly this kind of motivation which the Panslavic ideology was supposed to deliver. If wars of the future were to be national, what better method of motivating the Russian nation than a doctrine which proclaimed the superiority of the Slav? In the writings of military men connected with the Slavic Philanthropic Society, Panslavism was almost always connected with war. "United Slavdom," a 1908 pamphlet written by retired officer A. F. Rittikh and published by the society, is a good example. Rittikh predicted a great world war between all Slavs (led by Russia), England, France, and Denmark, on the one hand, and Germany, Austro-Hungary, Italy, Turkey, and Japan on the other. The result of the war would be the partitioning of all the latter states. A gigantic Russian-speaking Slavic confederation would be created with its capital in Constantinople.[58] We can discount Rittikh's chimerical schemes for Slavdom, but the unmistakable implication of his booklet is that by embracing Panslavism the Russian Empire would both become invincible in war and attain her historically mandated destiny.

Certain military figures shunted even further to the right in the quest for an inspirational ideology. One example was the Society of the Russian Borders, founded in St. Petersburg in the spring of 1908. This society was affiliated with the weekly newspaper, *The Borders of Russia*, which was characterized by its antipathy toward the Empire's ethnic minorities, especially the Poles and Jews. A small number of retired military officers participated in this society, among them A. M. Zolotarev and M. M.

---

[56] *SI*, no. 4 (1909): 46, no. 1 (1909): 155.

[57] TsGAOR, f. 102, op. 14, d. 104, 1913 g., ll. 10, 22, 23, 24.

[58] A. F. Rittikh, *Ob"edinennoe slav'ianstvo* (St. Petersburg, 1908), pp. 7, 13, 18, 23-24.

Borodkin.[59] As for officers who were sympathetic to such organizations as the Russian Society or the Union of the Russian People, we will have more to say about them presently.

This new sort of military professionalism did not totally eclipse the older variety. The official military publications and the traditional unofficial ones, such as *Razvedchik* and the society's *Herald*, continued to flourish and become loci of lively debate. Further, the newer military professional movements were smaller and feebler than those which had gone before: the editorial board of *Voennyi golos*, the Young Turks, and the neo-Panslavists taken altogether never represented more than a few hundred officers. Also, the new politicized officers had to confront the active and efficacious opposition of both the higher civilian and military authorities.

THE RESPONSE OF WAR MINISTRY TO OFFICERS' POLITICAL INVOLVEMENT

If officers engaged in politics with the interests of the army uppermost in their minds, why did the War Ministry object? The War Ministry itself recognized, just as did *Voennyi golos*, the Young Turks, and the Panslavists, that one of the Empire's critical weaknesses was the absence of military motivation among the population. For instance, in mid-1906, Rediger wrote that until the agrarian issue was resolved, the peasantry was unlikely to evince enthusiasm for military service.[60] In its report for 1911, the War Ministry would urge the "militarization of the population and the development in it of feelings of duty from childhood."[61]

But while it appreciated this point, the War Ministry still desired to remain in control of Imperial military policy. The politics which arose from the aspiration for military reform were dangerous since they could sow dissension among the ranks of Russian officers, and because such politics could lead, as Sukhomlinov discovered, to the formation of cabals directed against the ministerial leadership. When N. A. Danilov of the War Ministry Chancellery condemned Guchkov in 1913 for demoralizing the army, he was concerned precisely with political challenges to Ministry authority.[62]

Another danger arose from the army's presumed special relationship to the Imperial throne. The Fundamental Laws of 1906 had reserved to the Emperor the formulation and direction of military policy. Yet one

[59] *SI*, no. 1 (1909): 155 (advertisement).
[60] TsGVIA, f. 400, op. 15, d. 2344, ll. 34-35.
[61] TsGVIA, f. 1, op. 2, d. 171, l. 4.
[62] TsGVIA, f. 165, op. 1, d. 5255, l. 113.

uniform feature of the officers' politics we have been considering is that they were national politics, not autocratic politics. The Young Turks, the *Voennyi golos* group, and the neo-Panslavists placed the Army, the Nation, the Slav over the Emperor as the object of veneration, and they even challenged his military prerogatives. *Voennyi golos* saw the role of the Emperor as that of a mere figurehead; the Young Turks wanted to vest more control over the army in the Duma; the neo-Panslavists were appealing to the Russians to rally around the abstract idea of Slavdom, rather than the mystical concept of the Tsar. But the War Ministry had to work with the Emperor; to permit ideologies in which the Emperor was almost superfluous to flourish among the officer corps would therefore have been extremely impolitic. The Ministry and the politicized officers did share common assumptions about the causes of the Empire's military weakness, but the politicized officers alone dared pursue these assumptions to their logical conclusions, conclusions which implied changes in the government of the Empire so radical that the Imperial War Ministry could not possibly endorse them.

Thus it was that the War Ministry lashed out against political movements among officers whether on the right or on the left. One of the first political movements to attract ministerial attention was quite logically the one centered around *Voennyi golos*. In circular letter number 1060 for 1906, Rediger wrote that "in view of the given orientation of this paper, its further distribution may cause substantive harm." Rediger pointed out that because of its name, a variety of officers' libraries and even soldiers' tearooms had taken out subscriptions. Although Rediger could not forbid officers to read any legal journal, he exercised his power to interdict the distribution of any publication among private soldiers. *Voennyi golos* retaliated with a fiery editorial claiming that Rediger found the paper unpalatable because it truthfully declared that the War Minister was not master of his own house, since "his generals, his officers, his courts and his troops are controlled by the Ministry of the Interior."[63] In early September 1906, Rediger prevailed on the governor of St. Petersburg to suppress the paper.[64] Soon thereafter, the Main Staff bookstore took all volumes with the imprint of Shneur or *Voennyi golos* down from its shelves. All of these titles had been legally passed by the censorship. Although most concerned the Russo-Japanese War, the war was but a springboard for the discussion of military reform. It was the political content of these books which disturbed the Staff, despite the

---

[63] "Komu i pochemu my neugody?" *VG*, no. 146 (July 4, 1906): 1.
[64] "Voennyi golos," *VE*, vol. 6 (St. Petersburg, 1911), p. 584.

protests of Shneur and even such a conservative paper as *Novoe vremia (New Times)* against the Staff's arbitrary decision.[65]

We have already seen how Sukhomlinov disposed of the Young Turk movements. But to put pressure on the St. Petersburg governor to suppress books and to transfer officers to the oblivion of Asiatic garrisons were both possible without the invocation of Order number 804. The Ministry did in fact rely on the order in the struggle against politicized officers. Interestingly enough, in 1906, 1907, and 1908, the order was consistently employed as a wedge to split the army away from the Russian right. A comparison with the civilian ministries of state is interesting in this regard. Insofar as there was any civilian equivalent to army Order 804, it was the Council of Ministers' circular of September 14, 1906. This circular forbade all civilian government employees to participate in political parties or unions which were revolutionary, which opposed the government, or which called the people to a struggle with the government. As the articles of this decree imply, the measure was obviously designed as a weapon against the political opposition on the left. Under its provisions, provincial officials with Kadet leanings, for example, could easily be discharged from office. Yet there was no prohibition against civilian officials belonging to right-wing or monarchist organizations. It was only two years later that an Interior Ministry circular of May 19, 1908 informed the civilian police that they had to withdraw from association with any political groupings, including monarchist ones.[66]

The War Ministry, by contrast, was so committed to the ideal of an army above politics that it even proscribed right-wing organizations which it considered useful. On January 27, 1906, for example, the Main Staff reported to the War Minister on an organization called the *Russkoe sobranie* (the Russian Assembly). Founded in 1901, this society was intensely patriotic and employed as its slogan the old army battle cry "For Faith, Tsar, and Fatherland." But the Staff noted that "regardless of the character of the political program of the Russian Assembly, the Main Staff finds that the Assembly belongs to that group of political organizations forbidden to military men." The Ministry accordingly asked the Department of Police to inform the chairman of the Russian

---

[65] *Knizhnyi vestnik*, no. 12 (Mar. 25, 1907): 347-349; *Knizhnyi vestnik*, no. 15 (Apr. 15, 1907): 444. Among these works were F. F. Novitskii's *Sandepu*, D. P. Parskii's *The Reasons for Our Defeats*, A. Riabinin, *Infantry Guard Service*, N. Shneur, *Cavalry Patrol Service*, P. D. Girs, *Mounted Hunting Commands*, and A. V. von Shvarts, *From the Diary of an Engineer*.

[66] TsGAOR, f. DP, 4th deloproizvodstvo, op. 236 (II), d. 777, 1906, ll. 12, 41, 56.

Assembly that no soldiers would receive permission to join it.[67] In the same month, the head of the newly formed Kievan "Russian Brotherhood" requested War Ministerial consent for retired officers in uniform to participate. The organization was aggressively opposed to revolution and "criminal" propaganda. However, the Ministry declined this request, notwithstanding the Staff's observation that: "The value of such a society is indubitable, and the possibly broad participation in it of retired military men . . . is highly desirable . . . [yet] the basic idea of order number 804 was to separate the army from any participation in politics, and in particular to prohibit men in uniform, whether retired or not, from joining parties."[68] On October 16, 1906, the Ministry issued Order number 626, further stiffening Order number 804. Now not only was participation in political meetings forbidden; even casual attendance at nonpolitical meetings if organized by political groups was grounds for expulsion from service. A further clause, probably suggested by the *Voennyi golos* incident, made the expression of opinions by soldiers in the press (if contrary to government policy) an equally serious offense. The last clause made liable for discharge not only the offending officers, but also such of their superiors who knew of their involvement but did nothing about it.[69]

Pursuant to Orders 804 and 626, Polivanov rebuffed A. I. Dubrovin, head of the Union of the Russian People, when in 1907 the latter proposed that the Union help ferret out political agitators in the army.[70] When in 1908 a certain Morozov, head of the Armavirsk section of the Union, telegrammed the War Ministry requesting military guards and a military band for the anniversary celebration of the Union, Rediger declined.[71] The Union was not easily discouraged, however. Morozov approached the Emperor himself to ask that Rediger's decision be overturned. Rediger then had to explain to Nicholas II why it was that the Union's requests could not be satisfied.[72]

The Union of the Russian People persisted in making trouble for the War Ministry. In early 1908, Nicholas II received a forty-two man delegation from the Northwestern Section of the Union. The War Ministry was shocked when it discovered that one member of the delegation was Ioann Golubev, a military chaplain attached to the 27th infantry

[67] TsGVIA, f. 400, op. 15, d. 2617, 1. 383; TsGAOR, f. DP, 4th deloproizvodstvo, op. 236 (II), d. 777, 1906, l. 7.
[68] TsGVIA, f. 400, op. 15, d. 2617, l. 390.
[69] Ibid., 1, 311.
[70] Polivanov, *Iz dnevnikov*, p. 31.
[71] TsGVIA, f. 400, op. 3, d. 3087, l. 1.
[72] Ibid., ll. 5-6.

division. But Golubev's antics during his meeting with the sovereign were more alarming than the mere fact of his attendance. Golubev made a speech imploring the Emperor to permit the military clergy and military officers to join right-wing organizations, in contravention of Order number 804. To Rediger's horror, Nicholas gave his verbal assent to Golubev's proposal. (Fortunately, ministerial officials swiftly persuaded Nicholas to rescind his permission.) The Staff called for the exemplary punishment of Golubev; the army could do without military chaplains who believed that they had to belong to monarchist parties in order to fulfill their pastoral obligations. When Krshivitskii, Vil'na Military District commander, advised that to prohibit the membership of the military clergy in the Union or similar political groups was shortsighted, the Staff instructed him never to raise the issue again.[73] When the Union made its final attempt to secure an exemption allowing officer membership (midsummer, 1908), it was greeted with the War Ministry's adamant refusal.[74]

To be sure, the foregoing does not mean that the War Ministry was completely effective in its struggle with the rightist parties. Certain prominent officers espoused the doctrines of the right and protected reactionary movements. Gen. Baron A. V. Kaul'bars, Commander of the Kiev District, supplied arms to the combat unit of the Union of the Russian People in 1906-1907. General Gershel'man, Military District Commander of Moscow, secretly supported the monarchist organizations of Moscow in 1906. One official linked to him, Count Buksgevden, was implicated in the brutal murder of Duma deputy Iollos. The War Ministry may well have been unaware of these actions. Even if it had been apprised of them, military district commanders occupied an exceptional position, for only the Emperor himself could remove them. But not all district commanders were cut from the same cloth as Gershel'man or Kaul'bars. Sukhomlinov in Kiev, for example, forced Stolypin to remove the Kiev governor, Major General Veretnnikov, since the latter had publicly paraded in support of the Black Hundreds and even wore their insignia. All that can be said of the War Ministry is that it sincerely fought against officers' political action within the limits of the possible.[75] But try as it might, the Ministry was unable to check the politicization of Russia's military intellectuals. The politicization was in fact facilitated

---

[73] TsGVIA, f. 400, op. 15, d. 3224, ll. 26, 28, 34, 37-40, 42, 48, 52.

[74] Ibid., l. 58.

[75] A. Chernovskii, comp., *Soiuz russkogo naroda po materialam chrezvychainoi sledstvennoi komissii vremennogo pravitel'stva 1917 g.* (Moscow and Leningrad, 1929), pp. 227-228, 274-275, 71, 87; Sukhomlinov, *Vospominaniia*, p. 110; TsGVIA, f. 970, op. 3, d. 1505, ll. 4-6.

by the actions of certain other agencies of the state, principally the Department of Police.

THE DEPARTMENT OF POLICE AND OFFICERS' POLITICS

If the War Ministry was skittish about officer involvement in politics, the Department of Police became obsessed in the years after the revolution with the unmasking of the revolutionists and leftists who it presumed riddled the Russian officer corps. One noteworthy feature of the period after 1905 is the enormous expansion of police spying on Russian officers.

Police espionage within the Russian army was not a novelty. In 1902, for example, the police informed the War Ministry of a conversation between Colonel Porai-Koshits, commander of the 187th Khol'ma reserve infantry regiment, and some of his subordinates. In the course of his talk, Porai-Koshits apparently touched on the poverty of the Russian peasant, adding that "we military men live at the expense of the peasants and therefore ought to take measures to improve their material well being if we don't want to see a repetition of disorders such as the ones this spring in Khar'kov and Poltava provinces." War Ministry hostility towards such police actions was not new either. The police demanded that Porai-Koshits be discharged into the reserves. In fact there were very good reasons for disposing of Porai-Koshits other than those presented by the Police Department: he was notoriously cruel to his men, while his licentiousness had already provoked a scandal. Yet precisely *because* the police had initiated the attack on Porai-Koshits, the War Ministry and the Main Staff came to his defense.[76]

In the past the police had appreciated the army's sensitivity to external meddling in military affairs. In September 1904, for instance, the Police Department prepared a draft letter to the Military Justice Administration concerning sedition among the men of the 15th Krasnoiarsk infantry command. The original draft explained that this information had been collected by "secret agents"; the final version tactfully deleted any references to secret agents, disingenuously explaining that the information had been obtained "by chance."[77]

But the police were less cautious in the years after 1905. In 1906 the Gendarmes established a special military secret service with the sole purpose of spying on Russian officers.[78] This policy was presumed by some to be the brainchild of Sukhomlinov. In April 1912, Guchkov

---

[76] TsGVIA, f. 400, op. 15, d. 2273, ll. 211, 190, 230.
[77] TsGAOR, f. DP 00, d. 1885/02, ll. 87, 90.
[78] Denikin, *Tsarist Officer*, p. 200.

accused Sukhomlinov of founding a unit with liaisons to the Interior Ministry under S. N. Miasoedov to probe the loyalty and political reliability of officers.[79] Guchkov's charge has never been proven and there is good reason to take issue with it. Although police investigations into the politics of Russian officers intensified after Sukhomlinov came to office, heightened police espionage on officers began while Sukhomlinov was still district commander in Kiev—before he arrived in Petersburg as Chief of Staff, before he could have exerted any influence on the Ministry's policy. Although it would have been in character for Sukhomlinov to order investigations of officers' loyalty for his personal use, he was no less hostile to the new wave of police denunciations than his predecessor, Rediger. In the section of his memoirs devoted to his days in Kiev, Sukhomlinov expressed his disgust that the careers of numerous fine officers were ruined because of the false charges of the police.[80]

That view permeated lower echelons of the army as well; military officers throughout the Empire often displayed a sullen noncooperation when confronted with police accusations against their subordinates. On February 21, 1906, Interior Minister Durnovo wrote Rediger that the ataman of Ekaterinodar, Major General Savitskii, had received illegal political literature from abroad and, as chairman of the local Fine Arts Society, had encouraged the discussion of political topics. The War Ministry was compelled to look into this affair. But Savitskii's military superiors, the heads of Kuban oblast' (first General Odintsov, then General Babych), and the District Commander of the Causasus, Adjutant General Vorontsov-Dashkov, defended Savitskii. Besides reporting that Savitskii had repeatedly denied membership in any political parties, Babych volunteered that Savitskii was entitled to his private political opinions. Odintsev praised Savitskii's sterling military qualities, while Vorontsov-Dashkov advanced the suggestion (later adopted) that the War Ministry abandon the whole matter.[81]

While Savitskii evidently did express dubious political opinions, in many cases police accusations were either fantastic or trivial. The Police Department's investigation of the National Officers' Union in 1908, for instance, indicated as members one officer in Warsaw Military District, four sympathizers in Tiflis, and a paltry handful of other members scattered through the country.[82] This was hardly a subterranean plot of titanic proportions. Yet the police persisted in an almost hysterical sus-

---

[79] Pinchuk, *Octobrists*, p. 189; Stone, *Eastern Front*, pp. 26-27.

[80] Sukhomlinov, *Vospominaniia*, p. 129.

[81] TsGVIA, f. 330, op. 50, d. 1095, ll. 1, 3, 4-5, 14, 18, 19, 29-30.

[82] TsGAOR, f. DP 102, op. 9, d. 81, 1908 g., ll. 12, 19, 21-22, 25, 34.

piciousness of the Russian officer corps. In 1911, for example, the Poltava police accused General Zhdanov, head of the Poltava local brigade, of criminal and political offenses. Kiev District hotly described these charges as a tissue of lies, adding that "there is good reason to assume that the denunciation was written by an official of the civilian administration, who is extremely dissatisfied with the demands of Major General Zhdanov for the satisfaction of the lawful needs of the troops."[83]

In August of 1911, the Ministry of the Interior once again presented Sukhomlinov with another set of accusations. The Ministry had long been upset by the number of Polish officers, and Russian officers with Polish wives, who were serving in units on the Empire's Western frontier. These men, the Ministry darkly hinted, might turn traitor in the event of war with Austria-Hungary. The Ministry expressed particular suspicion about Colonel Symon, commander of the 19th Kostroma infantry regiment (Zhitomir). The Commander of Kiev District, Lieutenant General Ivanov, immediately exonerated Symon and the other Polish officers. Ivanov insisted that the majority of Polish officers could be relied on to discharge their duty in wartime unswervingly. Repudiating the Gendarme claims—that Symon had a fanatical hatred of Russia and persecuted Russian officers in his command—Ivanov declared that Symon was an outstanding officer, highly intelligent and talented. Taking action against Symon was preposterous.[84]

Yet the police retained the idée fixe of widespread left-wing subversion among the officers. A newspaper report of January 1910 declaring that a certain retired Colonel Tsimbalin had organized a "National Union of Officers and Bureaucrats" inspired a frantic search throughout the Empire for this nonexistent person.[85] The police continued to shower the War Ministry with gratuitous, officious, even insulting reports. In October 1912, the Interior Ministry wrote the War Ministry about the 124th Voronezh infantry regiment in Khar'kov. The officers of this regiment were somehow suspect for their conspicuous kindness to Jews. The police found the fact that Jewish clerks served in eight companies of the regiment to be especially damning.[86] The War Ministry ignored this letter.

Army tolerance for police intrusion was wearing thin. In April 1912, the police intercepted a letter by one Lieutenant Baklazhenkov which contained some remarkable comments about the recent shooting of workers at the Lena Goldfield. "I am glad that I wasn't there, and therefore

[83] TsGVIA, f. 400, op. 323, d. 38, ll. 67, 69, 71-72, 74.
[84] Ibid., ll. 86-87, 90.
[85] TsGAOR, f. DP 00, op. 240, d. 2451, ll. 1-18.
[86] TsGVIA, f. 400, op. 323, d. 38, l. 123.

214

didn't have to betray my oath. . . . when will the patience of the Russian people, these slaves in the past and present, finally give way?" Yet the army took no action against the author of these statements.[87] Again in 1912, the police examined a letter by Capt. Iu. A. Liperovskii, an instructor at the Kiev cadet corps. In his letter, Captain Liperovskii called himself a democrat and criticized (among other people) Plehve, Stolypin, and the notorious double agent Azev. Sukhomlinov, that supposed template of obscurantism, responded to the Police Department that he had no plans to punish Liperovskii, and further that if the Police Department could not supply any more damaging information about that officer, he planned to approve Liperovskii's promotion to lieutenant colonel.[88]

The police enjoyed little more success with its network of agents spying on private Russian soldiers. Certain district commanders flatly refused to allow police spies in their district. For example, General Samsonov, Commander of Turkestan District, said in 1909 that he would prefer "that the troops riot, rather than permit a gendarme secret service in the army." When he assumed the directorship of the Police Department in 1912, V. F. Dzhunkovskii severely reduced such espionage by abolishing the internal military secret service. The *Okhrana*, however, refused to obey Dzhunkovskii's command; at the end of 1913, Colonel Kotlen, head of the *Okhrana*, was fired for his noncompliance.[89]

After 1910 the Department of Police had a more substantive reason to fear sedition in the officer corps. The news of successful military coups in Turkey and Portugal had a certain, if modest, resonance among Russian officers. With the assistance of the Socialist-Revolutionary party, an "All-Russian Military Union of the Army and Fleet" was formed with branches in Petersburg, Kronshtadt, and Moscow. The police rapidly liquidated this organization in June 1910. In October of the same year, representatives of all the revolutionary parties, with the exception of the Bolsheviks, met in Zurich to consider the problem of the army. They decided to initiate a campaign to fill the military schools with "progressive youths," who, upon graduation and receipt of commission, could subvert the army from within.[90] Apparently, some leftists had already managed to penetrate the officer corps. In 1912, for instance, the police intercepted a letter by Capt. B. P. Bazilev, the acting Moscow District

[87] TsGAOR, f. 102, op. 13, d. 61 (1912), l. 10, 31.

[88] Ibid., l. 26-27, 92.

[89] P. E. Shchegoleva, ed., *Padenie tsarskogo rezhima; stenograficheskie otchety doprosov i pokazanii, dannykh v 1917 g. v chrezvychainoi komissii vremennogo pravitelstva,* vol. 3 (Leningrad, 1925), pp. 268-270, 275, 328-330; S. Ia. Svirskii, *Revoliutsionnoe dvizhenie v tsarskoi armii v Turkestane (1910-1914 gg.)* (Tashkent, 1960), pp. 12-13.

[90] TsGAOR, f. 102, op. 14, d. 291 (1913), ll. 1-2.

Court prosecutor. In the letter, Bazilev alluded to his refusal to prosecute in capital cases, discussed his revolutionary work, and proclaimed his allegiance to the cause of socialism.[91]

But the credit of the police with the army was low. Overt hostility to the police, born in the revolution, grew quickly because of police meddling in military affairs and the inquisitorial checks of the police into officers' loyalty. Contempt for the police spread like a contagion throughout the officer corps, even penetrating the great mass of non-professional officers who had no ideological reason to oppose the police. The phenomenon of negative corporatism continued strong in the years after 1907. In July 1909, Capt. V. L. Nikolaev attacked the peasant D. Guk in his garden in Simofropol' uezd, Tauride Province. After beating and reviling Guk, Nikolaev vowed to kill him "like a dog" if he did not display more respect for officers in the future.[92] However, one interesting feature of negative corporatism in the post-1907 period is the direction of it against the police and members of the civilian administration. It was not just civilians, but civilian bureaucrats who were perceived as conspiring against officers' honor. In December 1910 an officer of the 184th Warsaw infantry regiment made obscene advances to the wife of Doctor Solov'ev in the Shuia Noble Club (Vladimir Province). The club management, composed of local bureaucrats, banned all officers from the club until the malefactor was identified. But the guilty officer had already been discharged from service by a regimental court of honor and in fact the trustees of the club knew very well who the officer was. The officers of the regiment therefore viewed the club's demand as an attempt to humiliate the army. The regimental commander, Colonel Chistiakov, attributed the club's action to "the extremely hostile attitude of a significant segment of the civilians of Shuia to the military, which frequently appeared earlier with regard to many men of the regiment."[93]

In April 1910, when retired Lieutenant Shumanskii, a well-known cardshark, prevented a policeman from entering an Odessa club, the city *gradonachal'nik*, General Tolmachev, ordered his arrest. Odessa District was enraged by Tolmachev's exceeding of his civilian authority; he had no right to order Shumanskii's arrest. As for Tolmachev's attempt to strip Shumanskii of his uniform, the Odessa District Staff found it suspicious; the Staff went so far as to suggest that Tolmachev was suborning perjury to accumulate evidence against Shumanskii. Shumanskii himself

[91] TsGAOR, f. 102, op. 13, d. 61 (1912), ll. 21-22.
[92] TsGVIA, f. 801, op. 8/68, d. 15, 1910 g., l. 3.
[93] TsGVIA, f. 400, op. 15, d. 3713, ll. 1, 3, 5, 8, 14.

wrote "there is not one person in Odessa, and particularly among military men, who would not be shocked by these actions of the Odessa *gradonachal'nik*."[94]

In early 1911, Stolypin complained to the War Ministry that the military chief of Poltava, Colonel Baranovskii, repeatedly insulted the local civilian authorities in a shameless fashion. The Ministry retorted that the friction in Poltava was caused by the refusal of the civilians to satisfy the lawful needs of the garrison. "That difficult atmosphere in which this staff officer has to work—i.e., dislike for the troops, and the disregard for their lawful demands—partially justifies him."[95]

Perhaps most illustrative of civil-military relations in this period was the bitter and almost fatal clash of 1911-1912 in Karkaraly, a small town in the steppe region of Omsk Military District. In a dispute over cards at the local club, the head of the local command, Captain Povolotskii, considered that his civilian opponents had insulted him. In fact, so seriously did Povolotskii take this insult that he seemed temporarily to lose his mind. He burst into the club at the head of his soldiers and threatened various civilians there with violence. The intervention of the civilian uezd chief enraged Povolotskii all the more. In the middle of the night, he went to the chief's house with a loaded revolver in his hand. He changed his mind, however, and the planned assassination never occurred. What was the War Ministry's response to all of this? It neither pressed criminal charges, nor cashiered Povolotskii from the service. Instead it transferred him to another town and closed the case.[96]

Given the acute military sensitivity to civilian meddling, police espionage on Russian officers was not only counterproductive but was even dangerous, for it produced the very phenomenon it was designed to combat: the decline in officers' respect for the Imperial government. For many officers, an exaggerated sense of police espionage bore fruit in a feeling of unjust persecution. At the same time, many military commanders distinguished themselves by refusing to cooperate with the police. A Police Department memorandum from the end of 1912 noted that in questions of officers' loyalty, the Gendarmes were obliged to transmit information collected by their military secret service to the local military authorities. "Unfortunately, however, by no means do the field commanders always make use of the data provided by the Gendarmes; in general they treat the Gendarmes with skepticism and even hostility,

[94] TsGVIA, f. 400, op. 15, d. 3568, ll. 11, 17, 22.
[95] TsGVIA, f. 400, op. 15, d. 3719, ll. 1-3, 7-8.
[96] TsGVIA, f. 400, op. 15, d. 3944, ll. 3, 6, 7, 13, 16, 25-28, 128.

not supplying us with the unconditionally necessary assistance in the struggle against negative phenomena in the military."[97] The unity of goals and purpose between officers and police, ruptured in the years 1905-1907, was not reestablished after the revolution, and the rancor, misunderstanding, and alienation grew steadily worse.

[97] TsGAOR, f. 102, op. 14, d. 291 (1913), l. 3.

EIGHT

The War Ministry, the Duma, and Interministerial Politics, 1906-1914

THE WAR MINISTRY, like other agencies of the Imperial state, began the year 1906 in anxiety over those changes which would result from the establishment of an entirely new political system. A Duma with popularly elected representatives was shortly to assume an important legislative role within the apparatus of government. Yet, at least initially, the War Ministry showed a remarkable willingness to exploit the Duma to achieve its institutional objectives. Especially in satisfying the army's ballooning need for money, the Duma could prove a counterweight to the parsimonious Ministry of Finance and State Control. Yet to rely on the Duma in this way was dangerous, for too much cooperation with the Duma would arouse the suspicions of the Emperor, who soon came to despise all but the most right-wing of Duma deputies. Unhappy with the legislature he had granted the Empire, Nicholas II made several attempts in the ensuing years to recover some of those prerogatives he had signed away on October 17, 1905. He was particularly sensitive about his control of the Imperial Russian army. The War Ministry therefore had to balance its relationship with the Emperor against its relationship with the Duma. War Minister Rediger, weighed down by multiple worries—revolution, finance, and military reform—miscalculated: tilting too far in the direction of the Duma, he angered his sovereign and had to resign. Nicholas II then appointed V. A. Sukhomlinov to head the War Ministry, consciously choosing him as an anti-Duma candidate. Under Sukhomlinov's administration, the army edged away from the Duma, becoming more of a personal instrument of the Emperor. However, the operative word here is more; Nicholas never entirely repossessed the army. The tempo of professional military development was quite striking under Rediger, and although it slowed under Sukhomlinov, it did not cease. Sukhomlinov was personally less "professional" than Rediger in the terms of our definition. He was in addition handicapped by his shameless toadyism, which occasionally deprived him of any will to resist the monarch, whatever the issue or its importance. Still, even under Sukhomlinov, the army inched towards military professionalism. A chief example here is the fact that Sukhomlinov achieved the army's long-standing dream by almost completely extricating it from guard duty for civilians. However, as in the past, burgeoning military professionalism was inconsistent with the traditional autocratic principle. It was, moreover, inconsistent with the goals and the professionalisms of the other ministries of the Imperial state.

THE PROFESSIONALISM OF THE WAR MINISTRY AFTER 1905

We have already examined the ways in which individual Russian officers concocted schemes for the militarization of the Imperial population in the postrevolutionary years. The War Ministry was itself affected by this style of thought, at least under A. F. Rediger, who had tacit sympathy for the concept of mobilizing the entire nation for military service. However, for obvious political reasons, Rediger did not wish to move too fast, nor did he desire the impetus for reform to come from outside the Ministry. All the same, radical ideas for fostering a martial spirit in the Imperial population provided the hidden subtext of his reformism.

The War Ministry was still wedded to such traditional professional goals as the expansion of military maneuvers. Between 1903 and 1908 the budget for these exercises ranged from 2.4 to 2.8 million rubles a year.[1] Of course, owing to war and revolution, the War Ministry spent far less in certain years than the sums appropriated. As soon as was possible, however, the Ministry resumed planning for larger and more comprehensive maneuvers. Thus in 1909 Rediger managed to allocate 4.5 million rubles for maneuvers.[2] Thereafter the Ministry never spent less than 4 million rubles on maneuvers in any given year. Almost all units of the army now trained in summer camps; each year an ever greater number of units participated in mobile exercises. In 1910, for example, 611 battalions, 430 squadrons or sotnias, and 239 batteries were involved in mobile exercises.[3] In 1911, 1,098 battalions, 629 squadrons or sotnias, and 564 batteries took part.[4] By 1913 the army was spending over 11 million a year on training exercises of all kinds.[5]

In addition, the War Ministry worked for a more modern and effective military establishment through an increased emphasis on technical training as well as better pay, housing, and education.[6] A logical consequence of the army's thirst for competence and expertise was a greater influence

[1] TsGVIA, f. 400, op. 3, d. 4559, l. 4.
[2] TsGVIA, f. 400, op. 3, d. 4675, l. 4.
[3] TsGVIA, f. 1, op. 2, d. 170, l. 17.
[4] TsGVIA, f. 1, op. 2, d. 171, l. 18.
[5] TsGVIA, f. 1, op. 2, d. 173, l. 38.
[6] TsGVIA, f. 1, op. 2, d. 171, l. 4.

for the General Staff at the expense of the old privileged army elites—the Guards and the cavalry. In particular, General Staff officers came to occupy the majority of field command posts: by 1912, 62 percent of all corps commanders and 68 percent of all infantry division commanders wore the black insignia of the Staff.[7]

But Rediger's Ministry was committed to the new professionalism of mass mobilization as well as the old professionalism of education. In fact, Rediger aspired to a homogeneous patriotic army drawn fairly from all classes and nationalities in the Empire. He was not alone, as became evident in a very interesting case in 1906. In May of that year, the War Ministry learned that a bill on civil equality was about to be introduced into the Duma. The Ministry was aware that this would benefit persons of various estates, religions, and nationalities which heretofore had been the objects of army discrimination. The Main Staff consequently decided to poll each of the Ministry's Main Administrations for reactions. Some responses revealed a narrow-minded bigotry: the Main Engineering Administration, for instance, opposed the appointment of Poles and Jews to responsible jobs within the army engineering service. But many of the Main Administrations were more tolerant. The most liberal response came from the Main Artillery Administration, which welcomed the abolition of statutory restrictions against the "equality of all Russian subjects" in military service. It devoted a separate paragraph to the Jews, sensibly observing that "prejudice against the Jews cannot be dissipated so long as the stigma of alienation still lies on that nation." Noting that Jewish military doctors had already proved their loyalty and worth, the Artillery Administration favored extending the right of officer status to all Jews. According to a Main Staff memorandum of June 1906, most of the Administrations agreed that even if the law on civil equality was not enacted, discrimination against religious groups and nationalities had to be abolished anyway for the good of the army. Although it wanted to defer the question of admitting the Jews to the officer corps until calmer times, the Staff argued that "the War Department would doubtless be able to employ . . . the best talents among persons of different faiths."[8]

Rediger simultaneously wanted to streamline the Ministry of War by jettisoning nonessential offices and privileges, the incrustations of over one hundred years of haphazard ministerial growth. For example, in a remarkable departure from institutional imperialism, Rediger planned in 1906 to unload the civil administration of all Turkestan onto the

---

[7] Denikin, *Staraia armiia*, vol. 1, p. 13.
[8] TsGVIA, f. 400, op. 15, d. 2844, ll. 1, 5-6, 13, 26-28, 52-54.

Interior Ministry. Shortly thereafter, he proposed to close down the Main Administration of Cossacks and absorb the Cossack units into the regular army.[9]

As before, powerful forces impeded the realization of the Ministry's maximum program of military reform. The Ministry of Finance, now headed by the abrasive V. N. Kokovtsov, marshalled its considerable expertise to check the Ministry of War at every turn. And the War Ministry needed money. The reorganization of 1910, including the abolition of the reserve (*rezervnye*) commands and the first tentative gestures towards the territorial system, would require 1.3 million rubles in resettlement pay alone.[10] In addition, there were the unavoidable expenses of purchasing sufficient stocks of indispensable technical equipment for future war. The War Ministry still anticipated that the impending great European war could last no more than six to eight months.[11] In 1910 the Polivanov Commission on Supply Norms once again ruled that a long war was impossible.[12] This computation did not, however, obviate the need for modern weaponry. If war was to be short it had to be fought from a "standing start" with the materiel and munitions previously stockpiled. The official reports of the Ministry of War after 1907 are rich in discussions of gun purchases, ballistic tests, and the establishment of arms factories. In 1909 the army was rearmed with new quick-firing artillery while 214 mountain guns (model 1909) and 122 six-inch Schneider howitzers were on order.[13] In 1910 the army acquired 864 new heavy machine guns, and the Vickers light machine gun was adopted for standard use.[14]

The Ministry of Finance was alive to the fact that modern military equipment would be very expensive. While recognizing the Empire's security requirements, the Ministry nonetheless was perturbed about the solvency of the Empire and strove to restrain incontinent military investments just as it had in previous years. The Russo-Japanese War had cost the state almost three billion—nearly three times the bill for

[9] TsGVIA, f. 1, op. 1, d. 73539, l. 2.

[10] TsGVIA, f. 2000, op. 3, d. 295, l. 2.

[11] P. N. Krasnov, "Pamiati Imperatorskoi russkoi armii," *Russkaia letopis'*, vol. 5 (Paris, 1923), pp. 50-51.

[12] A. L. Sidorov, *Ekonomicheskoe polozhenie Rossii v gody pervoi mirovoi voiny* (Moscow, 1973), pp. 7-8.

[13] TsGVIA, f. 1, op. 2, d. 170, l. 4.

[14] TsGVIA, f. 1, op. 2, d. 171, ll. 8, 30. Clive Trebilcock, *The Vickers Brothers: Armament and Enterprise, 1854-1914* (London, 1977), pp. 121-134. See also L. G. Beskrovnyi, "Proizvodstvo vooruzheniia i boepripasov dlia armii v Rossii v period imperializma (1898-1917 gg.)," *Istoricheskie zapiski* (Moscow), 99 (1977): 92-93, 104-107, 110-111.

the war with Turkey of 1877-1878.[15] Kokovtsov later lied that his ministry had accepted all of the army's financial requests without demur from 1905 to 1914.[16] In reality, officials at the Finance Ministry were hostile to the army's pleas for increased appropriations. The clashes between the ministries of War and Finance assumed a particularly chronic and virulent character after the War Ministry's limited budget was abolished in 1908. Its hands freed from the bonds of appropriations agreed on five years in advance, the War Ministry would now needle the Finance Ministry for more funds for all of its programs.

Kokovtsov was unsympathetic and responded deviously. On April 20, 1907 he informed Polivanov that the army would receive no extra money to defray the costs of reform.[17] In December 1907, in separate meetings with Rediger and Polivanov, Kokovtsov declared that he expected Imperial tax revenues to rise by 75 to 150 million rubles in the following and all subsequent years. He was therefore prepared to offer the War Ministry an additional 25 to 30 million a year from this surplus. But Kokovtsov soon reneged on his promise. In mid-March 1908 he asked the War Ministry to submit a budget for 1909 no larger than that granted for 1908.[18] An enraged Rediger ordered the heads of the War Ministry's Main Administrations to insert every request they desired into the budget; as a result, the application for 1909 funding exceeded that of 1908 not by the 15 million rubles originally planned, but by 97.[19] If Rediger appeared childishly vindictive, the Finance Ministry exhibited its share of pettiness. In early 1908, the War Ministry, urged on by Grand Duke Nikolai Nikolaevich, requested 207 million rubles to replenish Russia's stocks of war materiel. Kokovtsov at first declined to reply but, when finally pressed for an answer, declared that this demand was unexpected and made the army a counter-offer for 7 million rubles.[20] Sukhomlinov also vied with Kokovtsov—at the end of 1909, 1910, and 1911. For instance, Sukhomlinov asked Kokovtsov in October 1912 to authorize 63 million rubles to strengthen the Empire's defenses on the Austrian frontier; Kokovtsov, however, indignantly refused and accused the War Minister of mismanaging the army's budget.[21] Shortly there-

[15] Bertrand Gille, *Histoire economique et sociale de la Russie* (Paris, 1949), p. 209.

[16] Fisher, *Memoirs of Count Kokovtsov*, p. 231.

[17] Polivanov, *Iz dnevnikov*, p. 27.

[18] Ibid., p. 36; TsGVIA, f. 280, op. 1, d. 6, p. 742.

[19] TsGVIA, f. 280, op. 1, d. 7, p. 762.

[20] Polivanov, *Iz dnevnikov*, p. 39; Shatsillo, *Rossiia pered pervoi mirovoi voinoi*, pp. 40-41.

[21] Fisher, *Memoirs of Count Kokovtsov*, pp. 342-343.

after the Finance Ministry excised 65 million from the War Ministry's request for 108 million rubles of extraordinary credits.[22]

Of course the War Ministry retaliated. One effective device was the exploitation of war scares. The Bosnian crisis of 1908, which resulted in widespread fear of war with Austria, enabled the War Ministry to snatch 299 million rubles from a reluctant Kokovtsov.[23] Rediger later ascribed the army's success in expanding its arsenal of machine guns to this 1908 war scare.[24] Sukhomlinov made a similar observation about the continuing Balkan crisis of 1909: he had been able to turn it to the financial advantage of the army. The Ministry of War's official report for 1913 bluntly confessed that the threat of war with the Central Powers, perceived as serious in 1912, caused a speed-up in military preparations and facilitated work on the Big Program for military investment approved by the Duma in 1914.[25]

If war or the threat of war was helpful to the War Ministry, so was the support it garnered from the government of France. After 1911, with Poincaré as president of the Republic and Joffre as Chief of Staff, an alarmed France insisted that its eastern ally upgrade its military establishment. Of great moment to the French was Russia's inadequate network of strategic railroads; the French constantly badgered the Russian government about remedying this deficiency.[26] It was partly due to these French remonstrances that the War Ministry secured the adoption of a 1913 plan for the development of the Empire's railways in the interests of national defense.[27]

But the War Ministry also availed itself of the traditional stratagems of bureaucratic infighting against the Ministry of Finance. A. S. Lukomskii once maintained that the worst failing of V. A. Sukhomlinov as War Minister was his insufficient assertiveness with the Ministry of Finance.[28] This is a curious judgment, for if Sukhomlinov's style was crude, it is impossible to fault him for lack of aggression. Typical of his methods was his calculated sloppiness in reporting a savings from the ministerial budget for 1909 in the hope of confiscating it.[29] Characteristically, Sukhomlinov also persuaded Nicholas II to decree in February 1911 that although the military had to report unspent funds to the

[22] Shatsillo, *Rossiia pered pervoi mirovoi voinoi*, p. 94.
[23] Ibid., pp. 41-42.
[24] TsGVIA, f. 280, op. 1, d. 7, pp. 751, 755.
[25] TsGVIA, f. 1, op. 2, d. 173, l. 2.
[26] Collins, "The Franco-Russian Alliance," pp. 776-778, 786.
[27] TsGVIA, f. 1, op. 2, d. 173, l. 27.
[28] Lukomskii, "Ocherki," p. 931.
[29] TsGVIA, f. 1, op. 1, d. 73413, ll. 30, 39-40.

Ministry of Finance, the latter had but two weeks to prevent the reversion of the money to the Ministry of War.[30] Nicholas II is supposed to have told Kokovtsov: "In your conflicts with Sukhomlinov you are always right. But I want you to understand my attitude: I have been supporting Sukhomlinov not because I have no confidence in you but because I cannot refuse to agree to military appropriations."[31]

In February-March 1913, the cunning Sukhomlinov once again withheld crucial information from Kokovtsov and then caught him off guard. At an important ministerial meeting, Sukhomlinov suddenly raised the issue of a one-time payment to the War Ministry of 350 million, plus an additional million a year. All other persons at the meeting, including representatives of the Interior Ministry and the Ministry of Foreign Affairs, had received a thorough briefing on this subject the previous week. Kokovtsov had not.[32] Perhaps Sukhomlinov's most presumptuous thrust against the Ministry of Finance came at the end of 1913 when he made an attempt to banish it from the War Ministry's budgetary process. Reasoning by analogy to the regulations which circumscribed the Duma's powers in military matters, Sukhomlinov argued that the Ministry of Finance, like the Duma, should have no right to question the substance of a particular War Ministry proposal. The Council of Ministers dismissed Sukhomlinov's suit, noting that in most cases there could be division of financial form and military content in the army budget.[33]

WAR MINISTRY AND DUMA

The judicious use of the Duma was another option for the War Ministry in its quest for money. From the day the First Duma convened the War Ministry had perceived the potential advantages of an ally against the Ministry of Finance and the Ministry of the Interior. In a secret memorandum of May 16, 1906, Lieutenant General Zabelin of the War Ministry Chancellery implied that the difficulties over the army's financial estimates regularly experienced in the Council of Ministers could be overcome if the War Ministry approached the Duma directly without first bringing the estimates to the Council. Rediger opposed this potentially dangerous procedure, but remained alert to the benefits of Duma support for military appropriations.[34] Similarly, the War Ministry was

[30] TsGVIA, f. 2000, op. 2, d. 333, l. 6.
[31] Fisher, *Memoirs of Count Kokovtsov*, p. 340.
[32] Ibid., p. 362.
[33] TsGVIA, f. 2000, op. 2, d. 333, l. 4.
[34] TsGVIA, f. 400, op. 21, d. 3621, ll. 6, 31, 37.

quite pleased when even the first two intractable Dumas introduced interpellations listing violations of the rules for civilian use of the troops, or exposing the arbitrariness (*proizvol*) of civilian officials in the same regard. Rediger approvingly cited the Duma interpellation of June 1906 when warning district commanders about rule violations at the beginning of July.[35] The Main Staff endorsed the justice of the Duma investigation of the misuse of Cossacks in the same month, while Rediger made pointed reference to it in a letter to Prince Odoevskii-Maslov, ataman of the Don.[36]

In Rediger's case, however, the source of his desire for amicable co-operation with the Duma ran deeper than cynical self-interest. A passage in his memoirs gives an insight into his thinking on this matter: "In the War Department, there is no room for dual power, or multiplicity of powers, neither at the center, nor in the provinces; this is especially important in view of the fact that the War Minister must give answers, not only before the Sovereign, but before the legislative institutions."[37] Unlike numerous other tsarist ministers, Rediger explicitly accepted the view that the War Ministry and the army were responsible to the Duma. Other members of the military elite also readily accommodated themselves to the popular assembly. As Denikin wrote: "Many [officers] saw in it [the Duma] one of the means to put the army on the path of broad reforms. . . . Several looked on the tasks of the Duma in a broader sense, presuming that only a general upsurge of national life—cultural and economic—could appropriately elevate the military potential of the country."[38]

Praise for the service rendered the army by the Duma imbues the military memoirs of this period. Gen. A. S. Lukomskii stated that work with the Duma went smoothly even in 1906, and he observed that the Third and Fourth Dumas rarely denied the army anything. Owing to the Duma, Lukomskii wrote, measures were enacted which the Ministry of Finance would otherwise have burked.[39] Rediger lauded the Duma Commission on State Defense (formed in 1907 under the Third Duma), for its "extremely benevolent" attitude towards the needs of the army. Rediger did not hesitate to tell the Commission the entire sordid tale of his struggles with the Finance Ministry; because of the "solidarity" of the Council of Ministers, he explained, he had previously been unable

[35] TsGVIA, f. 400, op. 3, d. 2814, ll. 1, 40-41.
[36] Ibid., ll. 50-52, 56; TsGVIA, f. 330, op. 50, d. 1232, l. 18.
[37] TsGVIA, f. 280, op. 1, d. 6, p. 736; I. I. Rostunov, *Russkii front pervoi mirovoi voiny* (Moscow, 1976), p. 38 also touches on Rediger's "loyalty" to the Duma.
[38] Denikin, *Staraia armiia*, vol. 1, p. 153.
[39] Lukomskii, *Vospominaniia*, pp. 28-29.

to make his grievances public.[40] Even Sukhomlinov paid tribute to the generosity of the Duma when the interests of the army were at stake.[41]

Indeed, the Third and Fourth Dumas repeatedly expressed solicitude for the army. In April 1908, for instance, the Duma and the Council of State approved the construction of the strategic Amur railway over the protest of civilian financial ministries.[42] When Kokovtsov allowed Sukhomlinov to ask the Duma for 299 million rubles to be spent from 1908 to 1915, the Duma trimmed only 6 million from this request.[43] The Duma played an important part in the adoption of both the Small Program of 1910 (715 million rubles for the army over a ten-year period) and the Big Program of 1914 (which envisioned the spending of some 433 million for army requirements from 1914 to 1917).[44] In short, the role of the Duma cannot be underemphasized in the striking improvement in War Ministry finances. The Russian Empire's direct military (including naval) expenses rose from 643 million rubles (24.8 percent of all state expenditure) in 1909 to 965 million (28. 5 percent) in 1913.[45] Military investment consumed about 5 percent of the Empire's national income in 1900 but absorbed over 7 percent in 1913.[46] In terms of army expenditure, Russia was outspending all of the states of Europe by 1913, yet per capita defense expenditure remained low (Table 15). It was obviously beyond the capabilities of the Russian Empire to achieve the level of preparedness attained by the German Empire in the span of a few years. Still, with a supreme effort of will, and the all-important assistance of the Duma, the War Ministry did take large strides towards rectifying the problems of the army—or at least, those problems which could simply be rectified with money. When war broke out in 1914, the Russian army possessed over 6,000 quick-firing field guns to Germany's 5,500 and 791 heavy guns to Germany's 2,000.[47]

However, several considerations prevented the War Ministry from becoming too reliant upon the State Duma. One inhered in the Duma's right of interpellation. From the vantage point of the General Staff building, this was a two-edged weapon. Rediger did approve of Duma inquisitiveness, especially when directed against the Interior Ministry

[40] TsGVIA, f. 280, op. 1, d. 6, pp. 733-734.

[41] Sukhomlinov, *Vospominaniia*, p. 180.

[42] TsGVIA, f. 280, op. 1, d. 7, p. 757.

[43] Shatsillo, *Rossiia pered pervoi mirovoi voinoi*, p. 42.

[44] A. Zhilin, "Bol'shaia programma po usileniiu russkoi armii," *Voenno-istoricheskii zhurnal* 16, no. 7 (June 1974): 91-96.

[45] Iu. N. Shebaldin, "Gosudarstvennyi biudzhet tsarskoi Rossii v nachale XX v (do pervoi mirovoi voiny)," *Istoricheskie zapiski* (Moscow) 65 (1959): 182.

[46] Calculated on the basis of ibid., pp. 165, 181-182, 190.

[47] Beskrovnyi, "Proizvodstvo vooruzheniia," p. 107; General Herr, *L'Artillerie: ce qu'elle a été, ce qu'elle doit être* (Paris, 1923), p. 12.

TABLE 15
Army Expenses in Europe, 1913

Nations	Millions of rubles	Percent of state budget	Per capita expenditure
Russia	709	21	5.5 rubles
Germany	634	14.05	12.6
France	369	17.71	13.9
Britain	267	14.43	15.3
Austria-Hungary	229	10.17	4.8
Italy	162	—	—

SOURCE: Calculated on the basis of *Ministerstvo finansov 1904-1913* (n.p., n.d.), *prilozhenie*, plates 5-9

for abusing prerogatives with regard to using the army. Yet the Duma was not content with this; its investigations could also result in disclosures that were embarrassing and damaging to the image of the army. The first two Dumas, dominated by radical elements, certainly did not exempt the army from their general assault on the institutions of the Imperial State. The unprovoked killing of the Podol'ia peasants, discussed previously, was a case in point. The War Ministry was similarly disconcerted when in mid-June 1906, the Duma challenged the legality of the mobilization of the forty regiments and fifty separate sotnias of Cossacks of the second and third reserves which were on active repressive service. Since the issue revolved around legal technicalities—whether the format of the mobilization order was correct and whether it had to be presented as an Imperial decree to the Senate, or could be a mere ministerial report approved by the Emperor—the Military Justice Administration's stable of clever lawyers was easily able to refute the Duma's charges.[48]

But acrimonious confrontation with the Duma was not always so easily avoided, and even the more conservative Third and Fourth Dumas included some avowed enemies of the army. Each of the first three Dumas, for example, made attempts to abolish the death penalty, the first in May 1906, the second in March 1907, and the third in August 1908.[49] Military jurists were, of course, uncomfortable with death penalties, but it was part of Rediger's unspoken bargain with Stolypin that the army

[48] TsGVIA, f. 330, op. 50, d. 1232, ll. 1-2, 10, 13, 16, 26.
[49] TsGVIA, f. 801, op. 39/45, d. 31, ll. 4, 84-88, 111.

impose them. This legislative initiative of the First Duma was rendered moot by the proroguing of that body, and the War Ministry informed the Second and Third Dumas that, under the Fundamental Laws of the Empire, the Duma had no authority to tamper with military law.

Even more discomfiting for the War Ministry were those occasions on which the Duma uncovered genuine evidence of military misconduct, wanton destruction of property, or taking of life. Such an occasion was the Duma's May 1908 investigation of the activities of Meller-Zako-mel'skii's punitive detachments in the Baltic two and one-half years previously. Neither the Chancellery of the Ministry nor the Main Staff had any detailed information about these detachments, and had to forward Duma materials to Meller-Zakomel'skii himself for an answer. Meller imperiously refused to respond to the Duma's questions point by point; he did, however, confess that in 1905-1907 military units in the regions under his control had killed 625 rebels: 66 were slain in battle, 356 had been summarily shot, and 42 had been rather dubiously killed "while trying to escape."[50]

The War Ministry was similarly embarrassed by a 1909 Duma investigation into the shooting of prisoners at the Riga Central Prison by military guards, and by a 1911 inquiry about the use of deadly force against suspected bandits in the Caucasus.[51] The political right in the Duma could also foment trouble for the War Ministry, as it did in sponsoring a late 1911 investigation of the alleged nonresponsiveness of the army to the insults and assaults which traitorous Finns were visiting on the troops quartered in their country.[52]

Thus it was that the War Minister could never be sanguine about what transpired in the Tauride Palace. The Duma was after all a political institution. The goals of its members were political, and ranged from the total destruction of the tsarist state to the establishment of a mystical absolute autocracy. The Duma was therefore dangerous, for its hectoring investigations might easily fix the public eye on sordid aspects of military life which the army preferred either to ignore or deal with quietly. But the politics of the Duma were replete with other hazards than these. Even self-proclaimed benefactors of the army, like the Octobrists, were motivated by concerns which surpassed the mere goal of upgrading Russia's military might. This is not to suggest that Guchkov was an unprincipled hypocrite. There can be no doubt of his sincere patriotism.

[50] TsGVIA, f. 400, op. 3, d. 3189, ll. 2-3, 28-30; TsGAOR, f. DP, d. 236g2/1908, ll. 4, 9.

[51] TsGVIA, f. 400, op. 3, d. 3330, ll. 2, 6, 13-14, 18, 30, 56; TsGVIA, f. 2000, op. 2, d. 954, ll. 1-16.

[52] TsGVIA, f. 2000, op. 2, d. 954, ll. 18, 20, 24-25.

Nonetheless, the Octobrist clamor for military reform represented in part a tactical ploy to capture a patriotic issue which would strengthen the party's hand in dealing with the center, the right, and the nationalist electorate in general.[53]

Coupled to the disquieting fact that military reform in the Duma was being supported or opposed for other than intrinsic reasons was the absence of military sophistication, if not egregious ignorance of military affairs, evinced in Duma debates. B. A. Engel'gardt, a former cavalry and Cossack officer, served in the Fourth Duma and reported to that body on Sukhomlinov's Big Program. Engel'gardt berated the majority of his colleagues for their disinclination, or incapacity, to make a serious study of the military reform proposals placed before them. No one could expect the average Duma representative to possess an authoritative grasp of ballistics, or engineering expertise; still, in Engel'gardt's opinion, rudimentary acquaintance with the significance of artillery in combat or the problem of logistics would not have been amiss.[54]

The military ignorance of most Duma deputies was not without its advantages for the bureaucrats of the War Ministry, for they could conveniently presume that appropriations would be granted without any intense scrutiny of their substance. However, given the absence of military expertise in the Tauride Palace, no honest partnership between army and Duma was possible. The Duma's uncritical acceptance of the wisdom of War Ministry reform measures might easily be supplanted by the antithetical attitude of suspicion regarding the competence of the War Ministry. This, of course, is precisely what happened shortly after Sukhomlinov's appointment as War Minister.

But perhaps the most dangerous impediment to a good relationship between army and Duma, and simultaneously perhaps the chief obstacle to military reform in Russia, lay elsewhere: in the antiquated values and ideas of the Romanovs.

THE ARMY AND THE IMPERIAL FAMILY

We have already discussed Nicholas II's conception of the Imperial army and its role. Counterproductive even in the period before 1905, this conception remained largely unchanged in the years after. Nicholas mulishly refused to accept that the Empire's population or the Duma had any claim on the army. To his mind, the army was his own personal

---

[53] Geoffrey Hosking, *The Russian Constitutional Experiment: Government and Duma, 1907-14* (Cambridge, England, 1973), pp. 74-80.

[54] B. A. Engel'gardt, "Potonuvshii mir," *Voenno-istoricheskii zhurnal* 9, no. 1 (Jan. 1964): 74.

fief, and nothing—the October Manifesto, the Fundamental Laws, the deportment of the Duma, the military situation in Europe—could shake this belief. Several of the Grand Dukes, Nicholas's nephews, cousins, and uncles, who had been assigned varying military responsibilities, shared the idea that a bond of affect linked the army and the dynasty, a bond that conferred on the Romanovs the privilege of intervening in military affairs while bypassing the chain of command. War Ministers Kuropatkin, Rediger, and Sukhomlinov were united in condemning the pernicious influence of the Grand Dukes.[55]

In a volume published in 1935, A. A. Mosolov, head of the Chancellery of the Ministry of the Imperial Court from 1900 to 1916, sought to exonerate the Grand Dukes from the charges levelled against them. He demonstrated that the majority of the Grand Dukes had been excluded from the formulation of military policy because of incapacity, morganatic marriage, lack of interest, etc.[56] But Mosolov's well-intentioned defense was subjective and untruthful. Several of the Grand Dukes were hindrances to the War Ministry, some through their activity in military affairs, others through inactivity.

Grand Duke Konstantin Konstantinovich was an exemplar of the latter category. An unworldly poet by temperament who published pseudonymously, Konstantin could not have been more unsuited for his post as Head of the Main Administration of Military Schools.[57] Nicholas's uncle, Vladimir Aleksandrovich, had a distant connection with the army through his honorific chairmanship of the Military Order of St. George, where he proved a nuisance. In December 1906, for example, he created a horrid scene for War Minister Rediger over trivialities concerning patents of admission to the Order.[58]

Other Grand Dukes who occupied more important military posts as inspectors of army departments followed similar patterns. Petr Nikolaevich, Chief Inspector of the Military Engineers, impeded reform by his inactivity, which resulted from broken health.[59] Sergei Mikhailovich was Chief Inspector of the Artillery Department. Although he contributed much to the development of the Empire's arsenal, he was an irascible individual who pestered Nicholas II with gratuitous advice about military policy. Further, his reputation was tainted with the suspicion of cor-

[55] "Dnevnik A. N. Kuropatkina," *Krasnyi arkhiv* (Moscow) 2 (1922): 48; TsGVIA, f. 280, op. 1, d. 6, p. 736; Sukhomlinov, *Vospominaniia*, p. 215.

[56] Mossolov, *Court of the Last Tsar*, pp. 67-97.

[57] Ibid., p. 33; TsGVIA, f. 280, op. 1, d. 7, p. 759.

[58] TsGVIA, f. 280, op. 1, d. 6, p. 664.

[59] Mossolov, *Court of the Last Tsar*, p. 92; TsGVIA, f. 280, op. 1, d. 6, p. 785.

ruption in the allocation of army contracts.[60] As powerful as these in-spectors were, Rediger was at least able to avert a catastrophic increase in their authority by defeating a 1907 legislative proposal which would have made them independent of the War Ministry. As finally enacted, the law subordinated them to the Ministry, while giving them the status of military district commanders.[61]

When Imperial War Ministers complained of Grand Ducal meddling after 1905, however, the person they chiefly had in mind was Nicholas II's great uncle, Nikolai Nikolaevich. A man of no mean intellectual gifts, Nikolai was nonetheless a neurotic man cursed with periodic bouts of anxiety and depression. His sway over the sovereign originated in 1905. It had been Nikolai who, according to Baron Frederiks, persuaded Nicholas to promulgate the October Manifesto and to summon Count Witte to be chairman of the Council of Ministers.[62] Nikolai was also behind the division of the General Staff from the War Ministry and the creation of the Council of State Defense (SGO); as chairman of that latter body, Nikolai had wielded enormous power over war planning, military appropriations, and reform. Rediger had to pander to Nikolai for support; in his memoirs, for instance, when he notes that in 1906 he saw Nicholas II eighty-one times, he immediately adds that he had thirty-six conferences with Nikolai Nikolaevich.[63] Kersnovskii, the au-thor of the most complete history of the Imperial army, deemed Nikolai's influence so pervasive that he described the years 1905-1908 as the "Grand Ducal period."[64] One way in which Nikolai exercised his influ-ence was his frequent and effective criticism of the War Ministry for contact with the Duma.[65] But once Nicholas II came to appreciate the inadequacies of Nikolai's SGO and the independent General Staff, Nik-olai's favor with the Emperor began to wane. On June 27, 1908, he was "retired" from the chairmanship of the SGO. Shortly thereafter he took command of St. Petersburg Military District. Even stripped of supreme authority over war planning, Nikolai remained formidable. In April 1912, when Nikolai fell seriously ill, former War Minister Kuropatkin confided to his diary his gleeful wishes for the speedy death of this "degenerate" and "evil genius of the sovereign."[66]

[60] Mossolov, Court of the Last Tsar, p. 94; TsGVIA, f. 165, op. 1, d. 5255, l. 100; Kersnovskii, Istoriia, p. 605.

[61] TsGVIA, f. 280, op. 1, d. 6, pp. 735, 737.

[62] Mossolov, Court of the Last Tsar, pp. 87-90; Mehlinger and Thompson, Count Witte, p. 44.

[63] TsGVIA, f. 280, op. 1, d. 6, p. 676.

[64] Kersnovskii, Istoriia, p. 589.

[65] TsGVIA, f. 280, op. 1, d. 7, p. 759.

[66] TsGVIA, f. 165, op. 1, d. 5255, l. 108.

Obviously, however, the Emperor's impact on the army was more important than that of the Grand Dukes. Nicholas was certainly ambivalent about the constitution he had been forced to grant; he understood that by doing so he had renounced a portion of his autocratic power. But one power which he still considered to be solely his was that of unlimited control over Russia's armed forces. And because of the irritating check on his authority represented by the Duma and the State Council, it was a power which he was determined both to guard jealously and to construe broadly. When he announced the dismantling of the Council of State Defense, on July 26, 1908, Nicholas stated, "I intend to take military affairs more into my own hands."[67] This had two meanings for the army in practical terms. First, Nicholas would continue to consider Russian officers as his personal vassals (thus once again frustrating the War Ministry's attempt to gain control over entrance requirements, qualification standards, and promotions). Second, Nicholas would regard friendly contacts between army and Duma with an extremely jaundiced eye.

The Ministry of War had formed the Higher Commission on Performance Reviews to rectify one of the principal problems exposed by the conflict with Japan: the problem of mediocre field commanders. As an instrument for purging the army of incompetents, this institution worked extremely well when allowed to operate without interference. Nicholas, however, could not refrain from interfering. Rediger displayed praiseworthy courage when he informed the Emperor in mid-1906 that Imperial patronage had prevented the discharge of three inept corps commanders.[68]

Another flagrant example of Nicholas's harmful meddling with reform was his 1909 decision concerning the *Voennyi sovet*, or Military Council. Before 1906, the Council, which on paper was entrusted with the promulgation of military legislation plus the inspection of troops and army departments, had consisted of an indeterminate number of generals, appointed for life. In practice, the autocrats had generally dispensed seats on the Council as rewards to elderly and revered generals. In 1905 there were 52 members of the Council; the average age was 70. The Council, which could have been one of the most meaningful components of the War Ministry, actually served as a sort of nursing home. In 1906, Rediger rewrote the Council's charter to set the number of members at 18 and the term of service at 4 years. But this step to fashion the reanimated Council into an efficient institution was undone in June 1909 when

[67] Polivanov, *Iz dnevnikov*, p. 49.
[68] TsGVIA, f. 280, op. 1, d. 6, p. 655.

Nicholas II arbitrarily raised the term of service to 6 years, permitted consecutive terms, and expanded the Council to 24 members. Nicholas made this decision over the heated protests of the Chancellery of the War Ministry. Imperial whim had emasculated an institution with important executive, legislative, and judicial functions. Nicholas desired to restore the Council to that earlier form which served the traditional paternalistic values of the autocracy by creating a mechanism for pensioning off trusty old servants. The interests of the War Ministry—in this case bureaucratic rationalization—were expendable.[69]

With regard to the State Duma, Nicholas left no margin for the misinterpretation of his views. When, in February 1907, Rediger informed the Emperor that he planned to attend the opening of the Duma, Nicholas bade him to meet the slightest insult to the army pronounced in the Duma with the strongest possible rebuff.[70] As it happened the Duma did subject the army to serious criticism. In the first two Dumas, the chief critics were deputies from radical or liberal parties. In April 1907, for instance, Kuz'min-Karavaev, a former professor at the Alexander Academy and now a member of the party of Peaceful Renewal, assaulted the military field courts from the rostrum of the Duma. In the same month, a Menshevik deputy, A. G. Zurabov, an ensign of the reserves, delivered a sarcastic address which impugned the courage and combat readiness of the troops.[71] This contumely, together with the discovery that certain Bolshevik deputies were conspiring with soldiers of the St. Petersburg garrison, provided pretexts to prorogue the Second Duma.[72]

In the Third Duma it was the Octobrists, and in particular the party's mercurial A. I. Guchkov, who emerged as the preeminent critics of government military policy. The first major outburst came during a discussion of War Ministry budgets, when Guchkov made an excoriating attack on the influence of the Grand Dukes in the War Ministry.[73] In direct contravention of Imperial orders, Rediger declined to reply. Rediger later excused himself by observing that since he agreed with Guch-

[69] TsGVIA, f. 1, op. 1, d. 73413, ll. 2, 4, 6-8, 19. Skugarevskii, *Ocherki*, vol. 3, pp. 19-21, falsely blames Sukhomlinov for this counterreform.

[70] Polivanov, *Iz dnevnikov*, p. 20.

[71] Ibid., p. 25. For a thorough treatment of the "Zurabov incident" see Manning, *Crisis of the Old Order*, pp. 311-313.

[72] TsGAOR, f. DP VII, d. 3234, 1907 g, ll. 27-37, passim. Alfred Levin, *The Second Duma. A Study of the Social-Democratic Party and the Russian Constitutional Experiment*, 2d ed. (Hamden, Conn., 1966), pp. 279-349, passim.

[73] Polivanov, *Iz dnevnikov*, pp. 46-48.

kov, his rebuttal would therefore have been so half-hearted and weak it might have stimulated still further controversy.[74]

Rediger, who had expected to be dismissed for his breach of express Imperial instructions, was surprised when Nicholas II decided to overlook his lapse. But Nicholas's patience had its breaking point. On February 23, 1909, Guchkov made yet another inflammatory speech in the Duma, condemning the quality of higher military officials. Rediger, who once again secretly sided with Guchkov (as we have seen, he resented Nicholas's intervention in the operations of the Higher Commission on Performance Reviews), gave such an inchoate and bumbling answer that he scandalized the rightists in the Duma and the Council of State, as well as the Imperial family. On March 10, Nicholas told Rediger that he had lost his confidence in him, and one day later he installed V. A. Sukhomlinov as War Minister.[75] Rediger's fall was widely interpreted as evidence of the deterioration of Stolypin's influence with the Emperor. This was not, of course, because of the friendship between these two statesmen. Rather Nicholas removed Rediger because of the latter's fondness for the Octobrists; Stolypin, too, had been working with them. And Nicholas was personally paying more heed to the voices of the Russian political right and such organizations as the United Nobility.[76]

The turning point in army-Duma relations came in April 1909. In that month, at the urging of right-wing elements, Nicholas II vetoed one of Stolypin's most important projects—the Naval General Staff bill. The bill, which involved the allocation of credits for the establishment of a Naval General Staff, had already been passed by the Duma and the Council of State. Yet since the bill also contained an organizational roster for this new institution, rightists were able to argue that, in backing the bill, Stolypin was conspiring with the Duma to undermine the Emperor's military prerogatives. Stolypin was now compelled to wash his hands of the Octobrists and hunt for new political allies on the right.[77] With the special relationship between the government and the Octobrists sundered, Guchkov abandoned all restraint and lashed out at army policy and, via these assaults, at the Emperor, with all the oratorical invective of which he was capable. Especially noteworthy was his May 1912

[74] TsGVIA, f. 280, op. 1, d. 7, pp. 758-759. The editorial board of *Razvedchik* also agreed with Guchkov's criticisms. See the lead editorial "Gosudarstvennaia duma i armiia" in vol. 21, no. 920 (June 10, 1908): 396.

[75] Ibid., pp. 819-824.

[76] Diakin, *Samoderzhavie*, p. 135.

[77] Hosking, *Russian Constitutional Experiment*, pp. 92-96; Alexandra Shecket Korros, "The Landed Nobility, the State Council and P. A. Stolypin," in *The Politics of Rural Russia, 1905-14*, ed. Leopold Haimson (Bloomington, Ind., 1979), pp. 132-134.

philippic against the Artillery Department, provoked by the dismissal of A. A. Polivanov, another War Ministry official whom he esteemed.[78]

Both the "Naval Staff crisis" and the change in War Ministers enheartened the obstreperous Russian right, which now began a systematic campaign to disrupt the Duma. Within the War Ministry itself, Rediger's downfall was Nicholas's signal to the army to eschew contact with the Duma. In conversation with his new Minister, Sukhomlinov, Nicholas was adamant on this point, and Sukhomlinov obligingly pledged himself never to attend a Duma session.[79]

At first, however, the Duma politicians misread the Sukhomlinov appointment. Assistant War Minister Polivanov observed that *both* the Octobrists and the Kadets were initially jubilant at the news, since both parties considered Sukhomlinov "their man."[80] But the Octobrists and Kadets were swiftly undeceived. On April 8, 1909, Sukhomlinov informed Polivanov that Nicholas had categorically forbidden him to go to the Duma. Sukhomlinov also summoned Guchkov and Krupenskii and advised them that since foreign intelligence services were battening on published Duma debates, they should discuss military matters less in the Duma.[81] But the issue at hand was not national security but autocratic prerogative. From the end of April 1909 it was increasingly apparent that Nicholas's desire was to limit the Duma's competence in military affairs. In the aftermath of the Naval Staff crisis, Nicholas commanded Stolypin to draft a set of rules to clarify article 96 of the Fundamental Laws of the Empire—i.e., that ambiguous article which defined the Emperor's powers over the Russian army and navy. The inevitable special conference went to work producing a document which the Emperor confirmed on August 24.[82] The new rules conceded the right of the Duma to consider the military budget but not the organization, administration, or planning of the military establishment.[83]

Even before the rules were published in August the Imperial government had begun to behave as if they were already law. On April 18, 1909, the head of the War Ministry Chancellery wrote N. G. Kondrat'ev, Chief of the Main Staff, admonishing all heads of War Ministry departments to use extra vigilance in their dealings with the Duma in order

---

[78] A. I. Guchov, *Rechi po voprosam gosudarstvennoi oborony i ob obshchei politike 1908-1917* (Petrograd, 1917), pp. 63-74.

[79] John David Walz, "State Defense and Russian Politics under the Last Tsar," Ph.D. diss., Syracuse University, 1977, p. 108.

[80] Polivanov, *Iz dnevnikov*, p. 63.

[81] Ibid., pp. 68-69.

[82] TsGVIA, f. 2000, op. 2, d. 333, l. 4.

[83] Hosking, *Russian Constitutional Experiment*, p. 96; Pinchuk, *Octobrists*, p. 76.

to prevent a recurrence of legislative encroachment on the Emperor's powers over the army.[84] At Nicholas's command and for the putative good of the autocracy, Sukhomlinov was redirecting Russian military policy.

THE SUKHOMLINOV PERIOD: RESOLVING THE PROBLEM OF SUKHOMLINOV

Sukhomlinov has long been a figure of opprobrium. In mid-1917 the Investigatory Commission of the Provisional Government found him culpable of negligence and treason. Since that time, a spate of books and articles devoted to World War I have stressed the huge personal responsibility borne by Sukhomlinov for the military disasters of 1914 and the great shell shortage of 1915. Whether portrayed as a sinister Machiavel from a Jacobean tragedy or a harebrained buffoon from a boulevard farce, Sukhomlinov until lately has suffered general condemnation.[85] In 1975, however, Norman Stone broke sharply with this tradition. Accusing Sukhomlinov's critics of bias and military incompetence, Stone made a daring but reckless attempt to completely rehabilitate this much-reviled minister. Walter Wilfong shortly thereafter provided another, though more cautious, positive appreciation of Sukhomlinov. Still more recently, Allan Wildman has argued that Sukhomlinov's personal contribution to the strengths and weaknesses of the army was altogether insignificant.[86]

Detractors of Sukhomlinov certainly have a case. The War Minister's personal life, scarred by episodes of adultery, extravagance, and peculation, does not stand up to close scrutiny.[87] It is also true that Su-

---

[84] TsGVIA, f. 400, op. 21, d. 3875, ll. 58-59.

[85] M. V. Rodzianko, "Krushenie Imperii," *Arkhiv russkoi revoliutsii*, vol. 17 (Berlin, 1926), pp. 79-99, passim; Major General Sir Alfred Knox, *With the Russian Army, 1914-1917*, vol. I (London, 1921), pp. 220-277, passim; N. N. Golovine, *The Russian Army in the World War* (New Haven, 1931), pp. 30-130, passim; also V. A. Apushkin, *General ot porazhenii V. A. Sukhomlinov* (Leningrad, 1925). One laudatory statement about Sukhomlinov was translated into English and distributed as a propagandistic tract early in the war: V. D. Doumbadze, *Russia's War Minister. The Life and Works of Adjutant-General Vladimir Alexandrovitsh Soukhomlinov* (London, 1915). For Sukhomlinov's service record, see TsGVIA, f. 409, op. 1, d. p/sp 362-573.

[86] Stone, *Eastern Front*, pp. 14-28; Walter Thomas Wilfong, "Rebuilding the Russian Army, 1905-14. The Question of a Comprehensive Plan for National Defense," Ph.D. diss., Indiana University, 1977, pp. 97 ff. and 170-171. Wildman, *Russian Imperial Army*, pp. 66-68.

[87] Polivanov, *Iz dnevnikov*, pp. 39, 50, 85; Shavel'skii, *Vospominaniia*, pp. 100-103; Wilfong, *Rebuilding the Russian Army*, pp. 111-113; Lukomskii, "Ocherki," pp. 571-575.

khomlinov did enjoy acquaintance with a coterie of raffish and suspicious characters—Lt. Colonel Miasoedov, the Austrian consul Altschuler, and others—persons who later came to be associated in the public mind with such crimes as forgery, espionage, and treason.[88] As for tales of Sukhomlinov's frivolity, they are legion. The favorite noun of Sukhomlinov's critics in this regard seems to have been *legkomyslennost'* (light-mindedness). To cite one typical anecdote, in 1911 Sukhomlinov saw a copy of the new journal of the Naval General Staff, assumed falsely that it was a publication of the War Ministry, and proudly displayed it to Nicholas II as such. When the Emperor corrected him, Sukhomlinov swore that he had made an honest mistake, that the Journal of the Army General Staff was similar in appearance. No such journal existed, and upon his return from Tsarskoe selo to Petersburg, Sukhomlinov commanded that the Army General Staff start a journal—and within five days print the first number in a format identical to that of the navy's.[89] It has been said of Sukhomlinov that even Nicholas II did not take him seriously, on occasion addressing him jocularly as "our hussar."[90]

Unlike Rediger, Sukhomlinov was also infected by an acute case of negative corporatism and hastened to the defense of officers or war departments accused of misconduct, whether rightly or wrongly. The Kaul'bars affair provides an example. In 1909 the Commander of Odessa Military District, Baron Kaul'bars, intimidated certain peasants into making overpayments for the estate of his friend N. N. Shchebinskii in Kherson Province. This fraud occasioned an angry letter from Stolypin to Sukhomlinov. Sukhomlinov, while admitting that Kaul'bars had acted as an agent in a private transaction while still on active duty, denied that Kaul'bars had committed any impropriety.[91]

Sukhomlinov was further a resolute supporter of the outmoded notion of officers' honor. When, in a quarrel over a woman in 1901, military medical student Konstantin Petrov collared cornet B. M. Miller of the Life Guard Dragoons, the latter felled him with a sabre. Petrov was hospitalized with eight serious wounds. Although Nicholas II personally quashed criminal charges against the hot-headed cornet, Petrov sued in civilian court and won a 1904 judgment: Miller was to compensate him with seventy-five rubles a month for the rest of his life. Miller continued

[88] M. D. Bonch-Bruevich, *Vsia vlast' sovetam, Vospominaniia* (Moscow, 1957), pp. 62-67; K. F. Shatsillo has brilliantly refuted the charges against Miasoedov in a masterful article, " 'Delo' polkovnika Miasoedova'," *Voprosy istorii* 42, no. 4 (April 1967): 103-116.

[89] Gerua, *Vospominaniia*, pp. 242-243.

[90] Gerua, *Vospominaniia*, p. 246.

[91] TsGVIA, f. 400, op. 15, d. 3455, l. 11.

his career in the Guards, while Petrov stayed within the Military Medical Administration, eventually becoming a doctor at the Dvinsk military hospital. Armed with the sympathy of his superiors in St. Petersburg Military District, Miller began to agitate in 1907 against what he thought was an unfair decision. Why, inquired Miller, did Petrov take a pension from a brother officer? Such an act was a breach of army etiquette. In addition, Miller complained that the burden of paying this pension (over one-third of his salary) could have no other effect than to drive him from the army. In April of 1908 War Minister Rediger ordered that Miller was to be bound by the court's decision, advising him to seek legal relief within the civil court system. The Ministry of War would not pressure Petrov on Miller's behalf. Just a year later, the new minister, Sukhomlinov, threatened to cashier Petrov unless he renounced his pension from Miller once and for all.[92]

Sukhomlinov's retrograde protectiveness of the military manifested itself in much more serious affairs. In the summer of 1908 Senator N. P. Garin started an investigation of all governmental institutions in Moscow with the exception of the Church. The investigation soon focused on the Military District of Moscow, with particular emphasis on the sordid transactions of the Intendancy. By March 1909 Garin had discovered that of the 150 million rubles' worth of contracts awarded through the Intendancy office in Moscow Military District since January 1904, at least 15 million had been expended in kickbacks and bribes. With Imperial consent, Garin expanded his inquiry to the districts of St. Petersburg, Kiev, Odessa, and Kazan'. Senators Neidgart and Dedulin conducted similar studies in Warsaw, and Senator Count Medem received powers to probe the Military Districts of Irkutsk and the Amur. In his correspondence with these senators and the Ministry of Justice, Sukhomlinov formally embraced the war on peculation; privately, however, he shared the irritation of War Ministry Chancellery Chief Zabelin, who declared that for the sake of the army's dignity members of the Military Council and representatives of the Military Justice Administration should have led these investigations. But realizing, as did Zabelin, that any attempt to wrest investigatory authority from the Senate would further discredit the War Ministry in the press, Sukhomlinov strove to shield the army from the overzealous senators. On April 30, 1910 Sukhomlinov urged Nicholas II to terminate the inquiries, pleading that the Main Administration of the Intendancy was becoming demoralized and inefficient because of them. Nicholas backed Sukhomlinov, who then pushed Stolypin and the Ministry of Justice to conclude the investigation

---

[92] TsGVIA, f. 400, op. 15, d. 2078, l. 42.

as soon as possible. At the same time, Sukhomlinov ruled against the distribution of "secret" information to the senatorial investigatory teams. Such information included data about the stocks of mobilization supplies; the Intendancy's acquisition and maintenance of these was in fact the key element in the scandal.[93]

Coupled to this hypersensitivity to criticism was Sukhomlinov's practice of upholding the vested interests of traditional military elites. He was notorious for flaunting his ties to the army cavalry and insisted on wearing a colorful hussar's uniform even after he had been raised to ministerial rank.[94] As Minister, Sukhomlinov took an intense interest in the operation of the Officers' Cavalry School to the detriment of more important duties, or at least so his enemies declared.[95] In 1906 Rediger began experiments with a new system of regimental purchasing which shifted fiscal responsibility from the regimental colonels to the central War Ministry. Rediger had high hopes for extending the new system to the entire army, partly to realize financial savings, partly to extirpate corruption (since a considerable number of colonels clearly pilfered the funds and doctored the books), but chiefly to dismantle the entire structure of the regimental economy which diverted so many officers and men from strictly military duties. Despite the wisdom of Rediger's reform, Sukhomlinov did not enforce it throughout the army; Rediger suspected that this was due to Sukhomlinov's links to the army cavalry, the nexus of intransigent opposition to the reform.[96]

Again, whereas Rediger wanted to transfer the civil administration of Turkestan to the Interior Ministry and had wanted to abolish the whole special status of Cossackdom, Sukhomlinov took a diametrically opposite stance. When a bill was introduced into the Duma in March 1911 to establish a civil administration in the Don, Sukhomlinov objected, averring that "in accordance with the status of the Cossack as a hereditary warrior, even at the lowest levels of administration, military and civilian functions are fused."[97] Far from abolishing the Cossack armies, or equalizing the position of Cossack and other officers, Sukhomlinov insisted on maintaining Cossack privileges intact.

Still, many charges against Sukhomlinov are based on distortions or misinterpretations. He has been condemned, for example, for possessing an overweaning confidence in Russia's military strength. Finance Minister Kokovtsov claimed that at a November 11, 1912 meeting of the Council of Ministers, Sukhomlinov had declared that Russia was fully

[93] TsGVIA, f. 1, op. 1, d. 7222, passim.
[94] Gerua, *Vospominaniia*, p. 246.
[95] Skugarevskii, *Ocherki*, p. 17.
[96] TsGVIA, f. 280, op. 1, d. 7, p. 815; John Bushnell, "Tsarist Officer Corps," passim.
[97] TsGVIA, f. 400, op. 21, d. 3989, l. 6.

ready for war with the Triple Alliance.[98] Kokovtsov's point, of course, was that Sukhomlinov actually believed this silly fiction; Sukhomlinov's statement on this occasion is hence entered as evidence of his intellectual flabbiness. Sukhomlinov may well have made this statement—but did so for tactical reasons (whatever these may have been). In fact, he was deeply pessimistic about the Empire's war preparedness. Less than two weeks after the incident cited by Kokovtsov, in a conversation with A. N. Kuropatkin, Sukhomlinov gloomily muttered that "we have made few preparations for war . . . the Sovereign, as at the time before the Russo-Japanese War, strongly believes that there will be no war."[99]

Again, in 1910 Sukhomlinov created an uproar when he called for the dismantling of the bulk of Russia's fortresses in the West. Sukhomlinov's critics, including the Young Turks and the Minister of Finance, decried this plan as plain idiocy.[100] Stone, arguing with the benefit of hindsight, such as his knowledge of the outcome of the battle of Verdun, applauds this measure as a stroke of military genius: Sukhomlinov alone foresaw that fortresses would be worthless in the conditions of World War I, while his opponents, incapable of this insight, revealed their essential poverty of imagination.[101] But the "fortress episode" must be seen in its true context. At the end of the nineties the Society of the Zealots of Military Knowledge had conducted a great debate on the value of fortresses. On that occasion, the "innovators"—including most of those who were later labelled Young Turks, came out against the fortress defense concept.[102] In 1909, Colonel Novitskii, one of the intellectual leaders of the Young Turks and the *Voennyi golos* movement, published a book in which he, too, demanded that the Western fortresses be razed.[103]

The Young Turks thus actually *agreed* with Sukhomlinov on the inutility of the fortresses. Indeed, it is difficult to discover a single issue of strictly military reform about which Sukhomlinov and his enemies were not in accord. One of the few exceptions was the reform of the Nicholas Academy of the General Staff. Sukhomlinov favored turning this school into sort of a military university, an institution for disseminating the most advanced military knowledge throughout the army. His opponents, on the other hand, Academy graduates to a man, were fiercely proud of the status of the Staff, and wanted to retain the Academy

[98] Fisher, *Memoirs of Count Kokovtsov*, p. 348.

[99] TsGVIA, f. 165, op. 1, d. 5255, l. 112.

[100] Apushkin, *General ot porazhenii*, p. 34; Fisher, *Memoirs of Count Kokovtsov*, p. 253.

[101] Stone, *Eastern Front*, p. 31.

[102] Gerua, *Vospominaniia*, p. 120.

[103] Novitskii, *Na puti*, pp. 85, 96-97.

as a special "finishing-school" for the army's intellectual elite.[104] In general, however, the Young Turks, and the other military opponents of Sukhomlinov were willing on occasion to betray their own cherished beliefs, preying on the credulity of the civilians (to whom the rationale for dismantling Russia's expensive fortress network was incomprehensible) in their desire to unseat Sukhomlinov; so deep was their loathing of Sukhomlinov, they would undertake almost any act to rid the army of him.

The root of the struggle between Sukhomlinov and his opponents within the army *was* ideological, but the nature of that struggle has been unfortunately buried under voluminous tracts about eight versus six gun batteries, fortresses, the territorial system, and all the rest. The chief ideological issue was that of a national army, a nation mobilized for war. The majority of Sukhomlinov's opponents embraced this concept; Sukhomlinov himself was both opposed to this concept in principle, and was mindful of his relationship with Nicholas II. By calling for a nation animated by patriotism (either right or left wing), the intellectual elite of the Russian army had moved up the ladder to a higher stage of military professionalism. Sukhomlinov elected to remain on a lower rung. This, then, is one of the reasons his fellow officers hated him. It is also one of the reasons that Stolypin, who had discerned the necessity for expanding the social basis of support for the regime, took such an aversion to Sukhomlinov. It is said that as Stolypin lay dying in Kiev, he implored Nicholas II to discharge Sukhomlinov as a man who was "unsuitable, unreliable, and incapable of inspiring respect."[105] This ideological conflict does not account for all of the animus against Sukhomlinov. Kokovtsov, for instance, had other good reasons to nurse a grudge against Sukhomlinov; the very structure of the Imperial government was conducive for rancor between the Minister of Finance and the Minister of War. There were also people who quite simply disliked Sukhomlinov on personal grounds. The ideological struggle is not the sole explanation for the vilification of Sukhomlinov as a German agent. Conspiracy theories are very comforting since they provide a simple answer to complex problems and allow those who adopt them to avoid facing unpleasant facts. As Shatsillo points out, if Sukhomlinov was a traitor, then Russian military defeat could be ascribed to his perfidy. Bad generalship, the Empire's weak industrial base, and the incapacity of Nicholas II could be excluded from discussion.[106]

---

[104] TsGVIA, f. 1, op. 2, d. 169, l. 3; Novitskii, *Na puti*, pp. 33, 107, 109; Grulev, *Zloby*, pp. 65, 69.

[105] Fisher, *Memoirs of Count Kokovtsov*, pp. 254, 314; Polivanov, *Iz dnevnikov*, pp. 75, 35; Apushkin, *General ot porazhenii*, p. 74.

[106] Shatsillo, " 'Delo'," pp. 115-116.

The fact that the majority of the most professional Russian officers opposed Sukhomlinov does not mean, however, that Sukhomlinov was himself incompetent, or unprofessional. He was less professional, but not unprofessional. It should be noted at the outset that although Sukhomlinov was highly unpopular with the Duma, he did work with it. Forbidden to attend Duma sessions without special Imperial dispensation, he nevertheless made shrewd use of A. A. Polivanov as his liaison with that body. He only dismissed Polivanov when he had accumulated irrefutable proof of Polivanov's treachery. Indeed, it is arguable that in his own admittedly peculiar way, Sukhomlinov respected the Duma. In November 1909 he commanded that the only War Ministry officials who were to testify before the commissions of the Duma and State Council were to be heads of War Ministry Main Administrations, or their assistants. He issued this order both in view of "the lofty position, occupied by the aforenamed institutions" and in view of "the unconditional necessity, that explanations . . . be given by fully empowered persons."[107] This order can quite plausibly be construed as an oblique tribute to the Duma.

Further, under Sukhomlinov the War Ministry did draft and implement significant military reforms from 1909 to 1914. Among them were the abolition of the territorial (*rezervnye*) troops and the fortress troops, which were reorganized into seven new front-line infantry divisions. Not only did this enhance the fighting strength of Russia's field army, it also regularized the Russian infantry. Most infantry divisions now possessed sixteen battalions; most rifle brigades, eight battalions. Sukhomlinov also initiated a territorial system of recruitment; the regiments, brigades, squadrons, sotnias, and batteries of the army were henceforth to be supplied with recruits from certain specified locales. This system, which had long been the rule in Britain, France, and Germany, was attractive because of its simplicity, cheapness, and the psychological boost it gave to army morale. In collaboration with A. S. Lukomskii, Sukhomlinov also made solid improvements in army mobilization planning. These were the chief reforms of Sukhomlinov; there were others. It is noteworthy that the greatest field commander Russia was to produce during World War I, Gen. A. A. Brusilov, gave Sukhomlinov full credit for them.[108]

Criticism of Sukhomlinov's reforms, such as that of Gen. Iu. N. Danilov, tends in retrospect to ring false. The main thrust of the criticism

[107] TsGVIA, f. 400, op. 21, d. 3875, l. 191.

[108] Kersnovskii, *Istoriia*, pp. 601-604; Basil Gourko, *War and Revolution in Russia, 1914-17* (New York, 1919), pp. 7-16; A. A. Brussilov, *A Soldier's Note-Book, 1914-18* (London, 1930), pp. 10-11; I. I. Rostunov, *Russkii front*, pp. 54-59; V. A. Emets, *Ocherki vneshnei politika Rossii 1914-1917* (Moscow, 1977), pp. 34-35.

was that Sukhomlinov did little to stockpile adequate supplies of munitions (principally shells for field guns and heavy guns). Yet as Brusilov observed, if Sukhomlinov was responsible for this so was the entire Main Administration of Artillery.[109] Further, if the Russian army held only six months' worth of artillery ammunition in August 1914, one must recall that practically no one in Europe expected that any war could last longer than that time. In Britain and Germany, purblind optimists predicted that the troops would be home in time for Christmas.[110] One can damn Sukhomlinov for his impulsiveness, his insouciance, and his vanity, but it is frankly unjust to condemn him for lacking the prophetic gift.

Sukhomlinov did not make the intellectual leap to the assumption that mass warfare implies mass patriotism and hence mass politics. Still, in important respects, he remained a professional. Indeed, in his early public writings, Sukhomlinov exemplified military professionalism. Again and again he exhorted the officers to study and demanded that they appreciate war as a science. And in 1905-1907 Sukhomlinov unswervingly insisted that the army had one purpose, the police another: the army's role was to defend the state from foreign enemies, the police's role was to cope with the internal foe. Capricious as he may have been, Sukhomlinov did not deviate from this idea after he arrived in ministerial office. He doggedly fought to free the army from police duty: in fact, under his leadership, the Russian army came close to realizing the old dream of professional officers—the total commitment of the army to external defense and its emancipation from the burden of internal repression.

The Army and Police Duty after 1907

In a protracted tug-of-war with Stolypin in 1908, Rediger had managed to bring more of the army back under War Ministry control. In March, Rediger was able to turn the authority of the Emperor against the Chairman of the Council of Ministers. One of Nicholas's hastily scrawled marginalia on a Staff report had endorsed the goal of a combat-ready

[109] Iu. N. Danilov, *Velikii Kniaz' Nikolai Nikolaevich* (Paris, 1930), p. 91; Danilov was less harsh on Sukhomlinov in his earlier work, *Rossiia v mirovoi voine 1914-1915 gg.* (Berlin, 1924), pp. 26-53; here he spreads responsibility for unpreparedness around a little bit. Brussilov, *A Soldier's Note-Book*, p. 10. Another favorable judgment on Sukhomlinov's reforms is to be found in the work of a gifted Soviet military historian, A. Kavtaradze, "Is istorii russkogo general'nogo shtaba," *Voenno-istoricheskii zhurnal* 14, no. 7 (July 1972): 92.

[110] Arthur Marwick, *The Deluge* (New York, 1965), p. 35; Gerald D. Feldman, *Army, Industry and Labor in Germany, 1914-1918* (Princeton, 1966), p. 52, points out that by October 1914, the Germans had exhausted their munition reserves.

army. Rediger naturally pounced on this remark and threw it back in Stolypin's face, appending that "for this purpose it is essential to furnish [the army] with the opportunity of occupying itself with its primary task, thus abandoning service which has no direct connection to the strengthening and development of its military capabilities."[111] Imperial support was a powerful card in Rediger's hand; so cleverly did he play it, for example, that he was able to remove 2,200 regular army soldiers from railroad guard duty, despite the protests of the Ministry of Transport and Communications.[112] The War Ministry continued to press civilian ministries on the issue of freeing the troops in 1909. In February, General Staff data showed that sixteen battalions of infantry and forty-two squadrons or sotnias of cavalry were currently on repressive service outside their home military districts.[113]

In April, the War Ministry sought relief through a time-hallowed method: the convocation of an interministerial commission at the Main Staff. There the Ministry of the Interior, to no one's surprise, supported those of its governors who wanted to retain their troops. The Moscow governor, for example, feared that unemployment in the province might result in riots without the restraining influence of troops; the Nizhegorod governor demanded troops since the time of the annual fair was swiftly approaching; the Kostroma governor was also worried about unemployment; the Ekaterinoslav governor said that the army units in his province might be withdrawn, but only very gradually.[114] Still, War Ministry negotiators were able to secure cutbacks in the military guarding of civilian prisons in twenty-four provinces and *oblasti*; they also obtained some concession with regard to military guarding of post and telegraph stations.[115] Yet the Ministry of War was unsatisfied. In July 1909, Sukhomlinov would indignantly write across the face of a letter sent him from P. Kurlov of the Interior Ministry that "it is essential to release all [officers and men] to their permanent quarters. Our Ministry has been asking about this for a long time and until now has not been able to achieve it."[116]

Sukhomlinov was not making an idle remark here. Although he and Rediger had success in 1909 in freeing such large units as battalions from special repressive service, civilian requests for assistance still represented an intolerable drain of manpower from the War Ministry's perspective. Sukhomlinov was simply alarmed when information con-

---

[111] TsGVIA, f. 400, op. 3, d. 3056, l. 50.
[112] Ibid., ll. 105-108; TsGVIA, f. 280, op. 1, d. 7, p. 778.
[113] TsGVIA, f. 400, op. 3, d. 3253, l. 46.
[114] Ibid., ll. 147-148.
[115] TsGVIA, f. 1, op. 2, d. 169, l. 21.
[116] TsGVIA, f. 400, op. 3, d. 3253, l. 224.

TABLE 16
Civilian Requests for Military Assistance, 1909

Month	Number of requests	Infantry	Cavalry	Artillery	Use of weapons
January	13,507	297.5 co 17 commands 139,622 men	14.75 sq/sot 1 command 23,041 men	249 men	1
February	11,271	332.25 17 129,652	13.75 10 14,171	140	1
March	7,829	367 330 149,383	25.5 0 21,857	63	0
April	10,872	349.25 17 174,522	39.25 0 19,966	140	3
May	9,185	83.25 13 158,592	32.25 2 14,968	0	0
June	8,998	139 12 143,506	30 3 15,855	12	1
July	9,118	79 15 142,803	21 0 16,148	0	1
August	8,778	139.5 9 141,958	45.5 6 14,666	34	3
September	8,652	138.5 1 143,375	28.5 0 15,190	46	0
October	8,863	238.25 2 148,090	13.5 0 16,004	48	0
November	8,487	122 14 134,941	23.75 0 17,927	46	0

TABLE 16 (cont.)

Month	Number of requests	Infantry	Cavalry	Artillery	Use of weapons
December	8,548	219.75	17.5	0	0
		23	14		
		129,377	17,382		
Total	114,108	2,505.25	305.25	778	10
		470	36		
		1,635,821	207,175		

SOURCE: TsGVIA, f. 400, op. 3, d. 3293, ll. 23, 56, 81, 110, 135, 160, 185, 207, 231, 255, 302, 332

cerning these requests passed to his desk. At first glance the figures, shown in Table 16, might convey the incorrect impression that the army was even more encumbered with repression than had been the case in the dark days of 1905-1906. In conformity with the regulations of November 1907, civilian requests for guard duty were to be aggregated along with requests for help to prevent and put down disorders. Because of this, the War Ministry stopped publishing detailed figures on military commands to aid the civilians in its annual reports for the years after 1908. What this table then records is the enormous amount of guard duty that the army was undertaking for civilian benefit. This supposition is reinforced by two deductions made on the basis of the chart. First, there was an extremely small usage of weapons relative to the numbers of soldiers deployed. Although late information from the Caucasus would raise the number of arms uses to seventy-six, this too, is still a relatively small number, which implies that the troops were not mainly engaged in the active crushing of unrest.[117]

The second striking feature of the table is the heavy reliance on infantry. As has been noted, when strikers, vandals, and the like had to be cleared from the streets, civilian governors preferred cavalry, especially Cossacks, for this purpose. But it is not only the heavy use of infantry that is significant, it is the way in which the infantry was deployed that catches the eye. Again, speaking relatively, there was less employment of large infantry units—such as companies, or even commands—by comparison to the staggering deployment of individual sol-

[117] TsGVIA, f. 1, op. 2, d. 169, l. 21.

247

diers. The army lost over 1.6 million man days in the course of 1909 as the result of this deployment of soldiers in formations of a platoon or less. The civilians, who had demanded huge numbers of military guards since 1905, had become habituated to this state of affairs. In a sense, they had become addicted to military guards and trembled at the very thought of losing them.

The table does demonstrate that the interministerial conference of April 1909 was not in vain, for civilian demands on the army began to fall in May. But the reductions were not speedy enough to placate the War Ministry, or the irate military district commanders. Sukhomlinov assumed office only in March 1909. Initially unsure of himself and preoccupied with consolidating his own position, he hesitated to force a showdown with the civilian ministers. In August 1909, Moscow District Commander P. A. Pleve wrote Sukhomlinov to inquire what could be done to release five squadrons and one sotnia (one-sixth of his district's cavalry) from repressive service in Nizhegorod, Kostroma, and Voronezh. Sukhomlinov replied through the Main Staff that the units would have to remain where they were and that the orders cut for special cavalry maneuvers near the village of Klement'evo would have to be annulled.[118]

Sukhomlinov would not long persist in this pliancy before the civilians, and by 1910 he was confidently denying the civilians guard duty details. When the Poltava District Court demanded an honor guard of four soldiers before the doors of an empanelled jury, Sukhomlinov refused.[119] In his report for 1910, Sukhomlinov applauded the reduction in military guard details generally, a reduction he ascribed to the "persistent attempts of the War Ministry."[120] Although the number of civilian requests for aid declined in 1910 (there were only 13,839 "extraordinary" above constant guard duty), and although weapons were used on only 42 occasions, the War Ministry was still displeased. Almost all offices, banks, and treasuries of the Ministry of Finance in the Caucasus, Turkestan, and Siberia were still under military guardianship. The army still protected civilian prisons, and not only *katorga* (forced labor) prisons either. Most noxious of all, the Ministry of Justice refused to assume any responsibility for order during the convoying of prisoners, even though that Ministry through its inspectors of prison transport exerted some control over army convoy commands. An interministerial conference had resulted in the predictable stalemate.[121]

[118] TsGVIA, f. 400, op. 3, d. 3253, ll. 189-191.
[119] TsGVIA, f. 2000, op. 2, d. 890, ll. 1, 3, 27.
[120] TsGVIA, f. 1, op. 2, d. 170, l. 18.
[121] Ibid., l. 18.

Sukhomlinov had been biding his time. Beginning in early 1911 he launched what can only be described as a powerful offensive against the civilian ministries of state. His objective was the unconditional freeing of the army from guard duty. In the pursuit of this goal, Sukhomlinov mobilized every department of the War Ministry and made shrewd use of every initiative from provincial military leaders.

A mass consensus, extending down to the garrison commanders, crystallized in 1911: the time to abolish military guard duty had come. In January, the General Staff told the Main Prison Administration to remove the military guards from the Saratov temporary *katorga* prison; in February, the Ministry stripped military guards from the post and telegraph stations of the Amur railway. When, in February, the Odessa District commander moved to end the military guarding of the Odessa treasury, he did so with the blessings of the General Staff.[122] In the same month the Amur River administration begged the War Ministry for fifteen Cossacks to assist in guarding the river near the "little Khingan." Its own watchmen there were regularly ambushed and murdered by Chinese bandits. It might seem that the Amur Military District could have spared fifteen Cossacks without unduly imperiling Russian security in the Far East, but Sukhomlinov thought otherwise. Manning the watchtowers on the Amur with Cossacks was "unacceptable," he wrote, "for it contradicts the interests of the army, the chief goal of which in peace is the appropriate training . . . [of soldiers] . . . in the event of war."[123] In March, the General Staff pressured the State Treasury to install electric signalling devices between its branch banks in Vil'na District and police stations, not army encampments, and preemptively withdrew the army guard which had been provided to the naval base at Kronshtadt.[124]

The Emperor unexpectedly came to the army's rescue in March. The Commander of Caucasus District had included an eloquent appeal in his annual report for the complete release of the army from the duties of guarding prisons, convoying prisoners, and aiding the police. This unresolved question, the commander observed, had been raised repeatedly for eighteen years. Mapping out what needed to be done (chiefly an expansion in the police of the Empire and the establishment of freely hired prison guard forces), the Commander stressed "that it is a grievous error to justify delays in the realization of these measures due to lack of funds, since the Ministry of War spends very large sums for the

---

[122] TsGVIA, f. 2000, op. 2, d. 890, ll. 31, 33, 35.
[123] Ibid., ll. 55, 56, 57.
[124] Ibid., ll. 58, 60.

troops serving [the interests] of the civil administration; and the main thing—it is completely impossible to appraise that enormous damage which is inflicted on the army by the removal from work of tens of thousands of instructors (officers and NCOs) and hundreds of thousands of private soldiers every year." Nicholas II underlined the text at various points, and pencilled its margins with comments such as "true" and "correct." The General Staff saw to it that a printed copy of this Caucasus report, complete with Nicholas's remarks, was on the desk of P. A. Stolypin by March 23.[125]

Capitalizing on the Imperial marginalia, the War Ministry circulated Order number 13404 on March 20 mandating the end of the guarding of civilian institutions by troops in towns or areas outside the immediate vicinity of their general headquarters.[126] Three days later the War Ministry took yet another audacious step: the General Staff instructed the military districts that detachments in aid of the civilian power were not to be increased—not even by one single soldier—without express Imperial permission.[127]

This aggressiveness produced results: from January 1 to the end of April 1911, the Ministry managed to release 7 officers and 1,408 men.[128] In April 1911 another interministerial conference on military guards met, and this time the civilians united in castigating the War Ministry for its irrational expectations. Emissaries from the Ministries of Finance, Justice, and the Interior said that although they were predisposed to cooperate with the Ministry of War, their fiscal resources were too small for them to shoulder the guarding burden at once. But Sukhomlinov and his subordinates were bent on sweeping soldiers from the guard posts before the civilian ministries conceivably could be ready to replace them.[129] Although unimpressed by these arguments, Sukhomlinov did retreat from his previous intransigent position on the issue of military guarding.

Indeed, he had already begun to relent. In late March when the Corps of Gendarmes protested the decision of the Irkutsk Military District to remove 14 officers and 114 soldiers from guard duty on key railway bridges spanning the Enisei, Kopa, Ufa, and Oka rivers, Sukhomlinov had quietly countermanded the Irkutsk order.[130] In late April, he tried to dampen the enthusiasm of Kiev District for relief from guard duty:

125 TsGVIA, f. 2000, op. 2, d. 903, ll. 2-7.
126 TsGVIA, f. 2000, op. 2, d. 890, l. 76.
127 TsGVIA, f. 2000, op. 2, d. 724, l. 1.
128 Ibid., l. 25.
129 TsGVIA, f. 2000, op. 2, d. 890, l. 47.
130 Ibid., ll. 61-62.

"Immediately terminating detachments to aid the civilian authorities can only evoke insistent complaints from the interested ministries and therefore is impossible."[131] Sukhomlinov also promised Stolypin in early April to honor the decision of the Council of Ministers of July 4, 1908: the War Ministry would continue to guard state financial institutions until the Ministry of Finance had raised, armed, and trained its own adequate forces.[132]

But these concessions did not signify that Sukhomlinov had renounced his deep-rooted opposition to guard duty. By means of Order 13404 Sukhomlinov had made it extraordinarily difficult for the civilians to *add* any soldiers to the military guard detachments which already existed. What was at issue was only the speed with which Sukhomlinov was intending to *subtract* them. If he could not emancipate the army overnight by executive fiat, he was resolved to whittle these detachments gradually down to nothing. The War Ministry's new moderation was less the consequence of civilian persuasiveness than of Sukhomlinov's own prudence. As the April note to Kiev District suggests, Sukhomlinov wanted to avoid too many explosive confrontations with his ministerial colleagues. In any event, his hostility to any increase in guard details was undiminished.

For example, in August 1911, the Commander of Omsk District requested permission to reinforce the guard details on crucial Trans-Siberian railway bridges. The General Staff was perplexed by the Omsk Commander's motivation: was he acting in his capacity as governor-general, and hence as a servant of the Interior Ministry, or was he acting on the basis of purely military considerations? (Russia was anticipating trouble in the Far East as a result of the Chinese revolution.) Whatever the rationale of the Omsk Commander, the Staff advised the War Ministry to disregard his plea and Sukhomlinov endorsed the Staff's decision.[133]

In late 1911 Sukhomlinov was still interested in reducing army police service. And at this juncture Finance Minister Kokovtsov unwittingly provided the War Minister with extra ammunition. Sukhomlinov rarely had reason to be grateful to Kokovtsov, but he must have beamed with pleasure when he caught sight of the 1912 budget—for the frugal Finance Minister had cut the sum earmarked for paying the military repressive bill from 1.5 million to 100,000 rubles. Sukhomlinov henceforth could deny civilian appeals for aid with a shrug and a reference to the mys-

[131] Ibid., ll. 77, 97.
[132] Ibid., l. 79.
[133] Ibid., ll. 136-137.

terious policies of the Ministry of Finance. Crying poverty could bolster the traditional military arguments against helping the civilians, as it did in Sukhomlinov's letter to Stolypin on May 27, 1911. After adducing the matter of the shrunken repressive budget, Sukhomlinov reverted to a more familiar theme, stating that detachments "to guard civilians have an extremely negative impact on the military preparation of the army, distracting troops from field exercises for the discharge of a duty unsuitable for them. . . ."[134] This latter sentence, with its allusion to training and the proper task of the army, could have been written by Rediger, Kuropatkin, Sakharov, even Vannovskii.

The second quarter of 1911 brought further good news to the War Ministry: guard-duty positions for the benefit of the civilians from May through August had registered another net decline (one officer and 318 men).[135] The tone of the War Ministry's annual report was openly self-congratulatory. Aside from the guarding of specific civilian prisons in European Russia, and the protecting of financial institutions in Siberia, the Caucasus, and Turkestan, civilian calls for military aid numbered only 8,908 for the year.[136]

If 1911 was the year of the central War Ministry attack on military police duty, 1912 was the year of local military initiative. Disagreeing with Sukhomlinov's new strategy of moderation, aggressive commanders in each of the military districts became contentious and provoked quarrels with the civilians over guard details. In early January, Odessa fulminated against military guards at the Nikolaev and Kherson *katorga* prisons. The commander of Kherson garrison held that these prisons could be guarded exclusively by the Ministry of Justice, despite the fact that Imperial law *obliged* the army to encircle *katorga* prisons with guard posts. On January 2, the Ministry of Finance complained that the Amur District refused to guard the Ussuri railway and called this a blatant violation of an order of the Council of Ministers. In February Sukhomlinov received a letter from the Ministry of the Interior, expressing incredulity that the Commander of Irkutsk District had declined to supply one soldier to guard the Kansk uezd treasury even though the governor of Enesei Province had unchallengeable evidence of a robbery plot directed against that bank. Later in the year, the Chief of Staff at Khabarovsk, Amur District, refused to add five guards to those at the branch of the state bank in Blagoveshchensk. In May military authorities in Warsaw wrote that it was essential "in the interests of the troops" to

---

[134] Ibid., l. 157.
[135] TsGVIA, f. 2000, op. 2, d. 724, l. 21.
[136] TsGVIA, f. 1, op. 2, d. 171, ll. 17-18.

abolish the detail of 1 officer and 137 men dispatched every day to guard civilian financial institutions in the district. In August, Vil'na insisted that its military guards be taken off state treasuries in the towns of Vil'na, Lidsk, Grodno, and Slonim, and that its soldiers be removed from the Riga katorga prison and from the Riga convoy command. Kazan' wrote in a similar vein in September. In October, Lieutenant General Babich, ataman of the Kuban, recalled military guards from the Arvmavich-Tuapsa railroad; he was acting on his own authority.[137]

War Ministry response to these local actions took two forms. First, the stream of pugnacious letters and telegrams from the provinces could be rechannelled to the civilian ministries. This technique was the centerpiece of the letter Sukhomlinov posted to the Ministry of Finance in June 1912. He wrote that in 1910 the Ministry of Finance had vowed to establish its own corps of bank guards, yet thus far had raised no such corps. Sukhomlinov curtly accused the Finance Ministry of intentional procrastination and referred to the enormous resentment against the Finance Ministry which was now brewing in the army.[138] But Sukhomlinov after all did have to work with the civilian ministers. The Ministry of War had projects other than the abolition of police service, and if Sukhomlinov wanted to make gains in one area he had to compromise in another. He therefore had to whip the insubordinate district commanders into line. To his horror, he rapidly discovered the limitations of ministerial power in this regard. On January 17, for instance, he instructed Odessa District to restore the military guards at Nikolaev and Kherson prisons. When his instructions were not obeyed, he repeated his request for compliance in March. Odessa once again discarded Sukhomlinov's letter. In August, a telegram from the War Ministry to Odessa dropped all the polite circumlocutions of official discourse and demanded the immediate restoration of the Kherson prison guard.[139] The Odessa case was the most flagrant example of provincial military disobedience in 1912. It was not, however, an anomaly.

Such was the anger of army commanders towards the civilians that the War Ministry's grip on its local bureaus and staffs was weakening. This ominous trend continued into 1913. General of Cavalry Samsonov, District Commander of Turkestan, removed all guards from the Ashkhabad, Kushka, Merv, and Krasnovodsk treasuries, and from the branches of the state bank at Ashkhabad and Kokand. He justified his decision on the basis of the "indifferent attitude of the civilian insti-

---

[137] TsGVIA, f. 2000, op. 2, d. 909, ll. 1, 14, 22, 63, 68, 75, 97 and passim.
[138] Ibid., l. 43.
[139] Ibid., ll. 5, 17, 61.

tutions to our military needs" for intensive field training.[140] Kazan' District entreated for the termination of military guard details attached to eleven civilian prisons, embellishing its request with specious legal fustian.[141] In March 1913, the frustrated Commander of Petersburg District, Nikolai Nikolaevich, pared down guard details at banks and treasuries in his district (especially within the city limits of Petersburg itself) on his own authority. Nikolai explained that the guard details were so large that training was suffering, and special units, usually exempt from this service, had to be used for it. But even these sacrifices were insufficient; there were still too few troops to go around. Soldiers were forced to stand guard shifts longer than the legal eight hours.[142] In April, the Military District Commander of Irkutsk proposed that the articles which prescribed military guards for civilian *katorga* prisons be expunged from the Code of Imperial Laws and the Code of Garrison Service. The Main Prison Administration, under constant military pressure, had modernized certain jails and correctional facilities. Better lighting had been installed and unnecessary outbuildings and structures in prison yards had been pulled down. The Irkutsk Staff had thus been able to eliminate 53 guard duty positions. But the district was still filling 336 posts for the Prison Administration which did nothing to establish its own guard services, since it was so convenient to hide behind the articles in the Code.[143]

In April, when the military governor of the Amur oblast' requested that a platoon of soldiers be sent to each of four gold mines, in view of the brazen attacks upon them by an elusive gang of mounted bandits, the District Commander rebuffed him.[144] In May, the Commander of the Caucasus appealed for an end to the military guarding of treasuries and great reductions in the number of troops assigned to protect branches of the state bank. The Caucasus was at the time maintaining 1,453 guard-duty positions for the benefit of the civilians; this was especially burdensome since 21 battalions, 28 sotnias, and 6 batteries were operating across the border in Persia, because of the anarchic conditions there.[145]

In 1913 civilians suddenly started to yield. In no case was this more dramatic than in the policy of the Chief Prison Administration. In July, that institution advised the War Ministry that military guards could be released from three prisons in Kazan' District. In September, the Prison

---

[140] TsGVIA, f. 2000, op. 2, d. 938, l. 1-2.
[141] Ibid., l. 6-9.
[142] Ibid., l. 10-11.
[143] Ibid., l. 12-13.
[144] Ibid., l. 14.
[145] Ibid., ll. 19-20.

Administration reported that the enactment of prison reform legislation on July 7, 1913 would result in the emancipation of troops from guard duty at thirty-nine prisons. These prisons were located in Omsk, Irkutsk, Kazan', and Turkestan, four of the districts which had most vociferously protested prison guard duty.[146] In October, the State Bank agreed to remove military guards from some of its branches, including its central facility in Petersburg.[147] By April of 1914, the army was finally on the verge of withdrawing all military guards from all state financial institutions throughout the Empire.[148]

Why did the civilians finally cave in to the military? The answer to this question comes in several parts. First, the Emperor Nicholas II had finally thrown his full weight behind the goal of freeing the army from police service, in striking contrast to the wild vacillation he had manifested in earlier years. In mid-1913 Nicholas wrote across the face of a report sent him from Turkestan that he required every civilian ministry to create its own guard forces. By his order the War Ministry transmitted this command to each of the civilian ministries of state.[149] The diplomatic and military crises of 1912 and 1913 were not auguries favorable to the preservation of European peace. And Nicholas, reflecting more deeply on the possibility of war, also listened more intently to the counsels of his military leaders. For instance, in the army's confidential post-mortem on the Japanese defeat, which Nicholas received in December 1912, Sukhomlinov warned that the army could be ready only if it were adequately funded and allowed to concentrate on training.[150]

But Imperial backing might be temporary. The advantages the War Ministry could derive from a scrap of Nicholas's marginalia could vanish if the Emperor rapidly forgot what he wrote or was persuaded by some other minister to change his opinion. However, on this occasion the civilian ministers did not carp overmuch, nor did they call for special conferences, which every bureaucrat knew could delay the resolution of a conflict for decades. This unusual conciliatoriness is explained by a special study of the stability of the Empire, conducted in 1912-1913 by the Department of Police.

In 1907, the Council of Ministers had debated enlarging the monetary rewards and expenses allowable to officers and soldiers who were on

---

[146] Ibid., l. 43.

[147] Ibid., l. 60.

[148] TsGAOR, f. 102 (DP OO), op. 236 (II), d. 175, t. 7, 1906 (sic), l. 150.

[149] TsGVIA, f. 2000, op. 2, d. 938, l. 8.

[150] *Vsepoddanneishii otchet o deiatel'nosti glavnykh upravlenii voennogo ministerstva, vyzvannoi voinoiu s Iaponiei v 1904-1905 gg. sekretno* (St. Petersburg, 1912), pp. 1, 11, 277.

long-term repressive assignments. Committee discussion of this problem in 1909 had resulted in a decision to increase these sums and the publication of the new regulations on June 11, 1910. There was a catch in these rules, however: clause 6 declared that they were only to become operable when all military units on repressive service had returned to their respective general headquarters, and the Empire was adjudged to be "calm" enough by the Interior Ministry to make large-scale military assistance to civilians unnecessary. It does not require much perspicacity to detect here the tight fist of Finance Minister Kokovtsov. The Department of Police was now charged to pay particular attention to civilian summons for military assistance. Exclusive of guard duty, the police uncovered the information provided in Table 17. The police supplemented this information with a telegraph poll of every governor in the Russian Empire (excluding the Caucasus). The results of this survey have interesting implications for the government's perception of unrest in the Empire on the eve of World War I. Writing in July 1913, the Police Department had no objections to the introduction of the new heightened military expense allowances, "taking into account the insignificant quantity of troops now detailed to help the civilian powers, and also [taking into account] the fact that, as monthly reports of the Governors received by the Police Department testify, the general mood of the population is calm, and there are no grounds to expect that a massive revolutionary movement will arise in the near future." A follow-up

TABLE 17
Military Assistance to Civilians, 1912 and 1913

1912		1913	
Province/ oblast'	No. of times	Province/ oblast'	No. of times
Petrokovsk	1	Olonets	1
Don	3	Tver	1
Irkutsk	4	Don	1
Tomsk	1	Tomsk	2
Zabaikal	2	Amur	2
Primorsk	3	Zabaikal	1
Semirech'e	1		—
Total	15		8

SOURCE: TsGAOR, f. 102 (DP OO), op. 236 (II), d. 175, passim

letter of October qualified this position somewhat: the police were not arguing that the country was firmly (*prochno*) calm; after all, there had been some disquieting episodes of unrest in recent years (demonstrations occasioned by the Beilis case, the Moscow tram strike, Lena massacre, etc.). Clearly, the total exclusion of the army from all forms of internal service was unattainable, since military force would always be required to deal with the infestation of bandits in the Caucasus. But the Caucasus aside, the police did state that the army could be freed *everywhere* else, as soon as the police reform planned to enlarge the number of policemen was enacted.[151] In other words, the police were expressing a cool optimism and faith in their abilities to control disorder in the Empire, without the crutch of the Russian military. There is no reason to doubt the sincerity of this document. Rather the reverse. One might have expected the police to emphasize the grave dangers to the social order which were lying dormant within the Empire, since such a tactic could have benefited them in wheedling money from the State Treasury. The Department of Police, like every other agency of state, was hungry for cash. That the Police Department and the Ministry of the Interior believed so strongly in the stability of the Russian Empire is also relevant for interpreting the massive upsurge of the workers' movement after April 1912. Such an upsurge occurred, but the army played a small role (comparatively) in dealing with it, at least until 1914. Since the civilian ministries traditionally appealed for army aid to help contain all disorders they considered serious, either they were fearful of appealing to the army, or they simply did not regard these workers' strikes and demonstrations as crises.[152]

In its annual report for 1913, on the first occasion in decades, the War Ministry did not even bother to comment on its help to the civilians, either in terms of preventing disorders, or in terms of furnishing guards.[153] Far too late, on the eve of August 1914, the Russian army was finally free to pursue its only goal in the minds of the professional officers: the defense of the Empire from its external foes. That this was so was due in some measure to the crafty bureaucratic maneuvering of Sukhomlinov; if he had done nothing else, the Russian professional

---

[151] TsGAOR, f. 102 (DP 00), op. 236 (II), d. 175, t. 7, 1906 g., ll. 1-2, 23-24, 30, 126-131.

[152] Leopold Haimson, "The Problem of Social Stability in Urban Russia in 1905-1917 (Part One)," *SR* 33, no. 4 (Dec. 1964): 619-642; for one Soviet view, see E. D. Chermenskii, *IV gosudarstvennaia duma i sverzhenie tsarisma v Rossii* (Moscow, 1976), p. 67. See also M. Balabanov, *Ot 1905 k 1917 godu. Massovoe rabochee dvizhenie* (Moscow, 1927), esp. pp. 275-327.

[153] TsGVIA, f. 1, op. 2, d. 173, passim.

officers should have expressed their gratitude to him. In a very real sense, by having its attentions focused on military developments beyond Russia's borders, the Russian army was at last truly *"vne politiki"* (out of politics). From the vantage point of the military professionals, the army now controlled itself rather than being controlled by the Ministries of Justice and Interior; it was also plentifully supplied with money, thanks to the liberality of the Third and Fourth Dumas. It only lacked one essential thing: time.

NINE

The Significance of Civil-Military Conflict in Tsarist Russia

CIVIL-MILITARY CONFLICT was a reality in late Imperial Russia. Arising in the early years of the reign of Alexander III, it grew in intensity throughout the nineties, was exacerbated by the multiple traumas of 1904-1907, and attained vast proportions during the constitutional period. The tsarist regime, which had so often underwritten the interests of the army in the past, largely reduced its support for these interests from 1881 to 1914. At the prodding of the Ministry of Finance, the Imperial government pursued a course of economic and industrial modernization in the nineties. In the opinion of the army's leadership, this led to budgetary allocations which gravely underfunded the military. Toward the end of the nineties, confronted by burgeoning challenges to its authority from the intelligentsia, the peasantry, and the working masses, the autocracy responded by employing the army to check and crush internal unrest on an ever increasing scale. During the 1905-1907 revolution, the regime dispatched troops not only to suppress disorders, but also to deter them through the intimidating presence of military guard details. At the same time, the military courts were themselves given over to repression, as cases involving thousands of civilian defendants crowded the dockets. The Ministry of War, however, accepted neither the erosion of its financial position nor its expanding repressive obligations. It fought, albeit not entirely successfully, for the funds necessary for improvements in armaments throughout the eighties and nineties, and it continued the fight with better results in the postrevolutionary period, when it even briefly allied with the State Duma in its quest for higher appropriations. Simultaneously, the Ministry's leadership insisted that the army be emancipated from internal service, and that the military perform no tasks which were justly the function of the police. A clerk who worked in the Ministry of the Interior in this period would have had little trouble detecting the steady hardening of War Ministry opposition to military police service.

The real heart of civil-military conflict in Russia inhered in the clashes between the autocracy, the civilian ministries, and the Ministry of War about the purpose of the army. Owing to the compartmentalization of affairs of state in tsarist Russia, civilian ministries tended to equate good government with the fulfillment of their own particular objectives; civilian ministers therefore tended to regard the army as a resource on which they could draw. Thus the Ministry of Justice viewed the army as a cheap and convenient source of penitentiary guards; the Ministry of the Interior saw the army as an auxiliary to the Empire's police forces; and the Ministry of Finance perceived reductions in the military budget as an excellent method of raising investment capital. As for the autocrats, they looked on the army as their personal possession, its officers as their sworn vassals, its traditional purpose the obedient discharge of any duties (including repressive ones) they assigned it.

Russia's increasingly professional military leaders, however, more and more adhered to the view that the army had one purpose and one purpose only: training for war. For this reason they were appalled when the government both denied them the revenue necessary for effective military competition with other powers and then sent the army to the Far East to fight a hopeless war for which it was ill-prepared. For this reason also, they came to loathe military repressive service, since it distracted the army from training, demoralized the troops, and destroyed the prestige of the army in civil society. These attitudes were founded in military professionalism. Military professionalism in Russia grew steadily stronger from 1881 to 1914. Regardless of the apathy and indifference of the majority of officers, there was a constant diffusion of professional ideas and attitudes among an ever-growing segment of the military elite. As military service grew more popular after 1908, as public hostility to the army cooled down, and as promilitary parties (like the Octobrists) and intellectuals (such as the *Great Russia* group) influenced the public mood, one gets the distinct impression that the army was attracting more officers with a nascent or developed professional consciousness. However, it is important to stress that the influx of professionals represented a trickle, rather than a stream. The total leavening of professionals within the Russian officer corps remained small. Thus when we consider military professionals as individuals and ask whether their professionalism constituted an ideology, we would have to answer that if it was an ideology, it was an ideology of self-esteem. In this early stage of professionalism the professionals favored improvement and progress rather than the status and conservatism often favored by professional groups which have firmly entrenched themselves. What was of great consequence for the tsarist polity, however, was the professional culture of the War Ministry itself. As we have seen, that professional culture was in part the creation of the professionalizing officers whom we have discussed. Clearly the Imperial Ministry of War could not establish a professional officer corps by decree. There were too many structural problems, inhering in Russian political, economic, and social backwardness, which militated against professionalism and which were scarcely amenable to abolition by executive fiat. Then, too, as we have also seen, the Ministry of War was at times as much a part of the problem as part of the solution. Yet the Ministry was situated to encourage and to reward "professional" behavior in the higher echelons of the military—among the district commanders, for example. Once again, we are only discussing a handful of individuals here—but the important thing is that these individuals had power. This is why, if the military professionalism of the War Ministry is viewed in the broader context of state policy, one of its outcomes was an intensification of civil-military conflict within the government.

In fact, in Imperial Russia military professionalism and civil-military conflict fueled each other. The more professional the military elite became, the more vigorously it pushed for the modernization of the military arsenal and the creation of a truly national, patriotic army. Conversely, the more the autocrats and civilian bureaucrats frustrated these goals, the more firmly officers adhered to their professional program. Russian military professionalism was essentially inward-looking, insular, and concerned with the general problem of governance only insofar as it directly impinged on the army. For professional officers the army became an end in itself, the preservation of the army a goal more important than the survival of the Romanov dynasty or the Empire. That the primary value of the professional officer was the army, not the regime, found striking expression in the War Ministry's resistance to repressive operations during the 1905 revolution. Another expression of this value was the politicization of military intellectuals in the post-revolutionary years and their flirtations with ideologies of mass mobilization.

There was, of course, no military coup in Russia during the period we have discussed, nor did any discernible plans for a coup exist. The personal loyalties of the great inert mass of Russian officers simply precluded such an event. However, as it has been often and correctly pointed out, the abdication of Nicholas II in March 1917 can in part be construed as a military coup. Nicholas decided to renounce his power only after almost all of his front commanders had urged him to do so. Explanations of the abdication tend to concentrate on the army's frustrations at the mismanagement of the war. In fact, as we have seen, officers' resentment against civilian treatment of the army had a pre-history which long antedated August 1914.

Civil-military conflict of the variety which emerged in late Imperial

Russia was, then, profoundly dysfunctional. This was not only because the tension underlying the conflict contributed to the downfall of the Romanov dynasty, but also because the energies squandered on this conflict could have been productively expended in the solution of other problems. Civil-military conflict damaged the combat readiness of the army, not only because civilian demands for guard details distracted the troops from training, but also because the War Ministry devoted countless hours to bickering with the civilians over what became in the end such trivialities as the posting of fifteen Cossacks to the Amur River. These hours might more efficiently have been invested in furthering the cause of military reform. The War Ministry's intransigence in the face of civilian repressive demands from 1908 to 1913 illustrates the degree to which the state's ability to count on the army as "its only refuge under heaven" had already atrophied, even before the outbreak of World War I. To be sure, the army rallied to the civilian aid in the last years before the outbreak of the war, as in the case of the great July 1914 strikes in St. Petersburg. But Russia's military intellectuals had understood since 1905 that the use of troops in certain repressive capacities sooner or later ruined them as a combat force. Even if Russia had somehow miraculously avoided participation in World War I, it is doubtful whether the military elite would ever again have supplied the regime with the protracted repressive service of 1905-1907.

An expansion in military professionalism was, of course, a feature of other European armies. But the Russian military professionals were almost unique in their lack of prestige and lack of natural allies. Unlike the Austro-Hungarian armed forces, the Russian army had no role as an agency for the resolution or the suppression of nationalism. Unlike the German officer corps, the Russian officer corps enjoyed low prestige and was popularly reviled by the educated classes. Unlike the French army, the Russian army could rely on little political support either from the left or from the right, at least until the Octobrists came to preeminence in the Third Duma. But Octobrist backing was contingent on amicable relations between Octobrist and ministerial leaders. With the change in leadership the War Ministry found itself under attack. By the summer of 1914 the relations between army and Duma, army and autocrat, and army and bureaucracy were characterized by mistrust and suspicion, which did not bode well for the conduct of the war effort.

Contrary to what has often been said of it, the cream of the Russian officer corps was politicized. But the capital weakness of the politics of the military elite was superficiality. Russian military politics was interest group politics. The military elite appreciated politics less for what they meant to the country and more for the possible benefits which could accrue to Russia's military potential. The politicized officers were lob-byists, not statesmen. I would hypothesize here that this fact may have helped to explain why at least some of Russia's top soldiers succumbed to the blandishments of Bolshevism or National Bolshevism. Once it was manifest that the young Soviet state was to possess a regular army, not a people's militia, a least some tsarist soldiers, such as Bonch-Brue-vich, Brusilov, and Barsukov could hope that Bolshevism might be ex-actly that mass political movement which could instill the patriotism which was the chief element in victory. There were opportunists who joined the Red Army, there were some whom Trotskii blackmailed into enlisting, but there is no reason to doubt that there were some sincere officers in addition to these.

The failure of the White movement has been ascribed in part to the political naiveté of Russian officers, which is often taken as equal to total political ignorance. This assertion needs to be further refined. Numerous officers who joined the Whites were new professionals. They were in fact politicized. But their politics were narrow and consequently flawed. The White movements did not have a unified political ideology. Mere opposition to Bolshevism was too barren a program to unify soldiers, politicians, and population. So, too, was a concern for the preservation of the army.

Further, the military policy of the Soviet state may itself have to be reevaluated in the light of this treatment of late Imperial civil-military conflict. Additional study is necessary to determine the extent to which the Soviet state sought to avoid replicating the mistakes of the Imperial regime which had led to conflict in the first place.

The real problem which military professionals confronted in late Im-perial Russia was the inability of the regime to find a place for them. The tsarist government was unable (and unwilling) to generate insti-tutions which could mediate between bureaucracy and army. Further, the autocracy was also unready to grant the army more autonomy, since military autonomy was in itself a contradiction of the autocratic prin-ciple. Civil-military conflict was the unavoidable result.

GLOSSARY OF RUSSIAN TERMS

Dvorianin (pl. dvoriane)   A member of the estate of the nobility

gornyi nachal'nik   Engineer in charge of mining operations in one of the mining districts of the Empire

gradonachal'nik   An official who headed the government in any one of a number of important cities; equal in authority to a governor

katorga   forced labor

meshchanin (pl. meshchane)   A member of the estate of petty urban traders and artisans

oblast'   Territory with its own administration separate from a province

ochered   In Cossack armies, designation of regiments: regiment of the 1st ochered (first line regiment), etc.

pod"esaul   Cossack rank, equivalent to second lieutenant

rotmistr   A Cavalry rank, equivalent to captain

sotnia   A squadron of Cossacks

ssylka   exile

uezd   A district. One of the components of a province

verst   A Russian unit of distance, equal to 1.06 kilometers

zemskii ispravnik   Chief of police in an uezd

APPENDIX

Approximate Peacetime Strengths of
Field Military Units in the Russian Army, 1890

INFANTRY

A company of line infantry consisted of 96 to 168 men.
Four companies comprised a battalion (384 to 612 men).
Four battalions made up a regiment (1,536 to 2,688 men).
Two regiments made up a brigade (3,072 to 5,376).
Two brigades comprised a division (6,144 to 10,752 men).
In 1890 there were 885 battalions and 1 company of field infantry totalling 482,000 men.

CAVALRY

A squadron or sotnia of field troops consisted of roughly 138 to 180 men.
Each of the four cuirassier regiments had four squadrons (552 to 720 men).
Each of the two hussar, two uhlan and fifty dragoon regiments had six squadrons apiece (828 to 1,080 men).
The two guard cavalry divisions had six regiments apiece (4,968 to 6,480 men).
In 1890 there were 350 squadrons or sotnias in the line cavalry with 63,000 men.

ARTILLERY

A separate field artillery park comprised 152 men.
A field artillery battery consisted of roughly 178 men.
Six batteries composed a brigade (1,068 men).
In 1890 there were 366 batteries and 57½ separate parks with 74,000 men.

ENGINEERS

A field engineer's company had 100 men.
Four to five companies made up a battalion (400 to 500 men)
In 1890 there were 31½ battalions, 3 companies, and 23 parks of engineers with 21,000 men.

SOURCE: Zolotarev, *Zapiski voennoi statistiki*, pp. 383-388.

SELECT BIBLIOGRAPHY

I. Archival Sources

As this book is based on over 450 archival files, I have chosen not to list them separately, but rather have provided a description of the *fondy* (collections) employed.

Central State Archive of Military History (Moscow) (TsGVIA):
fond 400.   Main Staff
fond 2000.   Main Administration of the General Staff
fond 1.   Chancellery of the War Ministry
fond 330.   Main Administration of Cossacks
fond 801.   Main Administration of Military Justice
fond 409.   Personnel records
fond 348.   Alexander Academy of Military Justice
fond 544.   Nicholas Academy of the General Staff
fond 280.   A. F. Rediger
fond 165.   A. N. Kuropatkin
fond 278.   P. S. Vannovskii
fond 970.   Imperial Chief Apartment

Central State Archive of the October Revolution (Moscow)(TsGAOR):
fond 102 or DP.   Department of Police
fond 601.   Nicholas II
fond 677.   Alexander III
fond 124.   Special Chancellery of the Ministry of Justice

Hoover Institution Archives, Stanford University:
A. S. Lukomskii collection
D. N. Liubimov collection

II. Archival Guides, Bibliographies

Beskrovnyi, L. G. *Ocherki po istochnikovedniiu voennoi istorii v Rossii.* Moscow, 1957.
Cherepakhova, M. S., and E. M. Gingerit, comps. *Russkaia periodicheskaia pechat' (1895-Oktiabr' 1917). Spravochnik.* Moscow, 1957.
Chernovskii, A., comp. *Soiuz russkogo naroda po materialam chrezvychainoi sledstvennoi komissii vremennogo pravitel'stva 1917 g.* Moscow and Leningrad, 1929.
Dement'eva, A. G., A. V. Zapadova, and M. S. Cherepakhova, comps. *Russkaia periodicheskaia pechat' (1702-1894). Spravochnik.* Moscow, 1959.
Grimsted, Patricia Kennedy. *Archives and Manuscript Depositories in the USSR. Moscow and Leningrad.* Princeton, 1972.

Grimsted, Patricia Kennedy. *Supplement I*. Zug, 1976.

Levasheva, Z. P. *Bibliografiia russkoi voennoi bibliografii*. Moscow, 1950.

Levasheva, Z. P. et al., comps. *Russkaia voennaia pechat' 1702-1916 gg.* Moscow, 1959.

Luchinin, V. *Russko-iaponskaia voina 1904-1905 gg. Bibliograficheskii ukazatel' knizhnoi literatury*. Moscow, 1940.

Lyons, M. *The Russian Imperial Army. A Bibliography of Regimental Histories and Related Works*. Stanford, 1968.

Putevoditel' po tsentral'nomu gosudarstvennomu voenno-istoricheskomu arkhivu. Moscow, 1941.

Tsentral'nyi gosudarstvennyi arkhiv Oktiabr'skoi revoliutsii i sotsialisticheskogo stroitel'stva. Putevoditel'. Moscow, 1946.

Tsentral'nyi gosudarstvennyi istoricheskii arkhiv v Moskve. Putevoditel'. Moscow, 1946.

Ukazatel' k voennomy i literatornomu zhurnalu Razvedchika za desiat' let, 1888-1897 gg. St. Petersburg, 1898.

Voit, S. S., comp. *Alfavitnyi ukazatel' k svodu zakonov rossiiskoi imperii*. Petrograd, 1916.

Zaionchkovskii, P. A., ed. *Spravochniki po istorii dorevoliutsionnoi Rossii*. Moscow, 1971.

III. Published Laws, Documents, Reports, and Encyclopedias

Adres-kalendar. Obshchaia rospis' nachal'stvuiushchikh i prochikh dolzhnostnykh lits po vsem upravleniem Rossiiskoi Imperii. St. Petersburg, 1881-1916.

Aleksandrovskaia voenno-iuridicheskaia akademiia. Pervoe dopolnenie k zhurnalam konferentsii (gody 1889-1891). St. Petersburg, 1891; *vtoroe dopolnenie . . . (gody 1891-1893)*. St. Petersburg, 1893; *tret'e dopolnenie . . . (gody 1893-1896)*. St. Petersburg, 1896; *chetvertoe dopolnenie . . . (s 18 sentiabria po 31 dekabria 1907 g)*. St. Petersburg, 1908.

Allgemeine Rechnung über den Reichshausalt für das Rechnungsjahr 1901. Berlin, 1905.

Biblioteka Aleksandrovskoi voenno-iuridicheskoi akademii. Sistematicheskii katalog. 3 vols. St. Petersburg, 1899.

Chistiakov, Major General, comp. *Nikolaevskaia akademiia general'nogo shtaba. Naznachenie akademii*. St. Petersburg, 1904.

Drezen, A. K., ed. *Tsarizm v bor'be s revoliutsiei 1905-07 gg*. Moscow, 1936.

Encyclopedia Britannica. 11th ed. Cambridge, England, 1910-1911.

Entsiklopedicheskii slovar'. Publ. F. A. Brokgauz and I. A. Efron. St. Petersburg, 1889-1907.

Godovoi otchet za 1-i god deiatel'nosti obshchestva revnitelei voennykh znanii. St. Petersburg, 1900; *. . . vtoroi godovoi otchet*. St. Petersburg, 1901; *. . . tret'ii godovoi otchet*. St. Petersburg, 1902; *. . . chertvertyi godovoi otchet*. St. Petersburg, 1903; *. . . za 6-i god*. St. Petersburg, 1905; *. . . vos'moi* *godovoi otchet*. St. Petersburg, 1907; . . . *deviatyi godovoi otchet*. St. Petersburg, 1908.

Gosudarstvennaia Duma pervogo prizyva. Portrety, kratkiia biografii i kharakteristiki deputatov. Moscow, 1906.

Izvlechenie iz vsepoddanneishego otcheta Ego Imperatorskogo Vysochestva, Glavnokomanduiushchego voiskami gvardii i peterburgskogo voennogo okruga za 1897. St. Petersburg, n.d.

Karavaev, V. Kuz'min. *Voenno-iuridicheskaia akademiia 1866-1891 gg*. St. Petersburg, 1911.

Kennard, Howard P., ed. *The Russian Year Book, 1908-1913*. London, 1908-1913.

von Laue, T. H., ed. "A Secret Memorandum of Sergei Witte on the Industrialization of Imperial Russia." *Journal of Modern History* 26, no. 1 (Mar. 1954): 60-74.

Maskevich, N. M., comp. *Raz"iasneniia glavnogo shtaba i drugikh uchrezhdenii po kvartirnomu dovol'stviiu voisk*. St. Petersburg, 1896.

Materialy po istorii studencheskogo dvizheniia v Rossii. 2 vols. London, 1906.

Materialy po peresmotru ustanovlennykh dlia okhrany gosudarstvennogo poriadka iskliuchitel'nykh zakonopolozhenii, vol. 11. St. Petersburg, 1906.

Ministerstvo vnutrennykh del. Departament politsii. Spravka o chislennom sostave politsii. St. Petersburg, 1913.

Ministerstvo voennoe. Doklad po glavnomu shtabu. Otdelenie v. stol 1. 22 maia 1898 goda. no. 6. Istoriia sostavleniia i utverzhdeniia Finliandskogo ustava o voinskoi povinnosti. St. Petersburg, 1898.

Ministerstvo voennoe. Glavnoe voenno-sudnoe upravlenie. Otdelenie 1. 31 avgusta 1894 no. 4025. St. Petersburg, n.d.

Nifontov, A. S., and V. V. Zlatoustovskii, eds., *Krest'ianskoe dvizhenie v Rossii v 1881-1889 gg. Sbornik dokumentov*. Moscow, 1960.

Obzor deiatel'nosti ministerstva finansov v tsarstvovanie Imperatora Aleksandra III (1881-1894). St. Petersburg, 1902.

Obzor deiatel'nosti voennogo ministerstva v tsarstvovanie Imperatora Aleksandra III (1881-1894). St. Petersburg, 1903.

Otchet Gosudarstvennogo kontrolia po ispolneniiu gosudarstvennoi rospisi i finansovykh smet za 1881, ff. St. Petersburg, 1882-1914.

Otchet po deloproizvodstvu Gosudarstvennogo Soveta za sessiiu 1892-1893, ff. St. Petersburg, 1893-1905.

Otchet voennogo ministra po poezdke na Dal'nyi Vostok v 1903 godu. 2 vols. St. Petersburg, 1903.

Pervaia vseobshchaia perepis' naseleniia Rossiiskoi Imperii 1897 g. Raspredelenie naseleniia. vols. 1 and 2. St. Petersburg, 1905.

Podrobnaia programma obucheniia molodykh i starosluzhashchikh soldat pekhoty. Sostavlena po prikazaniiu komanduiushchego voiskami kievskogo voennogo okruga. 29th ed. Kiev, 1908.

Polnoe sobranie zakonov Rossiskoi Imperii, 3d ser. St. Petersburg, 1882-1915.

Polozhenie ob ofitserskom sobranii ofitserskoi strelkovoi shkoly. St. Petersburg, 1907.

Resheniia glavnogo voennogo suda 1903-1908 gg. St. Petersburg, 1903-1909.

Revoliutsiia 1905-1907 gg. 20 vols. Moscow, 1956-1965.

Sbornik materialov po russko-turetskoi voine 1877-78 gg. na Balkanskom poluostrove, vol. 16. St. Petersburg, 1900.

Shapkarin, A. V., ed. *Krest'ianskoe dvizhenie v Rossii v 1890-1900 gg. Sbornik dokumentov.* Moscow, 1959.

Shchegolev, P. E., ed. *Padenie tsarskogo rezhima,* vol. 3. Leningrad, 1925; vol. 6. Moscow and Leningrad, 1926.

Sliusarskii, A. G., ed. *Krest'ianskoe dvizhenie v poltavskoi i khar'kovskoi guberniiakh v 1902 g. Sbornik dokumentov.* Kharkov, 1961.

Spisok vysshim chinam gosudarstvennogo, gubernskogo i eparkhial'ogo upravleniia. St. Petersburg, 1881-1914.

Spravochnaia kniga dlia iunkerov 2-go voennogo Konstantinovskogo uchilishcha na 1889/93 uchebnyi god (sic). St. Petersburg, 1888.

Statistika proizvedenii pechati vyshedshikh v Rossii v 1910 godu. St. Petersburg, 1911.

Statistisches Jahrbuch für das Deutsches Reich, herausgegeben vom Kaiserlichen Statistischen Amt. Berlin, 1881-1902.

Svod shtatov voenno-sukhoputnogo vedomstva. 4 vols. St. Petersburg, 1893.

Svod voennykh postanovlenii. izdanie 1859. St. Petersburg, 1859.

Svod voennykh postanovlenii. izdanie 1869. St. Petersburg, 1869-1898.

Svod zakonov Rossiskoi Imperii. izdanie 1892. St. Petersburg, 1892.

Svod zakonov Rossiskoi Imperii. izdanie 1906. St. Petersburg, 1906.

Tagantsev, N. S., ed. *Ugolovnoe ulozhenie 22 marta 1903 g.* St. Petersburg, 1904.

Tsarskii listok. Doklady ministra vnutrennikh del Nikolaiu II za 1897 g. Paris, 1909.

Ustav vnutrennei sluzhby Vysochaishe utverzhden 14 sent. 1902 g. St. Petersburg, 1908.

Varshavskii voennyi okrug pod komandoi general-ad''iutanta generala-ot-kavalerii I. V. Gurko, 1883-1893 gg. Warsaw, 1893.

Velichko, K. I. et al., eds. *Voennaia entsiklopedia.* St. Petersburg, 1911-1914.

Vsepoddanneishii doklad po voennomu ministerstvu 1880-1889; 1892-1893. St. Petersburg, 1881-1890, 1893-1894.

Vsepoddanneishii otchet chlena Gosudarstvennogo Soveta, senatora, tainogo sovetnika Manukhina po ispolneniiu Vysochaishche vozlozhennogo na nego 27 aprelia 1912 goda razsledovaniia o zabastovke na Lenskikh promyslakh. St. Petersburg, 1912.

Vsepoddanneishii otchet o deiatel'nosti glavnykh upravlenii voennogo ministerstva, vyzvannoi voinoiu s Iaponiei v 1904-1905 g.g. sekretno. St. Petersburg, 1912.

Vsepoddanneishii otchet o deistviiakh voennogo ministerstva za 1881-1913. 33 vols. St. Petersburg, 1882-1914.

SELECT BIBLIOGRAPHY

IV. MEMOIRS, DIARIES AND CONTEMPORARY WRITINGS

Andreieff [Andreev], Leonid. *His Excellency the Governor.* Trans. Maurice Magnus. London, 1921.
_____. *The Red Laugh.* London, 1915.
Anisimov, S. S. *Kak eto bylo. Zapiski politicheskogo zashchitnika o sudakh Stolypina.* Moscow, 1931.
Apushkin, V. A. *Russko iaponskaia voina 1904-1905 gg.* 2d ed. Moscow, 1911.
Articles on the German Army Maneuvers Reprinted from The Times. London, 1911.
Artzibashe, Michael. *Sanine.* Trans. Percy Pinkerton. New York, 1932.
Ashenbrenner, M. Iu. "Voennaia organizatsiia partii 'Narodnoi Voli'." *Byloe* 1, no. 7 (July 1906): 4-26.
Balabanov, M. *Ot 1905 K 1917 godu. Massovoe rabochee dvizhenie.* Moscow, 1927.
Bing, Edward J., ed. *The Letters of Tsar Nicholas and Empress Marie.* London, 1937.
Bloch, I. S. *The Future of War.* Trans. R. C. Long. Boston, 1902.
Bogdanovich, A. V. *Tri poslednikh samoderzhtsa. Dnevnik A. V. Bogdanovicha.* Moscow and Leningrad, 1924.
Bonch-Bruevich, M. D. *Vsia vlast' sovetam, Vospominaniia.* Moscow, 1957.
Brussilov [Brusilov], A. A. *A Soldier's Note-Book, 1914-1918.* London, 1930.
Cyril, H.I.H. The Grand Duke. *My Life in Russian Service—Then and Now.* London, 1939.
Danilov, Iu. N. *Rossiia v mirovoi voine 1914-1915 gg.* Berlin, 1924.
Denikin, Anton I. *The Career of a Tsarist Officer: Memoirs 1872-1916.* Trans. Margaret Patoski. Minneapolis, 1975.
_____. *The Russian Turmoil.* London, 1920.
_____. *Staraia armiia.* 2 vols. Paris, 1929-1931.
Dnevnik Imperatora Nikolaia II 1890-1906 gg. Berlin, 1923.
Dragomirov, M. *Dueli.* Kiev, 1900.
Durland, Kellogg. *The Red Reign: The True Story of an Adventurous Year in Russia.* New York, 1908.
Engel'gardt, B. A. "Potonuvshii mir." *Voenno-istoricheskii zhurnal* 9, no. 1 (Jan. 1964): 70-89.
Frantz, Gunther. *Russland auf dem Wege zur Katastrophe: Augzeichnungen des Grossfürsten Andrei Wladimirowitzch und des Kriegsministers Poliwanow. Briefe der Grossfürsten an den Zaren.* Berlin, 1926.
Galkin, M. *Novyi put' sovremennogo ofitsera.* St. Petersburg, 1907.
Garlinskii, D. N. *Mysli ob armii.* 5 vols. St. Petersburg, 1911.
Gerua, B. V. *Vospominaniia o moei zhizni,* vol. 1. Paris, 1969.
Gourko [Gurko], Basil. *War and Revolution in Russia, 1914-17.* New York, 1919.
Greene, Francis V. *Sketches of Army Life in Russia.* New York, 1880.
Grulev, M. *Zapiski generala evreia.* Paris, 1930.
_____. *Zloby dnia v zhizni armii.* Brest-Litovsk, 1911.

Guchkov, A. I. *Rechi po voprosam gosudarstvennoi oborony i ob obschei politike 1908-1917.* Petrograd, 1917.

Gurko, V. I. *Features and Figures of the Past: Government and Opinion in the Reign of Nicholas II.* Trans. Laura Matveev. Stanford, 1939.

A. A. Ignat'ev. *Piat'desiat let v stroiu,* vol. 3. Moscow, 1942.

[A. A. Ignatyev]. *A Subaltern in Old Russia.* Trans. Ivor Montagu. London, 1944.

Ivanov, S. A. "Vozniknovenie i padenie Durnoselovki. Epizod iz istorii krest'ianskikh dvizhenii 80-ikh godov." *Byloe* 1, no. 6 (June 1906): 33-40.

Kizevetter, A. A. *Na rubezhe dvukh stoletii. Vospominaniia 1881-1914.* Prague, 1929.

Kokovtsov, V. N. *Out of My Past. The Memoirs of Count Kokovtsov.* Ed. H. H. Fisher and trans. Laura Matveev. Stanford, 1935.

Korolenko, V. G. *Sobranie sochinenii,* vol. 9. Moscow, 1955.

————. *Tragediia generala Kovaleva i nravy voennoi sredy.* Moscow, 1906.

Korostovetz, J. J. *Pre-War Diplomacy. The Diary of J. J. Korostovetz.* London, 1920.

Krasnov, P. N. *Na rubezhe Kitaia.* Paris, 1939.

————. "Pamiati Imperatorskoi russkoi armii." *Russkaia letopis'* (Paris) 5 (1923): 5-64.

Kuprin, A. I. *Na perelome.* Nizhnyi Novgorod, 1929.

————. *The River of Life and Other Stories.* Trans. S. Koteliansky and J. M. Murray. Boston, 1916.

Kurlov, P. *Konets russkogo tsarizma. Vospominaniia byvshego komandira korpusa zhandarmov.* Petrograd, 1923.

Kvitka, A. *Dnevnik Zabaikal'skogo kazach'ego ofitsera. Russko-iaponskaia voina 1904-05 gg.* St. Petersburg, 1908.

Lamzdorff, V. N. *Dnevnik, 1891-1892.* Ed. F. A. Rotshtein. Moscow and Leningrad, 1934.

L'armee russe et ses chefs en 1888 par l'auteur du Marechal de Moltke. Paris, 1888.

Lenin, V. I. *Articles on Tolstoi.* Moscow, 1951.

————. *Collected Works.* 4th ed. vol. 8. Trans. Bernard Isaacs and Isidor Lasker. Moscow, 1962.

Lewenhaupt, Count Eric, trans. *The Memoirs of Marshal Mannerheim.* New York, 1954.

Lichnevsky, M., trans. *Lettres des Grands-Ducs à Nicholas II.* Paris, 1926.

Lindsay, A. B., trans. *The Russian Army and the Japanese War by General Kuropatkin,* 2 vols. London, 1909.

Littauer, Vladimir S. *Russian Hussar.* London, 1965.

Lukomskii, A. S. *Vospominaniia.* 2 vols. Berlin, 1922.

Mandel'shtam, Mikhail L'vovich. *1905 v politicheskikh protessakh.* Moscow, 1931.

Martynov, A. P. *Moia sluzhba v otdel'nom korpuse zhandarmov. Vospominaniia.* Ed. Richard Wraga. Stanford, 1972.

Martynov, E. I. *Iz pechal'nago opyta russko-iaponskoi voiny*, St. Petersburg, 1906.

Miliukov, Paul. *Political Memoirs*. Trans. Carl Goldberg. Ann Arbor, 1968.

Miliutin, D. A. *Vospominaniia*. Ed. W. Bruce Lincoln. Newtonville, Mass., 1980.

Mossolov [Mosolov], A. A. *At the Court of the Last Tsar*. Trans. E. W. Dickes. London, 1935.

Mstislavskii, S. "Otryvki o piatom gode." *Katorga i ssylka* (Moscow) 39 (1928): 7-36.

Naumov, A. N. *Iz utselevshikh vospominanii 1868-1917 gg.*, vol. 1. New York, 1954.

Novitskii, V. D. *Iz vospominanii zhandarma*. Priboi, 1929.

Novitskii, E. F. *Na puti k usovershenstvovaniiu gosudarstvennoi oborony*. St. Petersburg, 1909.

————. *Sandepu*. St. Petersburg, 1907.

Ognev, D. F. *Voennaia podsudnost': sravnitel'nyi ocherk*. St. Petersburg, 1896.

Pamirtsev, L. *Voina i Duma*. St. Petersburg, 1905.

Parskii, D. *Prichiny nashikh neudach v voine s Iaponiei. Neobkhodimye reformy v armii*. St. Petersburg, 1906.

Pimenova, E. *Postoiannoe voisko i militsiia*. St. Petersburg, 1905.

Pis'ma Pobedonostseva k Aleksandru III, vol. 2. Moscow, 1926.

Polivanov, A. A. *Iz dnevnikov i vospominanii po dolznosti voennogo ministra i ego pomoshchnika 1907-1916 gg.*, vol. 1. Ed. A. M. Zaionchkovskii. Moscow, 1924.

Polner, T. I., comp. *Obshchezemskaia organizatsiia na Dal'nem Vostoke*. 2 vols. Moscow, 1908-1910.

Polovtsov, A. A. *Dnevnik gosudarstvennogo sekretaria A. A. Polovtsova*, vol. 2. Moscow, 1966.

Rashevskii, S. A. "Dnevnik polkovnika S. A. Rashevskogo (Port-Artur, 1904)." In *Istoricheskii arkhiv*, vol. 10. Moscow and Leningrad, 1954.

Rediger, A., and A. Gulevich. *Komplektovanie I ustroistvo vooruzhennoi sily*. 3d ed. St. Petersburg, 1900.

————. *Zametki po voennoi administratsii*. St. Petersburg, 1885.

Rittikh, A. F. *Ob''edinennoe slav'ianstvo*. St. Petersburg, 1908.

————. *Russkii voennyi byt v deistvitel'nosti i mechtakh*. St. Petersburg, 1893.

Samoilo, A. *Dve zhizni*. 2d ed. Moscow, 1963.

Savinkov, Boris. *Memoirs of a Terrorist*. Trans. Joseph Shaplen. New York, 1931.

Sazonov, Sergei. *Fateful Years, 1909-1916: The Reminiscences of Sergei Sazonov*. London, 1928.

Seeger, Charles Louis, trans. *The Memoirs of Alexander Iswolsky*. London, 1921.

Shavel'skii, Georgii. *Vospominaniia poslednego protopresvitera russkoi armii i flota*. New York, 1954.

Shipov, D. N. *Vospominaniia i dumy o perezhitom*. Moscow, 1918.

von Shwartz, A. V. "*Vospominaniia.*" In *Russia Emigre Archives*, vol. 3. Ed. Alexander Pronin. Fresno, Calif., 1973.

Skugarevskii, A. P. *Ocherki i zametki*, vol. 1. Vilna, 1900; vol. 2. Vilna, 1901; vol. 3. St. Petersburg, 1913.

Smelkov, N. "Kak voznikaiut inogda krest'ianskie bunty." *Istoricheskii vestnik* (St. Petersburg) 105 (1906): 334-335.

Sukhomlinov, V. Piat' voennykh rasskazov. St. Petersburg, 1894.

———. Vospominaniia Sukhomlinova. Moscow and Leningrad, 1926.

Suvorin, A. S. *Dnevnik A. S. Suvorina.* Ed. Mikhail Krichevskii. Moscow and Leningrad, 1926.

Tkhorzhevskii, K. *Nadezhnye soldaty.* 5th ed. St. Petersburg, 1907.

Urussov [Urusov], Prince Serge Dmitriyevich. *Memoirs of a Russian Governor.* Trans. Herman Rosenthal. London, 1908.

Vassilyev [Vasil'ev], A. T. *The Ochrana: The Russian Secret Police.* Philadelphia, 1930.

Veresaev, V. *In the War: Memoirs.* Trans. Leo Wiener. New York, 1917.

Veselovskii, B. B., V. I. Pitchet, and V. M. Friche, eds. *Materialy po istorii krest'ianskikh dvizhenii v Rossii. Agrarnyi vopros v Sovete Ministrov.* Moscow and Leningrad, 1924.

Vitte, S. Iu. *Vospominaniia.* 3 vols. Moscow, 1960.

———. *Vynuzhdennyia raz''iasneniia po povodu otcheta Generala-ad''iutanta Kuropatkina o voine s Iaponiei.* Moscow, 1911.

Voznesenskii, V. N. *Teni proshlogo. (po tsarskim sudam). Iz vospominanii politicheskogo zashchitnika.* Moscow, 1929.

Witte, S. J. (S. Iu. Vitte). *Vorlesungen über Volks- und Staatswirtschaft*, vol. 2. Trans. Josef Melnik. Stuttgart, 1913.

Youssoupoff [Usupov], Prince Felix. *Lost Splendour.* Trans. Ann Green and Nicholas Katkoff. London, 1953.

Zolotarev, A. M. *Zapiski voennoi statistiki Rossii*, vol. 1, 2d ed. St. Petersburg, 1894.

V. PERIODICALS (other than those indicated in Sections III and VI)

Knizhnyi vestnik. St. Petersburg, 1890-1913.

Krasnyi arkhiv. Moscow, 1912-1941.

Novoe vremia. St. Petersburg, 1895-1907.

Pravo. St. Petersburg, 1904-1910.

Razvedchik. St. Petersburg, 1890-1911.

Russkii Invalid. St. Petersburg, 1888-1908.

Slav'ianskie izvestiia. St. Petersburg, 1908-1910.

Tiuremnyi vestnik. St. Petersburg, 1904-1905.

Vestnik Evropy. St. Petersburg, 1890, 1892, 1904-1906.

Vestnik obshchestva revnitelei voennykh znanii. St. Petersburg, 1891-1908.

Voennyi golos. St. Petersburg, 1906.

Voennyi sbornik. St. Petersburg, 1888-1914.

VI. Secondary Literature

Abrahamsson, Bengt. *Military Professionalisation and Political Power.* Stockholm, 1971.

Afanas'ev, V. *Aleksandr Ivanovich Kuprin.* 2d ed. Moscow, 1972.

————. "Sovremennitsa 'Poedinka.' " *Ogonek,* no. 36 (1960): 19.

Ageev. A. "Ofitsery russkogo general'nogo shtaba ob opyte russko-iaponskoi voiny 1904-1905 gg." *Voenno-istoricheskii zhurnal* 17, no. 8 (Aug. 1975): 99-104.

Aleksandrovskoe voennoe uchilishche za xxv let 1863-1898. Moscow, 1900.

Alexander, John T. *Autocratic Politics in a National Crisis: The Imperial Government and Pugachev's Revolt, 1773-1775.* Bloomington, Ind., 1969.

Anan'ich, B. V. *Rossiia i mezhdunarodnyi kapital 1897-1914 g.g.* Leningrad, 1970.

Andreski, Stanislaw. *Military Organization and Society.* 2d ed. Berkeley, 1968.

Apushkin, V. A. *General ot porazhenii V. A. Sukhomlinov.* Leningrad, 1925.

Balfour, Michael. *The Kaiser and His Times.* London, 1964.

Baluev, B. P. *Politicheskaia reaktsiia 80-kh godov xix veka i russkaia zhurnalistika.* Moscow, 1971.

Barkai, Haim. "The Macro-Economics of Tsarist Russia in the Industrialization Era: Monetary Developments, the Balance of Payments and the Gold Standard." *The Journal of Economic History* 33, no. 2 (June 1973): 339-371.

Bennett, Helju Aulik. "The Chin System and the Raznochintsy in the Government of Alexander III, 1881-1894." Ph.D. diss., Berkeley, 1971.

Beskrovnyi, L. G. "Proizvodstvo vooruzheniia i boepripasov dlia armii v Rossii v period imperializma (1898-1917 gg.)." *Istoricheskie zapiski* (Moscow) 99 (1977): 88-139.

————. *Russkaia armiia i flot v xix veke.* Moscow, 1973.

Best, Geoffrey, and Andrew Wheatcroft, eds. *War, Economy, and the Military Mind.* London, 1976.

Blinov, I. *Gubernatory. Istoriko-iuridicheskii ocherk.* St. Petersburg, 1905.

de Bloch, Jean. *Les finances de la Russie au XIX⁰ siècle,* vol. 2. Paris, 1899.

Bovykin, V. I. "Banki i voennaia promyshlennost' Rossii nakanune pervoi mirovoi voiny." *Istoricheskie zapiski* (Moscow) 64 (1959): 82-135.

Bushnell, John. "Mutineers and Revolutionaries: Military Revolution in Russia, 1905-1907." Ph.D. diss., Indiana University, 1977.

————. *Mutineers and Revolutionaries: Military Revolution in Russia, 1905-1907.* Bloomington, Ind., 1985.

————. "Peasants in Uniform: The Tsarist Army as Peasant Society." *Journal of Social History* 13, no. 4 (Summer 1980): 565-576.

————. "The Tsarist Officer Corps 1881-1914: Customs, Duties, Inefficiency." *American Historical Review* 86, no. 4 (Oct. 1981): 753-780.

Challeat, J. *Histoire technique de l'artillerie de terre en pendant un siècle,* vol. 2. Paris, 1935.

Chermenskii, E. D. *IV gosudarstvennaia duma i sverzhenie tsarisma v Rossii.* Moscow, 1976.

Chernukha, V. G. *Vnutrenniaia politika tsarizma s serediny 50-kh do nachala 80-kh g.g. XIX v.* Leningrad, 1978.

Collins, D. N. "The Franco-Russian Alliance and Russian Railways, 1891-1914." *The Historical Journal* 16, no. 4 (Dec. 1973): 747-788.

Cooper, Jerry M. *The Army and Civil Disorder: Federal Military Intervention in Labor Disputes, 1877-1900.* Westport, Conn., 1980.

Corvisier, Andre. *Armies and Societies in Europe, 1494-1789.* Trans. Abigail T. Siddal. Bloomington, Ind., 1979.

Curtiss, John Sheldon. *The Russian Army under Nicholas I, 1825-1855.* Durham, N.C., 1965.

Demeter, Karl. *The German Officer Corps in Society and State, 1640-1945.* Trans. Angus Malcolm. New York, 1965.

Diakin, V. I. *Samoderzhavie, burzhuazhiia i dvorianstvo v 1907-1911 g.g.* Leningrad, 1978.

Dixon, Norman. *On the Psychology of Military Incompetence.* London, 1976.

Domanevskii, V. N. "Revniteli voennykh nauk. Chastnyi pochin v voenno-nauchnom dele." *Chasovoi,* no. 5-6 (Mar. 1929): 15-17.

van Doorn, Jacques, ed. *Armed Forces and Society: Sociological Essays.* The Hague, 1968.

———. *Military Profession and Military Regimes: Commitments and Conflicts.* The Hague, 1969.

Doumbadze, V. D. *Russia's War Minister: The Life and Work of Adjutant-General Vladimir Alexandrovitsh Soukhomlinov.* London, 1915.

Eisen, B. I., ed. *Iz istorii russkoi zhurnalistiki kontsa XIX-nachala XX v.* Moscow, 1973.

Eisenstadt, S. N. *The Political System of Empires.* London, 1963.

Faleev, N. I. "Shest' mesiatsev voenno-polevoi iustitsii." *Byloe* 2, no. 2/14 (Feb. 1907): 43-81.

Falkus, M. E. *The Industrialization of Russia, 1700-1914.* London, 1977.

Feldman, Gerald D. *Army, Industry and Labor in Germany, 1914-1918.* Princeton, 1966.

Field, Daniel. *The End of Serfdom. Nobility and Bureaucracy in Russia, 1855-1861.* Cambridge, 1976.

———. *Rebels in the Name of the Tsar.* Boston, 1976.

Filat'ev, G. "Dorevoliutsionnye voennye sudy v tsifrakh." *Katorga i ssylka* (Moscow) 7, no. 68 (1930): 138-167.

Finer, S. E. *The Man on Horseback: The Role of the Military in Politics.* 2d ed. London, 1976.

Fridman, M. *Nasha finansovaia sistema.* St. Petersburg, 1905.

Frolov, B. "Russko-iaponskaia voina 1904-05 gg. Nekotorye voprosy voennogo iskusstva." *Voenno-istoricheskii zhurnal* 16, no. 2 (Feb. 1974): 83-90.

Gernet, M. N. *Istoriia tsarskoi tiur'my,* vol. 4. Moscow, 1954.

Gerschenkron, Alexander. *Economic Backwardness in Historical Perspective.* Cambridge, 1966.

Gille, Bertrand. *Histoire économique et sociale de la Russie.* Paris. 1949.

Gindin, I. *Gosudarstvennyi bank i ekonomicheskaia politika tsarskogo pravitel'stva*. Moscow, 1960.

Goldstein, Edward Ralph. "Military Aspects of Russian Industrialization: The Defense Industries, 1890-1917." Ph.D. diss., Case Western Reserve University, 1971.

Gooch, John. *Armies in Europe*. London, 1980.

de la Gorce, Paul-Marie. *The French Army: A Military-Political History*. Trans. Kenneth Douglas. New York, 1963.

Gosudarstvennyi kontrol' 1811-1911. St. Petersburg, n.d.

Gregory, Paul R. "Economic Growth and Structural Changes in Tsarist Russia: A Case of Modern Economic Growth?" *Soviet Studies* 23, no. 3 (Jan. 1972): 418-434.

———. "1913 Russian National Income—Some Insights into Russian Economic Development." *The Quarterly Journal of Economics* 90, no. 3 (Aug. 1976): 445-459.

———. "Russian Industrialization and Economic Growth: Results and Perspectives of Western Research." *Jahrbücher für Geschichte Osteuropas*, neue Folge 25, no. 2 (1977): 200-218.

Gribovskii, V. M. *Gosudarstvennoe ustroistvo i upravlenie Rossiiskoi Imperii*. Odessa, 1912.

Griffith, Paddy. *Forward into Battle: Fighting Tactics from Waterloo to Vietnam*. Chichester, 1981.

Haimson, Leopold, ed. *The Politics of Rural Russia, 1905-1914*. Bloomington, Ind., 1979.

———. "The Problem of Social Stability in Urban Russia 1905-1917 (part one)." *Slavic Review* 23, no. 4 (Dec. 1964): 619-642.

Harcave, Sidney. *First Blood: The Russian Revolution of 1905*. New York, 1964.

Harries-Jenkins, Gwyn. *The Army in Victorian Society*. London, 1977.

Hellie, Richard. *Enserfment and Military Change in Muscovy*. Chicago, 1971.

———. "The Structure of Modern Russian History: Toward a Dynamic Model." *Russian History* 4, pt. 1 (1977): 1-22.

Herlihy, Patricia. "Death in Odessa: A Study of Population Movements in a Nineteenth-Century City." *Journal of Urban History* 4, no. 4 (Aug. 1978): 417-441.

Hicks, James E. *French Military Weapons, 1717 to 1938*. New Milford, Conn., 1964.

———. *Notes on German Ordnance, 1841-1918*. 2d ed. New York, 1941.

Hobsbawm, Eric. "Peasants and Politics." *The Journal of Peasant Studies* 1, no. 1 (Oct. 1973): 3-22.

Hobsbawm, Eric, and George Rude. *Captain Swing: A History of the Great English Agricultural Uprising of 1830*. New York. 1968.

Hoffman, Walther G. *Das Wachstum der Deutschen Wirtschaft seit der mitte des 19. Jahrhunderts*. Berlin, 1965.

Hosking, Geoffrey. *The Russian Constitutional Experiment: Government and Duma, 1907-1914*. Cambridge, England, 1973.

Howard, Michael, ed. *Soldiers and Governments: Nine Studies in Civil-Military Relations.* London, 1957.

Hutchinson, J. F. "The Octobrists and the Future of Imperial Russia as a Great Power." *The Slavonic and East European Review* 50, no. 119 (Apr. 1972): 220-237.

Iasnopol'skii, N. P. *O geograficheskom raspredelenii gosudarstvennykh raskhodov Rossii,* Kiev, 1897.

Ignatovich, I. I. *Pomeshchich'i krestiane nakanune osvobozhdeniia.* 3d ed. Leningrad, 1925.

Istoricheskii ocherk Pavlovskogo voennogo uchilishcha, Pavlovskogo kadetskogo korpusa i Imperatorskogo voenno-sirotskogo doma 1798-1898 gg. St. Petersburg, 1898.

Istoriia 'dvorian' i 'konstaninovtsev' 1807-1907. St. Petersburg, n.d.

Jane, Fred T. *The Imperial Russian Navy.* Rev. ed. London, 1904.

Janowitz, Morris. *The Professional Soldier: A Social and Political Portrait.* 2d ed. New York, 1971.

Johnson, John H., ed. *The Role of the Military in Underdeveloped Countries.* Princeton, 1962.

Joubert, Carl. *The Truth about the Tsar and the Present State of Russia.* London, 1905.

Judge, Edward Henry. *The Russia of Plehve. Programs and Policies of the Ministry of Internal Affairs, 1902-1904.* Ph.D. diss., University of Michigan, 1975.

Kashkarov, Mikhail. *Finansovye itogi poslednego desiatiletiia 1892-1901 gg.* 2 vols. St. Petersburg, 1903.

Kazakov, M. "Ispol'zovanie rezervov v russko-iaponskoi voine, 1904-1905 gg." *Voenno-istoricheskii zhurnal* 13, no. 4 (April 1971): 44-45.

Kavtaradze, A. "Is istorii russkogo general'nogo shtaba." *Voenno-istoricheskii zhurnal* 13, no. 12 (Dec. 1971): 75-80; 14, no. 7 (July 1972): 87-92; 16, no. 12 (Dec. 1974): 80-86.

Kenez, Peter. "A Profile of the Pre-Revolutionary Officer Corps." *California Slavic Studies* 7 (1973): 121-158.

Kennan, George. *Siberia and the Exile System,* vol. 1. London, 1891.

Kennedy, Gavin. *The Economics of Defense.* London, 1975.

Kersnovskii, A. *Istoriia russkoi armii.* pt. iii (1881-1917). Belgrade, 1935.

Kipp, Jacob W., and W. Bruce Lincoln. "Autocracy and Reform: Bureaucratic Absolutism and Political Modernization in Nineteenth Century Russia." *Russian History* 6, pt. 1 (1979): 1-21.

Kitanina, T. M. *Khlebnaia torgovlia Rossii 1875-1914 g.g.* Leningrad, 1978.

Kitchen, Martin. *The German Officer Corps, 1890-1914.* Oxford, 1968.

Kobylin, V. *Imperator Nikolai II i General-Ad"iutant M. V. Alekseev.* New York, 1970.

Kokhn, M. P. *Russkie indeksy tsen.* Moscow, 1926.

Kon, F. "Voennye sudy v Tsarstve Pol'skom." *Katorga i ssylka* (Moscow) 19 (1925): 14-164.

Koniaev, A. *Finansovyi kontrol' v dorevoliutsionnoi Rossii.* Moscow, 1959.

Konovalov, V. I., ed. *Revoliutsionnoe dvizhenie v gody pervoi russkoi revoliutsii.* Moscow, 1955.

Korkunov, N. M. *Russkoe gosudarstvennoe pravo,* vol. 2, 6th ed. St. Petersburg, 1909.

Labe, Camille. *Le budget de la guerre en France.* Paris, 1930.

Lachappelle, Georges. *Les finances de la IIIeme République.* Paris, 1937.

Lang, Kurt. *Military Institutions and the Sociology of War: A Review of the Literature with Annotated Bibliography.* Beverly Hills, 1972.

Langer, William L. *The Franco-Russian Alliance 1890-1894.* Cambridge, 1929.

———. "The Pattern of Urban Revolution in 1848." In *French Society and Culture Since the Old Regime,* ed. E. M. Accomb. New York, 1966, pp. 90-118.

von Laue, Theodore H. "A Secret Memorandum of Sergei Witte on the Industrialization of Imperial Russia." *Journal of Modern History* 26, no. 1 (Mar. 1954): 64-74.

———. *Sergei Witte and the Industrialization of Russia.* New York, 1963.

Lazaresvskii, N. I. *Lektsii po russkomu gosudarstvennomu pravu,* vol. 2, pt. 1. St. Petersburg, 1910.

Le Donne, John P. "Civilians under Military Justice During the Reign of Nicholas I." *Canadian-American Slavic Studies* 7, no. 2 (Summer 1973): 171-187.

Leikina-Svirskaia, V. R. *Intelligentsiia v Rossii vo vtoroi polovine XIX veka.* Moscow, 1971.

Leslie, R. E. *Reform and Insurrection in Russian Poland.* London, 1963.

Levin, Alfred. *The Second Duma. A Study of the Social-Democratic Party and the Russian Constitutional Experiment.* 2d ed. Hamden, Conn., 1966.

Lincoln, W. Bruce. *Nicholas I. Emperor and Autocrat of All the Russias.* Bloomington, Ind., 1978.

Lovell, John P., and Phillip S. Kronenberg, eds. *New Civil-Military Relations.* New Brunswick and New York, 1974.

Luckham, A. R. "A Comparative Typology of Civil-Military Relations." *Government and Opposition* 6, no. 1 (Winter 1971): 5-35.

Lyashchenko, Peter I. *History of the National Economy of Russia to the 1917 Revolution.* Trans. L. M. Herman. New York, 1949.

McCormick, Frederick. *The Tragedy of Russia in Pacific Asia.* 2 vols. New York, 1907.

Manning, Roberta Thompson. *The Crisis of the Old Order in Russia: Gentry and Government.* Princeton, 1982.

Mansheev, F. A. "K 75-letiiu Nikolaevskoi akademii General'nogo Shtaba." *Voennyi sbornik,* no. 12 (Dec. 1907): 213-238.

Martov, L., P. Maslov, and A. Potresov, eds. *Obschestvennoe dvizhenie v nachale xx-go veka,* vol. 2, pt. 1. St. Petersburg, 1909.

May, Ernest, ed. *Knowing One's Enemies: Intelligence Assessment before the Two World Wars.* Princeton, 1985.

Mayzel, Matitiahu. "The Formation of the Russian General Staff, 1880-1917:

A Social Study." *Cahiers du Monde russe et sovietique* 16, nos. 3-4 (July/ Dec. 1975): 297-320.

————. "Generals and Revolutionaries, the Russian General Staff during the Revolution: A Study in the Transformation of a Military Elite." In *Studien zur Militärgeschichte, Militärwissenschaft und Konfliktforschung*, vol. 19. Osnabruck, 1979.

Mehlinger, Howard D., and John M. Thompson. *Count Witte and the Tsarist Government in the 1905 Revolution*. Bloomington, Ind., 1972.

Menne, Bernard. *Krupp. Deutschlands Kanonenkönige*. Zurich, 1937.

Meshcheriakov, G. P. *Russkaia voennaia mysl' v XIX v.* Moscow, 1973.

Metzer, Jacob. "Railway Development and Market Integration: The Case of Tsarist Russia." *The Journal of Economic History* 34, no. 2 (Sept. 1974): 529-550.

Migulin, P. P. *Ekonomicheskii rost russkogo gosudarstva za 300 let.* Moscow, 1913.

Mikhailovskii, B. V. *Russkaia literatura XX veka.* Moscow, 1939.

Miller, Forrest A. *Dmitrii Miliutin and the Reform Era in Russia.* Nashville, Tenn., 1968.

Ministerstvo finansov 1802-1902, pt. 2. St. Petersburg, n.d.

Mitchell, B. R. *European Historical Statistics, 1750-1970.* London, 1975.

Mitchell, Donald W. *A History of Russian and Soviet Sea Power.* New York, 1974.

Morrill, Dan L. "Nicholas II and the Call for the First Hague Conference," *The Journal of Modern History* 46, no. 2 (June 1974): 296-313.

Morskoi, A. *Voennaia moshch' Rossii. Predskazaniia general-ad"iutanta A. N. Kuropatkina i ikh kritika grafom S. Iu. Vitte.* Petrograd, 1915.

Mosse, W. E. "Aspects of Tsarist Bureaucracy: Recruitment to the Imperial State Council, 1855-1914." *The Slavonic and East European Review* 57, no. 2 (April 1979): 240-254.

Neymarck, Alfred. *Finances contemporaines. II. Les budgets 1872-1903.* Paris, 1904.

Obzor deiatel'nosti ministerstva finansov v tsarstvovanie Imperatora Aleksandra III (1881-1894). St. Petersburg, 1902.

Okamoto, Shumpei. *The Japanese Oligarchy and the Russo-Japanese War.* New York, 1970.

Orlovsky, Daniel T. *The Limits of Reform: The Ministry of Internal Affairs in Imperial Russia, 1802-1881.* Cambridge, Mass., 1981.

————. "Ministerial Power and Russian Autocracy: The Ministry of Internal Affairs 1802-1881." Ph.D. diss., Harvard University, 1976.

Perlmutter, Amos. *The Military and Politics in Modern Times: On Professionals, Praetorians and Revolutionary Soldiers.* New Haven, 1977.

Perrie, Maureen. *The Agrarian Policy of the Socialist Revolutionary Party from Its Origins through the Revolution of 1905-1907.* Cambridge, England, 1976.

Perrins, Michael. "Russian Military Policy in the Far East and the 1905 Revolution in the Russian Army." *European Studies Review* 9 (1979): 331-349.

Petrov, V. A. *Ocherki po istorii revoliutsionnogo dvizheniia v russkoi armii v 1905 g.* Moscow, 1964.

———. "Tsarskaia armiia v bor'be s massovym revoliutsionnym dvizheniem v nachale xx v." *Istoricheskie zapiski* (Moscow) 34 (1950): 321-332.

Pinchuk, Ben-Cion. *The Octobrists in the Third Duma.* Seattle, 1974.

Pipes, Richard. *Russia under the Old Regime.* New York, 1974.

Pogrebinskii, A. P. *Gosudarstvennye finansy tsarskoi Rossii v epokhu imperializma.* Moscow, 1968.

Pokrovskii, S. P. *Ministerskaia vlast' v Rossii.* Iaroslavl', 1906.

Polianskii, N. N. *Tsarskie voennye sudy v bor'be s revoliutsiei 1905-1907 gg.* Moscow, 1958.

Ponomareff, Dmitry. "Political Loyalty and Social Composition of the Military Elite: The Russian Officer Corps, 1861-1903." RAND Paper, ser. P-6052 (Nov. 1977).

Porch, Douglas, *March to the Marne: The French Army, 1871-1914.* Cambridge, Eng., 1981.

Purves, J. G., and D. A. West, eds. *War and Society in the Nineteenth Century Russian Empire.* Toronto, 1972.

Rabinovich, M. D. *Polki petrovskoi armii. Kratkii spravochnik 1698-1725.* Moscow, 1977.

Raeff, Marc. "L'état, le gouvernement et la tradition politique en Russie imperiale avant 1861." *Revue d'Histoire moderne et contemporaine* 9 (Oct.-Dec. 1962): 295-308.

———. *The Origins of the Russian Intelligentsia: The Eighteenth Century Nobility.* New York, 1966.

Raffalovich, Arthur. *Le marche financier en 1893-1894.* Paris, 1894.

———. *Le marche financier en 1894-1896.* Paris, 1896.

———. *Le marche financier en 1896-1897.* Paris, 1897.

Rieber, Alfred J., ed. *The Politics of Autocracy: Letters of Alexander II to Prince A. I. Bariatinskii, 1857-1864.* The Hague, 1966.

Rimailho, Lt. Colonel. *Artillerie de campagne.* Paris, 1924.

Ritter, Gerhard. *The Sword and the Scepter: The Problem of Militarism in Germany.* 2 vols. Trans. Heinz Norden. Coral Gables, Fla., 1969-1970.

Rostunov, I. I., ed. *Istoriia russko-iaponskoi voiny 1904-1905 g.g.* Moscow, 1977.

———. *Russkii front pervoi mirovoi voiny.* Moscow, 1976.

Rothenberg, Gunther A. *The Army of Francis Joseph.* West Layette, Ind., 1976.

See, Henri. *Histoire économique de la France. Les temps modernes 1789-1914.* Paris, 1942.

Senchakova, L. T. *Revoliutsionnoe dvizhenie v russkoi armii i flote v kontse XIX - nachale XX v.* Moscow, 1972.

Shatsillo, K. F. "'Delo' polkovnika Miasoedova." *Voprosy istorii* 42, no. 4 (Apr. 1967): 103-116.

Shatsillo, K. F. *Rossiia pered pervoi mirovoi voinoi (vooruzhennye sily tsarisma v 1905-1914 gg.)*. Moscow, 1974.

Shebaldin, Iu. N. "Gosudarstvennyi biudzhet tsarskoi Rossii v nachale XX v (do pervoi mirovoi voiny)." *Istoricheskie zapiski* (Moscow) 65 (1959): 163-190.

Shebalor, A. "Vopros o smertnoi kazni za politicheskie prestupleniia nakanune Pervoi Dumy," *Katorga i ssylka* (Moscow) 17 (1925).

Sidorov, A. L. *Ekonomicheskoe polozhenie Rossii v gody pervoi mirovoi voiny*. Moscow, 1973.

Skalon, D. A. et al., eds. *Stoletie voennogo ministerstva, 1802-1902*, vol. 1. St. Petersburg, 1902.

Skobennikov, A. "M. V. Frunze (Arsenii) na katorge i v ssylke." *Katorga i ssylka* (Moscow) 20 (1925): 250-254.

Sliozberg, G. B. *Dorevoliutsionnyi stroi Rossii*. Paris, 1933.

Solov'ev, S. M. *Istoriia Rossii s drevneishikh vremen*, vol. 12. Moscow, 1979.

Spencer, Herbert. *Principles of Sociology*, vol. 2. New York, 1895.

Stein, Hans-Peter. "Der Offizier des Russischen Heeres im Zeitabschnitt zwischen Reform und Revolution (1861-1905)." *Forschungen zur Osteuropäischen Geschichte* (Berlin) 13 (1967): 346-504.

Stone, Norman. *The Eastern Front, 1914-1917*. New York, 1975.

Svirskii, S. Ia. *Revoliutsionnoe dvizhenie v tsarskoi armii v Turkestane (1910-1914 gg.)*. Tashkent, 1960.

Taranovsky, Theodore. "The Politics of Counter-Reform. Autocracy and Bureaucracy in the Reign of Alexander III, 1881-1894." Ph.D. diss., Harvard University, 1976.

Tate, Merze. *The Disarmament Illusion. The Movement for a Limitation of Arms to 1907*. New York, 1942.

Teitler, G. *The Genesis of the Professional Officers' Corps*. London, 1977.

Trebilcock, Clive. *The Vickers Brothers. Armament and Enterprise, 1895-1914*. London, 1977.

Troitskii, N. A. *Bezumstvo khrabykh. Russkie revoliutsionery i karatel'naia politika tsarizma 1866-1882 g.g.* Moscow, 1978.

———. *"Narodnaia volia" pered tsarskim sudom 1880-1891 g.g.* Saratov, 1971.

———. *Tsarizm pod sudom progressivnoi obschestvennosti 1866-1895 g.g.* Moscow, 1979.

———. *Tsarskie sudy protiv revoliutsionnoi Rossii. Politicheskie protsessy 1871-1880 g.g.* Saratov, 1976.

Troitskii, S. M. *Finansovaia politika russkogo absoliutizma v XVIII veke*. Moscow, 1966.

Ulam, Adam B. *In the Name of the People: Prophets and Conspirators in Prerevolutionary Russia*. New York, 1977.

Vagts, Alfred. *Defense and Diplomacy. The Soldier and the Conduct of Foreign Relations*. New York, 1956.

———. *A History of Militarism*. Rev. ed. New York, 1959.

Volonter [M. Pavlovich]. *Russko-iaponskaia voina (prichiny, khod i posledstviia)*. St. Petersburg, 1905.

Vovchik, A. F. *Politika tsarizma po rabochemu voprosu v dorevoliutsionnyi period (1895-1904)*. L'vov, 1964.

Vrzhosek, S. *Zhizn' i tvorchestvo V. Veresaeva*. Priboi, 1930.

von Wahlde, Peter. "Military Thought in Imperial Russia." Ph.D. diss., Indiana University, 1966.

Walkin, Jacob. *The Rise of Democracy in Pre-Revolutionary Russia: Political and Social Institutions under the Last Three Tsars*. New York, 1962.

Walz, John David. "State Defense and Russian Politics under the Last Tsar." Ph.D. diss., Syracuse University, 1967.

Weissman, Neil B. *Reform in Tsarist Russia: The State Bureaucracy and Local Government 1900-1914*. New Brunswick, N.J., 1981.

———. "Rural Crime in Tsarist Russia: The Question of Hooliganism, 1905-14." *Slavic Review* 37, no. 2 (June 1978): 228-240.

White, John Albert. *The Diplomacy of the Russo-Japanese War*. Princeton, 1964.

Whittam, John. *The Politics of the Italian Army, 1861-1918*. London, 1977.

Wildman, Allan K. *The End of the Russian Imperial Army: The Old Army and the Soldiers' Revolt (March-April, 1917)*. Princeton, 1980.

Wilfong, Walter Thomas. "Rebuilding the Russian Army, 1905-14. The Question of a Comprehensive Plan for National Defense." Ph.D. diss., Indiana University, 1977.

Woodward, James B. *Leonid Andreyev. A Study*. Oxford, 1969.

Wortman, Richard. *The Development of a Russian Legal Consciousness*. Chicago, 1976.

———. "The Russian Empress as Mother." In *The Family in Imperial Russia*, ed. D. Ransel. Urbana, 1976.

Yaney, George L. "Some Aspects of the Imperial Russian Government on the Eve of the First World War." *Slavonic and East European Review* 43 (Dec. 1964): 69-87.

———. *The Systematization of Russian Government. Social Evolution in the Domestic Administration of Imperial Russia, 1711-1905*. Urbana, 1973.

———. *The Urge to Mobilize: Agrarian Reform in Russia 1861-1930*. Urbana, 1982.

Zaionchkovskii, A. M. *Podgotovka Rossii k imperialisticheskoi voine*. Moscow, 1926.

Zaionchkovskii, P. A. *Rossiskoe samoderzhavie v kontse xix stoletiia*. Moscow, 1970.

———. *Samoderzhavie i russkaia armiia na rubezhe XIX-XX stoletii*. Moscow, 1973.

———. *Voennye reformy 1860-70 godov v Rossii*. Moscow, 1952.

Zakharova, L. G. "Krizis samoderzhaviia nakanune revoliutsii 1905 goda." *Voprosy istorii*, no. 8 (1972): 119-140.

Zdobnov, N. V. *Russkaia knizhnaia statistika*. Moscow, 1959.

Zeldin, Theodore. *France, 1848-1945*. 2 vols. Oxford, 1973.

Zhilin, A. "Bol'shaia programma po usileniiu russkoi armii." *Voenno-istori-cheskii zhurnal* 16, no. 7 (June 1974): 90-97.

Zolotarev, V. A. *Russko-turetskaia voina 1877-78 gg. v otechestvennoi istorio-grafii*. Moscow, 1978.

Zuckerman, Frederic Scott. "The Russian Political Police at Home and Abroad (1880-1917)." Ph.D. diss., New York University, 1973.

INDEX

Abaza, A. A., 61
Abaza, A. M., 131
Abrahamsson, Bengt, 4
Adrianov, A. A., 180-181, 184
agricultural crisis, 55-56
aid to the civil power, 76, 107, 165-166;
against peasants, 76-77, 85-87, 89, 90,
92, 92n; burden of, 84, 102, 245, 253-
254; complaints concerning, 93-98,
103-106, 134-137, 141-142, 145-148,
200, 225-226, 249-250, 252, 254, 260;
cost of, 86-87, 135-136, 140; deployment and, 106, 155; guard duty and
police service, 81, 84, 95-98, 102, 104-
105, 130, 140, 144, 150-154, 165, 244-
245, 247-257; in cities and towns, 89-
92, 102-103, 149-150, 247; industrialists and, 102-103; in Western Europe,
76-77; landowners and, 150, 152; proposals for change, 98-100; rules for,
77-81, 90, 93-94, 98-100, 109-110, 134-
135, 142, 147, 156, 162, 255-256; statistics on, 81-84, 87, 88, 129, 130n,
144, 152-153, 246-248, 256
Alexander II, xviii, 7, 37, 61
Alexander III, xxi, 11, 14, 25-26, 42, 106;
character of, 39; coolness to army, 39-
40, 64; cuts military budget, 66-68;
subscribes to *Razvedchik*, 34; view of
officers' honor, 24
Alexander Academy of Military Justice,
11, 32, 123-127, 186-187, 190-191, 234
All-Russian Military Union (1905), 196
All-Russian Military Union (1910), 215
All-Russian Officers' Union, 196
Andreev, L. N., 143
Andreevko, 105
anti-Semitism, 109-110, 110n, 206, 214,
231. *See also* pogroms
Apushkin, V. A., 200
army, xxiv, xxv, 3, 58-59, 205; armaments and weapons, 7, 54-55, 57, 68-
69, 73, 222, 227, 243-244; cavalry, 20,
90, 99, 151, 155, 220-221, 240; con-

scription, 11, 48, 53; Cossacks, 19-20,
102-103, 105-106, 136, 146-148, 151,
153-155, 161, 163-164, 222, 226, 228,
240, 249; engineers, 92; Imperial
Guards, 15, 18-19, 41, 220-221; infantry, 20-22, 86-87, 89-91, 96-97, 136,
155, 243; inspectorates, 7, 134, 231-
232; provisions, equipment, and supplies, 53, 55-57, 147, 157; size of, 52,
67-68; strategic plans, 15, 53, 65, 222;
strategy and tactics, 6, 65, 132, 158,
201-202; training and exercises, 42-44,
78-79, 96-98, 105-106, 155-158, 160-
161, 165-166, 220, 249, 252-254, 260.
See also Main Administrations; Ministry of War; officer corps
Astrakhan Province, 104
Austro-Hungarian army, 43, 262
Austro-Hungarian Empire, 52
autocracy, xxii, 64, 66; army and, xxiii,
17, 24-26, 30-31, 107-108, 198, 199-
200, 207-208, 219-220, 230-231, 233-
236, 259-263
Avramov, V. A., 98

Baiov, A. K., 201
Baku, 92
Baltic territories, 137
Batum, 92
Bekman, Lieutenant General V. A., 109
Berezovskii, V. A., 33
Bershadskii, S. A., 125
Bessarabia Province, 109-110
Bezdna rising, 76
Bezobrazov, A. M., 131
Big Program (1914), 227
Black Hundreds, 211
Bliokh, Ivan, 5
Bloody Sunday, 133
Bobrikov, N. I., 98
Bobrovskii, P. O., 123
Bolshevik Party, 215, 234
Bonch-Bruevich, M. D., 201
Bosnian crisis (1908-1909), 205, 224

LIBRARY OF CONGRESS CATALOGING IN PUBLICATION DATA

Fuller, William C.
  Civil-military conflict in Imperial Russia, 1881-1914.

  Bibliography: p.
  Includes index.
  1. Civil-military relations—Soviet Union—History.
  2. Soviet Union. Armiia—Political activities—History.
  3. Soviet Union—Politics and government—1881-1894.
  4. Soviet Union—Politics and government—1894-1917.
  I. Title.
  JN6520.C58F85 1985   322'.5'0947   85-3493
  ISBN 0-691-05452-5 (alk. paper)